OUR GUYS

The Glen Ridge Rape
and the Secret Life of the Perfect Suburb

Men and Masculinity
Michael Kimmel, Editor

OUR GUYS

The Glen Ridge Rape and the Secret Life of the Perfect Suburb

BERNARD LEFKOWITZ

UNIVERSITY OF CALIFORNIA PRESS

Berkeley   Los Angeles   London

University of California Press
Berkeley and Los Angeles, California

University of California Press, Ltd.
London, England

Library of Congress Cataloging-in-Publication Data

Lefkowitz, Bernard.
    Our guys : the Glen Ridge rape and the secret life of the perfect
suburb / Bernard Lefkowitz.
        p.   cm. — (Men and masculinity ; 4)
    Includes bibliographical references and index.
    ISBN 0-520-20596-0 (cloth : alk. paper)
    1. Gang rape—New Jersey—Glen Ridge.   2. Mentally handicapped
women—Crimes against—New Jersey—Glen Ridge.   3. Sexism—United
States.   4. United States—Moral conditions.   5. Social values—
United States.   I. Title.   II. Series: Men and masculinity
(Berkeley, Calif.) ; 1.
    HV6568.G54L43   1997
    364.15'32'0974931—DC21   96-48276
                                                                                 CIP

Printed in the United States of America
9 8 7 6 5 4 3

The paper used in this publication is both acid-free and totally chlorine-free (TCF). It meets the minimum requirements of American Standard for Information Sciences—Permanence of Paper for Printed Library Materials, ANSI z39.48-1984.

For Becky

———

C O N T E N T S

ACKNOWLEDGMENTS

I am deeply grateful to the late Diane Cleaver, who was my literary agent during most of the research and writing of this book. She cared intensely about the issues the book raised and fought for its publication. I miss her.

I also appreciate the support and guidance of Steven Schechter, my attorney, whose enthusiasm cheered me through the final stages of this work.

I owe a huge debt to Diane Curcio Walsh, a splendid reporter for the *Newark Star-Ledger*. She opened many doors for me when they seemed permanently locked, and was a great friend through the seemingly endless course of this case. I also want to acknowledge the help of another colleague, Christopher Kilbourne, of *The Record* of New Jersey. Alan Ziegler, director of the writing program at Columbia University, was a supportive listener and a wise counselor throughout.

Harriet Barlow and Sheila Kinney welcomed me to Blue Mountain Center in the Adirondack Mountains of New York State, one of the most beautiful places in the world, where I wrote a large chunk of this book.

For more than six years, Linda Grant, Cherry Provost, Terry Webster, and Kathleen Middleton, among others in Glen Ridge, treated me with courtesy, kindness, and understanding. During that time I also mercilessly hounded the defense lawyers and prosecutors. And they responded to my never-ending questions with good humor, patience, and surprising tolerance of my legal deficiencies.

I will always be grateful to Naomi Schneider and William Murphy, my editors at the University of California Press, who rescued me from the nearly fatal embrace of Simon & Schuster, where the bottom line rules absolutely.

My wife, Becky Aikman, kept me going from beginning to end, even when it seemed that there never would be an end. Her intelligence and convictions are the soul of this book.

AUTHOR'S NOTE

The author has used the real names of people who were involved in the investigation and trial, who held public positions, and who were identified in news stories about the case. The author has used pseudonyms, denoted by an asterisk, to disguise the identity and maintain the privacy of the rape victim and her family, as well as others not centrally involved in the case. Any similarity between these fictitious names and those of living persons is coincidental.

The author recognizes that many of the facts in this case are disputed and will continue to be in dispute. While these disputed facts remain unverifiable, the author has presented the version of events he believes is most plausible in light of his research, legal testimony, and the jury's verdict.

INTRODUCTION

I spent much of the 1980s writing about the lives of poor children and adolescents. During that time I interviewed hundreds of youngsters and visited dozens of schools and neighborhoods throughout the country. One place I returned to often was the ravaged housing project in the Lower Broadway section of Newark, where a courageous youth worker struggled to bring a semblance of stability to the disordered lives of the children and adults in the community. During the days and nights I followed him around, I never knew that just fifteen minutes down the road was a beautiful little suburb named Glen Ridge, which, to any of the kids I was meeting, would have seemed like paradise.

I heard about Glen Ridge as most Americans did. On the night of May 23, 1989, a New York television station reported that authorities were investigating "rumors" that a group of Glen Ridge adolescent males had raped a seventeen-year-old retarded girl. Two days later, newspapers throughout the United States carried stories about the arrests of five popular high school athletes, who, police said, had penetrated the young woman's body with a baseball bat and a broomstick.

The stories conveyed a sense of shock that these atrocious acts could have happened in such a prosperous and tranquil town. If the charges were true, this was certainly an appalling crime. After thirty years as a journalist, I wasn't naive enough to believe that perfect towns produced only perfect kids. Still, I was curious about what had gone wrong in this perfect town—the antithesis of Newark—where children grew up with every advantage.

The follow-up stories added new information. First, this wasn't about just a couple of oddballs with a sadistic streak. A number of young men seemed to be involved. The papers reported that on March 1, 1989, thirteen males were present in the basement where the alleged rape occurred. There also were reports that a number of other boys had tried to entice the young woman into the basement a second time to repeat the experience. This was puzzling. Glen Ridge is a small place, and there were only a hundred or so students in the senior class. What were we talking about here— 20 or 30 percent of the senior males? The growing number of actual participants, would-be participants, and observers made me wonder about the environment in which they grew up. I wanted to know more about how this privileged American community raised its children, especially its sons.

I was also curious about the silence of the other kids—the Glen Ridge adolescents who had not been in the basement and would never have thought of going down there. The newspapers were saying that accounts of what had happened had circulated among the students in the high school for almost three months before the arrests, but that the kids had kept it to themselves. They hadn't gone to the police and they hadn't told their parents or teachers. Why was it so important to protect a bunch of classmates who enjoyed sticking a bat and a broom into a retarded woman? Weren't they worried about what had been done to her and what might happen to her in the future if the truth were suppressed?

Maybe the silence of Glen Ridge students was a symptom of grief and shame, colored by self-interest. Maybe they were thinking: Keep quiet for a couple of months and this will all blow over and we'll graduate and slip off to college. It was more difficult to understand the comments attributed to adolescents *after* the arrests. Some teenagers told reporters: "She teased them into it." "She asked for it." "She was promiscuous." Adults in the community were slightly more guarded in their comments: "She was always flirting." "This is Leslie just getting into more trouble." People in Glen Ridge were saying: The girl is to blame for all that happened to her. And it wasn't only a few people. The stories suggested that such views were widespread in the town.

Without doubt, a grave moral transgression had taken place in the community on March 1. Didn't the adults there see it the same way? Weren't parents worried about how their sons were growing up? Weren't they concerned about what might happen to *their* daughters? What kind of place was Glen Ridge anyway?

A large group of charismatic athletes. A retarded young woman. The silence of the students and adults. The inclination to blame the woman and exonerate the men. These elements seemed to be linked by a familiar theme in my life in journalism. I began to frame Glen Ridge as a story of power and powerlessness: the power of young males and the community that venerated them, and the powerlessness of one marginalized young woman—one woman whom I knew about from the media coverage. Maybe there were other young women with stories to tell.

The sense of social nihilism expressed by many youngsters in Newark was attributable, at least partially, to their economic condition and the social devastation it created. The immutable condition they all shared was poverty. Being poor was the ongoing trauma of their childhoods. You could draw a line from the rubble of the streets to the rubble of their lives.

Of course, Glen Ridge was different. It was a town where almost everybody was pretty well off. If I decided to write about this place, I would have to readjust my perspective. The prosperity of Glen Ridge didn't negate the impact of economics on the values of young people in this suburb. But instead of writing about the sense of impotency arising from generations of poverty, I might be writing about how affluence and privilege could inflate the self-importance of otherwise unremarkable young men, not always with good results.

This was all surmise from a distance. Before I decided to write about Glen Ridge, I wanted to take a closer look at the boys involved in the alleged rape, at the residents, and at the town. In the late afternoon of June 23, 1989, I boarded a number 33 DeCamp line bus from the Port Authority bus terminal in New York City. Forty minutes later, I got off at the intersection of Bloomfield and Ridgewood Avenues in Glen Ridge. I followed the crowd that was walking toward the field behind the high school, where the graduation ceremonies for the Class of '89 were about to begin.

My first mental snapshot: Glen Ridge was a squeaky-clean, manicured town that liked to display its affluence by dressing its high school graduates in dinner jackets and gowns. What impressed me most was the orderliness of the place. The streets, the lawns, the houses—everything seemed in proportion. There were no excesses of bad taste, no evidence of neglect or disrepair.

Although graduation was an emotional ritual, made more intense by the recent arrest of four seniors on rape charges, there were no outbursts of feeling, no overt expressions of anger, grief, or remorse. The adults and their progeny exercised near-perfect restraint.

It was as if these graduates had fulfilled the first requirements of a master plan for their lives. Their parents' success had secured them a place in this charming town. Now they would follow their parents down the same road, passing all the trailmarks that led to achievement, security, and fulfillment. The contrast with Newark was overwhelming. The youngsters I met there had no idea what they would be doing tomorrow, let alone five years from now. The teenagers in Glen Ridge seemed to exude confidence in the future. It was a future that included more years of higher education, then entrance into an occupation or career. After that, marriage, children, and, perhaps, residence in Glen Ridge or a place very much like it.

They were secure in the knowledge that they would be protected as they made their passage into adulthood. Most of them would have their college board and tuition paid by their parents. If they needed to buy new clothes or a car or to pay a doctor's bill, they could depend on a check from home. Most of them had the luxury of easing into independence.

That's what I thought on the first night I visited Glen Ridge. But I also recognized that, even with all these advantages, kids don't always fulfill their parents' expectations. Some people have the benefit of wealth and nurturing parents and a good education, and still wind up morally and financially bankrupt. There are no foolproof master plans for success. I knew that because of what had happened three months before in this town, only a few blocks away from where I was sitting on this warm, humid night in June. What I didn't know was why it happened. If I found that out, I might have an interesting theme for a book.

Later that night I got my first glimpse of some of the boys who had been in the basement. They showed up for one of several parties that the town was holding for the graduates. As these thick-necked, broad-shouldered young men circulated in the crowd of students and chaperones, I felt a surge of recognition. I knew these kids! I had seen them all my life. They were the kids on my block who had developed faster than all the other boys of their age. They were out driving cars and dating and having sex while I was still fussing with my stamp collection. They were the guys in the jock clique of my high school, louder and tanner than the students who never saw sunlight because they were always home studying so they could win the Nobel Prize in chemistry before they turned fifty.

The kids in Newark, black and brown, speaking Spanglish, hoods over their heads, wheeling their stolen cars over to the local chop shop—they were aliens in America. Strange, forever separate and separated from the American ideal. But these Glen Ridge kids, they were pure gold, every mother's dream, every father's pride. They were not only Glen Ridge's finest, but in their perfection they belonged to all of us. They were Our Guys.

And that was the way they were being treated that night at the graduation party. Parents and kids collected around them, slapping them on the back and giving them big, wet, smacky kisses. Who would have guessed from this reception that some of them had been charged with rape and more of their pals would soon be arrested? In the bosom of their hometown, they were greeted like returning warriors who had prevailed in a noble crusade. Or, if you prefer, martyred heroes.

It may have all been a bravura show of solidarity by a bunch of scared people who saw their world crashing down on them. But it looked real to me. The accused looked like a bunch of carefree kids who had just wrapped up high school and were heading off to the shore for some sun and fun before they started college. Then I heard a voice next to me saying, "It's such a tragedy. They're such beautiful boys and this will scar them forever." The man who said that drifted away before I could ask him a question, but others I spoke to repeated this sentiment: "It's such a tragedy." Often, they identified the victims of the tragedy. It was a short list: the young men who had been arrested, their families, and the good name of Glen Ridge. The list, more often than not, omitted the young woman in the basement and her family.

Tragedy was a curious word to describe what these young men had done. It was so carefully neutral. It made the experience in the basement sound like an act of God—a bolt of lightning or an earthquake. Even when they attached the word to the actions of individual boys—"It's a tragedy for Chris," "It's such a tragedy for Bryant"—it seemed to absolve the young men of moral responsibility. These Glen Ridge folks sounded as if they were talking about an inherited disease, a flawed gene, not a deliberate act that reflected patterns of socialization, years of social and cultural experiences.

The next morning, I woke up thinking that something was missing from the conversations I had in Glen Ridge. What was missing was a word I had heard often in Newark: character. When a teenager went out and mugged an old lady for her food stamps, the law-abiding, respectable residents of the Newark neighborhood would say: "He has a bad character." By that they meant he was responding to his defective environment: an irresponsible mother, an absent father, the gang culture on the streets, an indifferent police force. They weren't excusing his crime. They were only listing the risk factors that undermine the healthy human development of many youngsters living in poverty. They were only pointing out the obvious: Kids raised in squalor often make very harmful decisions.

But a few miles down the highway in Glen Ridge, people seemed to disconnect youngsters living in affluence from their environment. When they discussed the "incident," they substituted temperament for character. One of the guys in the basement was a "nasty" kid. Another was "hyper." And still another was always "upbeat." They seemed to be talking about inherited traits, a biological code they had no control over. But they didn't mention the life experiences that sensitize, magnify, and aggravate the predispositions of temperament; they didn't speak of the boys' characters.

That's what interested me: their characters. I wanted to know what they had acquired from the world around them and how their formative experiences found expression in a dimly lighted basement in Glen Ridge. What was it in their upbringing as children and adolescents—so seemingly comfortable and secure—that inclined them to take pleasure in the conscious degradation of a helpless woman? More particularly, I wanted to understand how their status as young athlete celebrities in Glen Ridge influenced their treatment of girls and women, particularly those of their age. I wanted to learn how the institutions of the community responded to them. What they did in the basement on March 1 was clearly a group enterprise, so I was especially curious about what license they were permitted as a clique of admired athletes and how that magnified the sense of superiority they felt as individuals.

But there were two parties to this story—victimizer and victim. This was also the victim's story. Although she was disabled, she was as responsive as the young men were to the culture of Glen Ridge. She, too, learned who was admired and who was despised; who counted and who didn't; what got you attention and what got you ignored. If she was as vulnerable as the boys were powerful, it wasn't only because she was intellectually impaired. It was because she received and accepted the message sent out by the kids and adults who lived in the "normal" world. And that message was that she was born inferior and would always remain inferior. She learned early that to be "accepted" by the popular kids in town, she would have to submit to their ever more elaborate demands. Other girls got the same messages, but they knew they had alternatives. Sooner or later, in Glen Ridge or elsewhere, they would find people who would reward them for their independence and individuality. The victim's experience in Glen Ridge left her with only two choices: submit or be cast out of the only world she knew.

In the summer of 1989, I began the effort that the adults I had met on my first visit to Glen Ridge seemed unwilling to undertake: an examination of the character of their community and the young people who grew up in it. During the six years it took to complete this work, I interviewed more than 150 people who lived or worked in the town. I am not talking about a single conversation with an individual or a family. I returned repeatedly to some people to broaden my understanding and clarify my thinking.

The "incident" became a fiercely emotional matter for them. Longtime friends and neighbors, even husbands and wives and parents and children, clashed over the ethical, legal, and moral issues raised by this experience. When attention shifted from the town to the response of the criminal justice system, I conducted more than one hundred interviews with law enforcement officials, cops, prosecutors, reporters, defense lawyers, psychologists, social workers, and psychiatrists. In these discussions I found that the issues generating such discord in Glen Ridge had now become part of a national conversation about morality, integrity, and justice.

When I started, I knew that much of my work would be concentrated in Glen Ridge. But I also recognized that the themes shaping character in this suburban town in northern New Jersey were representative of the social and psychological currents that form mainstream American culture. Every town has distinctive qualities, but there was nothing in Glen Ridge that set it apart from thousands of other upper-middle-class suburban communities throughout the country. What happened there could have happened in many other places—and probably has.

I know that now, because the natural course of the story carried it beyond the borders of Glen Ridge to the larger society. As the case slowly wound its way through the criminal justice system toward trial and judgment, the boundaries between the town and the outside world eroded. Millions of Americans discovered that Glen Ridge was not a foreign and alien culture, but all too closely resembled their own communities. Glen Ridge's test of character became America's test of character. Glen Ridge ultimately found that it could not insulate itself against the turbulence created by an outrage that in the past would have been hidden and buried. Like Glen Ridge, America has been forced in recent years to define what are fair, just, and principled relations between men and women. That has not been easy for Glen Ridge to do. And it hasn't been easy for America either.

PART I

The Basement

1

Ros Faber* didn't want to fret about her daughter, but she felt that familiar sense of uneasiness tug at her as she saw Leslie* running down the steps in her sweats. She's home from school ten minutes and she's leaving already, Ros thought.

"Where are you going, Les?" Ros asked.

"Shoot some hoops at the park," Leslie said without stopping as she detoured into the kitchen.

Ros watched her gulp down a glass of milk. She hesitated and finally said, "You know, if you're going to be late, you must call." Leslie was expected home at 5:30 on weekdays. That would give her time to help set the table for dinner.

"Don't worry," Leslie replied impatiently. She was seventeen, and she didn't want to be treated like a little kid. "You know I always get back on time."

Carrying her basketball and portable radio, Leslie opened the front door and started down the pathway to the street. "Bye," Ros called after her, trying hard to sound casual.

It was never easy for Rosalind to let her daughter go out alone. Leslie Faber was retarded.

To someone who didn't know her well, Leslie might appear almost normal: a friendly, outgoing teenager who loved sports. But Ros knew that Leslie's condition had left her impaired in a way that wasn't always visible. A lot of what people said in seemingly straightforward conversations went over her head and she was extraordinarily susceptible to suggestion and manipulation by anyone who seemed to like her.

In a big city, Ros thought, Leslie would have been vulnerable to the predatory stranger. But in 1989 Glen Ridge, New Jersey, retained the gentility of a more tranquil age; it remained a small, picture-perfect suburb where almost everyone knew everyone else. And that's what reassured Ros Faber. Today Leslie would be shooting baskets in the middle of the afternoon in a community playground that was a five-minute walk from her house. She had played in this park all her life. The other neighborhood children knew her well. They all came from respectable, well-off families like the Fabers themselves. The homes of many of the Fabers' friends were nearby. Strangers rarely passed through the sheltered streets of Glen Ridge. What could be safer than a couple of hours of healthy recreation in Cartaret Park?

The Fabers had moved to Glen Ridge fifteen years before and had never regretted it. When they learned that Leslie was retarded, it comforted them to know that they lived in the sort of place where the strong didn't prey on the weak. For Leslie needed protection, and the cruel streets of the city could inflict terrible injuries on a defenseless child. The Fabers believed that raising their daughter in Glen Ridge would keep her out of harm's way.

It was, in fact, just the sort of lovely, peaceful suburb many Americans dream about but few can afford. Many of the houses were neat and spacious, the streets were immaculate and picturesque, the schools were good, and the values of the community, Glen Ridgers would say with pride, were solidly planted in family, country, and the free enterprise system. On days when the urban swirl seemed overwhelming, Glen Ridge was the kind of place a New Yorker dreamed of escaping to.

Only 7,800 people lived in Glen Ridge. It was the second-smallest municipality in populous Essex County, consisting of just 1.3 square miles, and you could drive from one end to the other in five minutes. Set at the crest of a gentle slope rising from Newark Bay, the town seemed little changed in 1989 from when it was created in 1895. For the people who lived there, Glen Ridge remained a secure retreat in a contentious world.

A teenager walking the cobblestoned, leafy streets of Glen Ridge couldn't help feeling secure. Tranquility was so highly valued that the entire commercial life was limited to a couple of small stores housed in a single building near the commuter rail station. Indeed, when kids complained that it was boring to live in such a small, unexciting town, parents were quick to tell them that it was precisely the pastoral peacefulness of the suburb that made it a perfect place to raise children.

With her usual exuberance, Leslie trotted the short distance to the park. She was tall for her age, broad-shouldered, and somewhat overweight. Leslie was dressed in her play clothes: a West Orange High School shirt, purple sweatpants, and red-and-white sneakers. She was very proud of the radio she carried. It was about a foot and a half long, with speakers at each end. What made it special was its color—pink. It was a pretty radio, a feminine radio. That's why she had bought it. It was important to her because she had paid for it with her own money that she had earned mowing the lawn and raking leaves for her parents. She had plunked down the $35—her savings—at Crazy Eddie's about a year and a half ago; since then, the pink radio had been her constant companion whenever she went out to play.

Her walk to the park took her along Linden Avenue past the elementary school she had attended through the fourth grade. She walked one long block and turned left onto Cartaret Street, where she entered the playground. She had taken the same walk hundreds of times in her life.

Today the weather was cool and blustery, typical of the first day of March. The park was rectangular, about three hundred feet in length. Leslie headed for the basketball court in the southwest corner. She would remember later that as she walked toward the court, she noticed a stick in the grass. It was about a foot long, smeared with mud and flecked with red paint. She picked it up and threw it a few feet away. It was nicely balanced and carried well. She thought it would make a good "throwing stick" and decided to keep it.

Directly parallel to the basketball court, on the northwest side, was the softball diamond. At the other end of the park, the southeast corner, was the baseball diamond. Six rows of wooden bleachers, where spectators sat during Little League games, looked down on the first-base line.

At the baseball diamond a bunch of high school guys had formed two lines. The boys wore baseball gloves and cleats and trailed baseball bats behind them. Leslie, who was so devoted to athletics that she divided the year by the different sports seasons, knew what was going on. The guys on Glen Ridge's championship baseball team were going to have a preseason practice session, an easy drill without any adult coaches around. Loosen up, look sharp. The stars of the high school's other big-time teams, the wrestlers and the football players, also were there, hanging out, checking out the scene. This was very cool, Leslie thought. When she had left her house a few minutes before, who would have guessed that she was headed for jock heaven?

In a bigger town or in a city, most of these guys would be considered average athletes at best. But in the insulated world of Glen Ridge, they were the princes of the playing field. And that was the only world Leslie had ever known. These were the guys who acted as if they owned the high school. More than once, Leslie overheard girls saying they'd just *die* if the jocks didn't invite them to their parties.

It was a tough call to pick out the leader among all these handsome, popular guys, but Leslie guessed that it was Kyle Scherzer, although he wasn't her personal, true fave. Kyle, everybody said, would probably be picked as the best athlete in the senior class. Kyle was captain of the baseball team. He and his twin brother, Kevin, were co-captains of the football team. The Scherzers lived at 34 Lorraine Street, a white shingled house adjoining the park. From their backyard it was just a step onto the grass of Cartaret. Now, as she stood on the basketball court, Leslie could see Kyle on the back deck of his house, surveying the park as though it were his private kingdom.

Leslie knew that the deck was a pretty special place, although she had never stood on it herself. In whispers interspersed with giggles, her teammates on the girls' basketball and softball teams had explained the significance of being invited to a party on the Scherzers' deck.

For years now, Kyle and Kevin had invited their friends to deck parties after long afternoons of sports. Within the closed circle of jocks their spontaneous parties were famous. This was the closest thing the jocks had to a frat house. Here on the deck the guys celebrated a football or baseball victory, cooled out after a tough practice, or just gathered to goof around. Mostly, it was just the guys, but every once in a while one of the girls who trailed after the jocks would be admitted. The menu was usually soda and potato chips; occasionally, when no adults were around, there would be a few cans of beer. When the weather was cold or nasty, the guys would retreat downstairs to the Scherzers' semifinished basement to watch television or play Nintendo.

Leslie understood: If you got invited, it showed that you belonged. You were part of the gang. You counted. The teenage heroes of the town thought you were worthy of their attention. This honor had never been bestowed on Leslie. It wasn't because she was a newcomer to Cartaret or one of those kids who paid tuition to the high school and lived out of town. No, Leslie was as much a fixture in the park and in the town as the Scherzers.

She pitched for the girls' softball team and played guard for the high school girls' basketball team. She sold Girl Scout cookies door to door. In the spring she was there for the Memorial Day parade and in the winter she was there for the Christmas tree–lighting ceremony. At all times of the year, except when the snow got too deep, she could be seen riding around town on her bike, her brown hair blowing back from her forehead, her shoulders hunched over the handlebars, a big smile brightening her face as she called out "Hi" to all the people she knew and to people she knew not at all.

That was Leslie's special attribute: her buoyant personality. "If you smiled at her, she'd give you the world," said Christine Middleton, who was Leslie's teammate on the basketball team. "All she ever wanted was to be accepted by the other kids, to be part of the gang. And the kids she always admired the most, because she herself was good at sports, were the jocks. She'd see the other girls mooning after them and she'd want to do that, too."

Although she traveled freely throughout the small community, her most frequent destination was Cartaret Park. From the time she was a toddler, Leslie had watched the boys of Cartaret grow up. As a child, Leslie had lived near the eastern boundary of the playground. Then when she was in middle school, her mom and dad moved to their current house a few blocks away.

When Leslie was very young, Rosalind would bring her to the shady incline at the western end of the park where all the other mothers gathered with their babies and preschoolers. Rosalind would push her daughter on the yellow and red swings or watch her clamber in the miniature playhouse constructed of logs.

From Leslie's earliest memories, the Scherzer twins were always around. Whenever she was playing, they were playing. Whenever she was just a kid, not a dutiful daughter or an obedient student, the Scherzers were also being kids. Leslie was generally accurate when she later said of Kyle and Kevin, "I knew them all my life." She knew them, but only from afar. Leslie and the boys had followed separate paths through childhood and adolescence—Leslie friendless and alone, the boys clustered in the most envied and admired teenage clique in the town. Up to that moment, their lives had never converged.

Today didn't seem any different from most of the days of her youth. She played by herself on the basketball court, firing up some three-point bombs from behind the foul circle. Then, avoiding the puddles caused by last night's rain, she practiced her drives to the basket, shooting left-handed and right-handed, just like the pros.

A hundred feet away, the elite teenagers of Glen Ridge reveled in their male camaraderie. How many afternoons had she ended, from her vantage point under the backboards or in the top row of the wooden bleachers, watching Kyle and Kevin and their friends trooping happily toward the Scherzer house? But she was never included in that group. Look at it the way the guys did: If you invited a cute cheerleader, that boosted your romantic reputation. If you invited a not-so-cute brain, that might at least help you pass history and stay academically eligible for athletics. But what was the advantage of befriending a plain-looking retarded girl?

Sure, she played on teams, but she wasn't any star. Sure, she'd been hanging around for a lot of years, but she wasn't part of any popular group in school. In fact, she didn't even go to school in Glen Ridge anymore. The district had transferred her out to West Orange, where she attended a class for retarded kids. No matter how cheerful and friendly she was, no matter how desperately she yearned for one sign of recognition from her heroes, Leslie Faber could never expect to break through this invisible wall that separated her from the coolest kids in the school. She could never imagine being invited to one of the famous parties given by the Scherzer twins. No way. "Up until *that* day, I was never invited to a party at the Scherzer house," Leslie Faber would say later.

During the next half hour the baseball players rapped grounders, pegged bullets at each other, and chased down fly balls. The guys who were on other teams stood nearby in small groups, laughing, jostling each other, throwing mock punches. Guy stuff. They didn't seem to pay any attention to the young woman who was faking out an imaginary Michael Jordan over on the basketball court.

The few patches of blue were obscured by thick gray clouds, the wind picked up, and it looked as if it could rain again. The practice was breaking up. A bunch of the baseball players began walking in the direction of the Scherzers' house. Today was a good day to party. The twins' parents were in Florida all week. Aside from an elderly grandmother, the boys had the run of the house.

From the corner of her eye, Leslie could see five or six of the other boys, who weren't on the baseball team, walking toward the basketball court.

They stopped a few feet away, waving, smiling, all part of one happy group. The one boy who kept coming toward her was Christopher Archer.

Of all the kids who played at Cartaret, Leslie Faber probably knew Chris Archer and his brother, Paul, best. Leslie's parents were friends of the Archers' parents. Leslie would visit, sometimes unannounced, at their house down on lower Ridgewood Avenue. She would stay a while and talk with Chris and Paul when she was selling her Girl Scout cookies door to door.

Although she hadn't spent a huge amount of time with them when she was growing up, she had learned that there was a big difference between the two brothers. Paul had a kind smile and gentle, almost mournful, eyes. Eyes that melted you. He was a reasonably good football player and a captain of the wrestling team. And he was *very* good-looking. With all that, you might think he'd act stuck-up. But sometimes he'd talk to her, mostly about sports, and treat her just like any other girl in town. A few times he could be mean, but mostly he was nice. Paul was a really "cool guy." Chris, who was a year younger than Paul, had steel-cold eyes that always seemed to be looking beyond her. He almost never asked her about her basketball and softball, and he always had that sly grin on his face when he was making conversation with her.

Of the two, she liked Paul better, but it was important for her to please Chris; he might tell Paul she was nice. Chris was her link, her connection to Paul. Leslie never tried to hide her feelings about Paul. "I really liked him," she said later. "He's cute. He's handsome. He was my hero."

Chris chatted her up, his big smile radiating high spirits and camaraderie. He said to her, C'mon over to the Scherzer house, the guys just want to talk to you. C'mon over, we're all going to have a party.

Leslie considered this sudden invitation to attend a party with the most popular guys in town. Then she decided it wasn't such a good idea. No, I don't want to, Leslie said. Chris's invitation raised a question in her mind: Why would they want to take me down to the basement when they always called me retarded?

Chris, never at a loss for a new ploy, kept trying. "He said that his brother, Paul, was there," Leslie remembered later. "Chris told me that Paul would go out with me. I like Paul. So I went with Chris."

Gathering up her belongings—the stick, the radio, and her basketball—Leslie set out on the three-minute walk to the house. On the way to her "date" with Paul, Chris "walked with me, and put his arm around me," Leslie said. "He was like really romantic." When she was asked how Chris made her feel as he accompanied her to the Scherzer house, she replied: "Wonderful."

They passed the rear of the Scherzer house. The molded plastic chairs were stacked in one corner of the redwood deck next to a pile of tie-on canvas seat covers. The beach umbrella had been removed from its hole in the round picnic table and propped against a railing. It was too chilly on the first of March to hold an outside deck party; it would have to be in the semifinished basement.

A group of boys entered 34 Lorraine Street first. Trailing behind them were Chris and Leslie. Chris opened the door to the front entrance of the house. Leslie could feel his hand on her back, prodding gently but insistently. In the hall, just beyond the door, pegs had been set in the wall. The boys took off their red-and-white varsity jackets and hung them on the pegs. What a rush! Leslie could hang her own jacket on a peg, just as if she were also part of the team, just as if she were one of the pretty, effervescent girls who were always hanging around the jocks.

Chris led her forward, toward the stairs to the basement. On the way, she glanced into the kitchen, where she thought she saw the figure of an elderly woman.

Chris guided her down the stairs, past the younger kids who were clustered on the steps. As she reached the bottom, Leslie had a view of the entire basement. This was it: She had arrived. She was entering into the boys' special place, the "clubhouse" of the stars of Glen Ridge.

The room she entered now had a musty, wintry feel. It was lighted by a dim overhead bulb, turning ruddy outdoor complexions into gray pallor. The athletic trophies awarded over the years to Kyle and Kevin and their two older brothers were displayed on wall shelves, along with family photographs. One wall was unfinished, consisting of whitewashed concrete. Leslie would remember that three concrete blocks were piled near the wall. A sofa in the middle of the room could comfortably seat three. An area rug had been placed near the sofa. From the sofa you had a good view of a big-screen television. You could also watch TV from a wooden bench and maybe a half-dozen folding chairs. The entire basement was twenty-seven feet long and nineteen feet wide. There was only one exit, the steps to the front door.

In one alcove there was a refrigerator. Up against the wall, near the refrigerator, was a broom. Leslie, with her excellent memory for details, never forgot the color of the broomstick. She would always remember that it was "fire-engine red." In the back end of the basement, leading to the deck, the room was L-shaped. This area contained a bar, with three or four bar stools. There was a shelf at this end, and under it was a jumble of athletic equipment: basketballs, gloves, and baseballs and bats. Quite a few bats, including even a fungo bat used for practice. From her many years of playing softball, Leslie knew all about fungo bats: they were slightly narrower than a regular bat, but close to regulation-length.

Leslie would later remember that lots of boys were milling about in the basement. When she arrived, five of them, all seniors, were already down there. Among them was the one she adored—Paul Archer. Others joined them, including sophomore and senior baseball players and, of course, one junior, her friend Chris Archer. Some of them sat down or stood on the stairs.

The big attraction in the Scherzer basement in the winter and spring of 1989 was the Nintendo game, which at that time was still something of a novelty. Leslie could see a couple of the boys huddled around it.

Leslie also saw some of the boys arranging folding chairs in front of the couch. To her, it looked like they were getting ready to "watch a movie." A movie in which she was the star.

Chris leads her to the sofa where another senior heartthrob, Bryant Grober, is sitting. Leslie doesn't know him as well as she knows the Archers and Kyle and Kevin, because he lives on the other end of town and went to a different elementary school than she did. He comes to the park from way over on Forest Avenue and he isn't around all that much. She has seen Bryant play football, and she sometimes passes him in the corridors when she goes to Glen Ridge High School for basketball practice. She knows he is popular with the guys. She knows the girls think he is really cute. Sit here, Chris says, the idea man, handing her over to Bryant.

There is the hum of pleasantries exchanged in the basement.

Leslie, how's the basketball team doing?

Leslie, you gonna pitch again for the softball team?

But mostly the boys are talking to each other, chattering excitedly, like a group of kids rehearsing a student play.

After a while, Leslie hears the sound of footsteps on the stairs. She sees the adult she only glimpsed when she came into the house. The boys are saying, That's Kyle and Kevin's grandmother. She will always remember the old woman on the stairs—the presence of an adult makes the party seem normal just before it lurches out of control.

The woman, Leslie notices, has "white hair, sort of going bald." She is skinny and has a cane—"a silver metal cane with a green handle." This elderly woman, leaning heavily on her cane, walks halfway down the flight of steps. She calls out, "Kevin, you have a phone call." Kevin bounds up the steps, passing his grandmother, and disappears into the kitchen to take his call. This reassures Leslie: The boys wouldn't do something really bad, would they, knowing that the Scherzer twins' grandmother was bustling about in the kitchen right above them?

The kids are talking, but talking rather softly. For so many kids in a relatively small space, it is surprisingly quiet. Phil Grant, a senior baseball player, feels a hushed, expectant weight in the room, like the heavy silence before a storm.

Another boy, a fifteen-year-old sophomore, watches Chris Archer leaning over and whispering to Leslie. He sees Leslie sitting in the middle of the couch, Bryant on her right. Bryant pulls off his pants and then his underpants. The sophomore can't hear what Chris is saying to Leslie, but he can see what's going on. The sophomore looks into Leslie's eyes and sees what the others can't or won't see. He sees puzzlement and confusion and skepticism.

Now they have all taken their places—thirteen young men, the pride of Glen Ridge High, and Leslie. Some of the boys are seated on the folding chairs, a few feet away from the sofa. Others are standing to the side and behind the chairs. A few kids are watching from the stairs. For the moment Paul Archer is silent; he doesn't seem to be in any rush to ask Leslie out. Kyle is standing near the line of folding chairs. Kevin, who has returned to the basement after taking his phone call, is sitting on one of the chairs.

As Leslie begins to pull up her shirt, the sophomore who has seen puzzlement and confusion in Leslie's eyes turns to another of the underclassmen and says, "Let's get out of here." They leave together.

Phil Grant, the senior baseball player, also feels queasy as Leslie begins to disrobe. He is thinking, I don't belong here, it's just too weird. Phil exchanges looks with a buddy of his, another senior baseball player. They both start up the stairs together. Then Phil stops and turns and says to his childhood friend Paul Archer, "It's wrong. C'mon with me."

Archer says nothing in reply. He stays where he is, with his brother and his buddies.

At the top of the stairs, Phil hears somebody shouting, "Don't go. Don't miss this." Even though what his friends are doing makes him uncomfortable, he feels obliged to offer an excuse. "I got to go home," he says. "Seeya later."

Six young men have left. Seven young men, six seniors and junior Chris Archer, will remain in the basement with Leslie until they are done with her.

Yes, it is "just like a movie"—she attracting all the attention, the boys staring at her from their chairs, the other boys peering down at her from the stairs. But, as in all memorable movies, certain scenes would stand out.

Things she heard, things people did—images that would stay with her no matter how many times she was later questioned by the police, by investigators, by psychiatrists and psychologists, by grand jurors and prosecutors and defense lawyers. Some of what Leslie remembers:

The boys getting up from their chairs, crowding around the sofa, a circle of flushed, excited faces urging her, Go further, go further!

Phil and his friend and the younger kids leaving without saying a word to her.

Leslie left alone with the inner circle of jocks: Kyle and Kevin, Bryant Grober, Paul and Chris Archer, and two of their friends and teammates, Peter Quigley and Richard Corcoran.

Leslie feels a hand on her head. There is a penis in her mouth.

Leslie hears another boy shout, You whore!

The boys are laughing, snickering. How does it feel? a boy asks. Does it make you feel good?

Leslie hears the voice say, Let's play a joke on her.

A neighborhood boy, a boy she has known all her life, is walking toward the 'fridge, reaching for the broom with the bright-red handle.

A boy walks to the back of the basement, fishes through the pile of sports equipment, pulls out a bat.

A voice says, Stop. You're hurting her.

Another voice says, Do it more.

Leslie remembers: Everyone was laughing. I was crying to myself, but I had tears coming out of my eyes.

Leslie remembers: The boys say to her that this all must be our secret. We'll be mad at you if you talk about this, you'll get kicked out of your school, we'll tell your mother if you break our secret.

Then, all in a circle, they clasp one hand on top of the other, all their hands together, like a basketball team on the sidelines at the end of a time-out. Leslie would say: It was just like one-two-three win!

A voice announces: We're not going to tell anybody. This is our little secret.

A voice says to Leslie: Hurry up. Go. Get out of here.

After Leslie left the basement, she waited a while outside the Scherzer house. Then she went into the park. She waited there, walking back and forth between the baseball diamond and the basketball court. She waited and waited for Paul Archer, her dream date, to show up. But he never did.

She walked a few blocks into Bloomfield to visit one of her few friends,

Jennifer Lipinski. "She always stuck up for me," Leslie would say later. "I wanted to discuss with her what happened to me." But it was already late in the afternoon, long after she was expected at Jennifer's house. Jennifer had left, so Leslie spent a little time playing ball with Jennifer's brother. Then she went home.

Rosalind Faber was not pleased with her daughter. She had expected Leslie to be home by 5:30. Leslie knew she was supposed to set the table for dinner. That was her one daily chore. Routine provided continuity and structure for Leslie. But the table was not set and Ros's daughter was not there. 6:30. 6:45. Rosalind was getting nervous. It was dark outside. Where was Leslie?

When Leslie showed up at 7 o'clock, her mother did not try to hide her disapproval. "Where were you?" she asked, each word coated with ice. "Why didn't you call?"

"I was at the park, playing basketball," Leslie mumbled.

"I was worried."

"I'm okay," she said, looking down at the floor.

Glancing at the stick Leslie was holding, her mother asked, "What's that?"

"Oh, it's just a stick I found in the park," Leslie said.

"It's dirty. Why don't you put it in the garbage?"

"No, I want to keep it. It's good for throwing."

Rosalind took the stick from her. "All right, I'll keep it for you," she said. She put the stick on the top of the refrigerator, out of sight.

"I'm going up to change my clothes," Leslie said, starting up the stairs.

"I don't want you to do this again," her mother called after her. "You know it upsets me when you're not home when you're supposed to be."

Leslie, already upstairs, already going into her room, didn't answer.

At the dinner table, Leslie appeared distracted and withdrawn. She ate quickly and did not volunteer any information about her day. Her behavior made her parents uneasy. Leslie did not usually start a conversation, but she did join in when her mother and father initiated a discussion. Tonight she was quiet.

Charles Faber, who was a manager at a large corporation, knew how to draw people out, to find out what was bothering them. But with Leslie he was running into a wall.

"Leslie, what's wrong? Is anything bothering you?"

"Nothing," she said. "I don't know . . . Nothing's wrong."

Something's not right, Rosalind was thinking. She's trying to send us a signal, Charles was thinking, but what signal? The Fabers knew from experience that when Leslie didn't want to talk about a subject or when she was hiding something, it was not productive to push her. You had to wait for her to open up and then you asked a specific question. If you tried to press her, she would go silent on you or lapse into vagueness: Well, gee, I don't know . . .

Rosalind tried one more time. "Did you run into anybody at the park?"

Her response was sharp. "Why do you want to know?"

"I'm just asking, Leslie. Well, did you?"

"No. Nobody."

When they finished dinner, Leslie gathered up the dishes. Then she went into the living room to watch a rerun of "Gilligan's Island," her favorite TV show. After a while, Leslie said she was tired and went upstairs to get ready to go to bed.

At about 3 A.M. her parents heard Leslie talking in her sleep. Their bedroom was next door to Leslie's and the sounds could be heard through the wall. Words. Then what sounded like a muffled cry or gasp. They knew that when something disturbed Leslie, she would talk in her sleep. But she didn't often cry.

They got up and quietly walked into her room. They tried to make out what she was saying, but the words were indistinct. She was squirming in the bed—and groaning. Rosalind didn't want to wake her, but she was so concerned that she couldn't stop herself.

She shook Leslie. "Les, you're talking in your sleep. What's wrong?"

Leslie rubbed her eyes. "Nothing," she said. "*Nothing's* wrong."

Back in their bedroom, Charles Faber looked at his wife and said: "Something's happened."

That morning Rosalind tried to probe gently. "Leslie, you really had a restless night last night. Is everything okay? What were you talking about in your sleep?"

Leslie answered much as she had at dinner. "I don't remember. . . . Everything's okay. . . . I'm fine."

Months later she would recall that night after she came home from the Scherzers' basement and say, "I was embarrassed. I was too scared to tell my parents. They wouldn't understand."

2

Sheila Byron had just attended Easter Sunday Mass at Sacred Heart Church in Bloomfield, Glen Ridge's next-door neighbor. As she left the church this morning, March 26, her mind was definitely not on her job, which was working as a detective for the Glen Ridge Police Department. Her mind was on the week she had just spent with two girlfriends in Mexico, a Club Med vacation. Her mind was on white sand and turquoise water. As she crossed the street in front of the church, she met her boss, Detective Lieutenant Richard Corcoran.

"Hey, boss, how you doing?" she greeted him. "Was it a good week?"

"Oh, it wasn't a good week at all," he said. "There's something pretty serious going on."

It made sense that Lieutenant Corcoran would turn to Sheila Byron when he caught a tough case. Although she was only twenty-six, she was a rising star on the Glen Ridge police force. First of all, she knew the town well. She had graduated from Glen Ridge High in 1981 and had lived in town most of her life. During her four years on the force, she had handled some delicate cases, including wife battering and child abuse, with intelligence and sensitivity. Her style—direct, calm, and easygoing—was effective in tamping down a barroom fight or coping with the good-natured teasing of her fellow cops.

Sheila Byron stood out, and not only because she was a solid cop. She was a tall woman with sparkling eyes and long, thick hair. She was also a stylish dresser. In social situations she was outgoing and gregarious. In the department and the town, she was admired for her personality, beauty, and brains. During her brief police career, she had moved up from uniformed cop to juvenile officer to detective. One of only two women in the department, she was treated with professional respect by the men she worked with. She would need their respect on this case.

As Corcoran filled her in, the case impressed her as something unusual, something her relatively brief experience as a cop in a small, genteel suburb hadn't prepared her for. Bizarre accusations were floating around the school and the town, involving a bunch of high school guys, including the Scherzer twins, and a retarded girl. There were rumors that some of the guys might have done things to the girl with a bat and a broomstick. The police, Corcoran told her, already had the names of nine boys who might have been in the Scherzer basement on March 1. Maybe there had been a sexual assault. There wasn't enough to go on yet to be sure. One thing was clear, a lot of guys had been there. And the cops also had the name of the possible victim: Leslie Faber.

Byron had seen enough of Leslie Faber over the years to know she was different. But she wasn't sure how different. "The Fabers say they want a woman to talk to Leslie," Corcoran told her. "They were waiting for you to get back. They want to bring Leslie in tomorrow."

"I'll get in early and read the file," Byron said.

When she walked into the squad room the next morning, Sheila felt the tension. She didn't hear the usual wisecracks about who got poured out of the Town Pub on Saturday night. Nobody was asking her if she fell in love with one of the studs at Club Med. When the police chief, Tom Dugan, handed her the paper on the case, he seemed more nervous than usual. Dugan was a real go-by-the-book guy. Make sure you follow procedure. Don't leave anything out. He was always like that, but now he seemed strained. Something was eroding the armor of cop stoicism. Emotions swept across his broad Irish face: sadness, anxiety. And she caught that blink in his eyes; it was as close to fear as she had ever seen. All he said to her was "Get it all on paper. I want everything. I want it all."

She understood his concerns when she finished reading. The slim file began with March 22. That day, Charles Figueroa, a high school senior, told school officials that he had overheard students talking about a sexual encounter involving a number of athletes and a retarded girl. The vice-principal of the high school called the police. Detectives Richard Corcoran and Robert Griffin went to the school. There they interviewed the principal, the vice-principal, and Figueroa. Sheila knew Charlie Figueroa. His family lived near where she had grown up, and he was one of only three black students in the Class of '89. She had seen him play football and remembered that he had also wrestled for the high school.

Detective Griffin wrote in his report that, according to the school administrators, "a complainant who was a seventeen-year-old girl, classified as educable mentally retarded, may have been sexually abused by a group of juvenile males from Glen Ridge High School."

According to the detective's report, Figueroa recalled that the day after the experience in the basement, he had been standing outside the Scherzers' house with a group of other jocks. Figueroa said the boys told him what they did to Leslie, which the detective translated into legal terms:

"The complainant was reportedly penetrated . . . by baseball bats, broom-sticks, and a musical drumstick." The other jocks also reportedly told Figueroa that "oral sex" occurred during the incident.

Baseball bats, broomsticks, oral sex. The detective's account was shock-ing. But the next report in the file had even greater impact on Byron. This was Griffin's summary of his interview on March 23 with Margaret Sav-age, Leslie's swimming coach at West Orange High School. In effect, for the first time Byron was hearing the "victim's" account, albeit in a second-hand version from the swimming coach.

Savage reconstructed for Detective Griffin a conversation she had with Leslie three days after the basement encounter. Savage said Leslie told her that she had been at a "party in the basement with ten boys and they did things to me." According to Savage: "They asked her how many fingers could she put up [her] butt and then put 'something very big into me' and then they asked her to suck their dicks and said they wouldn't like her if she didn't do it and she would 'get into trouble.'"

Savage told the detective: "They [the boys] told her not to tell 'cause . . . they'd be mad and she'd be kicked out of school." Griffin noted: "Com-plainant told Savage that she was afraid to say 'no' and didn't know what to do." Leslie told the swimming coach that the boys had assured her that what they were doing was "okay," but Leslie wasn't so sure of that because, as she put it: "It hurt a lot."

What she read took Byron's breath away. If the allegations contained in these reports could be verified, you had the elements of a major crime. But that wasn't all. One other report in the file contained a list of nine names culled from the interviews with Figueroa and Savage.

Whoa. Wait a minute. She knew these names. She knew these kids. Archer, Scherzer, Grober, Quigley. They were popular, they came from good families, they were the best athletes in the high school. Some of them had been in a few scrapes with the law. Noisy parties, underage drinking— nothing major. As far as she knew, the worst thing you could say about them was that they were boisterous.

It was strange when you thought about it. These jocks, of all the teenagers in town, probably got along the best with cops. When she was on duty at sports events or keeping order at a high school dance, the Scherzer twins always made a point of coming over and saying hello. She remembered them as far back as the eighth grade.

The only word of caution came from a patrolman who knew the twins. He had told her, "Watch out for those two. They're pretty wild." But it sounded like nothing more than rowdiness, so she'd put it out of her mind.

She had been in high school. She had seen jocks acting as though they owned the place, obnoxious, arrogant. But now they were selling stocks, pushing insurance policies, married with a couple of kids, shouldering a heavy mortgage. You can't apply the same standards to a sixteen-year-old that you apply to an adult. You have to give him a few years to grow up.

Often in a small town, when you hear something bad about a kid, the first thing you do is check out the family. Are the parents big drinkers? Do they beat or abuse their kids? No hint of that with the families on this list.

The Archers? Doug Archer was Mr. Congeniality. A salesman of computer systems by trade, he was a big civic booster, along with his wife, Michaele, a nurse. They lived on Ridgewood Avenue, the town's grandest street, in a brick Colonial-revival house. Genial and outgoing, Doug and Michaele were popular in the upper reaches of Glen Ridge's church, civic, and social circuits, and they were friendly with Leslie Faber's parents.

Whenever Sheila met Doug at a school function or on some town committee, he gave her the big handshake with the simultaneous pat on the back and the ear-to-ear smile. Always, "Sheila, it's great to see you. You're doing a great job with the kids in town." And Michaele Archer, she was as nice as they came. Sweet, thoughtful, a loving mother. A good nurse, too, from what Sheila had heard.

Many parents didn't want to hear anything bad about their children. That wasn't true of the Archers. They had four children, all boys, all athletes, all popular with parents and kids in the community. Michaele was always up-front, telling Sheila, Let us know if the boys are problems; call us if they're at a party where there's alcohol. When Sheila did call, they always acted as if they were glad to hear from her, appreciative, very much the concerned parents.

The Scherzers? Jack, he was Mr. Jock. During the days he was a maintenance supervisor for the Otis Elevator Company in New York City. But after work, every season, every year, he was there for each game his kids played in. He was there even when his kids weren't playing. Lived and died with every pass, every base hit. Now, with Jack, you might not want to criticize his boys, because he seemed to think they were nearly perfect. But so did lots of fathers. When you showed up in the police car at a block party on Lorraine Street, Jack would be the first guy to show you around. Mrs. Scherzer, Geraldine, she was quiet, faded into the background. But a nice lady. Pleasant.

The Grobers? They were quiet people with a lovely house on Forest Avenue in the prosperous north end of town, a couple of streets away from the country club. Nate Grober was a doctor, with an office in East Orange.

Sheila had heard that his patients loved him because he really showed concern for them. Bryant was a football player and wrestler; his older brother had also been a popular jock—a wrestler, she remembered. The family probably had some money, but didn't show it off. Bryant's mom, Rosemary, was also a nurse, like Michaele Archer. Easygoing, cheerful. The kids in the neighborhood loved her cookies.

The Quigleys? Not as active on the social-civic-sports scene as some of the other families, but a pleasant, low-key couple. Michael Quigley worked as an accountant; his wife, Mary, had been a staff member at an early-childhood center near Glen Ridge. Mr. Quigley didn't show up for every game the way Jack Scherzer did, but he had coached in the town's preteen sports leagues. Peter had two brothers, one younger and one older, both into sports. Many in the town thought Peter was the most affable of all the boys in the jock circle; the seniors had voted him "best-looking" and "best body." He was also a co-captain of the football team, and if you took a secret vote of his teammates, they would probably pick him as the best pure athlete on the team. Solid family, lived a couple of blocks away from Cartaret Park.

Some of the boys listed in the police report had reportedly been in the basement. Others were rumored to have tried to talk Leslie into coming back a second time. Supposedly, there were even more kids involved, but the police didn't have all the names yet. These were the sons of lawyers, investment bankers, accountants, teachers—people who formed the backbone of the town. They weren't necessarily the old-line aristocrats of Glen Ridge; they didn't all run for public office or belong to the country club, but they held good jobs, volunteered for time-consuming civic activities, coached the community sports teams, and went to church. Cheez, they didn't just show up on Sunday; they sang in the church choir, they were vestrymen. They defined Glen Ridge; they made it what it was.

Sheila knew that the case could be dynamite. If you were a young cop and you wanted to hold on to your job for a while and maybe even had a secret ambition to become the first woman police chief of Glen Ridge, you'd better go slow. The potential was there for charging some of these boys with first-degree rape. Serious stuff. Putting aside what an accusation like that could do to a kid's future, it could tear a family apart, ruin something that these people had worked their whole adult lives to build. And it wasn't only them as individuals. If any of this was true, it could also savage the entire town. This wasn't about one or two kids going bad. What did you have here, many of the best-known boys in the senior class? The file she held in her hands struck at the heart of the way kids were raised in

Glen Ridge, at the basic values of the town. The paper in this manila folder was a ticking bomb.

She wondered how many more names might be added to the list. (Ultimately, as the investigation expanded, the police report would list nineteen names of Glen Ridge High School students.) As the town's juvenile officer, Sheila Byron had a good idea of who belonged to the different adolescent cliques. The guys on the list were all jocks, but one name in the group was missing. She knew he was tight with these boys. They were his best friends. He had played football and had wrestled. He had difficulty in school with his studies and with observing rules. He had the reputation of being something of a loudmouth. But so far nobody had put him in the basement. And, God, she hoped they wouldn't. The last name she wanted to see on the list was that of Richard Corcoran Junior. That would be some wonderful bonus: the son of your immediate boss, the son of Detective Lieutenant Richard Corcoran—a rape suspect.

The yellow light of caution warned her: Go slow, Sheila. Don't rush to judgment. The one consolation this Monday morning was that nothing was certain, nothing had been proved. All they had to go on were the fragments of a conversation reported by one student and what a young woman in a special ed class had *reportedly* told a teacher. Sheila hadn't talked to any of the boys who had been in the basement. And she hadn't talked to the young woman. Who knew? Cases could crumble in a hurry. Maybe when she met Leslie this afternoon she would have a clearer idea of whether any of this would stick.

For Sheila, a key question was: Did the boys force Leslie to perform these acts, or did she go along willingly? The matter of consent is a critical issue in most rape cases, except when the victim is so badly beaten that there can be no question that force was used. When victim and assailant know each other, the consent question can be difficult to answer. In this case, involving a supposedly retarded girl, it would be even more so. Did Leslie give consent or not? So far, the reports Sheila had read made it sound like Leslie had not actively resisted.

But if she hadn't, was it possible that she was incapable of giving consent? Was she too retarded to understand what consent meant? Did she realize what was happening to her in the basement? If she hadn't understood, then what? Was what the boys did a crime—or was it just a crummy thing to do? With Leslie, the detective believed that consent would supersede all the other issues in the case.

Byron finished reading the file. At 4:30 Mrs. Faber brought Leslie into the police station. As soon as Leslie saw Sheila, she walked away from her mom. It was obvious to Byron that Leslie didn't want to talk in front of her mother. Ros Faber seemed to sense that, too. After she introduced Leslie to Byron, she left the room. Ros knew that if Leslie was going to unburden herself, she would have to do it without her parents present. As the detective wrote in her notes concerning that first meeting, "She was very concerned about her mother finding out what happened."

Sheila led Leslie to a small room on the second floor of the Public Safety Building that was used for interviews. The furnishings were austere: a desk, a couple of chairs, walls unadorned except for an old map of Glen Ridge. There was one window, which looked down on a quiet residential street.

Leslie was dressed in play clothes: gym shorts, a sweatshirt, sneakers. She sat in a chair. Sheila sat next to her. For much of the next ninety minutes, Leslie would stare down at the wood floor. Often her remarks would drift off the subject. She'd compliment Sheila on her gold earrings. She'd get up and look out the window.

Byron decided that in this first meeting she would try to keep the conversation informal and relaxed. She wanted Leslie to feel comfortable with her. The detective wanted to gauge her competence, to see how credible she appeared.

She did not take a formal, signed statement from Leslie. It was her practice never to take a signed statement during her first meeting with the victim of a sexual assault. Often the traumatic impact of the experience distorted the victim's memory, confusing the chronology of what happened when and the sequence of who did what. At the second or third meeting, when the victim felt more comfortable, her recollection of the assault would be sharper and more complete.

Getting a complete account of what happened in the basement could wait for another day. For openers this afternoon, Sheila asked Leslie about her dog, her schoolwork, her softball and basketball practice. It was pretty clear from the start that Leslie liked her. She had always expressed an affinity for pretty, intelligent young women who had achieved a lot in a short time. And that described Sheila: a woman who radiated confidence.

And probably most important to Leslie, this terrific woman seemed to really enjoy her company.

After about forty-five minutes, the detective eased into the reason why Leslie was at the police station this afternoon: "You know, Leslie, some of the kids at the high school heard these boys saying they did sexual things to you."

Without hesitating, Leslie answered, "Yes, yes, yes. It's true. I did things with the wrestling team because I want them to be my friends."

From the list she had, Byron knew that not all the boys who were in the basement were wrestlers, but she understood why Leslie thought they were all on the team. Some of the guys were wrestlers: the Archer brothers and Bryant Grober. And this had happened on a day when the wrestling championships were going to be held later that evening.

Sheila took notes on a lined sheet of paper while Leslie filled in some of the critical gaps about the hour she spent in the basement. Leslie told Byron that it was Chris Archer who talked her into going to the basement. Leslie estimated that there were between twelve and twenty boys in the basement. She said that a broomstick and a bat, which were covered with bags coated with Vaseline, had been inserted into her. As Leslie described what happened, Byron wrote on the paper: "Vaseline on broomstick." She wrote: "White plastic bag covered whole bat."

When the subject of the broomstick came up, Sheila asked, "Where did he put it, Leslie?" Leslie pointed down at her vagina. "In front," she said. She doesn't know the word, Sheila thought; she doesn't know the word *vagina*.

As the objects were being inserted into her, Leslie recalled, one boy, Kyle Scherzer, said, "Let's stop this. You shouldn't be doing this to her." Leslie mentioned the names of different boys who she said had been in the basement: the Scherzers, the Archers, "Brian" Grober. To Sheila's vast relief, one person Leslie did not place at the scene was Richie Corcoran.

She also told Sheila that on the following day she had been approached by two Glen Ridge seniors who asked her to return to the Scherzer basement—and she refused. Leslie said she told the two boys that she was waiting for a friend, which she acknowledged to Sheila was a lie. The girl didn't cry as she told her story to Sheila Byron. She had no apparent bruises on her face and body. She didn't say that the boys had threatened her with knives or guns. She didn't say that they had tried to beat her up. But to the detective she seemed emotionally battered—fearful and confused.

That fear surfaced whenever Leslie brought up the name of one boy—
Chris Archer. She complained that Chris had been bothering her for a
while. He had been calling her on the phone, she said, talking dirty. "Chris
has been bothering me for a year and a half," she said. He had been asking
her to have sex with him at different locations in town, including a shed
behind one of the elementary schools. "I tell Chris, 'Leave me alone,' but
he says he wouldn't ever leave me alone," Leslie told the detective. "Please
tell his mother to make him leave me alone."

As Leslie began to fill in the picture, adding images and details to the
flat sentences in the police reports, she was also bringing something more:
her personality and the limits of her understanding. She had always
wanted to be liked—especially by the popular athletes—and what happened in the basement hadn't changed that. She told Sheila that she still
wanted the boys to be her friends. She was saying, in effect, "These guys
are my heroes; I don't want to get them in trouble." It's clear, Sheila
thought, that she's not going to say, as a normal victim would, "This is
what they did to me." She's saying, "This is what I did."

It created a predicament for a detective. The victim was reluctant to
blame the victimizers. What kind of witness would Leslie make? Would a
jury listening to Leslie ever believe that something criminal had happened
in the basement? Unless you were able to find independent corroboration,
this was going to be a very tough case to win.

But all through this first meeting, Sheila had to remind herself: This is
no ordinary case; Leslie is no ordinary adolescent girl. Her loyalty to these
boys, her need to be friends with them after all that has happened to her,
makes that clear. For successful prosecution of the boys, one would have to
argue that Leslie was retarded, that she did not possess the awareness and
maturity to know she had been exploited.

Was she, in fact, retarded? Sometimes in the course of her conversation
she appeared unfocused and illogical. But at other times her account was
precise and coherent. Sheila had wanted to meet Leslie to size her up. But
what was the sum total? What could the detective say—unequivocally and
definitively—about this seventeen-year-old woman's intellectual capacity
and emotional maturity?

Sheila was asking herself exactly that question when out of nowhere
she got her answer. It followed a casual remark that Sheila made just as the
interview was ending. Byron asked her, "Les, do you want me to make
these boys stop bothering you?"

Not missing a beat, Leslie said, "Yes. Please call their mothers and tell
them they're bad boys."

It wasn't that many years ago since Sheila herself was seventeen. She couldn't imagine using those words when she was that age. *Tell their mothers they're bad boys!* That's a child talking, Sheila thought. A kid in kindergarten. A first-grader. There was no way that Leslie Faber had the mental age of a normal seventeen-year-old.

With that answer all the surface layers were peeled away, leaving the core of a mentally retarded, emotionally unguarded child. Sheila had much more to do. She wanted to talk to the main actors in the basement and those boys who had observed them. She needed to talk to the kids who had heard about it in school. And there would be many more conversations with Leslie and her parents. But this was ground zero, the bull's-eye. No matter what Sheila heard later, no matter how many people she spoke to, nothing could shake her conviction that Leslie Faber didn't understand what was being done to her in the basement, and that a gang of boys had cruelly exploited her lack of understanding. That conviction was formed in the interview room of the Glen Ridge police station at 6 P.M. on March 27, 1989.

As Byron got up from her chair to signal that the interview was drawing to an end, she said, "Leslie, these boys are not your friends. You can't let them touch you in any way ever again."

"If anyone touches me, I'll tell you right away," Leslie promised.

She left the room and rejoined her mother. Ros didn't ask the detective what Leslie had told her. She didn't ask her where the investigation was going or whether there would be any arrests. Ros believed that this was a police case now, that it was in the hands of the legal system. She didn't want to interfere with the investigation, and also she couldn't bear hearing what had been done to her daughter in the basement. Silently, mother and daughter left the police station.

Sheila Byron's instincts as a woman and a cop told her that something terrible had been done to Leslie Faber. That helped her to uncloud her mind, bleach out the ambiguity. She knew she needed that confidence because this case wasn't going to be easy. Before it was over, it could get very nasty.

Sheila had never backed away from a challenging investigation. And this case certainly presented a mystery, she thought. More than one, really. The most obvious one had to do with crime and the law. What exactly took place in the basement? Did Leslie say "no" to the boys? Did she have the mental capacity to say "no"? What did the law say: Was this a crime?

Was it, in the strictest legal sense, a rape? These questions swarmed around her like angry hornets. Months of investigation might provide the answers.

But there was another mystery, too. It was a deeper, more troubling mystery than the police were either equipped or required to solve. But she couldn't drive it from her mind. The mystery was *why*. Why did such a thing happen? Why in this peaceful little town of all places? Why *these* young men, the most pampered and favored boys in a town filled with pampered kids? Crime or not, what these celebrated young men of Glen Ridge had done was ugly. It was barbaric. It was inhuman. It made Sheila sick. How could they do that to another human being?

She was a cop second, but a human being first. She had been shaped in large degree by her life in Glen Ridge. It wasn't only a place. It was a force that in significant part made her who she was. It was also the force that helped to mold these young men. And there was the mystery. How could this happen in a beautiful place like Glen Ridge? What made a bunch of friendly, likable boys—boys from fine families, boys with every imaginable advantage—do such a thing? A police investigation was always a whodunit. But the human story here, the living story, was a whydunit. Through more than four years of investigation and trial, Sheila Byron would ponder that mystery. Why did it happen? What went wrong in the perfect suburb?

PART II

Secrets

3

Italianate villas. High Victorian mansions. Million-dollar Tudor-revival houses. This is not the Bronx, Charlie Faber whispered to his wife. And it's *definitely* not Brooklyn, Rosalind whispered back.

It was 1964 and a real estate agent was showing the Fabers Ridgewood Avenue. They reacted as so many young marrieds would at their first exposure to Glen Ridge's most prestigious street: This is too rich for my blood. Charlie's boss had suggested that he might consider moving to Glen Ridge. But all Charlie could think of after this peek at the town's prime real estate was: Does this guy know what he's paying me?

Once the Fabers got off Ridgewood Avenue, they discovered that you didn't have to own a mansion to live in Glen Ridge. Other streets were still lovely, lined with shade trees and lit by graceful gas lamps, but with houses that were less imposing than the town's grand showcases. After three visits they decided to buy the first house they had liked, a three-bedroom Dutch Colonial in a pretty section of the south end that was convenient to that nice neighborhood park on Cartaret Street.

The price was $18,000, not exorbitant but in 1960s dollars still something of a stretch. After all, Charlie was only six years out of college, earning a bare-bones salary as a low-level manager for a northern New Jersey firm; Rosalind wasn't getting rich either, teaching junior high English and social studies. The Fabers were not risk takers, but there was something about Glen Ridge that was worth a modest gamble: It was the very opposite of Brooklyn.

Specifically, it was not Williamsburg, the Brooklyn neighborhood where Rosalind had spent her childhood. In the 1950s, when she was growing up, Williamsburg was a restless place. Other sections of Brooklyn, such as East Flatbush and Midwood, were urban neighborhoods, but they had a suburban tone to them: two-family houses, private garages, small lawns fronting the houses, even sandlot baseball fields. In these neighborhoods homes passed from one generation of a family to another. Williamsburg, just over the Williamsburg bridge from the immigrant struggles of the Lower East Side, was more transitional, a roadside rest stop where a family could catch its breath before it reached the suburbs.

Rosalind's family was solidly middle class, her dad a skilled machinist, her mother a public school teacher; together they had earned enough money to buy their half of a two-family house, which made them something of a rarity in a community of renters. For Rosalind the big drawback was that there wasn't much green to be found in Williamsburg. During the summer families took their ease on folding chairs set out on the sidewalk. Kids timed their football plays to coincide with the light turning red at the corner. For Rosalind the neighborhood playground was McCarren Park, a treeless place of asphalt and stone where she and her younger sister and brother went wading. McCarren Park didn't look much like Cartaret Park in Glen Ridge.

Rosalind met Charles when she was a freshman at Wagner College in Staten Island and he was a junior. Two city kids, he from the Bronx and DeWitt Clinton High School and she from Williamsburg and Washington Irving High in Manhattan. Two city kids, but with a twist. Chemistry aside, what drew them together was that they had both had enough of the city. They wanted to find a patch of green.

In 1960, right after she graduated, they got married. For the first couple of years, they satisfied their thirst for the outdoors by going camping, anywhere in Jersey and upstate New York that would allow them to bring along their dog. It was a conscious decision to begin their married life in Staten Island, which was about as far out of the city as you could get while still living in it. Then Charles found his job in Jersey, and the Fabers found Glen Ridge.

Charles and Rosalind Faber were devout believers in the perfectibility of life. This was their secular gospel: If you worked hard at it, if you played by the rules, you could make your marriage and your family and your work darn close to perfect. They believed that with concentrated effort and a dollop of good luck, they would be able to complete the passage begun by their parents back in Brooklyn and the Bronx. It seemed back then, in 1964, that they could do that in Glen Ridge. They signed the mortgage as though it was their first down payment on the good life.

So the Fabers joined earlier generations of newcomers who had seen in Glen Ridge the realization of their desire for a peaceful, civilized suburban community. That enticing image had been in the making since 1895, when well-to-do Glen Ridge seceded from the larger town of Bloomfield, located five miles from Newark and twenty miles from New York City. Glen Ridge declared itself a separate borough[1] because its leaders thought that they weren't getting the services their substantial taxes entitled them to. Many

1. In New Jersey the designation of "borough" was limited to municipalities of no more than 5,000 residents living in an area of four square miles or less. Under the borough system of government, power was shared by the governing council and mayor.

residents came to believe that their town was different—*better* was the word that Ridgers used in private conversation—from the bigger towns that surrounded it, including Bloomfield and Montclair. From its earliest days, Glen Ridge tended to view its neighbors with a measure of suspicion, hostility, and condescension.

To achieve their goals of creating a separate and better community, the town leaders zoned the town as predominantly residential. The idea was to keep industry and most businesses out of the town. From its start then, Glen Ridge was conceived of as a bedroom community. Robert Rudd, the town's first mayor, said, "We may confidently hope that Glen Ridge will become a residence section second to none." In the years that followed, more prosperous families began to build the stately homes that marked the town as the domain of the wealthy.

But after the turn of the century, the dominant political factions in the town—to the amusement of its neighbors—got into an ugly public squabble over money. "The peace, harmony, and good feeling, which for seven years have made Glen Ridge a second edition of the Garden of Eden, are, alas, no more," the *Newark Evening News* said in an editorial in 1902. "The pride of Glen Ridge is laid low and carping Bloomfield gleefully gloats over the humiliation of its aristocratic neighbor."

Personal invective. Public bloodletting. It was all so unseemly for proper Glen Ridge. One way to restore the appearance of serenity was to get rid of the two-party political system. In 1913 the political leaders formed a private organization that they called the Civic Conference Committee. Six times a year CCC members, representing different civic organizations, met under an oath of secrecy to select a single slate of candidates for public office. Except for a rare challenge arising from a heated local issue, such as the closing of an elementary school in the town, the political candidates selected by the organization were virtually assured of election.

The CCC expounded the "wise men" theory of government: Bring together a group of thoughtful, dedicated citizens, and have them meet in secret to select candidates for mayor, town council, and the board of education. The CCC also postulated that one way to banish greed from politics was to make sure that no one who held public office in Glen Ridge received a salary.

The Conference believed that both elected and appointed officials should share the central values of the community: propriety, orderliness, discretion, and continuity. The principle guiding the CCC was that private discussions among people committed to preserving the heritage of Glen Ridge would resolve any conflicts that might arise. No need to air disputes or scandals in public forums or in the press. As long as everyone agreed that the ultimate objective was to maintain Glen Ridge as a genteel and peaceful town, everything could be worked out—in private.

The CCC turned out to be a durable vehicle. It would control the civic life of the community throughout most of the twentieth century. One history of the town noted that some residents criticized the "undemocratic" and "establishment" nature of the Conference. But the historian also pointed out that the CCC had sustained the clean-government standards of the town's founders.

Other critics of the CCC argued that its approach to governing created a model for the relationship between individual residents and public officials. If the CCC, composed of the town's elite, operated in secret, why shouldn't any average citizen try to do the same? Why is it anybody's business if a citizen tries to arrange special privileges for his kid with a member of the board of education? Who has to know if a resident tries to work out a personal arrangement with a cop to avoid legal embarrassments?

In this "second edition of the Garden of Eden," as the editorial writer described the town, residents had been friends with officeholders for generations. They marched together in Memorial Day parades, grilled hamburgers at block parties, sent their kids to the same schools, and belonged to the same clubs. If you needed a favor, you didn't have to bribe some politician, as was known to happen in big cities. A friendly hello and a firm handshake might do.

Most Ridgers were not troubled by this invisible latticework of discreet understandings and confidential markers. What was most important to them was that the system, lubricated by friendship and neighborliness, worked. The streets were cleaned efficiently, the gas lamps were regularly serviced, the schools prepared students for college, and the police kept the crime rate low.

What made Glen Ridge Glen Ridge? The physical appearance of the town clearly set it off from its more populous and urban neighbors. For example, you didn't find gas lamps in Bloomfield and Montclair. In Glen Ridge 666 gas lamps cast a dim glow, equivalent to a fifty-watt bulb, across the streets. The first lamps were installed twenty years after the town seceded from Bloomfield, and during the next half-century Glen Ridge preservationists constantly scoured the country for discarded gas lights.

The preservationist spirit was also reflected in the houses and public buildings. In 1989 the historic district included 90 percent of the town—some 1,700 buildings, mostly residences but also a few government and commercial buildings. It was one of the largest historic districts in the state. As a result, the Glen Ridge of the 1980s looked a lot like the Glen Ridge of the 1920s—a town of tree-shaded streets, spacious parks and gardens, and commodious homes.

The typical Glen Ridge house was constructed in the Victorian or Colonial styles, although some fine examples of Tudor and Queen Anne architecture also could be found. Inside, there were usually four or five bedrooms, a family room, a dining room, and a kitchen. Most houses had a finished or semifinished basement that the kids used as a playroom. Often, enclosed porches looked out on sizable backyards ornamented by gazebos and swimming pools. The front lawns were neatly mowed; a resident who neglected his groundskeeping chores was likely to receive a stern rebuke from his neighbors.

If Glen Ridge thought of itself as special and distinctive, this sense of superiority was not rooted entirely in its architecture or historic preservation. Ultimately, what gave Glen Ridge its cachet was its people, especially its leaders. The town's earliest benefactors were captains of industry. Their successors in town government were almost all businessmen, with a sprinkling of lawyers.

Over the years the town's leadership included executives with Grand Union, Ashland Oil, International Telephone and Telegraph, Bell Telephone, and Consolidated Edison. Glen Ridge's respect for its businessmen-mayors was boundless. Its leaders were not social workers or union organizers. They were not educators or writers. They were not reformers, rebels, and critics. They definitely were not women. The chosen of the town did not dissent from the American Dream; they fulfilled it. Generations of young people in Glen Ridge learned from their fathers and from the civic and social elite of the town that there was one supreme goal in life: achievement.

Achievement was cast in distinctly masculine terms. It signified a man who made money and wielded power in his town and his house. If a single binding ethic defined the culture of this community, it was: Winning is a helluva lot better than losing. That said, the social code prescribed some specific guidelines for winning. In the Glen Ridge style, winners were assertive but not belligerent, self-confident but not boastful, and determined but not driven. The model for success, for the male society at least, was the Well-Rounded Gentleman. He might toil long hours in the executive suites of Manhattan, but he made time on an early summer evening for a game of croquet, capped by a round of chilled martinis on a friend's porch.

While the town's most notable residents usually had achieved success before they moved to Glen Ridge, a few became prominent *after* they left town. Eighteen-year-old Thomas Mapother broke into show business on April 18, 1980, when he played Nathan Detroit in the high school's production of *Guys and Dolls*. But it wasn't until after he left the town, acted in a few more roles, and changed his name from Thomas Mapother to Tom Cruise that he became a movie star.

More typical was Eddie Bracken, the comic actor of stage and movies. He was already famous when he bought a hundred-year-old house in town in 1983. "Sitting on my porch is like heaven," Bracken told the local paper. "In the summer, it's the best place in the world. If someone told me I would never have to move from here, I'd be the happiest guy in the world."

If there was an ideal image of Glen Ridge, it was captured by one of its residents, Ronald Travisano. As creative director of the Manhattan advertising agency Della Femina, Travisano and Partners, he belonged to the "Tuesday Team," which produced a series of skillful ads for the stretch run of Ronald Reagan's 1984 presidential campaign. The TV spots evoked a gloriously romantic America. A rosy-cheeked kid getting his first haircut. An elderly couple walking hand in hand down a country road, with the sun setting behind them. A small-town Fourth of July celebration. "Morning in America." Viewers, mindful of the devastation of the South Bronx, might complain that there was more to the country than the sweet simplicity the ads portrayed. Some might say that even Glen Ridge wasn't quite so sweet and simple anymore, if it ever had been.

In the main, Glen Ridge was faithful to its appearance of affluent White Anglo-Saxon Protestant gentility. But there was always a small minority of non-WASPS and lower-middle-class and poor people in the town. In the 1920s and 1930s, numbers of Irish and Italian Catholics of modest income moved into the less developed south end of town.

Then, in the 1950s, similar to the pattern emerging in suburban towns across the country, developers built less expensive houses in the south end. "But the new people in the south end were never really accepted in the inner circle of the town," one retired teacher recalled. "It was pretty snobbish. So they saved their money and bought a second house near a lake or down by the shore. That's where they had their real social lives."

Not everyone was rich, but hard-core poverty was rare in Glen Ridge.

In 1979 the U.S. Census found that there were forty families and thirty-two single people living below the poverty level.

If you didn't mind being excluded from the social elite, the town offered advantages to people of moderate income. For one thing, the presence of three elementary schools meant that every child could walk to school. When one of the schools was discontinued because of a decline in student population, a huge uproar ensued.

Overall, the town's population was ethnically and racially quite homogeneous. There were few Jews and still fewer blacks. In a total population of 7,855 in 1980, there were only seventy-six blacks, which amounted to less than 1 percent. The U.S. Census reported in 1980 that there were no black children who lived in Glen Ridge attending any of the schools. The joke going around Glen Ridge was that an invisible fence had been built around the town. The sign on the fence read WALL, an acronym for White Alliance for Leisure Living.

Over the years, the Glen Ridge police had earned a reputation for zealotry in the pursuit of nonresident motorists who exceeded the speed limit; speeding fines were a significant source of revenue for the municipality. This presented something of a dilemma for blacks driving through. If they drove too fast, they would get ticketed; if they drove slowly, they might get pulled over because a cop suspected that they were looking for a house to burglarize.

One resident of Montclair, a neighboring town with a more diverse population, employed a black woman as a babysitter. She would often let the babysitter go home early because the woman was afraid to drive through Glen Ridge: "It would take her a lot longer to get home because she had to go around the town. The word had circulated among blacks that you would be stopped and harassed if you were spotted in the town after dark."

For the wealthy and not-so-wealthy, one distinct advantage to living in Glen Ridge was the easy familiarity between residents and town employees. Longevity on the job by public employees in Glen Ridge made them accessible to many residents. In the 1970s a majority of the town's sixty-six employees had spent all their working lives in the service of Glen Ridge. There were twenty-two families in which two or more members had worked for the town.

The police department was a good example of job security. For forty-three years, from 1916 to 1959, two men, Patrick Higgins and his son William, ran the department. Then there were the Dugans. Patrick Dugan joined the Glen Ridge force in 1910 and retired thirty-four years later as a lieutenant. His son Norbert became a Glen Ridge cop in 1930 and remained on the job until he died of a heart attack in 1955. In 1964 Patrick's grandson Thomas became the third generation of his family to wear the uniform.

Twenty-two years later Tom Dugan was sworn in as police chief and became Sheila Byron's boss. "For a policeman there are incredible benefits to being raised and living in a town," Chief Tom Dugan said. "You know everybody, you know all the players, you have a sense of the town. But it can be very difficult. If Joe's my next door neighbor and we sit in the backyard on Saturday afternoon at a barbecue and next Saturday I have to go to Joe's house because he's beating his wife, it's tough. I know Joe's probably not going to strike out at me—that's the plus side. But it's 'Tom and Joe,' and I'm really stressed because Joe's my buddy. I'm the responding officer and I'm going to do what I have to do, but . . ."

In the years when Tom Dugan was rising through the ranks, Sheila Byron was growing up on Essex Avenue, a middle-income island in the sea of Glen Ridge affluence. In 1968 houses over on tony Ridgewood Avenue were going for as much as $80,000. But a few blocks away, on Essex, Sheila Byron's parents could find a five-bedroom Colonial for only $19,000. By the 1970s most of the people there earned between $10,000 and $20,000. In other neighborhoods the median income ranged between $35,000 and $40,000.

The Byrons' house was just a couple of blocks away from where Richard Corcoran, the cop, and his family lived. The people who bought on Essex didn't expect to join the town's aristocracy. It was a neighborhood populated by families of policemen and firemen, college teachers and electricians. The lawns were small and the backyards smaller. The sound you heard all day was that of children playing. So many kids lived there— twenty-five on Sheila's block alone—that Essex resembled a giant playpen. Growing up on Essex, Sheila was a part of Glen Ridge but not a full participant.

As a child of middle-income parents, she was always something of an outsider; so the subtler imperfections of Glen Ridge—its exclusivity, its snobbery, its pretensions—were more visible to her than to a more upwardly mobile family like the Fabers.

Sheila was the second youngest of six children. Most of the friends she made came from big blue-collar Irish families. Apart from ethnicity, what they had in common was the economic struggle. Her father, Harold, had held a variety of jobs—truck driver, school custodian, some real estate work. Later on, when she was a teenager, he tended a boiler all day in a county building. Her mother also worked, even though married women in those days usually stayed home. She was employed as an admitting clerk at Mountainside Hospital in Glen Ridge, on the border with Montclair. "We were definitely, as far as this town went, on the poor side," Sheila said. If you were on the "poor side," you were treated like an outsider—someone who would not be easily accepted by the wealthy and popular childhood cliques.

In elementary school there was no lunch program and all the students had to walk home for a meal. Sheila remembered her mother, Pat, saying to school officials, "It takes them so long to walk home, by the time I feed them and get them back up, the class is starting." And the official would answer, "Well, why aren't you driving them?" Mrs. Byron would say, "We only have one car and my husband takes it to work." Sheila would recall that the school administrator "looked at her like—'Oh, you poor woman! You only have one car.'"

When the school started selling lunches, the Byron youngsters were given a book of coupons, similar to food stamps, with which they bought their meals. One of Sheila's closest friends would whisper, "Don't let anyone see those tickets."

In the seventh and eighth grades, dress became a good indicator of family status. Sheila wore the same few pairs of pants and shoes. Some of the other middle-school girls were showing up in jackets and skirts. And *boots*. "The boots, boy, some of them were very fancy," she recalled.

That's about when the party scene started. Lots of kids. Lots of booze. Sheila heard about the big weekend parties, but she never went to them. With six teenage kids, her family ran a babysitting service. That occupied her nights.

Status in Glen Ridge derived from money and history. If you weren't wealthy and you were a relative newcomer to the town, you were treated differently in the schools. Teachers had taught one generation after another from the old-line families, and if you had an older brother or sister who had gone through the schools already, it could give you a little edge.

Sheila's sister, Beth, wanted more than anything else to be a cheerleader for the wrestling team. One afternoon after cheerleading tryouts, Beth came home crying. "I was just as good as the rest of them; why couldn't I make it?" she told Sheila.

The next day the faculty coach of the cheerleaders offered Beth the position of cheerleader manager, but Mrs. Byron wouldn't let her take it. Instead, she encouraged Beth to join the color guard of the band, which was Sheila's main extracurricular activity as well. "It was obvious to my mother that there was a certain group of people who were going to be involved in cheerleading, and that there [was] a certain group of people who were not. An outsider is just not going to get in. It's a clique just like many other things in town," Sheila said.

She couldn't help noticing that the town officials seemed to think there was only one class in Glen Ridge—the wealthy. One year, when Sheila was in high school, there was a controversy over a proposal to build a swimming pool behind the high school. Her dad thought it was a good idea, and went to the town council meeting to speak in support of it. But, one councilman kept repeating, "Why do we need a pool when the kids can go to the country club?"

"We don't all have the country club," Harold Byron said. "Many people in town will never be part of the country club."

The town never built the pool.

Sheila knew a family that was friendly with a local police chief. Wide-eyed, Sheila listened as the cop talked about police work. If you were a cop, you learned all the secrets in your town. And then when you knew the secrets, you used what you had learned to put the bad guys away. What a great job!

She was hooked. Eight months after she graduated from high school, Sheila got a job as civilian radio dispatcher for the Glen Ridge Police Department. After growing up as an outsider inside Glen Ridge, Sheila Byron was tying her future to the town. Fascinated by police work and familiar with Glen Ridge, she seemed, at the time, to have made the right career choice. How rough could it get in her boring old hometown?

4

When the Fabers set up their Glen Ridge household in the 1960s, family life in the town had had a passing resemblance to a TV sitcom. Young marrieds buying furniture. Mom's in the kitchen. Baby's in the high chair. Dad's catching the 5:25 commuter train.

At first the Fabers fit smoothly into this scene. They made friends easily, meeting people when they walked the dog or raked leaves or went to
the post office. They found their friends on their street or in their part of
town. Each member of their social group would host a dinner to welcome a
newcomer to the neighborhood or just for the fun of building a meal
around a theme: an Italian pasta dinner or an adventuresome Spanish
paella. When the Fabers had people over, the high point of the evening was
the singing. They loved to have a group singalong as they played the chord
organ. It didn't really matter if you had a lousy voice; the idea was to have
some wholesome fun.

Charles and Rosalind were both reserved, but once you got acquainted,
you would find them quite likable. He was a trim, athletic man, a little
tightly wound but with a pleasant sense of humor bubbling under the surface. She was softer, more accessible. Her gentle, round face, framed by
strawberry-blond hair, made her seem open, someone you could talk to.
"Their little group was called the 'Sunshine Club,' or something like that,"
a friend of the Fabers remembered. "It was typical of their outlook that
they'd come up with a name like that. When the group got together, it
wasn't gossip like 'Did you hear about so-and-so, she's doing this or that.'
It was more like Ros and Charlie saying, 'Did you know that so-and-so's
mother's in the hospital, what are we going to do for them?'"

As the Fabers established themselves in Glen Ridge, Rosalind became
involved in educational and cultural organizations, improving the local
library, working with the historical society. Charlie enjoyed playing softball and bowling and coaching some of the community sports teams. Rosalind enjoyed camping and picnics and working with her different civic
groups. They weren't country club people.

Within their home they found their pleasure in books and music. "As
long as we have our books, we can take our time buying furniture," Ros
Faber would tell friends. "That's what filled up the moving van—books."
Outside their home no activity was more important than going to the
Presbyterian Church every Sunday in Bloomfield. A quiet but unwavering
faith was the foundation of their life together.

The words people used to describe the Fabers were "modest" and "un-
pretentious." These were uncommon attributes in suburbia of the 1960s,
where people were eager to fill their "Hollywood" kitchens with every
modern appliance on the market. The Fabers' first principle of household
finance was: Don't buy on credit. "If you have the money, you go out and
buy it," Ros would tell her friends. "If you don't have it, you wait." Even

when they could afford them, their purchases were basic and simple—the sturdy couch, a few tasteful paintings. Expensive living room suites, flashy cars—that wasn't the Fabers.

Although they were not close friends, the Fabers had a lot in common with the Archers, who lived nearby. Both couples placed great faith in religion. They shared a strong sense of optimism; if it were at all possible, they would banish ugliness, unpleasantness, and incivility from their lives. Their optimism was expressed by their concern about the well-being of their friends; when other people had problems, the Fabers and Archers would be inclined to emphasize not what had gone wrong but how it could be set right.

Despite these similarities, the Archers and the Fabers were dissimilar in their personal styles. "If you went to a party, you would see the Archers working the room," said one woman who was a friend and contemporary of both couples. "They were very outgoing, very social. . . . The Fabers were quiet, conservative. You had to make an effort to get to know them. If you walked into a party, you'd probably see Ros and Charlie standing in a corner, talking to each other. They were two of the most private people I've ever met."

To people who met them for the first time—who saw Charles in his dark suits, white shirts, and sober ties, who saw Rosalind in her tailored suits and high-necked blouses—they seemed to step out of a nineteenth-century daguerreotype. "Conservative. The first impression is that the Fabers are extremely conservative people," said one Glen Ridge school official. "Mr. Faber just looks like your picture-perfect banker. Mrs. Faber looks like a Daughter of the American Revolution."

Their determination to guard their privacy separated the Fabers from the gossipy, sometimes malicious chatter that was a staple of social life in some circles of Glen Ridge. Oh, those Fabers, they never let their hair down, whispered some of the women who were polishing off their second gin and tonic at the country club. But the Fabers were comfortable with their style. They believed that marriage and family were strengthened by honesty and intimacy. If you had a secret to confide, a hurt to unburden, a sin to confess, it should be done inside the family. Why impose your problems on strangers when only you and your family could solve them?

That vision of the family as a sanctuary distanced the Fabers from a lot of people in Glen Ridge, distanced them even from their friends. When popular psychology decreed that it was healthy to "communicate," to "share intimacies," to "open up," the Fabers turned inward. Sometimes people in town misinterpreted their need for privacy as chilliness and aloofness. It was much easier to empathize with the sunny, gregarious Archers, who made you feel like a member of the family. And so the judgment was delivered: The Fabers were good people who did many good things for the town, but they were hard to get to know. When it came to popularity contests, the Archers were way ahead.

A few years after moving into Glen Ridge, the Fabers learned definitively that they would not be able to have children. In 1968 they adopted with relatively little effort their first child, a sixteen-day-old baby girl they named Carol.* Ros left her teaching job to devote herself to motherhood and civic activities. Three years later they began their search for a second child. This time it was harder. There was a scarcity of babies who had been placed for adoption, and they already had one while many couples were pleading for their first. They went from agency to agency. One agency they had registered with asked them if they had any specific requirements. There were only two: the child should be reasonably healthy and it should be Caucasian. They did not think a child of color adopted by white parents would grow up happy in a place like Glen Ridge.

The agency asked the Fabers if they would accept a disabled child, perhaps a little girl living in a foster home in Newfoundland, Canada. They said, Yes, if it's a correctable disability.

The agency worker was vague. She said that this child's development seemed slow, but the doctors had not been able to find a cause. We think, she said, that this problem will pass.

The Fabers were anxious. If a child is blind in the left eye, at least the defect is known. But this was so uncertain. How serious was the problem? Would it get worse as the child got older? Could whatever it was be treated? The agency and its doctors had no answers for them.

But if you wanted a child badly enough—If the Fabers passed on this baby, who knew when the next one would come along?—you could brush aside these shapeless anxieties. You could tell yourself, The baby is nine months old; there's plenty of time to overcome whatever is holding her back if anything really is. At least, nothing they could find in the background of the natural parents caused concern. No history of alcoholism or drug addiction or child abuse. No pattern of violence or criminality.

On March 24, 1972, they flew to Newfoundland to bring ten-month-old Leslie home. The plump little girl they held in their arms resembled a round, soft dumpling. In the cab to the airport, they joked that her baby formula must have consisted of potato chips. They laughed and said, She's so overweight because babies need an extra layer of fat to withstand a Canadian winter. The first thing they would do when they got back to Glen Ridge was to get their pediatrician to put Leslie on a diet of skimmed milk.

It had been a long day, but they never heard a peep from her. First they picked her up at the agency, and then they had to go to the American consulate and then to the airport, and then there was the long wait at the airport in Montreal to catch a connecting flight to LaGuardia. It was a Friday night and people were tired and hungry and eager to get home, and through all the noise and commotion Leslie smiled and ate and slept. Rosalind's parents met them at the airport in New York. They gushed over Leslie. What a sweet, perfect little girl she was. They all agreed that this was one of the happiest days of their lives.

Leslie's personality didn't change much in the next couple of years. She gurgled and smiled and ate when she was fed and almost always slept through the night. She hardly ever cried. But aspects of her development troubled the Fabers. At ten months she was having trouble sitting up, and she was never able to crawl more than a foot or two; but these problems were discounted because she was overweight. Rosalind told Charlie, "It's just a matter of teaching and encouraging, because you don't know how much encouragement she got in the foster home."

Their pediatrician said, Well, Leslie is down at the slow end of the normal range, but not that far off. She'll probably put on a spurt and catch up. The Fabers listened and nodded. They responded well to optimism.

When Leslie was three and four years old, she attended the Presbyterian Church nursery school in Bloomfield. She seemed to have motor difficulties with small objects. She couldn't tie her shoes and she couldn't fit a button into a buttonhole. The nursery school teacher mentioned that Leslie didn't show much enthusiasm for the activities the other kids seemed to enjoy. She would hang back when the others were cutting and pasting and coloring. Leslie would never make trouble, never bawl that she wanted her mommy. She just wouldn't join in unless you said, Now, Leslie, you have to try this. But if somebody said that, Leslie would go ahead and try. The bright side, the teacher said, was that she really enjoyed riding the bicycles and the toy trucks—a real physical kid. Who knows, someday she might be a star athlete.

The Fabers reported all this to their pediatrician. Maybe there's something there, he told them; maybe there isn't. Give it time.

5

The Fabers planted deep roots in the community, and so did the families of the boys who would later be at the center of the Glen Ridge sports crowd. When these families came to Glen Ridge in the late 1960s and early 1970s, there was no lack of organizations to join. You could pick from the junior league and the country club, the women's club and the Friends of the Glen Ridge Library, among many others. For the spiritually inclined, there were two churches in town, the Congregational and Christ Church, Episcopal. (Although the Catholic population was substantial and growing, there were no Catholic churches in the town. Neither was there a synagogue for Jewish residents.) But most of the young marrieds—few single people moved to the town—found that the natural way of meeting people was through the neighborhood and their kids.

The area around Cartaret Park at the south end of town was the neighborhood where most of the young people who were later involved in the case grew up. The Fabers, Archers, Scherzers, and Quigleys all lived there and later sent their children to Linden Avenue Elementary School. Nearer to the other end of town, the Grobers and the Corcorans brought their children to the Forest Avenue playground and, when they were old enough, to Forest Avenue Elementary School. These families—with the exception of the Grobers, who were probably the most affluent of them all—seemed to occupy roughly the same niche in the suburban hierarchy: one leg on a middle-class rung and the other raised to make the climb upward.

Michaele Archer had come to Glen Ridge from Virginia, where she had worked as a nurse. Her husband Douglas had grown up in Kansas. After completing college, he had enlisted in the Navy and was stationed in Newport Beach, where he met Michaele. A personnel position with a firm in the New York metropolitan area brought the Archers to Glen Ridge in 1970. What attracted them to Glen Ridge, Doug would recall later, was that it was a fine place to raise children. "This is a town that really loves its kids," he said.

Michaele put her nursing career on hold when she became pregnant with Paul, the first of her four sons. Paul was born on March 16, 1971, Chris on April 8, 1972. Michaele later had two more sons. Doug remained in the Navy Reserve, which provided the family with a second source of income.

Doug and Michaele were congenial, easy to talk to, easy to share a laugh with. Some of their closest friends consisted of the mothers (and their husbands) who belonged to a neighborhood play group. Although the Archers and many of their friends were new to town, they embodied some of the old Glen Ridge spirit. Doug Archer was a broad-shouldered man with an open, friendly face; despite his rimless glasses and retreating hairline, he always looked younger than his age. Michaele, a petite, attractive woman with dark-auburn hair pulled back in a bun or a pony tail, could put together a dinner party with a few hours' notice.

Doug was no longer on active duty, but he retained his military bearing. His posture was so straight that he sometimes looked as if he were about to be inspected by his drill sergeant. One Sunday morning when Doug and Michaele arrived at the Episcopal Church with Paul and Chris in tow, the choirmaster greeted them with "Doug, can I please see your parade permit?"

Doug's manner was softened by free-flowing exuberance. His style on the job—in the 1970s he worked in personnel, then in sales—was on display during social occasions. Guests at the Archers' weekend get-togethers at their cream-and-blue house on Victor Avenue remember them as evenings brightened by the hosts' high spirits. Sometimes the conversation would extend beyond the conventional bounds of family and children to the town and the outside world. June Gilliam,* a member of the Victor Avenue play group, recalled that although the Archers were proud new parents, they would rarely get stuck on "how Paul was learning to walk or how Chris said something cute. There was some of that, but there was also talk about the situation in Vietnam or what we could do to help a couple that was going through this really rough divorce. With Doug especially, but with Michaele too, you felt they had a real sense of social responsibility."

That social responsibility would be expressed in a variety of ways: Michaele's contributions to the blood bank and her stint as a classroom volunteer at the Linden Avenue Elementary School; the Archers' attendance at Home and School Association meetings; and Doug's membership in the Glen Ridge Task Force, an organization formed to discuss problems that kids in the town were facing. In later years Doug would be most active as a vestryman at Christ Episcopal Church in Glen Ridge. The Archers' civic involvement and likable personalities made them very popular on the town's social circuit.

After they had moved from Victor Avenue to a larger house on more prestigious Ridgewood Avenue, they would open their home to young-sters who were having difficulties with their parents. One teenager recalls a time when he quarreled with his father and stomped out of the house. He was walking down Ridgewood Avenue, unsure of where he was going to spend the night. Mr. Archer pulled over in his car and asked, "Where you going, Frank?" Frank described his differences with his dad, and Doug of-fered, "Why don't you spend the night at our place?"

"I wound up staying the whole week, until the thing blew over," Frank recalled. "There were a couple, three kids sleeping there. It was sort of like a halfway house for kids with problems."

The Archers' friends were impressed with their optimism. "For them the glass was always half full," said June Gilliam. Their optimistic outlook may well have been grounded in religious faith. Doug was Episcopalian; Michaele was a devout Catholic. The one weekly event that could never be canceled, she would tell friends, was Bible study class. She was deter-mined, she said, to raise her children as both Catholics and Episcopalians and would insist that they attend services at both churches. Her faith in the power of religion to conquer adversity never wavered. "The saints will watch over them," she said, speaking of her children.

Whatever the reason, Michaele Archer sometimes seemed to function at a remove from the usual anxieties that troubled other parents, friends recall. At a party in the early 1970s, the conversation turned to drugs. Drug abuse was a fairly common topic in conversations in Glen Ridge. In September 1971 the arrest of two Glen Ridge kids on narcotics charges had led police to a major drug bust, involving thirty-five youngsters in ten towns. The drug problem was considered sufficiently serious that an orga-nization had been formed in Glen Ridge called "Get Your Head Together," to counsel kids who were using drugs.

"It is troubling," June Gilliam was saying at the party, "all this talk of drugs in town." As Gilliam remembered, Michaele Archer didn't look as much worried as she did startled. "No!" she recalled Michaele saying. "In Glen Ridge? In *our* town? I don't believe it."

In their open and nonjudgmental manner, the Archers seemed to embody the values of a modern young couple raising a family in the 1970s. A "modern" couple tried to give their children room to experiment and discover their own identities. A "modern" couple tried to instill "moral" values in their kids, but they wouldn't preach at them. They believed in talking through every problem, and spanking was a last and extremely distasteful resort. They hoped their own behavior would serve as an example of the right way to live.

In Glen Ridge, though, there were clear limits to the progressive approach to raising children. Blue collar and white collar, upper middle class or lower middle class, a streak of social conservatism ran through most of the families. Tradition guided the way children were raised in Glen Ridge. The family was viewed as an impregnable fortress. Parents were suspicious of public institutions and government bureaucracies that tried to tell them what was good for their kids. Children were taught that loyalty is a desirable character trait. Kids were raised to stand up for their parents, and parents were supposed to be there for their children.

In the 1970s in Glen Ridge, as in much of American society, most families agreed on one point: the traditional roles of the sexes. Husbands whose wives worked accepted the fact that their wives' wages paid for the good things in life, from a second home on the shore to a second car. But when the good wife returned home from the job, her position in the household stayed much the same as it had always been. She did most of the housework, looked after the kids, did the decorating, and organized dinner parties. Her husband disciplined the kids and made the major purchases.

Lawrence Roder, superintendent of schools in Glen Ridge from 1973 to 1979, said, "When people in town talked to me about sticking to traditional values, they were talking about traditional ideas of what men and women should be. Outside of Glen Ridge, values toward men and women were changing in the 1970s and 1980s. But in Glen Ridge it was still the world of the '50s."

These traditional roles were bequeathed to the children. Boys were supposed to be vigorous, assertive, competitive; they were expected to test the boundaries of behavior within clearly established limits. Girls were supposed to be feminine, attractive, cute; later on, the cuteness might turn a bit seductive, but the parents hoped they would retain their virtue (read: virginity). Daughters would be encouraged to go on to college, but their destiny would be fulfilled in starting and nurturing a family. In their youth sons were permitted and even expected to raise a little hell. "There was a 'boys-will-be-boys' attitude that went back to the 1950s," said Dr. Roder. "And that was very slow to change."

Although a handful of Glen Ridge families had begun to rethink male and female roles and responsibilities, most Ridgers, like most Americans everywhere, clung to the old ways, the ways that had worked for their fathers and grandfathers.

That was the familiar road traveled by Jack and Geraldine Scherzer. Their acquaintances included cops and firemen, but there were also teachers, business people, and a lawyer. Most seemed to share the Scherzers' orthodox attitudes about masculinity and raising children, and their almost religious faith in the redemptive powers of athletics.

While Jack Scherzer fixed elevators in New York, Gerry Scherzer labored on Lorraine Street. She worked hard to keep the house spotless. From her earliest days in Glen Ridge, many of her conversations seemed to center on her two sons, Eric and Paul. And after the twins, Kyle and Kevin, were born in 1971, it seemed to friends that her existence was pretty much defined by the experiences and successes of all four boys. In their living room was a wedding photograph of the Scherzers, in which Mrs. Scherzer looks radiant. Some visitors remembered that Geraldine would pass over it and show off pictures of the boys and the athletic trophies they were rapidly accumulating.

An acquaintance of the Scherzers recalled a typical conversation she had with Gerry when Kyle and Kevin were in high school. "I asked what she did on Saturday night. And Gerry said, 'Saturday I was mopping the floor when the boys and Jack were out at the football game. And then Jack came home. And then the boys came home. And I served dinner.' She really seemed to live to make her husband and her boys comfortable."

In the 1970s Geraldine Scherzer's extended Italian family would gather for reunions. Jack would sometimes wear shorts, loafers, and a plaid sports shirt opened a few buttons down to display a gold chain. He always looked tan and robust, if a few pounds overweight. Gerry, also tending toward plumpness, wore simple print dresses or slacks and a blouse. Her dark hair framed a round face and glasses. She spoke more softly than Jack.

Tom Roselli,* one of her relatives who attended these gatherings, recalled that the family members would describe Jack and Gerry as the "golden couple": "Everybody in the family always said, 'They are such nice people; nothing could ever go wrong with them.'" Indeed, their four handsome boys, Jack's steady, dependable job with Otis, Gerry's obvious dedication to the family, their house in Glen Ridge and their place on the Jersey shore—all of it spelled success.

At these family gatherings the conversations always seemed to divide along gender lines. The men talked about jobs, money, and sports. The women talked about children, food, and household appliances. Both sexes talked a lot about how people looked. The thinking was: If you looked good, you were successful. The good looks of Kyle and Kevin seemed to dazzle the whole family. The one word everybody used to describe them was "gorgeous"—as in "The twins are gorgeous." They made Roselli think of Oscar Wilde's *Picture of Dorian Gray*. It was hard to imagine that they would ever change, that disappointment or sadness would etch a line on those smooth, sunny, perfect faces.

Over at the north end of town, the two families whose sons later became prominent in the jock crowd resembled in some respects the Archers and the Scherzers. Bryant Grober's family may have shared many of the values and beliefs of the Archers, while Richie Corcoran's parents seemed to have a lot in common with Jack and Geraldine Scherzer.

In the Scherzer family Kyle and Kevin learned what it took to be a boy and a man from their father and their older brothers. Young Richie Corcoran was the oldest boy in his family. His brothers, Sean and Kevin, who were twins, were two years younger. Like the boys in the south end of town—like Kyle and Kevin, Peter Quigley, and Chris and Paul Archer—Richie had no sisters. He learned his lessons in masculinity from his father, Richard Edward Corcoran.

But the hard, gritty work of raising three young kids was left primarily to Richie's mother, Claire. June Gallo,* who was also married to a Glen Ridge cop and was Claire's close friend, recalled, "You had a typical cop family here. Claire did the buggy-hauling and the diapering and her husband had his cop work." Claire was a tall, slender, taciturn woman who had grown up in Glen Ridge, in an Irish-Italian family of fourteen brothers and sisters. She married Richard Edward Corcoran a few years after graduating from high school. Claire remained at home when Richie and the twins were young. In their adolescence she took a job as a secretary in a shirt-manufacturing company.

Mr. Corcoran had grown up in town and had played football for the Glen Ridge High School team during its glory days. He was a massive man, packing close to three hundred pounds on a five-foot, eleven-inch frame. In high school he had been nicknamed "Face," because his face seemed disproportionately large, even for his ample body. Richard did more than just play ball. His presence on the football team was so substantial that, in the words of the editors of his high school yearbook, he formed "a sizable part of the gridiron line."

His football clippings undoubtedly impressed his son. But even more impressive was the fact that he was a cop. His authority was enforced with a certainty and conviction that few fathers could match. Not only within the family but in the town itself, he defined good and bad; he drew the line that separated order and chaos. He wore the gun.

To get a job as a Glen Ridge cop, it helped that you had a relative who worked for the township. Richard Corcoran's dad, James, was an affable, well-liked man who had been a fireman for many years. It also helped that you had been a high school athlete. Traditionally, a number of kids who played ball seemed to gravitate to the police department.

The town was never a hotbed of violent crime. There was the usual mix of burglaries and auto thefts, occasional muggings, noisy parties, and drunk drivers, with the rare rape or murder thrown in. The job was a lot less dangerous than, say, pounding a beat in the South Bronx.

If you passed a two-year course in police science at Essex County Community College, as Corcoran did, if you kept your record clean, if you were honest, you had a good chance of moving up the ranks in a force that had only about twenty-five men on it in the 1970s. But it would be inaccurate to attribute Richard Corcoran's advancement solely to longevity. "Richard Corcoran is a good cop," said his boss, Glen Ridge police chief Tom Dugan. "When he's working a case, he is a *bulldog*."

Forest Avenue, where the Grobers lived, was an affluent neighborhood. If any family in Glen Ridge was thought to have lived its life under a halo, it was the Grobers. To neighbors and friends they seemed like a happy, prosperous family. Dr. Nathan Grober had a general medical practice in East Orange, where he had grown up. He added to his income by serving as the designated doctor for the East Orange police and fire departments. Rosemary stopped working as a nurse when Bryant and his older sister and brother were still young. (She would resume her career when the kids were older.) Their house was a couple of streets away from the country club. Kids who visited the Grobers would tell their parents that Bryant lived in "this really plush estate."

That was something of an exaggeration, but the house was roomy and elegant. Oil paintings adorned the living room. The centerpiece of the room was a baby grand piano—a surprise Christmas gift to the family from Dr. Grober. Some of Bryant's friends found the atmosphere in the house more formal than their own. There were no baskets of dirty laundry in the laundry room. The food was carefully organized in the refrigerator. The area rugs always looked as though they had been vacuumed five minutes ago. The Grobers also owned a summer house on Bradley Beach on the Jersey shore, where young Bryant developed into a terrific swimmer.

Rosemary Grober was known for her friendliness and outgoing manner. Nathan was a quiet, soft-spoken man, slender with sharp features, a pointed chin, and sunken eyes. He combed his few remaining strands of hair across his scalp. Nate had firm ideas on what he considered a good diet. He believed in staying in shape. Friends regarded the Grobers as people who took seriously the business of raising children.

Dr. Grober seemed well liked by his patients. "My mother didn't have a dime," one former patient said, "and there's no doubt in my mind that he let us slide a lot. And you could tell a lot of people in the waiting room were in the same position. I thought he was just really a very caring man. When he sat at his desk he was absolutely surrounded by pictures of his children and his wife. Absolutely, literally, like a photo gallery."

Bryant's brother, Gregory, was four years older than Bryant. His sister was three years older. He also had a younger sister and brother. The older siblings were amiable children who made friends easily. According to the kids who grew up with them, the only time young Bry and Greg really got intense was when they were involved in sports; otherwise, life seemed like a lot of laughs.

In Glen Ridge religion was a matter that was taken seriously. Bryant's father was Jewish, his mother was Catholic. (Filling out a form when Bryant entered school, Rosemary gave her religion as "Irish.") There was still some subtle anti-Semitism in Glen Ridge, but it wouldn't be felt by a young child. To playmates at the Forest Avenue playground, Bryant Grober was simply the cute, cheerful, curly-haired boy next door, doing all the things that an upper-middle-class white suburban kid is supposed to do.

Caroline Franco,* a girl who lived nearby, would always remember those carefree days of childhood: playing Monopoly with Bryant on rainy Saturday afternoons; always picking Bry after a snowstorm to build the igloos in her backyard because he was the strongest kid on their street and could pick up the heaviest blocks of ice. "He was extremely normal," Caroline would say after she had grown up. "That's my clearest impression of Bryant. He was an absolutely normal kid."

Much later it would become a matter of some interest in Glen Ridge that of all the boys charged with sexually assaulting Leslie Faber, only Bryant Grober had sisters. The others grew up in families where males were the dominant personalities. It was their fathers and brothers who became their models of American masculinity. The absence of sisters and the powerful influence exerted by male kin made it more difficult for them to develop an understanding and empathetic relationship with girls in their early childhood. Brothers and sisters may not always get along, but they do get to know each other as friends and playmates, as equals within the family; they come to appreciate each other as complex individuals whose goodness is not judged solely by appearance.

Other boys who do not have sisters usually compensate by developing associations and friendships with girls in the playground and neighborhood and school. But the path selected for these boys led them toward membership in a fraternity segregated by gender. It led them toward the exclusively male Glen Ridge brotherhood of athletes; the masculine style established at home was reinforced on the town's playing fields. And that began when they were very young.

6

When it was all over, when the big jocks of the Class of '89 had graduated and had been hugged and kissed at the parties and had gone off to college, they could look back at one moment of their youth and say it captured a childhood in Glen Ridge.

It is a late afternoon, about 6 o'clock, on a Tuesday in June 1976. The elm trees are thick with leaves. The grass has come up rich and green in the outfield. Lined up at home plate are maybe thirty or forty little boys and girls, all five and six years old, some wearing oversized gloves, others dragging too-heavy bats behind them. Dutiful mothers have driven their excited offspring here from all over town. This is opening day of Bandbox softball.

Now the fathers take over. "Count off," says one dad. The idea is that the odd-numbered kids will play on one team and the even-numbered ones will play on the other. Organizing the teams takes quite a while because when the numbers get into double digits some of the kids can't quite remember which number follows the last one. But finally it's done, and one bunch of kids takes the field while the other gets ready to bat. Because there are so many youngsters here and everyone gets to play, there are fifteen or more to a side. There are two kids playing shortstop and three positioned between first and second; close behind them are half a dozen outfielders. In Bandbox softball the outfield plays very shallow.

In this game there are no balls and strikes. Each at-bat continues until the kid hits the ball. The fathers toss soft underhand pitches. Sometimes it can take fifty pitches before the batter makes contact. But the adults are patient; everybody gets a chance. Over in foul territory, sitting in the folding chairs they have brought from home, the mothers and fathers and older sisters and brothers shout encouragement. "That's it, bring the bat out to meet the ball. Atta way, run it out, run it out."

When a single batter is permitted fifty swings, the game usually doesn't last more than three or four innings. It's over when the purple shadows shade the infield; it's over when the mothers realize that the roast in the oven is about to turn into gray mush. Ostensibly, there are no winners and losers. It's just supposed to be a way of introducing little kids to team sports. Schuyler Grant, whose son Philip is playing tonight, would remember later, "You weren't supposed to keep score but all the kids did. And so did some of the parents."

For two years, every Tuesday and Thursday afternoon in June and July, all of them were there for Bandbox softball: Richie, Bryant, Kevin, Kyle, Peter, Chris, and Paul. There, amidst all the boys, was Leslie Faber, who loved nothing more than to play ball, to be on the same field with them. Leslie, her baseball cap flying off her brown hair as she circled under a popup. Leslie, her polo shirt smeared with mud after a hard slide into second base. Leslie, just one of the kids.

This experience in Bandbox softball wasn't the same for boys and girls. For the girls it was one exciting moment, participating in an "official" game sanctioned and organized by the Glen Ridge Athletic Association. When they reached third grade, they could pick up with softball and other sports. But few parents and coaches in the town equated boys' sports with girls' sports. Athletic activity for girls was healthy, casual recreation, one element in a well-rounded childhood. For boys, especially boys who showed some athletic potential, Bandbox was the first stage in an extended sports progression that could culminate in a starting spot on the high school football and baseball teams, with the local celebrity that went with that.

It would take a while: They would have to progress from B League baseball in the third and fourth grades to A League in the fifth and sixth grades and Bill Thorne League in the seventh through ninth grades. There were no girls' baseball teams. Boys of middle-school ages with an interest in football could join the Cobra League, based in Montclair. Similar age-based leagues were organized in basketball, wrestling, and soccer. Only in soccer could girls play on the same team with boys—as Chris Archer later did with Leslie Faber.

A kindergarten or first-grade boy might not project an evening playing Bandbox softball into high school stardom and a contract to play with the Mets. But an athletic boy would know it was something special. It was special because he was taking the first step toward becoming a man. When Kyle and Kevin took their first swings, they could imagine themselves in the spiked shoes of their brother, Eric, whose athletic trophies were displayed on a shelf in the Scherzers' living room and in the rec room downstairs. Eric, nine years and five months older than they, was on his way to playing three years of high school baseball and four years of football. He would go on to become captain of the football team. And he would enjoy a perk that seemed to go with the position: selection as the best-looking senior. The twins might be a little young to indulge in two of Eric's favorite pastimes, water skiing and listening to Led Zeppelin records. But they weren't too young to enjoy his other two favorite activities—eating and football.

Even without Eric's gleaming trophies, there was no mistaking the significance attached to athletic success in the Scherzer family. At dinnertime, friends of the family said, the Scherzers' conversation almost always revolved around that day's sports activities. When Kyle pitched and Kevin caught—"the Scherzer battery," as some of the kids referred to them— Jack would go over the game, pitch by pitch. Gerry Scherzer would try to get in a word about how messy Kevin kept his side of the bedroom. But it would be drowned out by the baseball discussion.

When the boys were young, football, not baseball, was king. In those years their bedtime stories were the legends of the golden era of Glen Ridge football—the William Horey era.

Horey, a broad-shouldered man who favored aviator glasses and colorful shirts with floral designs, was a very successful high school football coach. From 1956 to 1978 Horey's teams compiled an extraordinary record: 147 wins, 35 losses, and 3 ties. During that time his teams won six state championships and fifteen conference titles. Among small suburban schools Glen Ridge was a powerhouse.

Glen Ridge's most famous football player was Gary Cuozzo, the son of a local dentist, who was signed by the professional Baltimore Colts in 1956. But Cuozzo was singular. Few of the town's other graduates went on to star in college, and no others were signed to play in the National Football League. That was of little consequence to the football fans. As far as the town was concerned, what happened on Saturday afternoons offered plenty of excitement.

For the Saturday faithful, Glen Ridge was football. Without it, Glen Ridge was just another suburban town. Kids who didn't play football—and worse still, showed no enthusiasm for those who did—were treated as "nobodies." Adults who didn't find football and the hoopla surrounding it exciting were judged lacking in civic spirit. They would never be accepted as real Ridgers.

Susan Atkins,* a Glen Ridge teacher for twenty-four years, moved to the town in 1952. "I had never seen anything like it before," she said. "All the boys in town wanted to be athletes. They all went out for football just so they could be around Bill Horey. Football was king and if you didn't wear a football uniform you were a nobody." Perhaps worse than a nobody. Although the band members shared the field with the players for a few moments every Saturday, they certainly didn't share the glory. In town they were widely known as "band fags," even among many parents.

Many former members of the team, like the elder Richard Corcoran, would recall their football days as the shining milestones of their youth— milestones they would try to relive at every opportunity. At one team reunion the old grads watched their game films. Then, after the grainy, flickering images dissolved, they all stood up to toast their guest of honor—Bill Horey. The hostess would remember, "They were so excited, it was like they were all freshmen again, going out for the team. These were grown men, stockbrokers and doctors, and they were shy, humble even, in his presence."

Sports, especially football in the Horey glory years, was almost as good as money; it was Glen Ridge's version of a meritocracy. If, for example, Richard Corcoran's sons played ball, and they were good at it, they could claim a status the nonperforming wimpy sons of wealthy fathers could never achieve. A couple of fifty-yard runs, a couple of touchdown passes, and you could be elevated to the pantheon of true Ridgers.

Athletes were exalted for their exploits on the field. Especially in the 1960s and 1970s, the athletes also got bonus points for what they weren't—for not being hippies. Hippie was an extremely elastic characterization. It could even be applied to a kid who would rather play music than ball. To have your kid labeled a hippie in Glen Ridge was the social equivalent of leprosy. Teenage nonconformity usually wasn't more radical than growing a scraggly beard. Of course, there was drug use in town, but that wasn't confined to "hippies."

Their parents knew that, for the most part, this was a gentle rebellion; still, they were frightened. What frightened them was any departure from their own lockstep adolescence during the 1950s. To them, the jocks were a known quantity. The fathers and mothers understood the transgressions of jocks because they had experienced them themselves. Jocks got drunk at parties. Jocks acted boorishly on occasion. Sometimes jocks were a little more aggressive with girls than good manners permitted. Mainly, though, parents believed that this behavior fit within the boundaries of "boys will be boys." They expected a smooth transition from raucous adolescence to responsible adulthood. With maturity the boys' hormones would calm down and they would resume their progress toward sober citizenship. What the parents didn't understand was the drugs and the music and the self-conscious antimaterialism of the hippies. That was different, unnerving, and threatening.

Claire Corcoran's friend June Gallo said that Detective Corcoran had a buddy who was a cop in a nearby town that was a lot like Glen Ridge. "When Joe* and Richard would get together for drinks, Joe would start crying about his two sons," she said. "His boys were tall and skinny and wore their hair long and played music—it was Joe's worst nightmare."

From Richard Corcoran's point of view—and in the view of most other fathers in town—there was no more effective vaccination against hippiedom than athletics. But athletics wasn't just an activity reserved for kids. Corcoran had carried it over to his adult life, and so had many other fathers. When Claire would take her three young boys to church on Sunday during the spring and summer, friends of the family said, Detective Corcoran would head out to the playing field for a game in the Men's Softball League. "To him, it was the most important thing in the world," said June Gallo. "His philosophy was you didn't play to have a good time. You played to win."

And that's the way Richard Corcoran's son was taught to play the game. "At an incredibly early age, Richie would throw a temper tantrum if he was called out by an ump," said one father who coached kids' baseball in Glen Ridge.

Glen Ridge offered a network of child development that was separate from the schools. It fell under the catch-all rubric of recreation. The strictly sports activities were supervised by the town's athletic association. Other leisure activities were sponsored by the recreation program. Together, they offered a wide variety of diversions for kids.

In the spring and summer, there were baseball and tennis, volleyball and field hockey, roller skating and bowling, for youngsters of different ages. The fall and winter brought soccer and basketball, karate and cheerleading, wrestling and indoor track. On Friday nights recreation programs were held at the middle-school and high school gyms. Other activities required a moderate fee ($80 for ten art classes, $15 for five sessions of cheerleading instruction). Of course, in a town like Glen Ridge, there would be a few big-ticket items, like a $500 trip to Disney World in Orlando, Florida.

The fact that these activities were organized and supervised reassured parents. Their youngsters weren't just hanging out, like some wild kids in the projects in Newark. Their kids were playing by the rules, the game rules and the social rules. No waywardness, no improvisation, no accidental friendships with out-of-town kids. And no frivolity. This was serious recreation.

It was especially serious for the aspiring athletes. The kids had uniforms and team names; they had coaches and instructors; they had winning and losing seasons and rankings and championships. The winners moved up from the bush leagues to the big time—high school sports— and the losers wallowed in mediocrity and anonymity. The athletes' progress was certified, formalized, by the athletic association and the recreation program, year after year. The sons of the Scherzers, Corcorans, Archers, Grobers knew they were special because the town told them so. It was right there in the end-of-season stats, right there engraved on their trophies.

As children the boys who would later be involved in the Leslie Faber case met in every detail the idealized standards held by the town for its young males. Lawrence Roder, the school superintendent in Glen Ridge in the 1970s, recalled that "the Glen Ridge image was something everyone was measured against. The image was that the successful kid was attractive, well groomed, articulate, and doing well in school or in some enterprise, like sports. If you didn't meet these standards, you could be treated like an outcast." In fact, one of the kids who wasn't an athlete and wasn't part of the Cartaret Street playground group would tell his parents, "We're going to form our own club. It's called the 'Outcasts.'"

The Cartaret playground gang and its satellite members from across town didn't have to invent an identity. They knew they were winners. From their preschool days when "the guys" played on the streets, to the pick-up games in Cartaret, and later to the organized leagues in the athletic association, they built their reputation as winners.

The mothers, meanwhile, served an unheralded but essential purpose in the athletic scheme. They got their kids up at 5 A.M. to transport them to practice, and baked cookies as an after-the-game reward. For the boys the audience that counted most, however, was the men—the fathers who cheered them on and the older brothers who inspired them by their own athletic exploits. It was the men whom the boys performed for; it was the men they tried to impress with their competitiveness and aggressiveness and controlled daring. Their clothes and uniforms, their jibes and jokes, and, most of all, their unshakable loyalty to their friends were elements in a rehearsal for manhood—or that special definition of manhood they picked up from their fathers and brothers. By that definition, if you weren't a winner, if you walked around with the hangdog expression of a loser, you were less than a man. Kids who weren't versed in jock talk, kids who didn't run out a ground ball or who swung their bats lethargically, kids who carried a book with them to Cartaret would be labeled "queers" or "nerds." These kids would never be real men.

7

How would Leslie Faber fit into the hierarchy Glen Ridge had established for its children? When she entered kindergarten at the Linden Avenue Elementary School in 1976, her parents couldn't be sure.

At their first meeting with Leslie's teacher, they mentioned their concern about problems the nursery school teacher had observed. The kindergarten teacher said she would keep an eye on Leslie. Six weeks later she said she had noticed that Leslie wasn't fitting in academically and socially. Would the Fabers mind if Leslie was tested? No, the Fabers wouldn't mind.

They had assumed that Leslie's problems were correctable; their attitude was, Let's find out what the problems are and fix them.

Before you can fix something, you need to know what's wrong. That's what school evaluations were supposed to show: What, if anything, was wrong. Students could be tested by school psychologists to see whether they should be placed in a special education program. The findings would be evaluated by members of the Glen Ridge school system's Child Study Team, composed of three special education teachers, the psychologists, and a consultant on learning deficiencies.

Leslie's test results were maddeningly imprecise. The Glen Ridge Child Study Team reported that Leslie was suffering from static encephalopathy, which was defined as a nonchanging organic brain disorder. That sounded serious, but when they got down to the fine details — an attention deficit disorder, no evidence of hyperactivity, minimal brain dysfunction — it didn't sound so bad. There was medication that could help with attention deficiencies. Also, parental support, affection, and guidance could go a long way.

It was a judgment call. Leslie's test results could have been interpreted as evidence of mental retardation. But that's something the school never told the Fabers. The evaluators chose, instead, to place her in the less serious category of "neurologically impaired."

Rosalind and Charles didn't realize that they were hearing the best-case, most optimistic assessment. The diagnosis of neurological impairment suggested the possibility, however remote, of progress and recovery; if the school had classified her as mentally retarded, the Fabers would have had little prospect of improvement. To most parents mental retardation sounds like an awfully definitive and final verdict. So, as Leslie began her school years, the Fabers were encouraged.

Stanley Brod,* who later became a member of the school system's Child Study Team, describes the classification "neurological impairment" in terms that might well offer hope to the parents of a five-year-old: "It would mean there's a neurological breakdown or a developmental delay where the student may not be processing information correctly." Could the breakdown be repaired? Could the delay now be made up by acceleration later on? The Fabers had no certain answer to these questions, but just being able to ask them lightened the burden.

If Leslie's evaluation gave the Fabers some hope, so did the experience of other youngsters who had been classified as neurologically impaired and who the Fabers knew were only marginally deficient. These kids were popular. Some were good athletes and good students measured against their peers. A number of these youngsters had been classified for a while and then declassified when their academic performance improved. With good fortune and constant support, Leslie might progress as they had.

When she entered first grade, her speech, although slightly slurred, was understandable; her disability had not affected her physical appearance; she was extroverted and loved to socialize and mix with other kids. She was a tractable, cheerful child. Partly because of her warm, winning nature and partly because she had been evaluated as neurologically impaired, her parents directed her toward the mainstream of school and community life.

Their decision to expose Leslie to a "normal" childhood was influenced by their confidence in Glen Ridge as a great place to raise a child. The Fabers knew that Glen Ridge wasn't paradise. But it was, they believed, an exceptionally safe and secure world for a child to explore, even a child who was impaired. And why wouldn't they feel that way? According to Glen Ridge learning specialist Frank Ewald,* "Historically, this has not been a threatening community. This community is about as homogeneous, socially and economically, as you'll find anywhere in the world. The place is so small [that] the kids in school know each other, they play on all the sports teams—there's less of a need to feel protective. So you don't lack confidence if your kid goes down to the park to play, as Leslie did, or goes to a basketball game or rides across town on her bicycle—all things Leslie did. I don't think her parents ever felt the need to take extraordinary steps to protect her. And I think that's totally justified because this is not New York City."

When Leslie Faber was entering the Glen Ridge school system in 1977, a new approach toward the education and development of the retarded and the learning-disabled was being discussed nationwide. Proponents of the new thinking advocated a more independent life and a more mainstream education for all but the most seriously impaired.

When confronted with a problem, the Fabers could be methodical in their approach. Rosalind Faber would take notes when she read an article that was relevant to Leslie's development and show them to her husband. The Fabers did not leap to a decision, but the articles were ultimately persuasive in their overall conclusion that many children with mild to moderate disabilities should be encouraged to lead a relatively independent childhood, which could potentially evolve into a relatively independent adulthood.

The old approach would have isolated the impaired child at home, segregated her with other disabled youngsters in school, and then quarantined her with other disabled adults in workshops where she earned fifty cents an hour making brooms and baskets. When parents became infirm or too old, their disabled offspring would be institutionalized. All that was changing rapidly in the late 1970s. The new thinking was that moderately impaired students should be exposed to a variety of mainstream activities in the schools. When it came to employment, various organizations were placing thousands of retarded citizens in "normal" jobs, ranging from kitchen work in hotels to the assembling of computer parts. Other advocates for the disabled were testing various arrangements in independent and quasi-independent living that held out the promise of marriage and children and reasonably steady employment in semiskilled jobs.

In the autumn of 1977 most of what they read and most of what they observed of their younger daughter guided the Fabers in the direction of a self-assertive, relatively conventional childhood for young Leslie. They understood that they would have to let her mingle freely with the neighborhood kids and make her own friends. However protective they felt, they couldn't be hovering over her every minute. That's not what parents of normal kids did.

Even at that early age, Leslie loved to play in Cartaret Park. As much as any of the neighborhood boys, she was at home there; giggling, she'd roll in the grass for hours or climb to the top of the jungle gym in a great scrambling burst of energy. What set her apart in those first years of her life was her almost unslakable thirst for attention and affection. A smile, a pat, a wink, a wave—she loved it, reveled in it. Most children want attention; Leslie craved it. Watch me, see me run, see me jump. See me.

In 1977 the kindergartners and first-grade boys were already laying claim to the playground. The Scherzer twins, Peter Quigley, the Archer boys—they all acted as if the place belonged to them. As a girl, Leslie would never win full acceptance in this brotherhood. But her robust athleticism should have qualified her as an occasional playmate. Already large for her age, with a sturdier build than you would expect in a five-year-old girl, you could do a lot worse than have Leslie on your side in a game of tag or kickball. But she didn't get picked.

To the other kids she seemed different. Hard to put your finger on it. Was it her size? Or maybe her unflagging cheerfulness? Or her incessant, unfocused jabbering? The guys decided that if they gave her a little encouragement, she would stick to them like glue, because her need for appreciation and belonging was so unrestrained. It was annoying and embarrassing for the tough little men of Cartaret playground. Even if you felt that way, even if being liked was more important than anything else, you weren't supposed to show it—it was weak, it was *strange*. Different, weak, strange—labels she wouldn't comprehend yet, but whose effect Leslie could already feel.

The boys didn't totally exclude her. They included her just enough so that they could exploit her vulnerability. One afternoon after school, five-year-old Leslie was walking along her street, looking for someone to play with. A couple of boys, maybe a year or so older than Leslie, called to her to join them in their backyard. They had two friends with them, the Scherzer twins from over on Lorraine Street. The boys were huddled together, laughing.

Leslie ran over. She was wearing her biggest smile. They wanted to be with her. One of them was holding something out to her. Hey, Les, we've got something special for you, something really nice.

It was a ballpoint pen. The tip was coated with a dark substance. The boys told her that it was chocolate. Why don't you taste it, Leslie, you'll like it, they said. She picked up the pen and caught the disgusting smell. It wasn't candy. It was dog dirt. *They wanted her to eat dog dirt?*

She looked confused, uncertain of what to do. She didn't want to eat dog feces, but if that's what her friends wanted her to do, she'd do it. She'd do anything for her friends.

As Leslie Faber licked the point of the pen, her sister, Carol, passed by. She could see Leslie and the boys circled around her at the end of the driveway. "There was a pen in her hand and a look of disgust on her face," Carol would say later. "They'd made her eat dog feces."

Carol, eight years old, the older sister, ran down the driveway, grabbed Leslie's arm, and started pulling her back to their house. When they got home, Carol told her mother what had happened. "The kids are all picking on her," Carol said, her voice quavering with outrage. "The boys even made her eat dog dirt."

"What!" Rosalind shouted, not believing what she was hearing.

"Yes, she ate it."

"Les, I want to talk to you alone."

She took Leslie into her bedroom and asked her, "Is this true? Why did you do something like this, it's so awful?"

Leslie nodded "yes," it was true.

Rosalind's first impulse was to call the neighbors in whose backyard it had happened and to call Jack and Gerry Scherzer, whom she had met a few times before. But the more she thought about it, the harder it was to pick up the phone. She hadn't been there. She had to accept the word of two young children. She had this rule: You never complain unless you've witnessed it yourself. You couldn't be sure of what led up to it. Besides, the few times she had met Jack Scherzer he had impressed her as a gruff, tough man whose life revolved around his boys' exploits on the sports field. If she complained to Jack, she was afraid he'd get into a big argument with her about it.

The other consideration was: If you start complaining over everything, you call attention to Leslie's special condition. That's not what you want to do; what you want to do is treat her like an average child who is resilient, who can run the gauntlet of childhood slights and cruelties and come out stronger for it.

So Rosalind Faber didn't complain. Instead, she pleaded with Leslie not to play with these boys. "But Mommy, they're my friends," Leslie answered. "They like me."

Although she didn't call, the incident gave Rosalind the chills. What was going to happen next? That night, before she went to sleep, she wrote in her journal two sentences, as if by keeping a record of this experience she would find it more comprehensible. *An incredible thing happened. They made Leslie eat dog feces,* she wrote.

It wasn't an isolated incident. Other incredible things happened. A few weeks after Leslie ate the dog feces, neighborhood boys molded mud into the shape of a candy bar and told Leslie that they would be her best friend if she ate it. She did.

One evening her parents noticed that her arm was covered with red welts.

"What's wrong with your arm?" her dad asked Leslie.

"The boys were pinching me."

"Well, why didn't you tell them to stop," he said.

Her head hanging, Leslie said, "I don't know."

The secret was out in the neighborhood: You could do almost anything to Leslie and she would let you get away with it if you said you really liked her and would be her friend. One of the favorite things was to make fun of her name. "Hey, Brain-Les." "Hey, Head-Les." "Hey, retard" would come later.

After a while, Rosalind noticed that Carol was reluctant to constantly defend Leslie against the other kids. Carol wanted to live her own life. Sometimes when Carol would be playing with dolls with her friends and

Leslie would be standing on the side, "I'd be mean to her," Carol recalled years later. "I'd tell her to go home and leave us alone."

Although the Fabers would not tell friends and neighbors about their tribulations, they began to feel they needed help with Leslie. They decided to take Leslie to a child psychologist. They told him about the incidents with the dog feces and the mud pies and other things kids did to her. They hoped he could make some practical suggestions, point to a general direction that would give Leslie the best chance to grow up as normally as possible. But the psychologist—like the adoption agency people, like the pediatrician, like members of the school's Child Study Team, like so many counselors and teachers and social workers they would meet through the years—hedged his bets. He told them: "Lots of children have some problems. And then they outgrow them. Why don't we see if Leslie outgrows them." The psychologist did not say that when youngsters were trying to persuade a disabled child to eat dog shit and mud maybe it was they who had problems, not Leslie.

8

Uncertainty surrounded Leslie when she began her education, but the boys she knew from the park and neighborhood had every reason to expect that they would make normal progress in school.

The members of the Class of '89 entered first grade in their neighborhood schools in September 1977. Approximately sixty went to Linden Avenue; the others went to Forest Avenue. They would remain in elementary school through fourth grade in June 1981. Then they would go on to middle school, which they would attend for the next four years, grades five through eight. After that, in September 1985, they would move on to high school.

The boys' parents knew that the local schools had an excellent reputation. But right from the start, a group of boys in the Class of '89 began what became a pattern of misbehavior that followed the class through its schooling in Glen Ridge. The group included some of the budding athletes who would soon form the jock circle in the class. These boys were loud and defiant, and they dominated other students with their raucous conduct. From an early age in school, the jock clique commanded the stage.

That in itself wasn't unexpected. In many schools boys get more than their share of attention and create more than their share of discipline problems. In the fledgling Class of '89, however, parents and teachers thought this pattern was more pronounced than usual. And in the face of this challenge, teachers seemed more passive and submissive than they had been in the past. Some teachers, particularly male teachers, assumed that these boys were just exhibiting high spirits; as a consequence, they tolerated behavior from the boys that they would have punished had it come from a girl.

Certain names turned up on school discipline reports with some regularity—Scherzer and Corcoran. Also, less frequently, Archer, Quigley, and Grober, and some of their friends. As these and other boys attracted attention by their deviltry and by their disregard for authority, some of the girls who were their classmates began to feel that they were getting less attention.

In September 1981 all the students who would graduate in 1989 came together in one middle school, where they would spend the next four years. In the first year or so, the jock clique—now drawing new members from all over town, not just one neighborhood—took on a definite shape and personality.

The group numbered twenty to twenty-five boys, plus another ten or fifteen girls who buzzed around them. About two-thirds of the boys were in the Class of '89; the rest would graduate a year later. The younger kids were granted honorary membership because they were up-and-coming athletes or because, like Chris Archer, they had older brothers in the clique's inner circle.

The middle-school miscreants found many ways to express themselves. One day they smashed the science laboratory equipment, which was reduced to a heap of twisted metal and broken glass. Another day they interrupted their classes with smutty jokes. They treated female teachers and students with contempt.

One teacher, Susan Atkins,* evoked the experience of many of her colleagues when she said, "It's not just one classroom. It's every class. There's a core and you never know what they're going to throw at you. And the other kids watch, wondering if the 'core' is going to come after them."

David Maltman, the principal of the Glen Ridge Middle School, referred to the class as "troubled," but singled out the young athletes as the main instigators. "Troubled, that's exactly right," he said. "These kids would act up in class, disrupt the learning situation, set other kids up, get in fights with them, go after them back and forth to school. They were instigators in the classroom. In the fifth grade, they already had had a bad name for a long time."

Yet the jocks were popular with many of the students, who admired the way they challenged authority. Tom Allen,* a basketball player who was one year behind them, said, "The jocks were the popular people. Definitely." They were popular with Allen and others for a reason that's very important to a ten- or eleven-year-old. As a group, they acted as though they were special. While most kids didn't know where they fitted in, the jocks created their own fraternal society with its secret codes and inside jokes. Either you were with them or you were out of it. "They were the first people to have their own little group, in sixth grade even," Allen said. "Other people had four people, maybe, but their group was big and it was always getting bigger. They'd always have enough guys for a football game or a whiffle game at Cartaret. The winter was the worst. They would always be making their own plans and you had to find out what they were doing and sometimes you'd get left out."

Even then, they seemed stronger and brawnier than the other middle-school kids. "You were around them, it made you feel safe," Tom remembered. "A lot of them wrestled, and everybody knew you had to be strong to wrestle. Not too many people challenged them if they did something wrong."

If you weren't strong and what passed at that age for good-looking, you weren't accepted into the inner circle—except, maybe, if you had a popular jock older brother. Phil Grant, who years later would walk out on the encounter in the basement, didn't have an older brother. (Having an older sister, as Phil did, wouldn't win you any points with this gang.) He was short. He wore glasses. Phil had been friends with Paul Archer since kindergarten. But now Paul was ignoring him, pretending they had never hung out together.

"They were the cream of the crop, always the cream of the crop—and I wasn't," Phil said. "Paul began to hang out with Richie and Bryant. I'd played organized sports just like them. I was as good as any one of them in baseball, but it didn't matter. They still didn't like me because of the way I looked and because they thought I was a wimp. I wouldn't throw the eraser at someone's back. Paul said, 'I'm not going to associate with you anymore.' He made it very clear. And it was like I'd never known him."

If you were exiled from the group, you were instantly transformed from a friend into a target. "They were so proud of being the worst of the worst and if you didn't do the things they did, they'd take it out on you with the most annoying, stupid, obnoxious stuff," Grant said. "But it was more than that. The kind of stuff they'd do was hit a kid when he was down. Hit him again and again."

The jocks spent a lot of time clowning around to amuse their friends. They didn't worry much about their grades because they knew that no one got left back in middle school. So the teachers wound up handing out mediocre grades to them and, at the same time, filling their file cabinets with complaints about their behavior.

Kevin Scherzer had one of the thickest files. In elementary school Kevin did poorly and was falling behind his classmates. In the second grade the Glen Ridge Child Study Team classified Kevin as "neurologically impaired," and he was assigned to a class of children who had educational deficiencies. In fact, it is noteworthy that he received the same classification as Leslie Faber did when she entered school.

In the sixth grade, though, the Child Study Team declassified him. He was returned to regular classes. Kevin, the team found, was "functioning satisfactorily" in all subject areas. Moreover, "he is well accepted by his peer group and appears to have many friends."

But almost as soon as he was back with his jock friends, Kevin's schoolwork and conduct deteriorated. In one sixth-grade report forwarded to his parents, three teachers said he had serious behavior problems. By the eighth grade, teachers described Kevin's behavior as "compulsive, rude, disrespectful." If Kevin had been reclassified and returned to a special education class or if he had received therapeutic treatment, his parents and teachers might have discovered that he had more serious problems than disrespectfulness and rudeness. But adults responded to Kevin's difficulties as though they were only the normal growing pains of an average boy, rather than serious maladjustments that could worsen as time passed.

Teachers responded to Kyle much as they did to his twin brother, Kevin. Kyle's IQ of 106 was in the normal range, but he had difficulty behaving and paying attention to his studies. His school records contain such comments as "motivation is low" and "He . . . can be disruptive. . . . When he is addressed with the problem he denies it."

One exasperated seventh-grade teacher wrote of her experience teaching Kyle: "I am older than my years. Why should I sit here and take this? Life is short."

Richie Corcoran began school with an IQ that was above average, but his behavior problems undercut his academic progress. In a legal brief later filed in the Leslie Faber case, Richie's lawyer, Anthony R. Mautone, would write: "Richard Corcoran's school records reveal a poor academic background and poor social adaptation. . . . Document after document shows poor classroom behavior and one document on detention has various teachers critiquing his lack of control." And yet : . .

Richie could be perceptive and responsive when he became interested in a subject or an issue. But his temperament could also be highly volatile. "One minute he would be so charming you wanted to love him," says one of his middle-school teachers. "The next minute he was ready to fight." It was hard to know what set him off. But his face would flush without provocation or warning, his eyes would narrow, and he looked as if he were about to detonate.

Kyle and Kevin and Richie frequently explored the outer limits of propriety in middle school. But other members of the jock group were more discreet. While Chris and Paul Archer and their friends committed minor infractions, they got decent grades for the most part and avoided major scrapes in school.

Paul was an average student, but at times he showed flashes of above-average intelligence. Like many of his friends, he had an excellent sixth grade, a fair seventh grade, and a troubled eighth grade, when the jock clique really jelled. With some prescience one of Paul's teachers described him as a "follower."

Paul's younger brother, Chris, got the highest grades in the group. In the sixth grade his IQ score was 121, and a test that measured academic ability placed him in the top 10 percent of the population, for his age and grade. When he turned twelve and the testosterone started kicking in, Chris also entered a rocky stretch: a couple of Ds, grades averaging in the 70s.

In his last two years of middle school, his grades rose and most teachers thought he was a superior student. But one teacher also noted that he "tends to be hyperactive." What was hyperactivity to one teacher was exuberance to another. Charlie Kinzler,* a middle-school teacher, found Chris, with his good looks and icy blue eyes, a "cool kid." Some teachers did think that Chris had a "wise edge to him," Kinzler said later, "but he was never wise to me. But he did have that little swagger, and the girls liked that a lot."

Other teachers didn't think he was so cool. "Chris had that academic quickness; he could memorize the answer in a flash," Susan Atkins, one of his teachers, said. "He resented it that he wasn't placed in the top group of students. He felt above the kids he was with. And he always looked at me with a sneer."

Chris passed most of his classes with ease. His jock buddies, who were disrupting the middle school, had much more serious academic problems. But the unstated policy in Glen Ridge was that every kid would move forward with his classmates to the next grade level. Charles Kinzler had been a teacher at the middle school for a dozen years when the Class of '89 showed up. "Keep moving the 'bad' kids along and get them out of your hair—that's always been the philosophy in the middle school," Kinzler said. "So many teachers change kids' grades—just to avoid the shit. In Glen Ridge, if a parent hassles a teacher, the teacher'll give the kid an A. The teacher just doesn't want to get in the middle of a big fight."

School correspondence, evaluations, grades, and IQ scores provide a partial written record of a child's development. But there is also a verbal record of other youngsters' memories and recollections of that child. These are experiences that teachers and principals rarely hear about. For his schoolmates Chris was the fuse, always ready to set off a blast. But Chris was cool; he saves his best shots for after school, out of sight of the teachers who saw him as young Mr. Honor Roll.

Tom Allen recalled that "Chris was always the hyperest of all the guys. We'd be sitting around watching TV and he's the first one to say, 'Let's get out of here, let's go.' He can't sit still. We go to Great Adventure [amusement park] and he'd run to every ride. We'd be tired out at the end of the day and he'd still be running. We'd be leaving and he'd jump into the fountain, just to stay longer. And when we'd get home and we had a test the next day, we'd all be studying, but Chris wouldn't pick up a book and he'd get a 90." Chris, always raising the hurdles, always upping the stakes.

His behavior didn't improve during his last year of middle school, when most of his friends had already moved on to high school. On the evening of April 4, 1986, twelve-year-old Chris Archer led a guerrilla raid against the Glen Ridge Country Club.

He and five buddies piled into two golf carts, with Chris at the wheel of one. They tore up the tennis court, drove their golf carts into the walls of the garage, and vandalized the locker room.

The next morning, when the damage was discovered, the boys were already bragging about the lightning raid; the police heard about it and brought Chris in. At first he denied any involvement, but after a while he admitted what he had done. Juvenile complaints were filed against Chris and the other boys, charging them with burglary and criminal mischief.

Meanwhile, the country club was assessing the damage; a preliminary evaluation estimated it at about a couple of thousand dollars, maybe more. The boys went before a town board called the Juvenile Conference Committee. Its practice was to mete out reprimands and sometimes a penalty of community service to juveniles charged with relatively minor offenses. As almost always in Glen Ridge, the issue was settled, wrong was made right, by the transfer of cash. The families of the six boys agreed to make restitution to the club for the damage. The club agreed to forget about the whole mess.

Chris pulled his share of stunts, but for the girls who attended middle school with these guys, the one name that still jumps out at them is Kevin Scherzer.

Kevin did things that most of the other guys wouldn't dare to do. In middle school his transgressions took on a blatantly sexual coloration. And some of these were aimed at Linda Donaldson.*

"For four years in middle school, whenever he could get behind me in the hall, he'd snap my bra," Linda said. She made a point of walking down the hall surrounded by friends, and if she were alone she'd scout the passageway to make sure Kevin wasn't there. But she couldn't avoid him all the time.

Linda could dismiss Kevin as a nuisance, somebody who really didn't matter. Diane Carter* was more fragile. The middle-school years were difficult ones for her. Her parents had gone through an acrimonious divorce. Her mother had recently remarried. A new baby was on the way. There was a sense that the earth was crumbling beneath her. Her girlfriends would quietly sympathize with her. But Kevin took her unhappiness as opportunity.

She became an object of Kevin's ridicule because she hadn't developed by the age of twelve. "Every day—'There's Diane, flat as a board.' Every day—'Diane you're the pirate's delight—sunken treasure.' I would sit there and try to laugh it off," she said, "or just get upset and say, 'Stop it.' I felt there was nothing I could do, that no matter what I did, Kevin, and Kyle, too, would just continue with their behavior."

Karen Carter, Diane's mother, never forgot the look on her face when she came home after school. "It was agony," Karen said. "Pure agony. What Kevin said became the truth in Diane's mind. She was convinced that she was the only girl in her class who was never going to reach puberty. Twelve and thirteen are ages of a lot of sexual anxiety to begin with, and she was tormented, absolutely tormented."

And Diane remembered: "I was terrified of boys because of my experiences with the Scherzers. All guys were perverts—that was my thought. All guys are mean, all guys have shitty cracks to say. All guys care about is big boobs."

Then came French class.

Some of the kids were disruptive there. And the most disruptive of all, according to Diane Carter, was Kevin Scherzer. "He used to pull his pants down and moon, sit on his bare behind all the way through class," Diane said. "Then he used to, like, stand behind the teacher and pretend to be humping her, doggy-style. The teacher never saw him do that, for the whole year."

But most of the students saw it. Frank Leary,* who later became an academic leader of the Class of '89, said, "In French the class was really out of control. The teacher would be writing on the blackboard and Kevin would stand up in his seat and expose himself. She never noticed it."

Kevin's behavior had been repeated so often by the seventh and eighth grades that it had lost the power to surprise or offend many students. "Everybody else was laughing, so I figured there was nothing really wrong," Diane Carter recalled. "The other kids were saying, 'Kevin needs attention, that's why he does it.' But I always thought in the back of my mind there was something a little warped about it. It wasn't normal to me, even back then—but what the hell, you go along with everybody else and laugh."

But she did something that many other students would not do. She told her mother, Karen, about what Kevin was doing in French. Karen Carter brought up the matter during a parent-teacher conference. A few days later Diane saw Kevin leaving the middle-school principal's office. Kevin had been given a few days in detention class as punishment. Diane said, "Kevin was running down the hall, screaming, 'If I find out who blew the whistle on me, I'll kill the kid.' I kept a low profile after that. The outcome was that nothing changed. He just went on doing what he'd always been doing. If anything, it worsened."

Why was so much of his hostility directed toward girls? By middle school most of the members of the sports clique and its admirers lived in a hermetic all-male world of teams and friends and brothers and fathers. Their most intimate relationships were with other guys and men. There was the usual sparse offering of banal extracurricular activities that brought boys and girls together to work toward common goals, but these were shunned as "nerdish" by the jocks. They just didn't know girls as equals, as true friends, as people you cared about.

The school didn't identify the jocks' voluntary segregation as a problem with potentially serious consequences for both the boys and the young women whom they targeted. Glen Ridge wasn't unusual in this respect. Schools across the country just didn't think the everyday treatment of girls by boys was a serious issue that merited discussion among faculty and students. In Glen Ridge the school did not detect, or chose not to notice, that these young jocks had a callous, abusive manner with girls, that the divide between them had widened. A more probing examination of why the boys behaved insensitively and cruelly toward girls—why they seemed to treat them like the enemy—was never proposed. The kids were never given a vehicle by the school to examine themselves.

In Glen Ridge, as in most public schools, no issue was treated more gingerly than possible sexual misconduct by a student. In most public schools in the United States, a certain amount of sexual acting out was tolerated unless a student came forward with a concrete accusation of harassment.

In 1993 a national survey by the American Association of University Women found that 81 percent of female public school students said they had been sexually harassed in school. Most of these incidents happened in places that parents and teachers had a right to expect were safe—school hallways, playgrounds, and classrooms. Perhaps the most striking finding was that only 7 percent of those who were harassed told a teacher about it.

One inevitable consequence of the Glen Ridge school's aversion to confrontation was that Kevin Scherzer began to evoke grudging admiration from some fellow students who otherwise thought him obnoxious. The "good" kids, the obedient kids, the studious kids began to copy Kevin, copy the "bad" guys. If the "bad" guys could get away with all this stuff, why couldn't they? If being "bad" was the ticket to popularity, maybe they should give it a try. By their example the core of "bad" kids licensed most of the rest of the students to become nuisances—or worse. This was the reputation they got, deserved or not. Forevermore, the Class of '89 would be known as the "bad class."

9

The bad news circulated among parents in town: In the middle school the Class of '89 had more than its share of troublemakers, and the chief troublemakers were mostly the jocks.

A number of parents began to conclude that their children could receive a better education elsewhere, instead of spending five more years in the company of the "bad" class. Because of the reputation of the class, some twenty families, representing roughly 17 percent of the students, removed their children from the school system before they reached high school. Lila Greenburg,* a Glen Ridge teacher, tried to persuade the father of one of her students to leave his daughter in the school, instead of sending her to a Catholic high school. "You know Glen Ridge is a better school," Greenburg told him.

"You're right, I know it is," the father conceded. "But I want her away from this group. She's too impressionable. She doesn't have the strength to withstand that pressure."

Lynn Andrews,* who taught in a school near Glen Ridge, took her son, Daniel, out of Glen Ridge Middle School and enrolled him in a private school. Linda Grant, however, decided to keep her son, Philip, in the school. She thought he would make it through without too much trouble if he stayed away from the jock circle. "Don't think it didn't occur to me to get Phil out," she said. "So what do we do? Do we move, go through selling the house, go to another community? Do you send him off to prep school somewhere while you're still paying exorbitant taxes in Glen Ridge? So, almost by default we continue with Philip in Glen Ridge."

After one especially egregious incident, the principal, David Maltman, and the teachers came up with a plan: Students who needed academic, emotional, or social help would be placed in special education classes. Also, youngsters who needed it would be given professional counseling. Finally, the overall discipline in the school would be tightened. None of these approaches was specifically directed at deterring animosity expressed by the boys toward female classmates.

The first approach, classifying a youngster as a special education student, required the student to be placed in one of thirteen classifications, ranging from perceptually or neurologically impaired (for youngsters with relatively minor learning problems) to mentally retarded, emotionally disturbed, or socially maladjusted. These were regarded as much more serious learning and behavioral conditions.

To classify a youngster, the school required the approval of parents. Some teachers said later that they urged the Scherzers to have Kevin placed in special ed classes, but the parents refused. They could argue, with some justification, that Kevin had advanced to the next grade every year. They could say he was an average kid, moving at average speed.

"The parents had a point," says Eileen Norris,* who taught special education classes. "Our own never-fail policies came back to haunt us. Teachers would pass Kevin because they didn't want to have him in their class for another year. And then his parents would say, 'How can he be so awful when he's always passing?' The school really did send them mixed signals."

"Parents responded with anger," Maltman recalled. "'You're after my kid'—that kind of thing. Parents don't want the stigma. They look at it as a stigma that 'my kid is a classified kid.'"

The parents prevailed over the teachers and counselors. In the eighth grade Kyle and Kevin were not classified. They remained in the middle of the action.

To implement the second phase of the school's plan to restore order—providing ongoing counseling to youngsters who needed it—the teachers wanted to hire a crisis-intervention counselor. Just the idea that a crisis might exist that would require the intervention of a counselor was a controversial notion in Glen Ridge. As a public relations ploy, the school changed the title of the position to School Assistance Counselor, when he was hired.

The name change did not satisfy skeptical parents. Was the counselor going to get mixed up in a kid's private life, in the family's personal affairs? Glen Ridge parents were wary of nosy bureaucracies and of almost anything that might have a remote bearing on how a kid was raised or on his parents' values. For example, school officials rejected an innocuous recommendation that high school students' writing skills might be improved if they kept a personal journal. Parents had protested that a journal could infringe on their privacy.

Another example: A teacher who was awarded a national teaching prize in the early 1980s wanted to donate her $1,500 award toward establishing a student organization to heighten awareness of the dangers of drunk driving. Several Glen Ridge young men had been killed in auto accidents in the past decade. But the teacher was told to keep her money. The school system felt that the organization might lead some people to conclude that Glen Ridge had a teenage drinking problem.

That same insistence on keeping personal matters secret succeeded in eliminating the crisis-intervention counseling. At the end of the 1985–86 school year, when the Class of '89 was in its freshman year of high school, the school board voted to discontinue the position. Maltman said later, "If they had continued with the counselor, extended it into the high school, there is an outside chance that what ultimately happened wouldn't have happened. Kids who were being harassed by the jocks could have gone to the counselor and said, Hey, get this guy into some kind of therapy."

The school's third strategy for containing the damage done by the "bad" class was to impose tougher discipline. On back-to-school night in the eighth grade, Maltman presented to the parents a modest plan: Students who failed to bring in their homework would be kept after school to complete it. Students who misbehaved would have to put in time after school. In most American public schools, this would be considered fairly mild punishment. In Glen Ridge "All hell broke loose," Maltman said. "The parents thought these were Gestapo methods. These were the same people who always complained that we weren't tough enough."

Despite the opposition of some parents, there were others who argued for greater discipline. Among these were Doug and Michaele Archer. "I can't say whether they knew what their kids were doing when they weren't around, but I do know that they backed up the school when we were trying to enforce discipline," the principal said. With the support of these parents, the school managed to sustain a watered-down version of its discipline policy until the Class of '89 left middle school. The next year, the discipline policy was dropped.

The year after the Class of '89 graduated from middle school, Maltman decided that he had had enough. After twenty-one years, he resigned from the Glen Ridge school system. "We missed so many chances to do the right thing for the kids," he said. "I did not leave as a happy person."

Maltman talked about doing the right thing for the kids. If the reforms he had tried to implement had taken hold, would anything have been changed? "Honestly, I don't know," said Maltman. "If you asked me in 1984 whether these kids would get in trouble I'd say, Yeah, they'd be out drinking and get themselves into a car wreck. Could I predict the kind of thing that was going to happen? No. I wouldn't have thought that kids I knew for years would get into something like that."

10

The parents of the boys were faced with one set of problems as their children grew up. Leslie's parents were confronted by a very different set of problems.

Ros and Charlie received many different and sometimes conflicting evaluations and recommendations from Leslie's teachers and counselors. Was she neurologically impaired, as the school continued to classify her, or was she mentally retarded? Were her "severe" learning disabilities permanent, or could she realize her "strong intellectual potential"? Sometimes Leslie's apparent progress gave the Fabers hope; sometimes her difficulties made them despair.

For example, in the second grade Leslie started taking the drug Ritalin, which is often prescribed for children who have a hard time paying attention and are easily distracted. This medication seemed to help. Her schoolwork improved; she was better able to retain information, and her conversations stayed on subject longer than before. Then came a crusher: Leslie's fourth-grade teacher told Charles and Rosalind, Your daughter's learning will never progress beyond the second-grade level. Another way of saying it: Leslie's mental development will be stuck forever on the plateau of an eight-year-old.

Yet, when she entered middle school in the fifth grade, Leslie didn't seem stuck at all. She had a special education teacher who believed in challenging her students. Every two weeks, every month, there was a goal. If you didn't reach the goal, you would do the work over until you got it right. When her parents asked her how she was getting along with her teacher, Leslie would say, "I don't like her. She's boring. She makes us do the stuff over and over. I hate her." But look at Leslie's handwriting! It was *nice*. It was *legible*. With that taskmaster of a teacher who kept challenging you, Leslie for the first time demonstrated that she could do a full school year's work—that is, a full year's work for a learning-disabled student.

With another teacher in sixth grade, she began to backslide. By the seventh grade, the Fabers were spending most of their time trying to hack through the brambles of special ed politics. Many times in the next few years, Charlie would have to fight back the rage that came with the realization that Leslie was being treated like a stick of furniture. First, there were not enough kids in the middle school to form a separate class for neurologically impaired youngsters; so Leslie was moved to a special ed program in a school in a nearby community; then that program ran out of funding. Back to Glen Ridge; back out again. Always on the move, the exile always searching for refuge.

In Glen Ridge Middle School, Leslie was the odd kid out. The "dumb" kid. The "different" kid. Paul Archer, who didn't spend a lot of time thinking about Leslie, would remember passing her in the middle-school corridor and noticing that she was carrying textbooks that he had read for a class a couple of years before. Leslie was almost as old as he was, but she was doing the schoolwork of a little kid. Everybody knew about Leslie.

To some who saw her at the school, Leslie Faber seemed a lonely figure. During one lunch hour another student, Diane Carter, who felt isolated herself, noticed Leslie sitting by herself at a table. "It just made me so mad," Diane would say later. "She was the brunt of everybody's shit, she was the reject. She always sat alone at lunch. She tried so hard to attach herself to the popular kids. But she was always being mocked; they were always pretending to take her seriously, but laughing at her behind her back."

Diane turned and walked back to where Leslie was sitting. "C'mon, Les, they rang the bell. You'll be late for your class."

"Thanks for telling me," Leslie said. "I appreciate that. You're always so nice to me."

The schoolwork and the lessons might fade, but she would have an exact memory of every expression of affection, of every time someone was nice to her. Mary Romeo, who usually taught in the high school, was asked to teach "adaptive" physical education to the younger special education class. Like many youngsters with developmental problems, Leslie seemed to respond well to tactile sensations. The teacher would hug Leslie, stroke her hair, squeeze her, hold her hand. Years later, even though Leslie was attending classes outside of Glen Ridge, she would come to the high school in the late afternoon and visit Miss Romeo in the phys ed office or in the gym. "You were always so nice to me," she would tell her. "You always gave me a big hug."

Out of school her parents tried hard to involve her in activities in which she would be relatively successful and which would help her make new friends who were not impaired. She pitched in the girls' junior softball leagues in elementary and middle schools and later for the girls' softball team. With her parents and her sister, she attended services at the Presbyterian Church-on-the-Green in Bloomfield and joined the church's youth group. She was enrolled in the summer-reading program in the public library. Leslie was not a stay-at-home.

Leslie is bigger and stronger than many kids of her age. It is a Saturday afternoon in June 1980. Leslie Faber is making her pitching debut. Even during the warmups, the other team is yelling: Reeetard . . . Brain-Les . . . And not one of the parents there to cheer their kids on seems to hear it. The tittering stops with Leslie's first pitch. Whoosh. Whoosh. One blur after another. One batter after another never gets her bat off her shoulder. For a nine-year-old Leslie is one sweet pitcher.

Just before her last inning of pitching, a player on the opposing team comes over to talk to Leslie. Gail King,* a little girl who lives down the block from her, asks in her best sugar-coated voice: "Les, won't you please, please let me hit one? If you let me hit it, I'll be your best friend forever."

So, of course, the next inning the first two batters get on base, and Leslie throws a watermelon up to her new best friend, Gail King, and Gail drives the ball into the outfield, and Leslie's team loses the game. But Leslie is not depressed. She's lost the game, but she's won a new buddy. She thinks.

On the sidelines Charlie Faber thinks, Leslie, why didn't you walk up to home plate and hand her the ball to hit? And then he smiles. Well, that's Leslie. Anything for a friend. And nobody's ever going to change that.

Leslie's difficulties in making friends with children her own age meant that she often had to seek companionship among younger boys and girls.

In 1981, when Mary Daniels* was a junior in high school, she volunteered to tutor kids in the public library's summer-reading program. All the youngsters in Mary's group were five years old. The only one older was Leslie. She was ten. The kids were reading *Curious George*. It saddened Mary that Leslie was clearly not able to read and understand a book that kids five years younger had pretty much mastered. Nevertheless, Daniels was impressed by Leslie's determination to please her parents. Leslie showed up for every reading session.

The incentive for Leslie was that she could get some attention and that she was accepted as a member of a group, although the other kids were much younger than she. Sitting at the blond wooden table in the street-level children's floor of the library, Leslie sometimes appeared impatient.

She would squirm in her seat, speak rapidly when she got excited. Leslie would show her enthusiasm by hugging one of the kids. Such sudden bursts of emotion seemed to frighten some of the little ones.

Curious about the other children, she would stare intensely at them. She had difficulty expressing herself. "Her behavior was not easily understandable to the kids, but I really liked her," Daniels said. "She was so spirited; she had a life to her. Les was always friendly and she could be funny. And I thought she was quite observant of other people. But I worried about her loneliness. She'd tell me she felt bad because she wasn't doing well in school. The kids in the library, they were civil to her, but she wasn't their friend. She didn't have the facility to connect, except for trying to attract attention. Here I was, my life was filled with people who would go on to college and have nice lives. But when you saw this real great, spirited person who just was going to be—it was going to be hard for her, very hard."

At eleven Leslie was about five feet, four inches tall—taller than most of the girls in her class and some of the boys. Her large head and muscular build gave her the appearance of ungainliness. Actually, her various athletic coaches over the years found that she was well coordinated. But her size combined with her developmental difficulties made her an opportune target for mockery.

When Leslie was in middle school, she enrolled in the summer junior tennis program, conducted by the Glen Ridge Tennis Club. Her instructor was Andrew Provost, a twenty-year-old college student. Provost assembled the kids in groups of ten. Leslie was the only girl in her group; among the boys were Chris and Paul Archer and Phil Grant. Leslie held her own as a tennis player. As always, though, she was held back by her short attention span. Sometimes she seemed less absorbed by the game than by earning her teacher's praise. She would run off the court and plead, "Andy, Andy, look at me serve." And after she served: "Watch me again, please, Andy. Please look."

At the beginning of the summer, Provost had more than a hundred kids to teach. But as families left for vacation, the numbers thinned, and he began to notice something he had missed earlier: how Chris and Paul were taunting Leslie. When she began to serve, they would throw tennis balls at her and shout: "Hey, special ed, can't you catch." Chanting: "Les-is-a-retard. Les-is-a-dummy." Then Les would forget about serving and throw the balls back at them. Sometimes she threw her racquet. Then she cried. But usually she would dry her eyes after a few seconds and go on playing.

Provost threatened the Archer boys, who seemed to be the most blatant offenders: "If you don't cut it out, I'll tell your mother." That didn't seem to cow them. The moment he was distracted, they went after her. Finally, wanting to end the taunting, he offered to move Leslie to another group. She refused. "I don't mind," she told him. "I can take it." Then when the boys started to ridicule her again, she burst into tears.

Andy wanted to do something to show his support for Leslie. On the last day of the tennis program, awards were handed out. "Aaaand to Leslie Faber goes the Good Sportsmanship Award." Proudly, Leslie accepted the six-inch-high plastic award with her name engraved on the base, just below the words *Good Sportsmanship*. Later on, Andy Provost would say, "We never had this award before, but we felt we had to give it to her for putting up with all the crap she took from the boys."

A few days later Rosalind Faber confided to Andy's mother, Cherry Provost, "You know, Leslie is neurologically impaired. It's going to be very tough on her. Tennis is something Leslie's good at, and she's just thrilled to get the award because she feels she's something special."

Something special. Leslie's need for affection, recognition, and inclusion would sound familiar to many parents of retarded children. Her eagerness to make friends and to earn their affection is typical of retarded youngsters, who often feel inadequate and alone. But as Leslie got older, these needs to be liked and accepted became more problematic.

They occasionally took the form of what teachers and psychoanalysts would call "inappropriate behavior." As she approached adolescence, she had to work hard to be noticed by kids of her age. So sometimes she would try to shock them by doing something that broke the rules for proper behavior in Glen Ridge.

Years later, when Leslie was interviewed by Dr. Susan Esquilin, a psychologist employed by the prosecutors in the Glen Ridge rape case, Esquilin observed that Leslie was "willing to do almost anything to gain a modicum of social acceptance," and that she saw "her own sexuality as a means of pleasing others."

Inappropriate behavior was not an unknown phenomenon among preteens and adolescents of both genders in Glen Ridge. One element that made inappropriate behavior inappropriate was that it occurred in public.

Kids who demonstrated the social control to conduct inappropriate activities in private often escaped adult scrutiny—and possible retribution. But it required a sense of discretion to distinguish between behavior tolerated in public and behavior best kept private. And that discretion eluded Leslie.

Frank Ewald, the Glen Ridge school official who assessed Leslie's educational and social progress and knew her well, would say, "Talking about sex is something Leslie would consider okay because it would give her access to other kids, a form of friendliness. Now, it may be that her social judgment is not the best in the world. But I've seen boys and girls with lots worse social judgment than Leslie. The social judgment of most of these boys who knew her stinks. But they were slick enough to get over with it."

Leslie was close enough to the buddy system of preteen girls to hear the crackle of gossip about flirtation, dating, and sex, but she was never close enough with the girls in school or the girls who prowled Willowbrook Mall to recognize that most of these tales were vastly exaggerated. There was no buddy Leslie could count on to separate the drama and myth from reality and truth.

The snatches of distortion Leslie overheard in school and in the playground resembled the way life was depicted by television. Some studies have found that in a single year television transmits some twenty thousand sexual messages. A report by the National Institute of Mental Health in 1982 estimated that 70 percent of the references to sex on television are to prostitution or extramarital sex. "On TV, you're either shooting somebody or you're trying to get them into bed," said Frank Ewald. "And Leslie saw that and accepted that because she couldn't make the separation between make-believe and reality."

Within the nineteen-inch frame, men and women weren't friends; they were sex partners. Within the nineteen-inch frame, the American economy ran on the heat generated by erogenous body parts. That's what TV taught Leslie. "Most kids can filter out the fact that obviously you don't spend all your life in the sun on the beach," Ewald said. "Life isn't a beer ad. Kids basically understand that. But for her, life is what TV says it is because her ability to make those distinctions isn't as good."

Innocently accepting of television's nightly *Decameron* and Glen Ridge's teen gossip, Leslie would sometimes try to mimic those folks who were always having such fun. In one instance, a group of ten- and eleven-year-old girls from Glen Ridge went out to Girl Scout camp at Fairview Lake in New Jersey. On their second afternoon there, it rained. There were ten girls lounging about in their cabin. Some were playing cards. Suddenly, Leslie leaped out of the bathroom. She was wearing only her bra and panties. She ran from one corner to another of the cabin, laughing at each startled girl.

Caroline Franco,* a camper and fellow student at the middle school, said later, "I didn't know Leslie then, I didn't know she was in a special class. All I could think of was, Why is this girl acting crazy? Later, I understood that Leslie just wanted everybody to look at her. If she stood out, she thought, everybody would want to be her friend."

Joey Drew,* a boy who was Leslie's age, saw her on Monday nights when he showed up for Scout meetings at the Linden Avenue Elementary School. A lot of the guys arrived early, hoping to flirt with the girls. To pass the time, they'd hit a tennis ball against the school wall or play basketball. Joey saw Leslie, standing off to the side, wanting to be noticed, eager to be asked to play. According to Joey, Kevin and Kyle Scherzer would shout at her: "Les, c'mon, take off your blouse. Show us your breasts. Leslie, show us how to French kiss. I bet you don't know how to pull down your pants. You going to moon us, Les?"

When Leslie stared back at them, they'd laugh and go back to their game. "She would never get angry at them, and they'd degrade her in every way possible," Joey said. "I mean, back then when they were eleven, twelve, it was all verbal. It was perfect for them. Since she was slow, she was someone they could pick on without her going home and telling her mom and getting them into trouble. Maybe it was hard for her to tell if they were being friendly or if they were making fun of her. But I could tell."

Joey would grow up to become an iconoclastic teenager, but even he was reluctant to stand up to the highly popular jocks and defend a not very popular girl. "I'd think, something could happen to Leslie if somebody doesn't stick up for her, and I'd want to say something to the Scherzers and their friends. But I didn't. I guess I didn't want to stand out."

11

Something did happen to Leslie. In April 1983 a tall, muscular high school kid began showing up at Cartaret Park. What struck some people as a little odd was that Michael Barone* had grown up in town but didn't seem to have any good friends. He was frequently seen wandering around alone, looking dazed. Sometimes he'd spend hours standing on the sidelines watching the other kids play. That was the other unusual thing. Michael was a big, strapping eighteen-year-old guy, and the kids he buddied up to were all six, seven, eight years younger.

On the late afternoon of Thursday, April 21, 1983, a cool, brisk wind came up, dragging heavy dark clouds across the sky. There were only a few people in the park. One of the people who refused to be chased by the weather was Leslie Faber, who was doggedly shooting foul shots. Another person who didn't seem to want to leave was Michael Barone.

The official Essex County prosecutor's complaint, later filed against Barone, said that he grabbed Leslie, who was then eleven years old, fondled her breasts, forced her to sit on his lap, and kissed her. He unzipped her pants, the complaint said,[1] and pulled them down to her ankles. He then exposed his penis and pinched her buttocks. Leslie, crying, pulled up her pants and ran away from him.

The minute Leslie walked into her house, she told Ros, "A bad thing happened in the park. This bad kid was there."

"What did he do that was bad."

"He was bad to me. He did bad things."

"What bad things?" Each sentence had to be dragged out of her.

"He grabbed me and . . ." She was crying now.

Before she finished, Ros was on the phone to the police.

Nineteen-year-old Sheila Byron, who took Ros Faber's call, had worked as a civilian dispatcher at the police station for a year. A dispatcher didn't get many calls like that in Glen Ridge—a woman, fighting to keep the hysteria out of her voice, saying her daughter had just been molested in Cartaret Park.

Byron was trying to keep her cool, telling Mrs. Faber, if she wouldn't mind, would she put her daughter on the phone. In just a few minutes, Leslie described to Byron the young man in the park, what he was wearing, the color of his bicycle. The dispatcher relayed the description to the supervising officer, who sent one cop to the Fabers' house to take a statement from Leslie and another to the park to see whether anybody had spotted this guy.

1. This description of Michael Barone's assault of Leslie is drawn from information provided by law enforcement officials and from material contained in a legal brief filed by attorney Anthony Mautone, who was representing Richard Corcoran, Jr., a defendant in the 1989 rape case.

There were no female officers on the Glen Ridge police force in 1983. The male officer who questioned Leslie was gentle and sensitive; reluctantly, Leslie told him what had happened. Police work in a town as small as Glen Ridge can be efficient. Within an hour the cops knew whom they were looking for.

They went to his house to pick him up, but only his father was home. The cops told the man what they had heard about his son. The father said he would bring his son to the police station as soon as he got home. Barely a half hour had passed, and Sheila Byron looked up from her switchboard to see the older man and the teenager walk into the police station.

That night when her dad got home from work, Leslie was furious. She wouldn't eat, she wouldn't look at her mom. Again and again, she repeated, "Why did you make me do it? Why did you make me tell the policeman about it? I don't want to talk about it."

Her parents tried to explain that when something bad happens you have to explain it to the police, because they have to punish the bad person and stop that person from doing it again. But Leslie could not be assuaged. As she paced back and forth, crying and shouting, her parents, trying to stitch together the broken phrases, realized she was blaming herself. Not blaming herself for what Michael Barone did to her. But blaming herself for always causing them grief. Leslie often had these feelings toward her parents as she was growing up. Sometimes she felt almost like a stranger among them. Sometimes she wished she could disappear because they looked so sad and worried about her. She wished she could make them happy all the time the way other kids seemed to make their parents proud and happy. But she didn't know how to do that.

Before she went up to her room, Leslie told her parents, "If anything like this happens to me again, promise me you won't make me tell anyone." Then she covered her face with her hands, trying to hide.

Leslie may have possessed the foresight that others lacked. She may have sensed that all she was made to go through, all the talking to her parents, then repeating the story to the cops and investigators from the prosecutor's office and grand jurors—that all of it would achieve so little.

The Glen Ridge police arrested Michael Barone. He was charged with second-degree "sexual assault by contact." Additionally, he was charged with public lewdness because he allegedly exposed himself. If he was found guilty, Barone could be sentenced to a minimum of ten years in jail.

The case was transferred to the Essex County Prosecutor's Office, as was customary when police in small municipalities like Glen Ridge had to investigate serious felonies. Under questioning by investigators, Barone signed a statement admitting that the accusations against him were true, according to sources in the prosecutor's office.

Barone's arrest came at a time when the law governing charges of sexual assault committed against a minor was changing. The new law provided that if the assailant was four or more years older than the victim and the victim was younger than thirteen, the charge would be elevated from third-degree to second-degree sexual assault. Barone was eighteen with he was arrested. Leslie was one month short of her twelfth birthday. Michael Barone fell within the reach of the new, tougher statute.

The Essex County grand jury returned an indictment, but it was for the lesser, third-degree, charge of aggravated contact. The change was significant not only because it shortened the potential prison time but also because the defendant could now apply for a program called Pre-Trial Intervention (PTI).

PTI was designed to avoid the expense and time of a trial for first offenders charged with less serious crimes. The defendant had to get counseling, perhaps perform some public service work, and not get arrested again. The criminal files of a PTI defendant—including, in Barone's case, his signed admissions—would be expunged after a specified time, usually no longer than three years. The only trace of his involvement in the case would be a single, dusty file folder—the "jacket"—that listed his name, the charge, and the disposition of the case. The folder was stamped PTI.

Years later, when the Essex County Prosecutor's Office was trying to understand what had happened in the Barone case, the prevailing view was that the grand jury had been misinformed about the new statute and therefore had mistakenly indicted Barone on the lesser charge.

By approving PTI for Michael Barone, the justice system was betting that the defendant would not repeat the crime. Judges and prosecutors were often willing to give the benefit of the doubt to a defendant who was working or going to school and whose family was stable. By these standards Michael Barone was a very good bet, and, in fact, he was not arrested again for a sexual offense.

Barone was a student at one of the most prominent prep schools in the state. The football coach at the school was one of the most successful high school football coaches of his generation in New Jersey—John Barone.*

He was Michael Barone's father. In his tenure of more than thirty years at the school, Barone's teams won almost three times as many games as they lost. His victories included many state championships.

An official in the prosecutor's office said later that John Barone's prominence did not influence the disposition of his son's case in 1983. According to this official, the reduction of the charges against Michael Barone and his admission into the diversion program were a result of administrative bungling.

The fact remains that the prosecutor who handled the case did not seek a prison sentence. The prosecutor did not seek probation. Both options would have left the young man with a permanent criminal record. The option the prosecutor selected wiped Michael Barone's crime off the books.

Leslie may have understood intuitively what critics had been saying for years about the criminal justice system's response to sex offenders: that it treats them more gently than muggers and drug dealers. Her parents might repeat for the next hundred years that she had nothing to be ashamed of, but the reality was that the outcome of the legal process—an outcome that attributed little if any responsibility to the offender—would raise doubts about her account of what Michael Barone did to her.

People talked in Glen Ridge. People saw the son of a famous man, a member of a fine, upstanding Glen Ridge family, wandering free in the streets again, acting as if nothing important had happened. And they saw Leslie acting as she usually did. What conclusions should they draw? One conclusion some people drew was that Leslie had not been molested— that, actually, she had been a consenting partner. Some people went further: They said that Leslie had seduced this slow, hapless young man.

Six years after the assault, various descriptions of what had happened in 1983 still circulated around town.

The mother of an eighteen-year-old boy who was in the jock circle in Glen Ridge described the 1983 assault as "just another Leslie story," and added, "Leslie made it all up. Nothing ever happened."

Even a boy who was sympathetic to Leslie doubted that she had been victimized in 1989, because of what he had heard about that first sexual assault: "I heard that Leslie was early on involved in a case with somebody and she said that the guy raped her," he recalled. "He definitely hadn't. They proved he hadn't. She had lied. So I don't know what her credibility is."

The police had taken seriously what Leslie told them in 1983; and, in the early stages at least, so had the prosecutor. The incident demonstrated once more how vulnerable Leslie was.

Ros and Charlie Faber thought the rational thing to do was to treat the 1983 assault on Leslie as an isolated aberration. The victimizer was a young man with a history of psychiatric problems, a "sick" kid. If you believed that most of the kids in Glen Ridge were not "sick," the future appeared much less threatening. But even as they tried to persuade themselves that this had been a one-time experience, they could feel the fear rising. Would their Leslie ever sacrifice a milligram of attention or feigned affection to protect herself? They could warn her, but they couldn't change the underlying needs that made her passive and compliant.

They needed a concrete way of changing her behavior, so they enrolled Leslie in an assertiveness-training course. After a short time the instructor recommended that Leslie should drop the course. There was no way, she said, that you could ever teach Leslie Faber to be assertive.

If she couldn't be taught to be assertive, Ros and Charlie would at least try to instill some awareness of potential danger. They lectured Leslie on the need for alertness when she was alone. Listen very hard to what people you don't know are telling you, they said to her; make sure they're not trying to harm you. Don't go places with people you don't know. They pleaded with her to be careful with strangers. But they didn't say anything about the young men Leslie thought were her friends.

1.   Kevin Scherzer (*left*) and his twin brother, Kyle, pictured in the 1989 Glen Ridge High School yearbook, were co-captains of the football team and among the most popular athletes in the school. State Exhibit: *State v. Christopher Archer et al.*

2.   Kyle Scherzer (*left*) and his friend Mari Carmen Ferraez were voted best athletes in the school. Ferraez, who ran track and played on the basketball team, was
a teammate of the alleged rape victim. State Exhibit: *State v. Christopher Archer
et al.*

3. A teammate of the defendants in the rape case, Charles Figueroa, shown in his yearbook photo, was the only student to disclose to his teacher and to police that he had been told about the rape. State Exhibit: *State v. Christopher Archer et al.*

4.   Bryant Grober, the son of a doctor and one of the leaders of
the Jock clique in the high school, wrestled and played football.
The senior poll said he had the "nicest eyes." He later became a
leading suspect in the rape investigation. State Exhibit: *State v.
Christopher Archer et al.*

5. Paul Archer (*left*) and Richard Corcoran, Jr., were mainstays of the group of athletes who dominated the high school. A poll of seniors found that Archer had the "nicest smile" and that Corcoran was the "loudest" and "most obnoxious." Both were present during the alleged rape and were suspects in the police investigation. State Exhibit: *State v. Christopher Archer et al.*

6. Paul Archer was regarded as one of the best-looking and most congenial Jocks. Leslie Faber once described him as "my hero." State Exhibit: *State v. Christopher Archer et al.*

7. Paul Archer (*left*) and his brother, Chris. Chris, a junior when this yearbook photo was taken, wrestled and played football. The brothers had known Leslie Faber since she was a child. State Exhibit: *State v. Christopher Archer et al.*

8. A former star athlete from Glen Ridge High School, Christopher Archer leaves Essex County courthouse in Newark, New Jersey, in 1993 at the end of the rape trial. AP/Wide World Photos.

PART III

All-American Guys

12

Twenty feet into Glen Ridge High School the jocks found their niche. In the hall right across from the principal's office were the glass cases displaying shelf after shelf of sports trophies, a glittering tribute to Glen Ridge's athletic triumphs. The cases could not contain the entire display, and the overflow adorned the shelves of the school's main office and the library, a cornucopia of bats and gloves and baseballs and footballs and plaques and cups and statuettes. Nowhere visible was last year's student honor roll.

Some of the one hundred or so groggy freshmen from the Class of '89—they would attend the school for the next four years, from grades nine to twelve—may have imagined the faint scent of locker room liniment as they entered the high school for the first time on Thursday, September 5, 1985. It wasn't only because of the clunky concrete-block walls or because the main corridor dead-ended into a row of boys' lockers. A strong muscular attitude permeated the building.

The bilevel building was designed in the stolid suburban bunker style of the 1960s. It was intended to hold up to 660 students, but in 1985 there were only 380. Student enrollment had declined sharply in recent years because families were smaller and because the population of the town was aging.

The center of command in the school was embodied in the two men standing there in the vestibule, waiting to greet the jaded returnees and the fumbling newcomers. They were the principal and the vice-principal. Both men had strong ties to the wide world of sports in Glen Ridge.

James Buckley, the principal since 1969, had been an assistant to the legendary football coach Bill Horey. During his long tenure in the town, Buckley had earned a reputation as a brilliant chemistry and physics teacher and a sensitive administrator who was reticent about meting out harsh punishment to misbehaving students. He was also known to cast a charitable eye on the shenanigans of rambunctious jocks.

John "Jack" Curtis, the assistant principal, had been the basketball coach at the high school. Curtis was a tall, beefy man with a ruddy complexion and the watchful eyes of a veteran detective. Which is how the sports crowd in the school sometimes viewed his job. For Curtis's primary task was maintaining discipline at Glen Ridge High. And one way he accomplished that was by functioning as school truant officer. The scariest sight in the world for some kid who decided to cut a few classes was the long shadow of John Curtis slanting across his front door.

The third member of the governing troika was, of course, Bill Horey himself. Horey, no longer football coach by 1985, served as athletic director. He was in the twilight of an enviable career, but his moral and athletic judgments were still influential. An athlete who crossed the line would receive appropriate judgment, but if Horey believed that one of his "boys" was falsely accused or that his misconduct was exaggerated, Horey would defend him to the last bullet.

These men had known each other for so long, worked so closely together, that they seemed joined at the waist. If a student angered one of them, or won praise from another, the news would flash instantly through the chain of command in the school.

These were the caretakers of *all* the students in the school, both boys *and* girls. Nevertheless, those young women seeking assertive role models—seeking a responsive and comprehending school elder to whom they might whisper an intimate confidence about how young women were treated by certain male classmates, would not find that confidant in the old-boy administration of the school. To recall a female authority figure in their school lives, they would have to think back to elementary school four years ago, a past life as time is measured in preadolescence. In the middle and high schools, there were no women at the top. In high school there were only three middle-aged males, all former coaches.

No question about it: In Glen Ridge High School, jocks ruled. And it had been that way for a long time. In fact, forty-four years before, in 1941, a study by Yale University's Education Department had found that the school placed "too great emphasis on producing winning teams at the expense of important social values."

The game of choice for most of the jocks coming out of middle school was football. Some planned to go out for other sports, such as wrestling and baseball, in the winter and spring. Paul, Richie, and Bryant would also wrestle, and Kyle would play baseball. But football was the high-profile one; history and tradition in Glen Ridge trained the spotlight on the football players.

So there they all were, grinding out the yardage, pounding away at each other in jayvee football practice: Paul Archer, Bryant Grober, Richie Corcoran, Kyle and Kevin Scherzer, and Peter Quigley. (Chris Archer, a year behind his friends, was in the eighth grade. He planned to play football and wrestle.) They would all play on the jayvee team for a year or so and then, barring setbacks such as failing grades, would move on to the varsity.

Barely a couple of weeks into the school year, the walls of Glen Ridge

High vibrated with a rumble that built day by day into a huge roar. The approach of Homecoming Day. On the horizon: the big game. Time to stomp Glen Ridge's hated rival, Mountain Lakes.

On the Friday before the game, Kyle and Kevin and Paul and Richie and the other freshman jocks would pass the houses of the varsity players, checking out the decorations on the fences and doorways, prepared with loving care by the cheerleaders. It was a tradition for the girls to decorate the homes of the varsity players before a big game; the guys also knew that the girls gave special attention to decorating the bedrooms of the senior players.

You couldn't get much algebra done this Friday. The varsity players wore their jerseys in school. The teachers couldn't miss the group of seniors dressed in red and white, acting smugly superior in the back of the classroom. On this day everybody seemed to know who ran the school, and it sure wasn't the grown-up in front of the blackboard.

Between classes the students got other reminders of whom the day belonged to. For example, each locker assigned to a varsity football player was decorated by a cheerleader. There would be signs exhorting the player to heroics on the field and drawings of hearts pierced by arrows. In front of the lockers, the cheerleaders and other fans would leave their offerings: mounds of candies, slices of cake covered with Saran Wrap. Some favored players would find in their lockers more personal messages—"I love your body"—and even some intimate garments, including bras and panties. The tie between sex and football heroics was very strong in Glen Ridge.

In the afternoon the entire school settled into the gym bleachers for sports assembly. Most of the rhetoric and applause were directed toward the varsity football players who paraded across the stage one by one in their game jerseys, flashing their toothiest smiles at their adoring public. Perhaps not all adoring. Sizable numbers of students sat on their hands, sneering at the attention the school was lavishing on a mediocre bunch of jocks. But they were the marginals, the ones who listened to the Grateful Dead and joined the chess club. "Catch the Spirit," the sign stretched above the stage said—and most students did.

The freshman players didn't really mind that right now they were lower than scrubs, not even bench-warmers. In another year or so, if everything worked out, they'd be out on the stage, too, waving to their fans.

That night before the game, the Homecoming dance was held in the school cafeteria. It wasn't a dress-up dance the way the Candy Cane Ball was later in the winter, but the kids caught the spirit, sweating through their shirts and tops after a half hour of dancing under the red-and-white streamers. Standing at the edge of the dance floor, Peter and Paul and the Scherzer twins and Bryant watched as the King and Queen of Homecoming, usually the football captain and the most popular cheerleader, were crowned. These first-year kids still looked so young in their pullover shirts and khakis. They didn't have varsity jackets yet, but already they were attracting a following—the girls who had been their friends since grade school and the guys who wanted to invest in a friendship that would assure them of popularity by proximity during the next four years.

In the town the football clan gathered. Homecoming was taken seriously in Glen Ridge. People came home from out of town and out of state for the game. Older brothers and sisters relived past glories at their parents' dinner tables and even older Ridgers camped at friends' and relatives' houses, delighted to show their old game slides against any bare wall.

Before game time hundreds of people were already in the stands, waving their Ridger pennants, roaring "Down the Lake." Now the Red and White galloped onto Hurrell Field to do battle. The marching-band members, red-and-white sashes pinned to their chests as though they were conventioneers, paraded to the fifty-yard line at halftime, clutching their wide-brimmed, conquistador-like hats and white plumes against the breeze. The preening, cartwheeling cheerleaders chanted the fight song, while the junior varsity cheerleaders hawked programs and the booster mothers dispensed hot dogs and grape juice at the refreshment stand.

Soaking up the scene, the freshmen knew they were about to enter the celebrity phase of Glen Ridge athletics. The hearty camaraderie of their fathers and brothers and friends, the frankly appraising looks from the hottest girls in the school, the pampering from their mothers and sisters— this was the payoff. This was what they had been priming themselves for ever since they were five and six years old and had stepped up to the plate in Bandbox softball. The 5 A.M. wake-up calls for morning practice, wallowing in the mud during a Cobra League football game—now it all was paying off. For a moment you felt like you had the town in the palm of your hand. Ridger proud.

After the game ended, as soon as the players showered and changed, one honking motorcade wound its way to Bloomfield, to the Town Pub, where parents of the players and just plain boosters reconstructed every scoring drive.

Other groups went to the homes of senior players, where a huge spread of food and drinks had been laid out. The football players, the cheerleaders, and assorted hangers-on joined friends, neighbors, and relatives. The parties flowed out onto the porches and backyards. The kids drank their sodas decorously as the parents got red-faced and misty-eyed with nostalgia. Then when the old folks started yawning, the players said their goodbyes and headed for their own parties, as the royal retinue, the cheerleaders and other girls, trailed in their wake.

The whole weekend was one big dream, even for the freshmen kiddos. They were reveling in the attention they received as heirs apparent to the football royalty of Glen Ridge. But for a bunch of guys who hadn't even started to earn their varsity letters, the high-stakes competition they were entering had to provoke some anxiety as well. What if they didn't live up to everybody's expectations? You couldn't miss the real meaning of Homecoming weekend: To the sports-obsessed crowd of Glen Ridge, you were a jock or you were nothing.

13

Within a few weeks of their arrival, the one hundred freshmen had found their places in the social constellation of Glen Ridge High. It wasn't hard to figure out who fit in where.

Every afternoon at about 2 P.M., a chattering, giggling, jostling mass of kids poured out of the exits onto the smoking patio and the lawn of the school. As a group they looked like nothing more than standard-issue suburban teenagers: a wave of Spandex and sweatpants, faded Guess jeans and pastel Benneton blouses. But these youngsters didn't constitute an undifferentiated bloc. The easiest way to distinguish the tribal styles of the kids was to watch how they divided up, the groups they formed naturally, easily on the lawn; who shared cars with whom, who walked together down Ridgewood Avenue.

When the students left the school building, they drifted over to the piece of turf that was claimed by their group. The Freaks, known in Glen Ridge as "Giggers," gathered on the smoking patio. The Greasers, here called "Guidos," sauntered over to the Glen, a grassy area close to the school, where they could consume their stash of beer without adult interference. The "Achievers," except for those involved in after-school clubs, lingered briefly on the lawn and then hurried home. They had homework to do. Meanwhile, the "Jocks" held court in the parking lot. Homework was not their highest priority.

Not many kids drifted from one group to another. They had formed their alliances as early as the elementary and middle grades, and once they found their place on the social map of adolescent Glen Ridge, they stayed there.

First there were the Achievers, whom less motivated students contemptuously labeled as "nerds" or "geeks." They talked softly and carried heavy book bags. Their collars were button-down, their sweaters crewneck and occasionally cashmere. They took part in many school activities—the band, student government, Model United Nations Club—but were consumed by only one: studying. Their industry was recognized by a place on the high honor roll and ultimately admission to Princeton or Skidmore.

The Achievers tolerated, at a distance, the Giggers. The Giggers got their label because they called their parties "gigs," as though they were jazz sessions. At the more radical end of the Gigger spectrum was one guy who planned to join a back-to-the-earth commune in Arizona. Other Giggers were bound for artsy colleges like Pratt and the Fashion Institute of Technology in New York.

In truth, the most radical kids in the high school were another small minority. The Guidos, a disrespectful term once directed specifically at blue-collar Italian youths in neighboring Bloomfield, had been broadened to include youngsters who openly rejected the college-and-corporate-success ethic of Glen Ridge.

They wouldn't be caught dead in the loafers and Docksiders favored by the Achievers or the bodyshirts and sneakers worn by the Jocks. Their uniform ran to work boots and T-shirts that advertised their heavy-metal enthusiasms: Anthrax, Iron Maiden, and Guns 'n' Roses. They weren't taking advance-placement classes or going out for the football team; their program was filled with pre-voc courses. Out of school they spent a lot of time fighting with their parents and hooking up with other alienated kids in Bloomfield and Montclair and Kearney, kids who had started scoring drugs when they were twelve or thirteen and who had graduated to Jell-O shots, a vodka drink potent enough to induce the appearance of paralysis after a few refills. When they weren't stoned, they were busy scheming to find a job that paid enough so they could afford to move away from home and buy a Monte Carlo with a double bass. Collectively, they amounted to the town's version of an adolescent underclass, not poverty-stricken but living the Greaser style.

The Achievers, Giggers, and Guidos had their friends and admirers, but they were not at the pinnacle of the social pyramid. That rarefied perch was occupied by the Jocks. Otherwise known as "the hunks." With their robust good looks, they partied with the flashiest and, some said, sexiest girls in the school. After a game, especially a winning game, some male teachers fawned over them almost as much as the cheerleaders did.

To those unfamiliar with the high school scene, the word *Jocks* was synonymous with athletes. That wasn't entirely accurate. Not all students who played sports were Jocks with a capital J. Some kids who participated in sports—most Glen Ridge students played on one team or another—gravitated toward the Giggers or the Achievers and, infrequently, the Guidos. But that hard core who considered themselves "real Jocks" did not treat athletes who identified with other social groups as equals. Only certain athletes felt they were truly worthy of the title *Ridger.*

There were two essential criteria for acceptance in the inner circle. First, you had to participate in at least one—or, better still, both—of the two most aggressive and physical sports: football and wrestling. A few baseball players made it into the inner sanctum, but members of the tennis and golf teams were not highly prized by the real Jocks.

The other quality that guaranteed certain kids popularity in Jock circles was an unmistakable style, most dramatically demonstrated by the "Jock Strut." Going over to the Jock dining table in the cafeteria, or joining their buddies in the parking lot, they didn't amble or shuffle or stroll. They strutted.

The peacock image they projected was not something they had picked up overnight in high school. They had spent years perfecting it. For these young men, the essence of jockdom was a practiced show of contempt for kids and teachers alike. They tried to humiliate any wimpy guy who got in their way, but they reserved their best shots for girls who ignored them or dared to stand up to them.

The only students spared their contempt were the "Jockettes." They were the natural satellites of the Jocks. True Jockettes would not be caught dead at a Gigger party. They basked in the reflected glow of the Jocks. Despite the feminine connotation, the Jockettes consisted of males and females. They were kids who hungered for an invitation to a Jock party, who attended every practice session, cheered them in every game. Jockettes treated their Jocks with an almost maternal loyalty and protectiveness.

They were both fan club and palace guard. Over the years, the Jockettes had come to consider the Jocks as not just "the guys." To them, they were always: *Our Guys*.

For a fourteen-year-old freshman surveying the social arrangements in the school, the only cliques that seemed to count were the academic elite and the Jocks. If you didn't fit into one of the two, where were you? Nowhere. The only thing worse was not belonging to any clique at all. Then you got treated like a lost soul, a friendless wanderer.

The elitist social hierarchy was firmly embedded in Glen Ridge tradition. As far back as the Yale University study of 1941, researchers had noted that the high school resembled "an efficient private college-preparatory school."

The researchers also said that in this environment secret fraternities and sororities in the school exerted a "highly undesirable" influence on the students. As time passed, state legislation prohibited secret fraternities and sororities. But their place had been taken in the school by the informal cliques. These cliques had a much more profound influence on the values of students than did the occasional "family life" or "civics" class.

Like many towns and schools, Glen Ridge was proud that the majority of its students went on to college. Parents and educators understood that admission to college had become a prerequisite for a successful career. The town didn't look down on high academic achievers. But a youngster, to win adult respect, had to pursue a carefully defined and prescribed regimen of academic study. An independent mind, iconoclastic intellectual inquiry, unconventional social and political ideas, and unorthodox scholarship were not widely encouraged. Adults wanted the kids to do just enough to meet the school's (and a college's) standards, but not to get carried away. Except for a few families and teachers, most Ridgers didn't swoon over exceptional scholars; their cheers were reserved for the quintessence of youthful masculinity—the exceptional athlete and the winning team.

During the forty-four years since the Yale study was conducted, the school never changed its priorities. It still prided itself on generating successful college applications and producing winning teams. As always, it left the development of character to family, community, and the kids themselves.

Glen Ridge High continued to act as if it were an exclusive prep school, which, by accident of birth, suffered the indignity of relying on taxpayer funds. In the 1980s it still fed on competition among different student elites: The rich versus the near-rich. The academic track versus the athletes. Who was "scoring" with which girl and who wasn't? Who was invited to the best parties? If you weren't crowned a "winner" at Glen Ridge High, you were a "loser" who left high school with a taste of ashes.

The few audible dissenters in the town did not exert great influence on the school. One was John McFadden, minister of the Glen Ridge Congregational (Episcopal) Church. He was troubled by the way children were raised and educated in this community. "For years I had been watching this upper-middle-class peer pressure unfold in the high school and the community, this constant academic competition and social competition," he said. "Achievement was honored and respected almost to the point of pathology, whether it was the achievements of high school athletes or the achievements of corporate world conquerors. The kids were being taught: 'We have achieved this, no one can take it away from us.' And what was this achievement? The achievement was that they were living in Glen Ridge. That very fact was supposed to make you feel very good about yourself. It was a strange message the schools were teaching these kids— this tremendous pride of place. We decided we didn't want our children to grow up in Glen Ridge." After nine years McFadden and his family moved out of the town.

You either wormed your way into the "in-crowd" or you spent the next four years in social Siberia. And you really got into trouble if you thought or acted differently. For such kids Glen Ridge High School could be torture. One boy, Gerald Rosen,* had a neurological disorder whose symptoms were facial tics and twitches. Physically unattractive, smart, *and* Jewish—Gerald had the makings of the complete outsider in Glen Ridge High.

"Gerald would start these funny twitches, and the kids would snicker, and then he would get all agitated," a classmate recalled. "The teacher would say, 'Gerald, cut that out,' instead of saying, 'Frank'—who plays football and is handsome and wealthy—'Frank, leave if you can't leave Gerald alone.'".

Gerald's parents took him out of the Glen Ridge school system after his freshman year. Day after day, students in the school were learning that it was better to be strong than to be weak. Compassion for the weak wasn't part of the curriculum.

14

Were the Jocks comfortable with the roles they were asked to play in the culture of Glen Ridge? A compelling argument can be made that the hyper-masculine style they were asked to assume by parents and brothers and sports enthusiasts was a heavy burden for a kid to carry through adolescence.

Most of these boys did not demonstrate great talent for athletics. They were kids who liked to throw a ball around or wrestle in the mud with their buddies. Yet they were touted by everyone who counted in their world as future stars. More than once, they asked themselves, What if I don't meet my father's expectations? What if I'm not even as good as my older brother—or, worse, my younger brother? When the school upped the ante, when it staked its reputation on their performance on the playing fields, it added significantly to the already outsized image that had been superimposed on a group of young and immature boys.

Then there was the matter of the social role that Glen Ridge conferred on its young athletes. That role decreed that they had to be popular, handsome, desirable to girls. But how many insecure adolescent boys believe, deep down, that they can live up to all that? They must have asked themselves: What if that cheerleader turns me down? What if I'm left out the next time the crowd has a party? They also might wonder whether the love and respect they received from adults and peers was conditioned largely on their athletic performance. If I fail, they might ask, will anyone love me?

The swagger they affected—the Jock swagger—was a handy way to camouflage their doubts. It served three purposes: It compensated for their limitations as athletes by allowing them to pretend they were stars. It was a distorted exaggeration of how they thought dominant men—real men—were supposed to behave. And, conversely, their defiance of authority may well have been a disguised growl of resistance against being programmed to conform to the myths nurtured by the community.

Young men have many social, psychological, and sexual insecurities. The myth of the future jock king added to the list. If they sensed they weren't going to be great athletes, they might try to conceal their insecurity through a show of childish bravado; they might try to lead by intimidation, not merit. If they weren't allowed to grow into their own masculine identity, they could develop their own grotesque version of manhood.

Some kids never openly resisted the roles they were being groomed for. The Scherzer twins, Richie Corcoran, Paul Archer—they seemed comfortable with the Jock persona. They were already big and brawny and had been raised to flaunt the Jock style of manhood. Besides, they couldn't see any alternative to the role of athlete-leader. They weren't cut out to be scholars, and whatever other talents they possessed weren't encouraged. What was the alternative to joining the Jocks: making like a "band fag" in a feathered hat at the halftime show?

But some of their Jock friends did perceive that they had choices, that they were not predestined to be sports stars. They were given a license by adults to explore different social styles. To the extent that they were granted that freedom, they expressed uneasiness with the Jocks' macho image of bluff and swagger. That didn't mean they rejected the Jocks outright. It meant that for some, like Bryant Grober, it would take longer to feel comfortable in the clique.

Many kids who knew Bryant when he was younger weren't sure if he would follow in the Jock mold. His brother had been a prominent athlete at the school, but his father, the slender, scholarly Dr. Grober, didn't seem like the football booster type. His mother and sister provided some feminine influences. And other kids pegged Bryant as basically an unassuming little boy. But the social pressure to belong, combined with his interest in sports, drew him in, and by high school he had become one of the most popular members of the clique.

His looks had a lot to do with it. As Bryant got older and filled out, he seemed to get more handsome by the day. Curly light-brown hair. Striking blue eyes. A slightly hooked nose that gave his face a rugged cast. Some kids said his features reminded them of pictures they saw in their textbooks of ancient Greek and Roman busts. But many more just thought of Bryant Grober, wrestler and football player, as good old-fashioned American beefcake.

Charlie Terranova,* a Gigger, had been a childhood friend and neighbor of Bryant's. When Charlie listed Bryant's assets, it sounded as though he were casting Bryant for the role of America's teen heartthrob. "Bryant had like the ideal situation for a high school kid," Charlie said. "He's a really incredibly good-looking guy, and he's very athletically inclined. Every girl in this town loved him. Besides that, the parents are both wonderful people, his father a doctor and his mother a nurse. And the family lives in this really nice house in one of the best parts of town. Not only that: Bryant Grober is hysterically funny. It was like, 'At any minute I could come out with something that would put you on the floor.' Bryant had it all."

The kids who knew him well agreed that for all of Bryant's good looks, wealth, and athleticism, he was not a leader. "He was a really, really good friend of mine," Terranova said. "I loved the kid to death. Honestly. But I have to tell you, Bry was the ultimate crowd-follower."

The younger, gentler Bryant Grober began to disappear. One of his classmates, Jacqueline Davis,* had been friendly with him since she was old enough to cross the street by herself. "What I liked about Bryant in the years before high school was he always saw me as an individual, not just a girl who was part of a group," she said. "He'd talk to me on an equal basis. He was definitely not in Kevin and Kyle's group. He didn't belong in that crowd."

Davis was smart. She was pretty. She was the equal or better of most boys on the track and the softball field. The only strike against her was that she was black. In middle school she had already felt a barrier separating her from the white preppy kids of Glen Ridge. She remembered a game of spin the bottle at an after-school party in the sixth grade. When the bottle pointed to her, all the boys refused to kiss her. All but Bryant. He asked the others, "What's wrong with Jackie?"

"Well, if you don't know," one of the kids snickered. But Bryant defied them, saying to Jacqueline Davis: "If it's okay, I'll kiss you." And he did.

As Jacqueline Davis, age twelve, left that house that afternoon, she was thinking: I love Bryant Grober to death.

Fade-out: Bry Grober kissing Jackie Davis. Fade-in: Bry Grober, high school football player, wrestler, handsome jock-about-town. There weren't many one-to-one talks anymore between Jacqueline and Bry. Jackie was busy with track, with her own set of girlfriends. And Bry had his friends. "I guess he didn't think it was cool to be friends with your childhood friends," she said.

She was sitting with her friends in the lunchroom. Fifteen or so elite Jocks made their grand entrance, muscling their way to the long table reserved for athletes. Kyle leaned over and said loud enough for everyone to hear: "Jackie, you getting too much sun these days. You're getting dark enough to be a Negro." Kevin offered, "Jackie, I saw a black guy down the street. You know him? You must know him, he's black." Now it was Bry's turn. He asked Jacqueline: "Buckwheat, what did you do to your hair? Buckwheat, we saw a whole bunch of niggers at Blimpie's last night. Your family eating there these days?"

The guys around Bryant were laughing, slapping his back. *Bryant* was saying this to me, Jackie was thinking. *Bryant*, who saved me at that stupid kissing party when I was twelve. She was also thinking: Bryant's more the leader of the Jocks than Kyle. When he talks, they all listen to him. Even Kyle listens to him.

Jackie wondered: What has happened to Bryant Grober?

Phil Grant, who played baseball and football, wasn't sure he wanted to conform to the Jocks' standard of behavior. Yet Phil knew what happened if you showed the slightest hesitance about sports or about adopting their style: You were left out in the cold.

Phil recalled that Richie Corcoran had been friends with a boy since elementary school. Then the boy lost interest in high school sports and quit the football team. "Richie just stopped talking to him," Grant said. "As far as Richie was concerned, he didn't exist. This guy was quitting something Richie was part of, that Richie thought was the most important thing in school—not only in school, but in Richie's life. And Richie couldn't understand that. Out of all the people on the team, I was the only one who told this kid, 'Hey, don't worry about it. I don't care if you play football; I'm still gonna be your friend.'"

Phil never fit in perfectly. If there had been a category in the senior yearbook for the "WASPiest" kid in the class, Phil Grant probably would have won by a landslide. His preppy clothes and his quiet, almost reserved manner led some kids in town to describe him as "starchy."

During his first two years of high school, his subdued personality distanced him from the Jocks. If he wanted to go out with them on Friday night, he would have to call them; he wasn't their first choice for a party invitation. When their style made him uneasy, he would overcome his qualms by reasoning: I'm on the teams and the Jocks are the coolest kids, the most popular kids in the school. If they want *me*, why shouldn't I want them?

Phil's family pressured him to keep his distance. Unlike many of the families of the leading Jocks, women exerted a powerful influence on him. His mother, Linda, and his older sister, Sarah, disapproved of the belligerent style that many of the Jocks displayed even before they reached puberty.

Linda Grant tried hard to counterbalance the appeal of the Jock clique. She was reasonably confident that his upbringing, the moral code she and her husband, Schuyler, had worked so hard to instill in him, and the innate sense of propriety that distinguished their family would guide his behavior.

Linda and Schuyler were charter members of the town's core leadership. Schuyler's father, Chauncey, had been mayor of Glen Ridge in the 1960s. Although Schuyler commuted every night from New York City, where he was an investment banker, he found time to coach Little League baseball teams and to participate in the Civic Conference Committee, the town's dominant political organization.

Linda Grant had been prominent in virtually every campaign for civic betterment: landmark preservation, fund-raising for the town library, steering the school board and the Home and School Association (the town's version of the Parent-Teacher Association). The word in Glen Ridge was that if you wanted your cause to succeed, you had better get Linda Grant involved. If any two people personified the title "Ridgers," it was the Grants. "When you come into our house," she would tell out-of-town visitors, "you are in heartland Glen Ridge."

Some of her concerns were unconventional for the socially and politically conservative gentry of Glen Ridge. These had been shaped by a feminist perspective. For example she had worked with the Junior League to help establish the Essex County Prosecutor's Sexual Assault and Rape Analysis unit, which was responsible for investigating and prosecuting all sexual crimes in the county.

Phil's sister, Sarah, saw him hanging out at school with the Jocks when he was a sophomore and she was a senior. At dinner she said, "They get away with murder, Mom, and I don't like Phil being a Jock, and I can see he's going to be a Jock." But Phil responded testily that he could take care of himself, thank you very much big sister.

Linda, on the other hand, saw Phil changing directions, growing up, showing maturity. Now, if he could only get through the next few years without trouble. Raising a boy, you could never be sure when the job was done.

If Phil, whose family was one of the most prominent in Glen Ridge, had difficulty resisting the Jocks, it was even harder for Charlie Figueroa. You could count the number of blacks in the Class of '89 on the fingers of one hand, and Charlie was one of them.

It wasn't easy for the Jocks to figure Charlie out. He hadn't spent all his life, as most of them had, in Glen Ridge. He had attended private schools and Catholic schools. His mother, Mary, had worked in administrative positions in hospitals and banks. His father, Julio, was an electrician. When

Mrs. Figueroa took a new job in Essex County, the family—which included Charlie's younger sister, who was in grade school— bought a house
in Glen Ridge, on Osborne Street, not far from where Richie Corcoran
lived and where detective Sheila Byron had grown up. Although Mary
Figueroa had heard disquieting stories about the attitude of some townspeople toward blacks, she decided to move to Glen Ridge primarily because
it was supposed to have good schools.

The Figueroas moved into town as Charlie was about to enter high
school. Charlie told the kids he met about experiences that were foreign to
them. He described how he had hunted for rabbits and possums in Missis-
sippi and Arkansas. He would also tell them about some of the tough kids
he knew in Newark, the Other World.

Because he was black, they would have definitely written Charlie off
as an outer-space alien if not for one fact: Charlie Figueroa was one
committed Jock. A huge barrel-chested kid, in his freshman year Charlie
wrestled, threw the javelin for the track team, and played offensive and
defensive tackle for the football team.

"When I came to the school, it was a lot like the private schools I'd gone
to, where all the kids' parents are lawyers and doctors and executives,"
Charlie said. "You can get along with these kids if you're friendly and
smile and act nice to them."

Mary, Charlie's mother, said, "Growing up, I was accustomed to racial
slurs. In Glen Ridge I kept saying to Charlie, I don't want any trouble.
Don't fight, I told him. If there's a problem—back off. I didn't want him to
be a troublemaker because you're in the minority group. You don't want to
cry racism and stick out all the time. And for a while that worked."

While Charlie, like Phil Grant, decided to hang out with the Jocks, they
both did so warily. And that caution was largely due to the formative feminine guidance—a dimension missing from the childhoods of many of
their teammates—directed toward them by the women in their families.
In Charlie's case, his mother and his godmother, a clinical psychologist,
had dynamic personalities and were successful in their work. Mary
Figueroa was a strong mother. Both women were deeply skeptical of the
values with which some young men in Glen Ridge were brought up, especially the Jocks.

A friendly, unthreatening, athletic black teenager, Charlie was so popular that he was voted sophomore class president. As he beefed up the football and wrestling teams, Charlie won the cautious acceptance of the Jocks.
"Charlie was in the group and he was not in the group," Mary Figueroa
said. "It was hard for them to accept a black kid, but he did play sports."

He was invited to some parties and sat at the Jock table in the cafeteria, but Charlie didn't believe he was fully treated as an equal by the Jocks. In his freshman year the football team played a school that had an outstanding linebacker who was black. "On the line our guys were piling on this kid," Charlie said. "All our guys were saying, 'Get that nigger, stop that nigger.' On the bus back to Glen Ridge the players were saying, 'We showed that nigger,' and the coach said, 'You guys ought to apologize to Charlie.'"

Remembering his first two years at Glen Ridge High, Charlie said, "I had some good times and I had good friends, but I kinda did hate it." Perhaps the Jocks sensed that. He was black, he came from out of town, he was friendly with a lot of different kids. He had multiple allegiances. It made some of the Jocks wonder, Could Charlie be trusted? Could they depend on him to keep his mouth shut? In the future, Charlie could turn out to be a problem for the Jocks. He had a conscience.

15

In Mary Romeo's high school health class, the subject is "fun things kids can do during their weekends." Romeo mentions movies, music, theaters, trips to New York. One Jock holds up a hand to interrupt her. "Miss Romeo," he says, "we might as well end this discussion, because over the weekend we get drunk, we have as much sex as we can have, and on Monday we come back to school. That's what we do."

By the time they were sophomores, the Jocks were already veterans of the Glen Ridge party scene. They had been giving and attending parties since the first years of middle school. For them, the essential components of a successful Glen Ridge party were:

Alcohol.

A house where adults were not present.

Girls.

Music, decorations, and food were add-ons, nice but not required.

Booze was definitely required. But the idea of arriving at a party with a couple of cases of Piels and Bud (the drinks of choice because they were cheaper than premium brands) did not originate with the Jocks in the Class of '89. Detective Sheila Byron, who became the Glen Ridge juvenile officer in 1987, said, "Booze has been a Glen Ridge thing since forever."

And it wasn't strictly a juvenile phenomenon. Over the years, there were few social events in town, except perhaps those held by the churches, that weren't lubricated by alcohol. On the first day of school in 1986, one mother in town held a breakfast for some friends. Some of these mothers had children in the Class of '89 who were beginning their sophomore year, and others had kids in the middle school. "I thought it would last maybe an hour," she recalled. "I had carafes of coffee, pastries, fruit for about forty women. Gossip a little, talk about the schools, end of party. I was wrong. I had to kick these women out at 2:30. They came in gunning to party like you would remember partying when you were eighteen. They set up bar in the kitchen and they wouldn't leave the room. They went through a two-liter bottle of vodka, four bottles of wine, they put a good dent in my rum and even found a couple of bottles of champagne. One woman brought a blender and made strawberry daiquiris because she found out I didn't have a blender. Some of the women would rush out at 11:30 because their kids were coming home for lunch, and they'd be back an hour later." Watching their parents, some teenagers got the message: Grown-ups got happy, celebrated life, by tanking up.

Adolescents understood that there were occasions during which they would be forbidden to drink, and that they had to plan ahead for these dry stretches. One of the best athletes in the Class of '89 would remember, "Always before dances at the school, you got drunk at somebody's house because you never went to a dance sober. *Never.* Then you'd have to act straight if you talked to a teacher or a parent at the dance. But I think they knew—they just didn't want to say anything."

The reaction of parents to adolescent drinking was not entirely consistent. Publicly, parents said that kids should be punished for drinking and so should their fathers and mothers who tolerated it. Then they said: But not necessarily my kid and not me.

In 1988 Doug and Michaele Archer were among a group of parents who signed a public pledge not to serve alcohol to youths under the age of twenty-one. But it was also Doug Archer, Detective Byron recalled, who sent a letter to the police proposing that it should be left up to parents, not the police, to determine whether a kid had actually been drinking and should be charged. The fact that Chris and Paul Archer were athletes and could be suspended from their teams if they were caught drinking could have had something to do with his letter, Byron said.

In 1984 a parents' organization that called itself the Task Force was formed to enlighten residents about the extent of teenage drinking. In a public letter to parents, the organization said: "Untold numbers of young people abuse drugs and alcohol in their homes and the homes of friends."

A flurry of meetings and petitions followed. But then interest waned, high taxes became the big issue in town, and the drinking went on as before. Four years later a controversy flared when a letter was sent to the local newspaper by Alice and Steve Golin, the parents of Joshua Golin, a member of the Class of '89. The Golins wrote:

> When you are 14 your social life is the most important thing to you. In Glen Ridge there is no social life without drinking. . . . There's a law in Glen Ridge: you can't be a popular kid unless you drink. There are no exceptions, except for athletes during the season. You don't have to drink if you're 14 or 15; you can always sit home and feel like a loser.
>
> By the end of freshman year, most kids have been initiated into the alcoholic culture, often by older kids. . . . Figuring out which house to go to and how to get the stuff and whom to invite become normal activities of normal Glen Ridge kids.
>
> When the kids are caught, as sometimes they are, we ground them for a while. And then they go back to drinking while we pretend we don't know.

Dianne Brookes, the alcohol and drug prevention counselor at the high school, said later, "Parental resistance is my main problem; parents just don't want to hear about alcohol and drugs. How can parents not know? They go away for the weekend and their house is trashed. What do they think happened?"

The issue of alcohol consumption by kids who played sports for the high school had divided the town for decades. Parents of boys who didn't participate in the marquee sports often voiced their suspicion that there was an implicit understanding among educators, the local police, and parents that permitted Jocks to get away with drinking while other kids were penalized. The police, like school board members and school administrators, reflected the dominant values of the people they served. And many people in town didn't want their varsity players suspended for drinking, leaving the teams they planned their weekends around decimated. The cops also knew that the town abhorred scandal—and it would be something of a scandal if the best players in the school were busted.

The cops were also following their own instincts. Many had had similar experiences in high school as these teenagers did. They hadn't been great in their studies and, like these kids, they had earned recognition on the ball field, not in the classroom. For just a couple of years of their lives, they had been boys being boys, boys who were allowed in this aristocratic town a bit more leeway than other kids because they could throw a football or hit a baseball. The cops thought: Let these boys have their fun just as we did; life gets hard very fast. It was among these athletic kids and their parents that the cops felt most at home.

"When I was first on patrol," said Sheila Byron, "I was probably guilty of being more lenient with kids involved in athletics, because they were so visible. I happened to love the baseball team and I used to go to all the games. These were the kids you got to know. I remember always thinking that to give a kid a break would be a better thing to do."

On 34 Lorraine Street—Kyle and Kevin Scherzer's home—the deck parties were sometimes hard to ignore. On a September afternoon a dozen or so football players stood on the deck drinking beer. The cops busted the party. The kids ran, but identification was no problem. These were the visible kids, the friendly guys. There were consequences: A couple of them were suspended for a game or two. A couple of guys had to see Mrs. Brookes for counseling. But the whole incident was soon forgotten at the school, except by the guys themselves, who made note of it in their remembrances in the high school yearbook.

A vacant house, as indispensable to a good time as booze was, always seemed to be available to the dedicated partygoers. The 1980s were the Gold Rush decade in Glen Ridge as they were all over suburbia. New Money was there to spend. Frequently, the money went for a brief vacation in Florida or the Caribbean. Maybe there would be an older brother or sister to watch over the young ones in the parents' absence. Or maybe not. Maybe a fourteen-year-old was left in charge over the long weekend or the long week.

Randy Leisey, minister of the Congregational Church, was separated from his wife and raising his daughter alone. When she was fifteen, he had to officiate at a night wedding and he gave her permission to attend a party at a friend's house. When he got home, the minister found beer cans in the bushes, a case of beer in the basement, towels dripping with alcohol in the bathtub, and four or five empty liquor bottles in the trash. Apparently, some boys had suggested moving the party to Leisey's house, where no parents were at home.

The minister wrote seventeen letters to the parents of the kids at the party. Did they know where their kids were on Friday night? Did they care? About a third bothered to call him. "The impression I got from most parents was they wanted the community to raise their kids," Leisey would recall. "They didn't want to hear what kids were doing in a vacant house. They didn't want to ask why it was vacant and nobody was watching a bunch of fifteen-year-olds."

Along with booze and an empty house, the other essential ingredient for a party was girls. For the Jocks, finding girls to party with was easier than finding an empty house. When Chris Archer and his friends from middle school entered the high school in September 1986, they expanded the number of up-and-coming Jocks and Jockettes to about fifty kids; roughly half of them were young women. An outsider could wrangle an invitation—especially if she was pretty—or give a party, but the core group of partygoers was drawn from the kids who took turns sitting at the long table in the cafeteria reserved for Jocks and their fans.

By custom, in this group of teenagers, the party was the main arena where relationships developed between the sexes. The girls who came to the party fell into two groups. There were those the guys had known for years and rarely had sex with. These girls provided companionship but without any pressure to perform sexually. And then there were girls whom the guys didn't consider friends and didn't especially want to be seen with in public, but who were available for a quick sexual release without any pressure for the male to be a fully involved companion.

The party was an ideal setup for a group of insecure guys. As the gatekeepers of the town's elite adolescent social set, their status allowed them to escape the normal pressure of having to court a girl. No need to make that stomach-churning phone call to ask her out and risk rejection. No need to dress up or pay for a night at the movies.

The girls in Glen Ridge didn't seem to get much out of the deal. The guys controlled the scenario, and the girls had to play their part or go to the back of the line. Many went along with the script to spare themselves from what they were sure would be social oblivion. If they did have misgivings, their parents, the schools, and their friends kept assuring them that they were entering the clique of cliques. And so they joined the line.

And what assets, exactly, did they need to be invited to a Jock party? The girls knew that looks counted for a lot, as did a nice body. God forbid, a girl should binge out and put on an extra twenty pounds. Hair styles were also important. In the late 1980s the modified Farah Fawcett style was still popular in the suburbs: long hair, with lots of layers permed to form a frothy, frosted mane. Many girls wore bangs that they sprayed up from their faces for added height. As the hair spray wore off, the girls blew puffs of air to keep tendrils from drooping onto their foreheads. Makeup—eyeliner especially—was a must.

As far as brains went, it didn't matter whether the girls had them, as long as they weren't exercised at social events. It was not a good move to put the boys at a disadvantage.

For the girls, the one nonnegotiable prerequisite for admission to the charmed circle was that they had to be unquestioning defenders of the guys. The boys would permit them a squeal of protest when they did something to them that most adolescent girls would consider offensive. But the protest had to be brief and lightened with a giggle or laugh. From where the Jocks stood, their ideal girl was easygoing, perky, patient, and uncomplaining.

Just because these girls were always hanging around didn't mean that they were all equal in the guys' rating system. And it didn't mean that the top-rated girls were the prettiest, sexiest, or most obsequious. First among the two dozen or so young women were the Old Friends who had evolved in their adolescence into what might be called the "Little Mothers."

As the boys became teenagers, they were naturally disengaging from their mothers. The Little Mothers who circled around them served in some respects as surrogates. They showed up at their games, made them late-night snacks, signed their casts, and bought them ice cream when they got hurt on the playing field. They helped them with their homework, offered sisterly advice about their relations with girls, and inflated their egos when a girl or a teacher put them down.

The girls gave so much. And what did they get in return? The Jocks kept them as friends even though other girls were now intensely competing for their affections. The Jocks invited them to their parties although they spent much more time going after the sex objects than they did talking to the Little Mothers. And they gave them a complimentary seat at the Jock table in the cafeteria.

That's what the girls got in return. For the guys it was pretty much a no-lose proposition.

One young woman who often went to parties with the Jocks said later that the boys invited the Little Mothers for the same reason that they rarely ventured outside of Glen Ridge. "The guys were afraid that they'd get beaten up by some kids from another high school who thought they were snobs," she said. "They didn't like to go to parties out of Glen Ridge because the girls weren't all that impressed with them. They knew we were loyal to them."

If you were a Jock, these girls were perfect. Unlike real mothers and sisters, they weren't censorious or judgmental. Because they were cast in the maternal role, they were not usually regarded as potential sexual partners. For a teenage guy who might be insecure about his sexual performance, the last thing he wanted was to have to perform with a girl who could tell everybody he knew about his shortcomings in the sack.

Basically, the Little Mothers were faithful friends, real pals. (But the Jocks, of course, were not as close to them as they were to their male friends.) But more than that, too. They served as a security force that protected the guys against their worst critics, excused their misdeeds to their mothers and fathers, and scrutinized the credentials of all the outsiders who clamored to join the clique. "There were two tests to get into the inner circle," Phil Grant remembered. "If I was a jerk to teachers in class, didn't do my homework, and abused anybody I could take advantage of—that might help me. Mostly, it depended on whether certain girls liked me. If Angela Termini thought I was okay, I'd be golden."

Angela Termini* was one of the original Little Mothers. She had become friends with Peter Quigley first, back in middle school, and then with Kyle and Kevin. Angie skied with the guys at Hunter Mountain, camped on the beach at Point Pleasant, got sick on a little too much beer on St. Paddy's Day in New York City.

The payback for inclusion was constancy and loyalty. You didn't visibly show interest in a guy who was outside the circle. When she was a freshman, she and a friend started to spend a little time with a couple of cute boys who were juniors. "Our guys were really starting to get mad at us," Angie said. "And they were like, 'Well, where are you going tonight?' We'd have to say, 'Well, we don't know.' We could never tell them we were just going to a party with Don or somebody. They were just like, 'Life has to be all of us or none of us.'"

Life meant that the Little Mothers had to be around and ready when the guys needed them, but the word *dating* just didn't appear in the guys' vocabulary. It wasn't until Angie was a freshman at college that she went out on her first real date. "On weekends I'd go out with my girlfriends and the guys and we'd hang out. It was never a *date*. So if Richie came up to me and said, 'Would you go out to dinner?' I'd probably laugh—'What are you talking about Richie? Okay, what's the joke?'"

Kelly,* another Little Mother, would lament that hardly anybody in the crowd dated, but was resigned to the fact that the guys prized their intimacy with each other far above what could be achieved with a girl. "Personally, I would've liked to have someone I could be really close with, but I think the guys were really close only with each other."

Sometimes a girl new to the scene would harbor the illusion that she was being asked out on a date when a Jock would call and invite her to a party. Irene* was flattered when Kyle started inviting her to parties. But once she got to them, they weren't a lot of fun. Kyle and his friends would stand off in the corner drinking, playing a coin game, or talking sports, basically ignoring the girls. "We would walk in together, he'd go sit down and drink with all his friends, and I would be there with the girls, hanging out," she recalled.

As the party wound down, Kyle would tell her, "I'm going out with the guys. You'll have to make it home on your own." At the end of the evening, she often would find herself pleading with the other girls to give her a lift home.

He didn't always wait until the end of the party to break the news. Sometimes he'd walk over to her and announce: "I'm going to the 7-11 with Richie and buy some dip." And he would never come back.

"That was something you had to accept when you were with these guys," she said. "It was like Kyle didn't know how to treat someone. He didn't feel too obligated. It was strange. It wasn't even a relationship; it was just go to the party and be in the same room."

Dating might have stirred feelings of affection, empathy, and tenderness. But the Jocks reserved those feelings for each other. They were surgical and functional in their dealings with girls. "The guys always had to be in control," Phil Grant recalled. "The way they did that was by segregating the girls into different groups." They used the Little Mothers for tea and sympathy. They used some girls as party decorations, to be displayed and dismissed. And they used others for a blend of sexual release—not to be confused with sexual relations—and abuse. If the Little Mothers represented purity, their own private Madonnas, other girls—frequently thirteen- and fourteen-year-olds—served as their sex toys.

"They'd use the same words with Angie and another girl," Phil Grant said. "But what was behind the conversation was different. With Angie, it would be just friends. With the other girl, they were trying to get something going for later and you could see it because after they were done talking, Kev would roll his eyes and Kyle would smirk and Chris Archer would be looking down at the floor, trying to hide his grin."

The guys invented a distinctive vocabulary to describe what they had planned for their targets that night or what they had already done. A girl who gave them oral sex was "Hoovering"—like a vacuum cleaner. Another young woman who supposedly affected great enthusiasm for oral sex was called "the Helmet Wash Queen." They would often refer to girls who were available as "animals." A girl who gave blow jobs to a group of guys one after the other was nicknamed "Seal." This meant, according to one of the Little Mothers, that the girl was behaving "like a trained seal in the circus, doing whatever they commanded." When they saw one of the marks coming toward them from across the room, the guys would put on their beer goggles and chant: "Oink, oink, oink."

At these parties it wasn't enough to get what you wanted from one of the girls. It was fun only if you could tell your teammates about it and better still if you could pass her on to your friends. Angie would remember nights when one of the Jocks would go upstairs with a girl and come down a little while later and declare loudly to his buddies: "I just got a blow job from her." Then he'd cock his head toward the stairs, as if to say, You're next in line if you want it. Another link in the chain of fraternal bonding.

For athletes, the guys were remarkably passive in their activities. Face-to-face intercourse, sharing pleasure equally, was rare. Sex was something that was done to them, not something they actively participated in. Hand jobs and blow jobs—*jobs* that girls performed at their bidding. The guys were the foremen supervising their work crew.

The Little Mothers and some of the other young women who were at the parties never mistook what was going on for passion or lust. In their minds it was pure function. About as sexy as urinating. "I don't know how much the guys got laid," Angie said. "They just got off a lot."

If the guys had any overt reaction, it was derision. And they found an odd way to express that. When a couple went upstairs, some of the guys would wait a few minutes and then follow them up, standing outside a door that would be left partly ajar by their buddy. They would watch the couple for a while through the opening and then come rushing down, shouting, "You gotta go up and see what they're doing upstairs. She's unbelievably gross."

Perhaps the harshest judgment on these sexually compliant young women was delivered by Tara Timpanaro, one of the cheerleaders. "Sometimes, guys will do something they shouldn't do. At parties when you walk in, I'd have like five different guys pinching my ass," she said. "So I'd turn around and tell them to fuck off. I think it's disgusting for a girl at a party to go upstairs with a guy to a bedroom."

The way Tara saw it, you couldn't hold the guys responsible for what happened; you had to expect a high school guy to act crudely. It was up to the girl, Tara thought, to control the situation, to exercise moral restraint. "The girls who do these things are just stupid. I would never do that," she said.

With a certain amount of ill-concealed pique, the Little Mothers and other Jockettes acknowledged Tara as the voice of authority. That was because she was special. She was one half of *The Couple.* The other half was

Peter Quigley, who was, arguably, the best-liked athlete in his grade. The different cliques in the school agreed that if there was one Jock who was least objectionable, it was Peter.

Other Jocks said they had girlfriends. But their attention was less than constant, and the cafeteria and homerooms of the school were rife with rumors of their infidelities. These other Jocks and their so-called girlfriends didn't walk the halls of the school hand in hand, as Peter and Tara did. They didn't go out for dinner to a *restaurant*, as Peter and Tara sometimes did. Compared to the other mechanistic and largely functional alliances, Peter and Tara represented true romance. They had their ups and downs, but this was as close as you got to Young Love in Glen Ridge High.

And it happened so quickly, it just about took your breath away. Tara had transferred to Glen Ridge from West Caldwell at the beginning of the sophomore year—an outsider, a stranger, and before you had a chance to blink she had made the cheerleading squad, got invitations to all the right parties, and caught the eye of Peter.

Tara had certain advantages. The Jockettes had to concede that she was very pretty, with her piercing gray eyes and blond layered hair. And she knew how to dress, too, the girls noticed—no shabby, raggedy jeans for her. When she became a senior, Tara would be voted as the "Best Body" of all the girls—a perfect match for Peter, who would be designated "Best Body" among all the guys. Yet, with some justification, she detested being labeled the "blond bombshell cheerleader." Sure, she was a cheerleader and would later become captain. But she was also a science and math whiz, making high honor roll in her junior and senior years; after graduation, she would go off to Purdue University to study engineering. The other thing she had going for her: she was the daughter of Vincent Timpanaro, an industrial arts teacher and a favorite of many students at Glen Ridge High.

Peter, the son of an accountant, looked like anything but. He was a square block of concrete, built like one of those kids who came out of the steel mills in Pennsylvania or the coal mines of West Virginia. Muscles on muscles: big chest, big shoulders, thick neck. In keeping with the rest of his trunk, his face had a squarish shape that was often softened by a wide guileless grin. Here was a body made for football, made for grinding out the yards as a fullback or, on defense, putting a hard hit on a runner. But Peter's popularity stemmed more from his pleasant nonthreatening manner and country-boy, Tom Sawyerish personality.

Tara got the feeling that the other kids spent more time following the progress of her romance than they did worrying about their own social lives. There was a snippiness—all right, call it jealousy—to how the other girls dissected her relationship with Peter. It wasn't only that in one lightning strike the attractive newcomer had snared the handsome fullback. What nettled the girls was that Peter and Tara acted as if they were roughly equal. Equal relationships were rarities in the Jock circles.

Tara did her part as Peter's helpmate. She tutored him in his class assignments, helped him write letters to the school when he was in danger of losing his athletic eligibility, and cheered mightily when he ran two yards. But Peter contributed his share to the relationship, too, as the reliable companion. When he and Tara went to parties, he talked to her and didn't spend all his time with his buddies. He never disappeared into the night. When he went fishing or camping, he included her.

Tara and Peter shared top billing in their romance. But other girls in the group were relegated to bit parts by the Jocks. At a time when they were supposed to be having fun, they could be treated like overworked and underappreciated housewives. And no one more so than the Little Mothers. Even those who closed their eyes to the most obvious failings of the Jocks couldn't help wondering why they always got stuck with the grunge work.

When the parties broke up and Peter and Tara slipped away together, Angela Termini, who had been Peter's best female friend in middle school, went back to her house alone. Just as she was settling into a deep sleep, the phone would ring. Kevin calling. "Angie, can we come over?"

A few minutes later the doorbell was ringing. And standing outside was the whole gang, three-quarters in the bag. Suddenly they were streaming into the kitchen like an army of ants discovering a sugar bowl. The refrigerator door was open and a dozen hands were reaching for the ham and the potato salad. "Guys, please don't make a mess," she pleaded.

But they didn't listen. They ate and drank and left the soda and beer and scraps of meat and dirty dishes all over the kitchen counter. And then they'd say, "Angie, we're sorry for the mess but we gotta go now. We'll see you later."

On nights like this, after the guys finally left, Angie would crawl into bed, stare at the ceiling, and ask herself: Why can't you just say "no" to the guys? Tell them, You can't come in here and raid my kitchen, acting like my feelings don't count at all. She'd berate herself, Why can't you get mad at them?

But she knew the answer to that question: What else could she do? Be a reject—like Mary Ryan?

16

There was nothing about Mary Ryan* that would have qualified her as a Jockette. A year older than the students in the Class of '89, she was extremely shy and spoke in a whisper that could turn into a whine when someone was mean to her; she dressed conservatively in white blouses and pale-blue and tan cardigan sweaters; she did not wear much makeup, and her brown hair was not permed or streaked or frosted or sprayed into an arabesque monument, as the popular girls did with theirs. Mary Ryan was never known to call attention to herself—except for one time, and that misjudgment would change her life.

In the Jocks' sophomore year, during the first week of February 1987, the shy junior stood up in the school cafeteria and said: "My parents are going to be away next week. I'm going to have a big party. Everybody come." Mary Ryan's secret wish was to be popular, to have people notice her. In Glen Ridge people noticed you if you threw a party when your parents were away. But giving advance notice within the hearing of a hundred or so high school students could be dangerous.

The risk was heightened if the Jocks weren't good friends with the hostess. "First of all, she was a girl none of us liked," Tara Timpanaro recalled. "If someone didn't like you, they're not going to have respect for your home." Charles Figueroa, a wrestler and football player, wasn't her close friend, but he liked Mary. "She smiled a lot and tried to be nice to you, but people wouldn't accept it. She had a kind of weak way about her. She tried not to offend anybody, so people thought they could roll right over her."

There were decorous nonalcoholic parties in Glen Ridge. There were rowdy alcoholic parties. And there were parties that turned violent. Before Tara transferred to Glen Ridge, she "had known for years that Glen Ridge was a major party town. Somebody is always having a party. I can remember my father telling me a guy jumped through a bay window during a party."

Fights often broke out at parties. But what got the Jocks really mad was being barred from a party. One of the proudest moments for the '89 Jock clique—a moment that was celebrated in their senior yearbook—was the time they beat up older boys on the lawn of a host's house in Glen Ridge.

The reason for the fight: The boys who lived in the house didn't want the Jocks at their party. Indeed, earlier in their sophomore year, on October 11, 1986, Kyle and Kevin were reported to the police when they crashed a party, refused to leave, and "had to be forcibly removed."

Parties could turn ugly when the adolescent partygoers decided they would use the party as a vehicle to hurt, one way or another, the party-giver, who in almost every case was a young woman. These scenes became known among the youth of Glen Ridge as "revenge" parties. The specific reason for the punishment seemed less important than the opportunity to hurt the girl. "If you're a girl and they don't respect you and they don't like you, forget it," said one of Chris Archer's wrestling teammates. This wrestler and other Jocks described what had happened to one of the Jocks' Little Mothers when she drank too much at a party. Like a bag of garbage, the girl was dumped in a closet as the party wound down; the guys locked the closet door and left her confined in the dark to gag on her vomit. Again, the Jocks noted the incident in the yearbook as one of the bright moments of their school years.

Kids who weren't in the cafeteria when Mary Ryan issued her invitation heard about it soon enough, and word traveled swiftly to students in other communities. February was the wrestling season, and high school wrestlers for miles around were told of the impending party. That's how it worked. Wrestlers told wrestlers; cheerleaders told cheerleaders in other towns. Why so much excitement? Parties with parents absent were not uncommon. But this one had the makings of something special. For Glen Ridge kids, the big attraction was that Mary Ryan, a tuition student, lived just across the town border in East Orange. They thought that if the cops busted the party, the guys' parents were less likely to find out. "When you go out of Glen Ridge, you go crazy," one of the athletes recalled. "There are no neighbors to stop you or tell your mother."

The other inducement was Mary's passivity. She was not known as a strong-willed kid, she didn't have many friends to protect her, and her family was not friends with the families of the Jocks. "If Mary said 'no,' who'd listen to her?" Charlie Figueroa said. "She didn't have anybody who'd fight for her."

Along with everything else, the timing was perfect. The date set for the party was Saturday, February 14, 1987, Valentine's Day. That Saturday also fell in the middle of a three-day weekend, Monday being Washington's Birthday. "It was, like, a party that could go on forever," one Ridger said.

Instead of on Saturday, the party began spontaneously on Friday, February 13. By sundown every parking space for three blocks around the Ryans' house was taken. There were kids from Caldwell, Montclair, Bloomfield, and Verona. From private schools and public schools, from middle school and high school. There were older guys who had graduated three or four years ago. There were even kids from East Side High School in Newark. There were Jocks and Guidos and Giggers, cheerleaders and majorettes, and even a few "band fags." There were girls who looked too young to get into a movie alone and some who seemed old enough to be married and have kids. There were kids who brought bottles, and kids who lugged cases of beer on their shoulders, and some who rolled kegs up the front steps into the kitchen.

They all converged on a narrow three-story white shingle house with a semifinished basement and a small balcony facing a nearby park. The location was perfect for a nonstop party. There were only a few other houses on the block, and they all adjoined the park. You could make as much noise as you wanted with little likelihood of interference.

The kids who got there early made for the upstairs rooms. It was the only place where you could hear yourself talk. The ones who arrived by 10 or 11 o'clock wedged themselves into the kitchen or basement. Sixty or seventy kids jammed together, drinking, smoking, and screaming. Mary Ryan had given up asking who the kids were and where they came from.

Despite all the kids and booze, there was relatively little damage on Friday night. One guy did take out all the crystal glasses and pitchers in the kitchen cabinets, line them up on the table, and fling them, one after the other, against the wall. But that happened at a lot of parties. It was nothing to get excited about.

John Maher, a student who later would be indicted on a charge of conspiracy in the Leslie Faber case, was working on Friday night. "My friends were saying it was a great party, the best," he would say later. "I couldn't believe what was happening. So I made sure I was there Saturday."

Saturday night, February 14, Valentine's Day. More kids. More booze. There were so many bodies in Mary Ryan's house, so many kids jammed into a small smoky space, that they had to open all the windows and the doors. With all the runs to the fridge, the beer couldn't be kept cold. So they gave up on the fridge, cleared everything out, and left the door hanging open.

They started taking the furniture apart. Within an hour the legs had been broken off everything that was standing—coffee tables, kitchen chairs and table, side tables. A couple of guys got the idea of using a leg from the kitchen table as a battering ram. One-two-three—charge. The leg smashed through the plasterboard, leaving a hole the size of a saucer. Back up and start all over. The hole got bigger and bigger, maybe two, three feet in diameter. Okay, let's start on the other wall.

Then some people decided that the amputated remains of the furniture were cluttering up the place. In five minutes every tabletop and chair seat had been heaved into the backyard.

One wall was covered floor to ceiling with a bamboo stand to hold decorative objects. The stand had been attached to the wall. "Betcha can't break that in half," one Jock challenged another. As if he were working out in the school exercise room, the other Jock stood with his back to the bamboo, his arms raised behind his shoulders. A deep breath and pull. The entire bamboo stand, with everything that rested on it, came crashing to the floor. A few minutes later some guys were breaking pieces of the bamboo over their heads and using them as swords in make-believe duels.

One guy stood in front of the fish tank. Thinking. Then he went into the kitchen and returned with a container of Comet detergent. He emptied it into the tank. A half-hour later another kid saw the fish floating dead in the water. He and a friend carried the tank to the door and emptied its contents into the snow.

Mary Ryan would wave her hand in a futile plea to halt the destruction. But one of the girls would take her by the shoulder and guide her out of the room. "We'll help you clean up later," she'd tell her.

Sunday night, February 15, 1987. It seemed as if the whole world under the age of thirty had turned up for the third act at Mary Ryan's house. Among the new notables were the wrestlers from Glen Ridge. They had been forced to miss the Saturday-night festivities because they were competing in a match. Rock-solid and brimming with energy, they could always be counted on to liven up a party.

It was a true gathering of the clan: Richie Corcoran and Kyle and Kevin; Peter Quigley, his companion, Tara, and Peter's older brother, Sean; Chris and Paul Archer. They had no problem finding the house. "You could hear the noise from like a mile away," said one Glen Ridge wrestler. "When you got on the street, it was amazing. It was so cold out and snow was on the ground and there were dozens of kids standing outside. One of the kids I recognized was holding a neon tube over his head and then he smashed it right on his skull. All the lights were on in the house, and you could see people in every window. As I was walking in, part of the frame over the door was hanging down and I almost ran into it.

"There were like a million people in there, all of them drunk. And right away I saw all the wrestlers from the school and I know they can get a little crazy at a party, and I thought, Whew, there's gonna be all sorts of shit tonight. I kept thinking, I'm walking into a movie."

Charlie Terranova, one of the Glen Ridge Giggers, stayed about fifteen minutes. "I went into this place and the things I saw I could not believe. I once worked for a construction company, and there were rooms in this house that looked like a construction crew had gone in there with the crowbars and the pikes and just destroyed the place. I just left. I couldn't stand it."

Some kids may have experienced a letdown when they surveyed the wreckage on the first floor. Really, what was left for them to do? The people who had been there the first two nights seemed to have exhausted all the possibilities. But, on reflection, it was apparent that they hadn't. There were two upstairs floors and a basement, and that left lots of unfinished work.

Chris Archer took the basement. People who were there remembered him rushing down the stairs with a can of spray paint in his hand and spraying every wall with painted graffiti. Another Jock, partygoers recalled, charged upstairs, followed by a pack of football players and wrestlers. First thing they did was dismantle Mary's parents' bed. One kid had the idea of setting the mattress on fire, but another thought that was a stupid idea since it was a waterbed. Let's puncture it, one guy suggested, and start a flood. Some guys began stabbing it with a screwdriver and a kitchen knife.

Other kids carried the bed frame to the top of the landing and, using it as a makeshift toboggan, tried to slide down the stairs. But the frame was too wide to make for a level ride. The kids smashed all the balusters that held up the stair rail. Now there was enough room. The guys sat on the frame, their legs straddling the sides, and slid down the slope.

Mary Ryan had retreated upstairs to her parents' bedroom, where she sat on the floor with another girl and Charlie Figueroa. They heard a roar coming from downstairs and rushed to the door; they saw a bunch of kids charging up the stairs as the boys were sliding down on the bed frame. The boys leaped over the mattress and burst into the Ryans' bedroom. There, they pulled open the dresser, flinging the underwear, blouses, and other clothing on the floor.

Holding their findings over their heads, they marched down the stairs. "Hey, wait a second," Mary shouted, fear in her voice. But who was listening? They put up on the mantelpiece all the personal possessions they had taken from the Ryans' bedroom dresser. Mary sank down in a corner of the room, her knees up against her chest. "She looked to me like she was getting smaller and smaller, like she wanted to disappear," Charlie said.

Now dozens of kids formed a row, and began snake dancing past the mantel, as though they were performing a religious ritual before an altar. Someone had come up with the perfect description for what was going on. And the snake dancers began to chant it, as they weaved through the room: Ryan's Wreck. Ryan's Wreck. Ryan's Wreck.

It must have got through to Mary that the party was out of control. This had to stop. It wasn't only her life that was being trashed; it was her parents' life, too.

Now she saw a boy pick up her cat by the back of the neck, hanging him high for the crowd to see, and then push him into the microwave. She heard one terrible yowl, smelled burning flesh, burning fur. She screamed: "Stop, you've got to stop." Somebody pulled the cat out, but few people were listening to Mary Ryan.

Mary ran up the stairs, rushed into a room, and flung open the window. She stepped outside onto the balcony. It was not very high, ten feet or so above the ground, but high enough so she could hurt herself if she fell. She leaned against the rail of the balcony and peered down through the darkness at the mob of teenagers who had gathered on the snow-covered incline. "Oh, my God, my house, my house," she screamed. "If you don't stop, I'll jump."

Alarmed, one girl urged her, "Come on, come back in, Mary. Everything's okay. We'll go home." But instantly the sound of her voice was drowned out by dozens of kids chanting: Jump. Jump. Jump. Jump.

Charlie Figueroa, standing in Mary's bedroom, decided that all this had to stop. He knew that what he was about to do would break the first rule of Jock solidarity—never squeal. Charlie called the police anyway.

At about 11:15 Officers Chwal and Marinelli, patrolling in East Orange police car number 23, got a radio message: "Loud party in progress. Proceed to the scene." A second police car was also dispatched. When the police got there, kids were still standing beneath the balcony urging Mary Ryan to jump. But they weren't there for long. As soon as they saw the two flashing reds wheeling around the corner, the kids scattered.

The party was over. "Ryan's Wreck" had now passed into the folklore of Glen Ridge High School.

East Orange has a lot more crime than Glen Ridge. The East Orange cops weren't going to spend time chasing a hundred or so kids through the brambles of a park at midnight. But even these experienced cops were impressed by what they found in Mary Ryan's house and recorded in their report: "The reporting officers noticed the front door wide open and the downstairs in shambles. . . . Further investigation showed the entire residence, three floors, in shambles."

The two officers called the crime "malicious mischief" and described the "weapon" used to commit the crime as "physical force." The police detained eleven juveniles, all from Glen Ridge or Glen Ridge High School. These included a boy who would be selected as one of the captains of next year's football team and another football player, Peter Quigley's older brother, Sean, who had already completed his football career at the high school. Also held for questioning was James "Tucker" Litvany, a Class of '89 football player, who would be later cited as an unindicted co-conspirator in the Leslie Faber case.

These youngsters were questioned briefly, their parents were informed, and that was the end of that. None of them was charged with a crime. None of them was punished or reprimanded by Glen Ridge High; none of them lost his athletic privileges or eligibility.

Mary never came back to Glen Ridge High. Her parents moved out of their house, and she was reportedly sent to live in another part of the state. A sophomore recalled that one of his teachers heard about the party and briefly discussed it in class: "The kids commented on how drunk people were, how they were breaking things, but how Mary deserved it. Nobody said they were sorry. Nobody offered to clean up the place. And nobody wanted to pay for the damage."

Two years later the memory of that party remained fresh in the minds of the Jocks and the Jockettes of the Class of '89. In a section of their yearbook, where each student listed personal highlights, many of them cited their participation in "Ryan's Wreck" as an outstanding event of the past four years. "It just showed what can happen to a girl when we didn't like her," one Jock would recall. John Maher, another Class of '89 football player, would say years later, "That's a party that everybody still talks about."

For that nucleus of sophomore Jocks, this was not a formal initiation rite on the order of their first high school football game. But it was a benchmark experience in their high school years. There had been destructive parties before in Glen Ridge, and there would be others later. But it was under the tutelage of upperclassmen—older, admired football players and wrestlers—that they learned at Mary Ryan's party how much they could get away with. They also learned that the girls who attached themselves to the Jocks could be as pitiless as they were.

The primary lesson was that a bunch of high school kids could raise hell and inflict tremendous pain without being penalized at home or in school. But the party also taught a more advanced lesson. To one father whose daughter was in the Class of '89, the boys who participated most enthusiastically at the party behaved as if they were gaining more legitimacy and authority as a group each time they victimized a woman. "If I think back about that period, I can see the group getting stronger, closer, every time they got together and humiliated a girl," he said. "What they enjoyed in common wasn't football. *This* was their *shared* experience. For them, this was what being a man among men was. My daughter would come home with stories—I'd just shake my head and wonder if they thought a girl was human."

17

Mary Ryan was an outsider in the teenage world of Glen Ridge, but Leslie Faber was completely off the social radar screen. To most of the kids her age, she was little more than a rumor. By the time she reached high school, Leslie was further than ever from her goal of being accepted as a normal teen.

Still classified by the school system as neurologically impaired, Leslie was moved to a special education program at Columbia High School in the nearby suburb of Maplewood. Officially, she was still enrolled as a student in the Glen Ridge system, and therefore could participate in the high school's athletic activities. But she would spend her high school years apart from the familiar faces she had known since kindergarten.

Not that they missed her. The kids she most wanted to be her friends ignored her or made fun of her. Sometimes Leslie didn't understand that they were laughing at her. But at other times she knew and tolerated it because that was the price she had to pay for acceptance. "I'd just let it fly," she would say later.

Despite her limitations in school, Leslie appeared to people who didn't know her well to be an ordinary suburban kid. Her speech, although mildly slurred, was understandable; a slightly drooping eyelid, caused by problems with her eye muscles, did not significantly affect her physical appearance. When she was talking about something she had personally experienced, describing a basketball game or somebody's new car, Leslie expressed herself lucidly and coherently. Leslie had an excellent memory for details. She sounded very much like an average self-conscious, hyperventilating teenager. Average—unless you had grown up with her, watched her day to day, year to year. Then, you knew, as a clergyman in Glen Ridge put it, that Leslie Faber was one of "God's innocents."

Although she was physically big, she had a child's view of friendship. She told a psychologist who interviewed her after her encounter with the Jocks that a friend was someone who played "nicely" or who "plays sports with me." In a sense Leslie was saying that a friend is somebody who would play in the sandbox with her. An adolescent developing normally would have a more complex understanding of friendship. She would regard a friend as a confidant, as a person who shared many experiences with her, who visited her frequently, and who talked with her about conventional teenage concerns—school, boyfriends, plans for college and career.

But Leslie found it difficult to respond to another person on this level. "Her concept of friendship is one that is typically found in children substantially younger," the psychologist wrote in her report. "Younger children count as friends those with whom they engage in activities and those who do not behave aggressively toward them; with such a simple definition, anyone who plays with you peacefully, even for a short . . . time, is a friend."

When the psychologist asked her to name her friends, Leslie could think of only two: the wife of the family's minister and a young woman in Bloomfield.

Her social life was much more circumscribed than that of other kids. One young man, a high school classmate, would visit Leslie occasionally, and they would watch television together. A few times, her parents would drive Leslie to his house, where the two kids would spend the evening eating ice cream and watching her favorite programs, "Alf" and "Gilligan's Island."

Otherwise, Leslie's main social outlet was youth activities sponsored by her church and vacation trips with her parents. But the one activity that gave her most pleasure was athletics. For most of her four years playing on the Glen Ridge High School basketball team, Leslie was on the jayvee squad. She usually didn't get into games unless the team was winning or losing by a lopsided score. She was an enthusiastic player, but she lacked poise. Sometimes she would run to the wrong end of the court. The other girls might laugh at her when she made a silly mistake, and a few may have resented the coach's willingness to give her a couple of minutes of playing time.

But Charlie Faber attended every game, training his video camera on Les during pregame practice and when she got to play. Of all the hours Charlie taped during Leslie's years on the team, one second stands out. Leslie was playing in the fourth quarter of a home game. The defensive player was guarding her closely, and Leslie dribbled backward toward the mid-court line. Instead of passing to a teammate, Les, motivated mostly by panic, fired up a shot from close to half-court. Swish. All net. The spectators cheered. She jumped up and down with excitement. If he could have, Charlie would have stopped time. It was the moment a father wants to freeze forever.

A few years later, Leslie might forget who the opponent was that night, who won, even whether the game was at home or away. She would remember the shot, the pleasure of seeing the ball go through the hoop, of hearing the applause and the cheers, of seeing her dad smile. Her reaction and her memories were similar to those of many disabled children.

For retarded youngsters like Leslie, experts say, beating your opponent is relatively unimportant. Many, in fact, don't even understand how a game is scored and may not realize afterward which team has won. But lots of retarded teenagers, who feel lonely and socially bereft, love sports for the camaraderie it offers them.

Ray Raphael, a social analyst investigating male rites of passage in America, recalled the experience of a man who coached disabled youngsters. One of the youngsters on this coach's basketball team hit a shot with a few seconds left in the game: "So my team jumps up thinking for sure they've won the game. We made the last shot so there's no doubt about it: We are champions. . . . The actual score was like thirty-six to two. That was the first and only basket we made, but it didn't matter—it came at the appropriate time."

Another coach reflected, "None of these teams could keep score, so it's absolutely irrelevant. The fact is, you've played, you've played well, and if you're lucky enough, the ball might have gone in the basket."

This was Leslie's game. It was great to make an impossible shot and bask in the appreciation of the crowd, but it was just as great when everybody on the team put hands on hands after a timeout and the captain shouted, "One, two, three—win." That was team spirit, and she was part of it. The way Leslie felt about it, winning or losing was almost incidental; everybody won because they were all "friends" with each other. Youngsters like Leslie are "blessedly relieved of the burden of using games to prove their superiority over others," Raphael wrote. "For these people alone a game is still truly a game, a 'positive-sum' event where everyone can come out on top."

That couldn't have been more different from the outlook of the mainstream athletes in Glen Ridge; for them sports was a means of gaining supremacy. But Leslie didn't care about becoming a leader of the crowd in Glen Ridge. She prized inclusion, if for no other reason than that she was so often excluded. But as much as she sought acceptance, she also wanted to share her pleasures. That's what you did with friends; you included them in your good times.

The Lipinskis were special to Leslie because they were truly her only good friends. Leslie met Jennifer Lipinski when she was eleven. Jennifer, who was a few months older, was an excellent basketball player for her age. As their friendship bloomed, Jennifer became her protector against the boys who tried to ridicule Leslie. Chris or Kevin or one of their buddies would take a basketball or tennis ball and throw it down to the other end of the playground and tell Leslie, "Go get our ball." And Jennifer would be right there, snapping at them, "Go get it yourself; you think she's your servant?"

What made Leslie's friendship with Jennifer different from her other teenage relationships was that it didn't stop there on the court. The Lipinskis lived just over the town line in Bloomfield, and their house was only a few minutes away from the Fabers' house. Leslie made that walk often; she visited two or three times a week, often staying for dinner. In turn, Jennifer, somewhat less frequently, would drop in at the Fabers'.

Dinnertime at the Lipinskis was a spirited event, with five preteen and adolescent kids all trying to make themselves heard above the din. Dawn, the oldest of the five Lipinski children, recalled that Leslie's presence didn't change the way the family acted. "She wasn't a special guest that we pampered," Dawn said. "She kinda fit right in. We were constantly joking, kidding around. And Les would kid us right along. When you see mildly retarded people, they don't have that outside stimulation, they're closet cases, they are introverted. But being around us, she was able to come out of the introvert a little bit. She'd never been around a big family, a family with three girls in it, and she just joined in."

When the Lipinski kids were talking about subjects Leslie understood, she was spontaneous and animated. But often she was a beat behind. "My mother'd be yelling at my brother Greg, and Les would be laughing when she wasn't supposed to be laughing," Dawn said. "Everyone'd be talking about politics and somebody'd say, 'What do you think, Les?' She'd try to answer, but not knowing anything about it. Everyone in the family knew that you talk to her on a more general level. But then there was her sense of humor, her curiosity, her generosity—and the differences would evaporate."

Les's generosity, that was something you could count on. Putting dinner together for seven (eight if you counted Leslie) could be a scramble. Leslie was always eager to do her share. Washing dishes. Taking the garbage out. Walking the dog.

In later years Dawn's mom was stricken by cancer. At the hospital, at home, Leslie was a frequent visitor, bringing with her a homemade card, flowers, a cake her mother had baked. "Les'd see me stressed out or trying to keep everything together and she'd say, 'Is there anything, anything at all, I can do to help you?' She was very, very emotional," Dawn said.

The only special effort the Lipinskis had to make with Leslie involved getting her home safely. "We'd never let her walk home alone at night," Dawn said, "because she really wasn't capable of taking care of herself. She's not afraid of people, even like I'd be if I were alone with a stranger. She is just so giving, so ready to make a friend that she doesn't—didn't— see anything as a threat. Which could be deadly. Which is deadly."

18

In high school the Jocks extended the pattern they had set in middle school: poor to middling grades and scourges of the classroom. But high school was different from middle school in one important respect: students had to get passing grades to remain eligible for sports.

The school required athletes to maintain a 1.75 grade point average. To qualify for athletics, their average had to be at least in the C− range. They also had to pass all but one of their major courses. They could repeat in summer school the courses that they had failed. If that didn't work, they could ask an appeals board to reverse the decision. Ultimately, it was up to the principal to approve the appeal.

Some of the Jocks had to mount letter-writing campaigns to get school officials to waive the requirements. One way or another, most of them succeeded in staying on the teams. Kevin was a case in point. During the spring term of his freshman year, it looked as if he was going to fail a couple of courses and lose his athletic eligibility. During an especially tense parent-teacher meeting, Jack Scherzer reportedly told one of Kevin's teachers: "Hell, if he can't pass your class, what good is it how he does in the other classes? He won't be able to play football."

Faculty members said later that at conferences with Jack and Geraldine Scherzer they pressed their case for evaluating Kevin, to determine whether he should be classified. But his parents, these school officials said, were fiercely resistant.

When it looked as if he would fail, Kevin made one more plea. He wrote to the assistant principal: "I am requesting this appeal because I feel that my grades have improved . . . an extra-curricular activity will help me improve even more."

However reluctantly, Kevin's teachers in his freshman year passed him, albeit with three Ds, three Cs, and an obligatory A+ in physical education. In fact, only one of the Jocks ever failed to maintain his eligibility for sports. Richie Corcoran was not allowed to play football in his sophomore year because of the poor grades he received when he was a freshman.

Kevin's athletic eligibility had been threatened by his near failure. But no one had threatened to disqualify him for his *behavior*, which was notorious among Kevin's classmates and among his more perceptive teachers. His school records show a number of complaints about his misconduct. For example:

> *May 13, 1987:* A teacher notes that Kevin "was kicked out of class today" and urges his parents to meet with her "immediately." But that meeting was not possible because, as a school official noted, "[Kevin's] parents in Florida."
> *October 23, 1987:* ". . . 'dangerously' immature . . ."

February 25, 1988: "He accused the teacher of being 'crazy, go to an insane asylum' in loud voice in front of class. Was sent to principal."

Kevin's classmates noticed even more problems than appear in his school records. As Kevin built his reputation, he also built his body. Almost halfway through high school, he was about six feet tall, big across the chest, muscled up after all the hours at the gym. His brown hair, spiked at the top and combed back at the sides, would fall across his forehead in a way the girls thought was cute. An adenoidal problem kept his mouth open much of the time, giving him a stunned, almost dumbfounded look. That may have influenced his classmates to vote him the "most gullible" member of the Class of '89.

Kevin used his body to get the attention of other kids. He started showing up in school wearing sweatpants. Sweatpants tied with a drawstring at the waist, making for easy access. Sweatpants made of cotton, perfect for showing off the outline of his erection. It got to be more of a habit in his later years in high school, but even when he was a freshman, students remembered Kevin tapping a girl on the shoulder during a class and pointing down to his crotch, where his other hand was stroking himself under his pants. Kevin usually wasn't happy with only one girl noticing his movements, his former classmates recalled. His buddies in class would pass along his message to three or four girls, and Kevin would angle his long legs into the aisle so everybody had decent sightlines. If he could get just one girl to react, to blush or bury her face in her hands, it made his day.

In a sophomore science class, Kevin sat near Charlie Terranova. "As soon as the teacher turned her back to class—boom! Kevin would start right in," Charlie said. "The thrill of his whole day was when he would unzip his pants, show himself, and try to get the girls in the front row to turn around and look at him. I wanted to say something, but my friends were telling me, Shut up, these kids'll kick your ass. So I kept quiet the next three years, just like lots of kids."

With fourteen kids in the average classroom, it's hard to imagine a student who didn't witness Kevin's behavior and the behavior of other Jocks. Terranova's depiction of Kevin's activities closely resembles the earlier accounts by girls in the middle school. Such odd behavior over such a long time. And no one in authority seemed able to stop it—or acted as if they were even aware that it was going on.

But some were aware. When a movie informed the curricula, teachers would show it in class. One girl remembered that when the lights went on after a showing of the film *Passage to India,* she saw Kevin smiling, as his hands moved under his sweatpants. The student recalled the teacher's saying, in a gently mocking tone, "There's Kevin, with his hands down his pants."

Yet another student remembered sitting down in her morning detention class and seeing Kevin masturbating with his penis exposed. "He was just jacking off," she said. "There were ten, eleven kids in the class and he was opening his fly and pulling his penis out. I didn't think anything of it because he did it so often. But I remember thinking, If Kevin ever tries to touch me, his ass'll be in jail."

Sometimes Kevin seemed to be making progress in curbing his "habit." On May 9 of his junior year, a teacher reported to a school official that Kevin "likes to show his body—is very physical—has stopped putting his hands in his pants." That's it: In all his school years, there is only this one notation in the school records explicitly describing how Kevin fondled himself.

Ben Tantillo, who was then vice-principal for discipline, later recalled a teacher telling him during the junior year that a student "had his hands in his pants and was scratching. I brought that person [Kevin] in and said, 'What the heck were you doing?' So then the kid said, 'I was itching.' So I brought him to the nurse and said, 'This kid might have the crab lice problem. Call his mother.'" Tantillo said that no other instances of Kevin's touching his crotch in school "were ever reported to me."

If the school had demonstrated its displeasure with Kevin's behavior, it might at least have protected other students from constantly witnessing it through middle school and high school. But what about Kevin himself? Didn't it occur to school officials that his aberrant conduct might signal a need for psychological intervention? The school, apparently sidestepping another embarrassing situation, did little, and Kevin continued to attend classes and play on the football teams. Ultimately, he was selected as co-captain.

Like his brother, Kyle stayed on the football team and also played baseball, despite receiving mostly Cs and Ds through his high school years. But some of his teachers' comments suggest that Kyle was more selective than Kevin in his abuse of other students. With people he didn't know well, especially adults, Kyle appeared shy. A girl he hadn't met before could make him blush and stammer. Kyle's features were finer, more delicate appearing, than Kevin's, although at six feet, 180 pounds he had an athletic physique. During a conversation his brown eyes would gleam with anticipation. Kevin would always be interrupting; Kyle would lay back, wait for the talker to finish, before he jumped in with a cutting put-down.

Among the Jocks Kevin was the twin you laughed at. Kyle was the one you listened to.

The leading Jocks—Peter Quigley, Bryant Grober, Kevin, Richie—all had their academic troubles, even with basic-level courses. Paul Archer, with an assortment of Bs and Cs, was a modest exception. But only Paul's brother, Chris, in the class behind, had a record of real academic accomplishment.

Some of their parents seemed responsive when the school asked for their help. When Paul slipped below a C average, Michaele Archer was on the phone immediately, asking his teacher what she could do to help. "Don't pull any punches," she reportedly told a teacher at one conference. "I want to know everything. *Everything,*" she emphasized, squeezing Paul's arm, her son already towering over her at fifteen. "One call and I'll be right here."

Rosemary and Nathan Grober also expressed concern about Bryant's slow progress—two Ds and two Cs in his first year, and five Ds and an F in his sophomore year. As the Grobers were leaving a conference with Bryant's teachers, Nathan lingered for a private word with a teacher who had taught Bryant's older brother and sister. "I missed out on the other two," the teacher recalled him saying. "I wasn't involved enough. But I'm not going to miss out on this one. You have to promise to let me know what's going on with Bryant."

Apparently, there was a lot going on that never appeared on the students' written record. The older they got, the more callous and domineering the Jocks became toward other kids, especially the girls. They were often singled out for the Jocks' displays of domination and sexual exhibitionism. Sometimes the girls were willing participants; often they were not.

Young men and women in the Class of '89 recalled times when the Jocks pinned girls against a locker or a wall in the school hallway and ground their bodies against them, simulating copulation. One young woman remembered how she hated passing the student lockers at the end of the school day. "Frequently, there'd be one of the Jocks on the floor with a girl under him and they're *writhing,*" she said. "Sometimes a teacher who'd be finishing her work for the day would come out of her room and see the squirming mass. She might say a cursory, 'Stop, don't do that.' But she would not say, 'Stop, I am going to escort you to the principal's office, where you'll get 8,000 days' CD [central detention].'"

Teachers (most of them female) said they saw certain Jocks rough up some of the young women students. They roughed them up emotionally and physically. As far as the teachers knew, the girls' bones weren't broken—but you'd have to be blind not to notice how the guys used their brawn to intimidate young women who tried to stand up to them.

In rare instances, the aggression toward young women in the Class of '89 was noted in the school record. On February 24, 1988, a school official wrote that Kevin Scherzer "slapped" a female student "across the mouth (after they were exchanging conversation) and then profusely apologized." The school official observed that "he [Kevin] appears to be 'out of control' emotionally."

One female student, Diane Carter, who was slender and quiet and looked much younger than her age, had been pushed around by the Jocks since middle school. What irritated them was that she tried to ignore them. One of Diane's friends recalled, "Poor Diane. They just kept going after her. They'd knock her down, shove her against the lockers, steal her stuff, punch her in the shoulder when she asked for it back. There were times I'd actually see her stagger when they hit her. And it was all because she dared to complain when they did something."

In late November of her junior year, Diane said, she was sitting in her seat, waiting for her English class to begin. One of the Jocks who had been harassing her all that fall came up to her, Diane recalled, and said, "Come on, Diane. Suck it, blow it, put it in your mouth." Then, she said later, "He took my hand and he put it on his crotch."

Diane said her first reaction was to laugh. "I laughed because I was shocked, and because I'd seen him do it to other girls. After he got a laugh, he left me alone, walked over to another girl sitting at her desk, pulled his pants down, and exposed himself. I saw it."

Later that day, as she thought about what had happened, her reaction changed. "I still felt degraded," she said, "but I also felt in a way accepted because I saw them doing these things to the popular girls. It was like I was part of the crowd."

The Jocks also went after young women who were supposed to be their friends. Irene, one of their classmates, had gone out with Kyle for a couple of months and had had many talks with Kevin. She knew them. So why, she asked herself, did they treat her as they did?

It was hot the day Irene left her accounting class and she was wearing a T-shirt and boxer shorts. Suddenly she felt her arms being squeezed. "My books got thrown out of my hand," she said. "Kyle and Kevin, they're grabbing me by my hands and legs and dragging me through the hallway of the school. They are carrying me off the ground, and they're trying to pull off my pants. I'm screaming my head off, and this teacher sticks her head out the door and she doesn't say anything because none of the teachers wanted to deal with them. So nobody did anything until they finally let me go."

Irene held her thumb and index finger about an inch apart. "Make you feel this big," she said. "Not one of them had any feelings for girls. They'd tear your feelings right out of you."

Much later, when Glen Ridge detective Byron was investigating the Leslie Faber case, she spoke to some of the young women in the Class of '89. "These girls were saying they were actually afraid to be going to school," Byron said. "I thought I knew this town, but these girls were giving me an education."

19

The academic reviews in their report cards were insignificant to the Jocks, except as they influenced their athletic standing. The reviews they kept—the reviews that they and their parents and the cheerleaders pasted into scrapbooks—were those that appeared in the hometown paper. Since middle school, they had been getting lots of ink in the local paper, which was filled with praise for their athletic endeavors.

But their performances on the football field weren't living up to their advance billing. When they were all juniors, except for sophomore Chris Archer, and playing varsity football, the team had one victory and eight defeats. However, some of the "lesser" teams did pretty well. The wrestling team had a good season with a 10–3 record, and Chris showed he was the equal of his older teammates by making it into the finals of the Christmas tournament. Other Jocks who wrestled were Paul Archer and Bryant Grober.

The baseball team, which included juniors Kyle Scherzer and Phil Grant, had a terrific season, winning the state baseball championship in its division. Kyle, playing center field, stood out in the semifinal game with a two-run homer and three runs batted in.

Perhaps the real stars of the junior year were the basketball players. The team, with a 24–3 record, won its first state championship in thirty years. But the Jocks hardly paid attention; they and their closest buddies weren't on the team.

In the Jocks' junior and senior years, the football team won only three games out of eighteen played. Their blustering and bullying were at their nastiest just as their football performance hit bottom. Yet, whether it was wrestling, football, or baseball, coaches and teammates praised all the Jocks, including even the lowly sophomore, Chris Archer.

"There was something about Chris," a football teammate said. "He was just fearless. He was the hardest hitter on the football team. And the way he carried himself on the mat. He'd break the ultimate rules of wrestling—never step left because you'll get caught—and he'd step left and get away with it. In football, the coach says, Don't shoot the gap. And he'd shoot the gap, and every time he'd get away with it. Like he was blessed."

Chris always played hard—even in practice. "Before the game the coach wanted to psych you up so you had to butt heads, right under the goalposts with everybody watching," said another football player. "I'm butting heads with Chris, he's a year younger than me. He's doing it to the point I'm saying to myself, I wish this kid would stop. Like I'm light-headed. But Chris says, 'That's the way you gotta play—with reckless abandon.'"

The coaches joined the players in their appreciation of Chris. "A tough kid" was the way one coach described him. "Won't back down."

Other members of the Jock crowd also drew the admiration of their coaches, too. What other kids in the school might call bullying, the coaches praised as "toughness."

"Kevin was a tough kid," an assistant Glen Ridge football coach said. "He was a charismatic young man." Classmates might find his antics offensive, but the coach thought Kevin was amusing. "He was a funny kid, fun to be around. He'd make light of a situation to break the tension.

"Kyle was an average football player," this coach went on. "He could be very quiet, but the kids rallied around him. He had those qualities to spark you, to get you going.

"Peter Quigley was one of the finest young men I've ever met in any of my coaching environments. He's a kid who played injured. He's a hard-nosed kid, an outstanding football player. He had a little more on the ball than the others, a little more mature. The kids rallied around him, too.

"Richie, a tough-nut kid. He was better than anything else we had. And he did an admirable job. Above-average toughness. Some kids can't play through pain. Richie could. He had a severely sprained ankle and I'd tell him to go to the doctor, but he'd play every week."

The boys' cliquishness also pleased this coach. "They were all friends," he said. "This whole group of kids were very tight-knit. They were dedicated. We started with twenty-eight kids on the football team and ended with twenty-eight kids on the team. As dismal as the seasons we had, everyone stuck it out. It's very easy to quit a loser. And these kids didn't. That shows a lot of character."

Character. This assistant coach prided himself on being a good judge of character. "A coach would know a kid better than a classroom teacher," he said. When the coach was asked about reports of drinking, parties, and girls being abused by some of his players, he said, "Never heard a word about it. I never socialized with these kids. I just spent 3 to 5:30 every day coaching. The locker room is on the first floor, the coach's office is upstairs. So you don't hear a lot of locker room whatever. All I know is that every kid who played did what he was supposed to—on the field."

The school administration apparently did not have a different opinion. Kevin and Kyle were selected as co-captains of the football team, and Kyle was chosen as captain of the baseball team for the upcoming senior year. No administrator openly questioned whether they had the ethics, the values, the *character* to hold leadership positions as captains, a position that ostensibly required traits of character, such as integrity and compassion.

Reports of questionable behavior had no effect on the way the school managed its athletic program. Nobody attempted radical surgery, such as setting new academic and behavioral standards for eligibility. Why did grades count, but not conduct? Why was drinking the only behavioral grounds for suspension or expulsion from a team? Why wasn't an athlete thrown off a team if he drove a teacher crazy, exposed himself to female students, or wrecked a classmate's house?

One thing the pressure to achieve academic eligibility demonstrated: The guys would bust their gut to raise their grades if they were threatened with losing something that really mattered to them—playing sports. If the same threat of being barred from team sports was contingent on their behavior, would they have found a way to restrain themselves? Wouldn't they have had a better chance of building real character if their eligibility had, at least in part, been determined by real qualities of leadership—principle and integrity?

Suppose eligibility was partially conditioned on behavior: What could happen? The guys might try to straighten themselves out. Or, if they didn't, student athletes who demonstrated traits of leadership and decency would take their place on the team. In either event, school policy would serve an important purpose: to educate students about the importance of character.

But this is speculation. In 1987 and 1988, Glen Ridge educators seemed to agree with the way the school handled athletics. Teachers might cavil at the boys' classroom behavior, but the Jocks rarely heard anybody with power warn them that their behavior could affect their participation in sports.

The coach's words: hard-nosed, tough, streetwise. Institutionally, the school seemed to agree with him that these were virtues the Jocks possessed in abundance. But individually, privately, there were faculty members who worried.

Two new administrators had arrived at the high school in the last two years, and the Jocks' antics made them edgy. In the sophomore year, Michael Buonomo replaced James Buckley as principal of Glen Ridge High School. Buonomo had taught social studies in the more urban East Orange High School and had been assistant principal in suburban Hanover Park. A year later, when the students in the Class of '89 were juniors, the vice-principal, John Curtis, was replaced by Benedict Tantillo, an energetic, straightforward man who had gained his schooling experience in Bernards High School in the wealthy New Jersey town of Bernardsville.

At Bernards, Tantillo had taught Family Life and had been head football and baseball coach. He joined a long line of Glen Ridge High School administrators who had a background in school sports. Tantillo, replacing both the vice-principal and the athletic director, would now be responsible for both directing athletics and maintaining discipline at Glen Ridge High. In appearance, he didn't look much older than some of the Jocks he was supervising.

Both Buonomo and Tantillo recalled that their mandate was to tighten discipline in the school. The new administrators identified as their two biggest behavior problems alcohol consumption by teenagers and misbehavior by athletes. "Glen Ridge had a reputation that the athletes were getting away with everything they wanted to," Tantillo said. "I tried to change that."

Over the bitter opposition of some parents and teenagers, the administrators stiffened the rules on drinking by athletes, and on truancy and lateness. "The year before I got here there were eight suspensions from school," Tantillo said. "The next year there were sixty-eight and the year after that seventy-two. I'm not one to take much crap from any of the kids."

But Buonomo and Tantillo didn't question the basic culture of school life in Glen Ridge. They didn't deemphasize the hoopla surrounding school sports. And they didn't make good behavior a prerequisite for participation in athletics. Essentially, they played the cards they were dealt; they didn't ask for a new hand.

20

The teenage Jocks were starting to build a record of petty legal offenses to match their academic rap sheet. And that gave the cops in Glen Ridge a little taste of what the guys were like.

On April 22, 1986, Kyle, Kevin, and a third boy were stopped by police after a BB pellet was fired through a picture window of a house. The pellet narrowly missed an occupant. The complainant preferred to seek restitution for the damage rather than file a juvenile complaint against the twins, adhering to the traditional Glen Ridge practice of resolving conflicts with teenagers by an exchange of money.

When the Jocks got into trouble with the law, it usually concerned buying or drinking booze. Bryant Grober, for example, was arrested on November 20, 1987, for "concealing two six-packs of beer in a vehicle in which he was riding," according to law enforcement reports. The Glen Ridge Police Department subsequently decided not to file a juvenile complaint against him.

Other Jocks were not treated quite as leniently.

On Friday, June 5, 1987, three Glen Ridge athletes were lined up at the checkout counter of the Grand Union supermarket in Bloomfield. They were Peter Quigley, John Maher, and Paul Archer, according to police records. John Maher later recalled, "We went to the store that day and hoped we could get some beer. We thought we could get away with it." It was a fairly substantial purchase—eight six packs of Miller's, plus several twelve-ounce bottles.

Their hopes had been raised because the cashier on duty at 4:15 this Friday afternoon in June was Richie Corcoran. Being a conscientious worker, Corcoran went to check the correct price and then rang up the purchase. He made only one mistake. The sale of beer to his underage buddies was being closely watched by the store's plainclothes security guard, an off-duty Glen Ridge cop. "Richie was the cashier, but there was a cop on the other side of the register waiting for us," Maher said.

Within a few minutes, the three boys were taken to the police station, where they were charged with attempting to buy alcohol when they were minors. Richie Corcoran was not charged. Although he had rung up the purchase, he had not deposited the money for the beer in the cash register. He did, however, lose his job at Grand Union.

John Maher, one of the three kids at the checkout counter, was living in Bloomfield then, and he later said he was required to do some community service there. Since Paul Archer and Peter Quigley lived in Glen Ridge, the town's Juvenile Conference Committee, which determined the penalties meted out to teenagers charged with relatively minor offenses, required them to do twenty hours of service to the community.

That is how Sheila Byron, the town's juvenile officer, got to know Paul Archer and Peter Quigley. The two students were on spring break from school, and Byron arranged for them to work off nine hours of their community service by doing clerical tasks for the town administrator. They were asked to stuff envelopes with forms notifying town residents that they had to register their dogs. "That afternoon the administrator came back to me and practically threatened me that I was going to be fired if I ever gave him any kids again," Byron said.

The official had been riffling through the envelopes when he saw some handwriting on the forms. His curiosity aroused, he opened one envelope, then another. What he saw made his eyeballs pop. Across the top of the forms had been scrawled: "—— sucks dick."

After some intense investigation, Byron found out that the guys thought the notices on which they wrote the obscene messages were being sent to the family of a kid who played on the football team. They got the right last name but the wrong family.

That ended the town's experiment of assigning juvenile offenders to work in township offices. After the parents of Quigley and Archer were informed of their sons' unusual approach to doing penance, Byron made sure the young men finished their community service under her direct supervision.

Quigley, Corcoran, and Archer included the Grand Union bust in their collection of noteworthy high school memories in their senior yearbook.

21

Sometimes school officials missed or ignored the Jocks' antics in the school, but they had to be aware of one major test of character that the Jocks failed—the 1987 Candy Cane Ball.

For the girls of Glen Ridge High, the Candy Cane Ball was the closest thing to a certified, legit date. It was the one social occasion where these young women had a chance to exercise control. The girls had control because they paid for this date.

Candy Cane was a Sadie Hawkins type of affair. Held every December in Glen Ridge, it was considered a more elaborate and more elegant event than the spring prom. The girls took their dates out to dinner at a restaurant or at their homes before the festivities began. The dance itself was held in the dignified sixty-two-year-old Georgian-style home of the Glen Ridge Women's Club.

Many of the young women hired limousines to pick up the boys and take them to dinner, to the dance, and then to whatever after-dance festivities had been planned by different groups of kids. These festivities could be expensive. Some girls used their parents' credit cards to reserve suites of hotel rooms for all-night parties where drinks other than ginger ale were consumed.

When the students in the Class of '89 were juniors, the Candy Cane Ball was held on Saturday night, December 19, 1987. By 8 P.M. the driveway was jammed with limousines. The uniformed drivers hustled out of the front seat to open the doors. The guys stepped out wearing dinner jackets and tuxedos, complete with cummerbunds and black (or red) tie. Some of the girls' dresses were pretty spectacular: black velvet, floor-length, spaghetti-strap silk, strapless plaid taffeta, feathered boas.

They entered into a main room where red-velvet curtains were drawn back from the windows and the walls were painted in Williamsburg blue-and-white trim. Wreaths had been hung on the walls, and strips of red velvet and sprigs of holly and mistletoe adorned the columns. A balcony with a gold rail overlooked the room, and chairs and tables had been pushed aside to create a dance floor. At one end of the room was a raised stage for the deejay.

As the couples walked into the room, they were greeted by a receiving line that included the principal, the vice-principal, members of the women's club, and the faculty adviser to the high school's "girls' club." These were the chaperones. That night there were ten of them, and one was Detective Sheila Byron, who was moonlighting to make a little extra money.

It was unclear who was in charge. Students, teachers, and administrators were present; that made it sound like a school function. But it was held off school grounds at the club; that suggested it was more of a women's club affair. Proper supervision had become more important each year as more kids seemed to show up drunk or stoned.

There was no question who did the work: the young women who belonged to the girls' club and the older women who belonged to the women's club. The boys were there for the good time.

When the music started, the girls left purses and coats on the chairs along the wall or on the floor nearby. They were sure their belongings would be safe. They were among lifelong friends, neighbors.

Midway through the dance, one of the junior young women noticed something strange. She was standing on the balcony, and looking down at the dance floor she could see a wall-to-wall crush of kids dancing—except for a few. These few were Jocks and they were all clustered at the end of the room where the girls had left their handbags. "Why aren't these guys dancing?" she asked her date, who also was a member of the Jock group. He whispered, "Let's forget about it. We're supposed to have a good time tonight."

At approximately 10 o'clock, one girl approached Principal Michael Buonomo. At roughly the same time, another girl approached Vice-Principal Ben Tantillo. A third was engaged in animated conversation with Officer Byron. All three girls appeared flustered. All three were saying much the same thing: *My money's gone from my purse.*

Not only money was taken. Someone's gold cigarette case, borrowed from her mom, was gone. A girl had taken her pearl earrings off and put them in her purse. They were gone. A few guys had left their wallets in their jackets, which they had hung over chairs. The wallets were gone. But most of the victims were girls. The girls would be carrying more cash because they had to pay the limousine drivers at the end of the evening. If they went someplace else when the dance was over, the girls were supposed to pick up the tab.

Buonomo, Tantillo, Byron, and officers of the women's club asked kids if they had noticed anybody hanging around in the dimly lighted area where the purses were left. It didn't take long for suspicions to center on the boys who often seemed to be involved in the troubles at Glen Ridge High.

The school officials and Byron told some of the parents who were chaperoning, but the parents and officials of the women's club urged them not to spoil the evening, to let confrontation and punishment wait until Monday morning; making an arrest in the elegant quarters of the women's club was so unseemly. Byron fairly erupted. "Do it now," she shouted. "I will not do this on Monday because on Monday we'll never get the kid to admit he did it. We're going to get the money back now."

The students' answers to the school officials' questions narrowed the search to a few boys—principally Kevin Scherzer and John Maher, who was a football player and dedicated Jockette. When the kids crowded into the parlor room, Buonomo asked, "Well, who did it?" All eyes turned to Kevin.

Watching the students shuffling their feet, Byron couldn't contain herself. She walked toward Kevin, telling the other adults, "I'm going over to him, and I'm going through his pockets and I'm going to get the money back."

Byron said later, "So that's what I did. I probably did it in a way that was not as legal as it should have been, but at that point I said, I don't care, because I'm not dealing with this on Monday when the money's gone."

Sheila found some cash on Kevin. He admitted that he had stolen it, she said. It looked as if other students may have also been involved in the thefts, but no one would admit it. School officials decided to impose punishment later.

Kevin and his friend John Maher were asked to reimburse the victims. Three years later, the recollections of the school administrators and Byron varied as to exactly how much money was stolen. Buonomo put the total at $450. Ben Tantillo estimated that it was $480 to $490. Sheila Byron, who was leading the investigation that night at the women's club, said $600 was stolen.

Whatever the amount, John Maher contended that he became the fall guy, taking the rap for something Kevin did. "I had to get money from my parents to pay for that. And I was no part of it," he said later. But not all the money was returned on Saturday night. There was a discrepancy between what was reported stolen and what Byron found in Kevin's pockets. In the following days other Jocks reported that they had found money, which they returned to Buonomo. "Obviously, there were other people involved," Byron said, "because Kevin didn't have all the money with him. But he wasn't giving anybody up."

Angie Termini, the Little Mother who had cooked all those night meals for Kevin and the other Jocks, was especially angry. "Was I upset?" Angie said. "Yeah, I was upset. I was upset first of all when my money got stolen and then when I found out it was Kevin, I was just like, 'How could he do that? How could he do that to me, to *Angie.*'"

When Angie had confronted him in the crowd of dancers, he had turned his back and gone on dancing. "What could I do?" she asked. "I mean, what's a girl going to say?"

Buonomo said he met with Jack Scherzer the Monday following the dance, and Kevin's father told him he would reimburse any money that wasn't turned in to the principal. Although Buonomo later said he was "horrified" by the thefts that occurred during the school dance, he did not press criminal charges against Kevin Scherzer. The women's club, where the thefts took place, did not press charges. No student whose money was stolen pressed charges. Byron was frustrated. If someone had stepped forward to press charges, the amount of money stolen would have been sufficient to return a felony indictment against an adult suspect. A minor like Kevin, if found guilty, could have wound up spending time in a juvenile institution.

On December 21, 1987, two days after the Candy Cane Ball, Vice-Principal Ben Tantillo wrote to Jack and Geraldine Scherzer: "This is to inform you that your son Kevin is suspended from Glen Ridge High School for two days—December 22 and 23. The reason for this suspension is that Kevin was stealing at a school function—the Candy Cane Ball—on December 19, 1987. Kevin is to return to school on Monday, January 4." John Maher said he was also suspended for two days.

Kevin's two-day suspension immediately preceded the Christmas holiday. Instead of having a six-day break from school, as all the other students did, he had an eight-day break. Tantillo also required Kevin to visit the school psychologist.

Three years later, Tantillo himself questioned whether the penalty fit the offense. "What would I do now, three years later?" he asked. "Have him arrested. Have him arrested on the spot." Of course, by then Kevin was awaiting trial on a charge of rape.

Theoretically, Tantillo could have suspended Kevin for all or part of the next football season. But he didn't. "If it was during that [1987] football season, I would have done something," Tantillo said. "But the season was over. In education you kinda take the point where everyone makes mistakes and how long do they pay for it?"

In Sheila Byron's view there was inconsistency in how students were

penalized. A few years later a young woman got drunk in public, Byron recalled, and the school removed her from her position as president of two
prestigious organizations related to her interest in law. "So she lost everything. She was extremely intelligent and she screwed up once. Whereas
these boys—a two-day slap on the wrist. Doesn't seem fair, does it?"

22

The Jocks dreamed of achieving all-American status in sports. But in
the sexual sphere their performance didn't measure up to the all-American
model of dating and courtship. In fact, as the guys advanced through adolescence, their relationships with girls deviated further from that romantic
ideal. Their approach to sexual relations became darker, more twisted.

Much of the sexual behavior by the leaders of the clique revolved
around acts that put them at an emotional distance from individual girls,
acts that reflected an unrestrained enthusiasm for pornography and
voyeurism. These acts allowed them to escape judgment on their sexual
performance and also allowed them to avoid ongoing relationships of any
intimacy with girls. And they wanted to avoid such intimacy because only
one relationship meant anything to them: the close tie with their male
buddies.

By junior year, Jock parties followed a common pattern: The boys
would all go into one room, pop a videocassette into the VCR, and watch a
porn flick for an hour or so. It was a strict rule: Porn was for men only.
Meanwhile, in another room, the young women at the party would chat or
dance with each other, waiting for the boys to appear.

For the Jocks, watching pornography wasn't regarded as a secret,
shameful vice. In the 1980s an X-rated video could be viewed by any
teenager who had the money to rent or buy one. You might not want to let
your parents know what you were watching, but there was no reason to
hide it from your friends—or from a girl you were trying to hit on.

Rumors circulated around the school. On nonpractice afternoons, some
of the Jocks would gather at a house where the parents were gone and
watch porn, as they all masturbated together. In fact, Leslie Faber later told
of stopping one day at the Archer house, when Mr. and Mrs. Archer were
absent, and being invited in by a group of Jocks to watch a pornographic
movie. A story—possibly apocryphal—that made the rounds of the parking lot and cafeteria was that at one of these afternoon viewings, the Jocks

stood in a circle watching a porn movie, each jerking off onto a slice of bread. Then, the story went, they brought the bread into school and tried to get some unsuspecting kid to eat it, as they once talked Leslie Faber into eating dog shit.

A couple of years later, some teachers speculated that the Jocks' interest in pornography may have encouraged their aggressiveness toward women. A Glen Ridge teacher who was close to some of the Jocks spent many hours thinking about how pornography might have nurtured feelings of violent misogyny. "Pornography is almost always about power and aggression," he said. "Women are always having vibrators and other inanimate objects thrust into their bodies. You get kids who can take this stuff, giggle, shrug it off, and say it's make-believe. But these Jocks were aggressive to begin with. Football and wrestling are aggressive. They were put on this earth to stomp anyone who was weaker than them. Girls were an easier target because they weren't as strong as them, and they had been taught not to complain about how they were treated. Girls were their toys. But suppose a girl decided not to act like a toy. What do they do then? Slap her around? Whack her on the head? What? That's what happens in the porn flicks. Maybe, just maybe, they thought what they saw in the porn videos was real life. Or, at least it was *their* real life."

The Jocks found pornography exciting because it could be shared by the entire viewing audience. It wasn't an individual experience. It was group onanism. But the ultimate team experience for the Glen Ridge Jocks went beyond pornography. It was a practice they called "voyeuring."

Here's how it worked: At a party one Jock would convince a girl to accompany him upstairs to the bedroom for a sexual encounter. But first he would tip off his buddies. They would go up and hide in a closet, under the bed, or behind a door. They also liked to hide out in shower stalls or outside windows where they could watch girls using the bathroom. It was all planned ahead of time. One football player recalled the Jocks in the locker room urging other teammates to "go voyeuring with us this weekend." The player said, "They'd ask as many people over as they could get."

After the encounter with Leslie Faber, friends of the Jocks would say, Why would they go out and rape a retarded young woman when a number of girls in the school were eager to offer them sex? But the defenders of the Jocks missed the point. Voyeurism was a way for these guys to create their own porn movie. Four guys crawling along a narrow ledge under the roof of a house so they could watch a couple having sex in a bedroom or a girl urinating. A Jock cracking up when three of his friends burst out of a closet after a Jockette has given him oral sex. The closet Jocks yelling: "Can we have one, too? That was great, do it to us, too." Getting a fifteen-year-old girl to go to a garage and perform oral sex on four boys. Telling two girls that they could gain membership in the clique if they had sex with each other while the guys watched. And jerked off.

One Jock recalled the enthusiasm for voyeurism: "There were different Jocks voyeuring each weekend. You wouldn't voyeur on the same girl each week. If a Jock liked a girl enough, he would make sure no one was watching during sex. But if it was a one-night stand, they probably wouldn't even care if the girl got mad and left during the screwing." Girls knew all about the practice, he said. "It was always a big thing for girls to say, You sure no one's in the closet, I'm scared someone's watching."

This Jock excused his own participation in voyeuring. "So many kids have done it. It's the people who keep doing it and doing it and doing it— that's when it gets real bad." What, exactly, happened? "It's always the same," he said. "You go in and watch and usually someone sneezes and the girl finds out and the guy who's making it with her says, 'I didn't even know they were there.' And he's lying his ass off. More than half the times the guy would know the others were watching them. Sometimes the guy would even say, 'We're going up to that room there.' And then three or four guys would go up and hide. And then the guy'd ask the girl to go up. Kevin, all of them would do it. It was the favorite thing to do."

Some girls were horrified when they realized that they had been suckered. But others seemed to understand the risk of "being voyeured" and accepted it. Irene, who came to some of these parties with Kyle, said, "If I'd been the girl upstairs and these guys were spying on me, I'd have said: You scumbag. But a lot of these girls would giggle or make a face and say, like the guys were just being a little naughty: Oh, you're a bad boy! Which just encouraged them."

The second act was usually performed on Monday mornings in school. It was there in Mary Romeo's phys ed class that the guys would recount in precise detail what they did and what they had seen over the weekend. "I'd hear it every week," Romeo said. "They would make asides to each other, but loud enough so everybody could hear. 'Were you in the closet?' 'Were you hiding under the bed?' 'We were behind the bushes in the Glen, but she knew we were there all the time.' You hear the asides, but, as a teacher, what do you do?"

Voyeuring was such a popular sport in this crowd that some of the Jocks memorialized it in the 1989 yearbook as one of their favorite memories. It did not make the girls' yearbook listings.

Voyeurism provided the Jocks with a sense of power and control. As directors, they shaped and controlled the action. The one problem with all the exhibitionism and voyeurism was the absence of a visual record. That's what the guys thought was so great about snapshots or, still better, porn films. For example, one of the Jocks had a friend photograph him and a girl having sex on the golf course. Then, according to students, the Jock slipped the snapshot into a display case in the high school, where every kid on the way to class could get a good view. But that was a one-time novelty and only a still photograph at that. How about actually making a movie? Not so easy. The girls who spent time with the guys could be compliant, but there were limits. Starring in a porn film probably exceeded the limit.

Then along came Arlene Meadows,* and the boys started to wonder whether they could actually get it together and make their own porn movie.

Arlene was a short, slender, attractive young woman. Her parents worked in white-collar jobs. Arlene did fairly well in school. When she was fifteen, she remembered, she was driven by one goal. "I always wanted to be the center of attention," she said. "I wanted everything to focus on me." Toward the end of her sophomore year in the Class of '89, Glen Ridge teachers began to notice a change in Arlene. "She came to school in X-rated clothes," one teacher said.

The change, Arlene said, took place after she had sex one day with several members of the wrestling team of a nearby high school. "I might have been a little drunk, but that's not why I did it," she said. "I was willing."

"It ruined my reputation in Glen Ridge," she remembered. "I had sex on a Friday night, and by Monday everybody in Glen Ridge knew." Later, when she was a senior, she would write in a friend's yearbook, "Me at ——'s party. That was the biggest mistake of my life."

What made this different and extra titillating to the Glen Ridge Jocks was the rumor that Arlene's sexual activity had been videotaped. Arlene denied it. "The room was absolutely pitch-dark. If someone had a video camera there," she said, "there would be no light, no way to see anything."

The story that circulated in Glen Ridge High was different. What the kids were saying and what eventually some teachers heard was that the episode took place during the state wrestling finals in Princeton. And everything that went on had been videotaped.

Once a rumor got started, it was hard to stop it. Arlene went out with a football player who was part of the Jock clique. Later, she occasionally went to parties with Kevin Scherzer.

The stories about "Arlene's sex movie," as it came to be called, were so widespread that they eventually reached her own mother, according to Arlene. "One day my mother came home crying. A boy she works with told her there was a videotape of me. I told her, Mom, it's not true, it's not true."

But Arlene also realized that the rumors of the sex videotape could inspire some of the Glen Ridge Jocks to make a movie of their own. "With them growing up, they had been watching pornos and reading things and voyeuring, and in their minds they had different fantasies—everybody has fantasies—and probably they could find a girl who was willing," Arlene said. "And they could act out all their fantasies with her. I hate to say it, if I was willing they would have done these things with me. But I would not be that stupid, especially not with them. They have the biggest mouths."

Arlene Meadows might deny forever that she had been filmed having sex. But the Jocks wouldn't take her denials seriously. They wanted to believe that she had been videotaped. And once they believed that, competition seized them. They needed to demonstrate that they could do what their wrestling rivals did—and do them one better. Their "movie" would be much more imaginative and creative than plain old oral sex. In Glen Ridge they could always find a vacant attic or basement. Male actors were no problem. Lots of kids could put their hands on a camcorder. They could find whatever props they needed. All they lacked was a leading lady.

23

In December 1987, when many of the students in the Class of '89 were excitedly selecting the tuxedos and gowns they would wear to the Candy Cane Ball, Leslie Faber was harshly reminded of how different and separate she was from other teenagers. Leslie was fifteen now, and for the past year and a half she had been attending Columbia High School in Maplewood. There she had been placed in a class for neurologically impaired students.

She had done fairly well in her studies at Columbia, compared to how other special ed students were doing, and she liked her teachers and classmates. Columbia appealed to her because she could attend classes and school activities with nondisabled handicapped students.

But socially she wasn't fitting in with mainstream students. Leslie's undisguised need to make friends, combined with her meager understanding of how to interact with other kids, made her behave inappropriately at times. In a high school full of adolescents pursuing their newfound interest in sex, Leslie became a natural target for teasing and mockery—and also for sexual banter that she couldn't fully comprehend.

As Ros Faber told Les's school counselors, her daughter had a tendency to "play the fool" when she was around other kids. She would act silly or do something outlandish to get a reaction from students. "She'd be the class clown," Ros would say later. "She didn't mind putting herself up to ridicule." And then Ros would add: "She does not know how to respond to sexually active boys."

The teachers at Columbia High School were learning how easily Leslie could be manipulated by other students. The incident that crystallized their concerns took place in December in the school cafeteria. During lunch hour Leslie would often wander over to the table occupied by the school's football players. "In Leslie's mind they were friends because they shared sports," a teacher said. One day teachers overheard the boys making sexually suggestive remarks and Leslie responding provocatively. The teachers often saw students flirting, but this exchange alarmed them because of the imbalance in understanding. The boys who spoke to Leslie knew what they were doing, but, in the view of one teacher, Leslie "didn't understand that her body was very private. If somebody she thought was a friend came up to her and touched her body, she thought it was a nice thing."

The teachers also noticed that one boy in her special ed class had made suggestive remarks and seemed to be taking an extraordinary interest in her. "We were concerned that this young man could do something to her," a teacher said.

Every three years, Leslie's intellectual and social development was reevaluated by Glen Ridge's Child Study Team. She had entered Columbia a year and a half before, functioning at a second-grade level, and she had not progressed. In December 1987 she was reevaluated, and her IQ was measured at 49.

Stanley Brod, a learning specialist on the Glen Ridge Child Study Team, compared the current findings with earlier assessments. He looked at the results of the personal interviews with Leslie, her impaired motor skills, her academic performance, her relationships with other students in school—what psychologists call an adaptive behavior scale—and her IQ.

"Lo and behold, there were some differences between the assessments at different ages, but we were getting the same IQ score as the person who did the assessment in the past—49," Brod remembered. "The exact same score. And my response was, 'She's MR—she's mentally retarded.'"

In her first assessment back in kindergarten and in subsequent examinations, Leslie met the three criteria for the classification of mental retardation listed by the *Diagnostic and Statistical Manual of Mental Disorders*, which is regarded as the definitive work in this field. These criteria are "(1) an I.Q. of 70 or below; (2) difficulty in meeting the standards expected for her age in areas such as daily living skills, personal independence, and self-sufficiency; (3) onset of these symptoms before the age of 18."

As Brod went back through all the assessments of Leslie, he realized that almost every aspect of her intellectual and social development conformed to the criteria for mental retardation and not the classification of "neurologically impaired."

Brod said later, "A student who's only neurologically impaired, you get a lot of variation in their abilities. That wasn't Leslie. A mentally retarded student will have a very flat intellectual profile, inability to think in abstract terms, not a lot of practical sense, an inability to improvise. And that basically described Leslie."

What is the significance of an IQ of less than 50? The significance is that Leslie Faber's IQ was in the bottom 1 percent of the population of the United States. Experts in mental retardation point out that 98 percent of the population falls between 70 and 120 IQ. Only 1 percent is above 120, and 1 percent is below 70.

Brod and his colleagues on the Child Study Team reclassified Leslie from "neurologically impaired" to "educable mentally retarded." Given the serious and permanent nature of her limitations, why did it take ten years for the school to make that determination? Brod posed that very question to his colleagues. A longtime member of the team told Brod straight out: "The study team that did the evaluations before was trying to spare the feelings of the parents."

Members of the Child Study Team called the Fabers in to tell them. Ros could barely hold back her tears. For the first time in Leslie's life, the word *retarded* was officially linked to her name—and it was devastating for both Leslie and her parents.

For fifteen years the Fabers had nurtured the hope that Leslie could overcome her disabilities. But the new evaluation suggested that her development would be limited and that she would require some form of supervision for the rest of her life. To spare her feelings, the Fabers tried to play down the findings to Leslie. They told her that the school people were just trying to find the best place for her to learn. They told Les that her teachers liked her and everybody thought she was nice.

They might have been able to persuade her that her new classification was merely a technical adjustment that wouldn't really affect her schooling and social relationships. But then the officials at Columbia High School informed the Fabers that she would have to be transferred to an all-day, self-contained class for retarded youngsters. No more mixing in social activities with "normal" students. No more gym classes and music classes with average kids. What was worse, Columbia did not have a self-contained class. Les would have to transfer to West Orange High School in another town, which did have a class for retarded students.

The decision to transfer Leslie once more was not based solely on her stunted intellectual development. School officials were worried about her well-being. "Once we thought she was retarded, we could not guarantee her safety," Leslie's guidance counselor said later. "For academic and personal reasons we insisted she leave the building."

The school psychologist who evaluated Leslie in December 1987 observed that she "exhibits poor social judgment when in an unstructured setting. She may be easily influenced by peers and may not be fully aware of the consequences of her behavior." The psychologist noted that "there is an immature or childlike quality to her perception of social protocol. Although she has an interest in establishing social relations with others, she appears to lack the social skills to do so."

The classification of Leslie as retarded saddened the Fabers. But the school officials used a phrase that frightened them. They told Ros and Charlie that they were concerned "about Leslie being raped." That was the first time anyone in authority had actually said: "We're concerned about her being a victim of a sexual attack." This so alarmed Ros that she began giving Les birth control pills.

It was a bleak Christmas season for Leslie Faber. The guidance counselor called Les into her office to discuss her transfer.

"Why? What did I do wrong?" Leslie asked.

"You didn't do anything wrong," the counselor said. "We just don't have the program here that will allow you to succeed in life."

"I don't want to go," Leslie said. "I love Columbia. I know it's my fault.

I shouldn't have talked to those boys. Can't we wait a while? Maybe I can do something to stay."

But the counselor explained that she would have to leave. Later the counselor would say, "I could never convince her it was not her fault." For a few weeks during January 1988, Leslie was taught at home while the paperwork was completed for her admission to West Orange High School. Again and again, she asked Ros, "Why are they doing this to me?" And then she would answer her own question: "Because of the cafeteria. That's why they're kicking me out."

She told her mother she didn't want to be in a class for retarded children. "I'm not retarded," she said. "You know I'm not retarded." To her mother she seemed inconsolable.

But once she started at West Orange, her optimism returned. "The kids're nice at school," she told Ros. "They all like me."

Although she felt bad about being placed in a program limited to retarded students, the program was more suited to her social skills, and sheltered her from the uncaring acts of unkind high school kids. Now her life was more structured. She awoke every day at 6:30, had juice and cereal, and left for high school in West Orange forty-five minutes later. Leslie rode to and from school in a car provided by the West Orange school district. She was transported in the car because Glen Ridge was off the route traveled by the bus that took disabled students.

Her school day began at 7:50 in the morning and ended at 2:10. She spent most of her time in the self-contained class of retarded youngsters, which studied math and English and basic science. The class operated a school store where students bought stationery and pens and candy. Leslie liked the store because it gave her a chance to talk to students who weren't retarded, but she always had difficulty figuring out the right change when a kid made a purchase. By 2:30 each day she was back home with her mother.

The problems that retarded children have in socializing with nonretarded youngsters are made more difficult when their peers become sexually active. The retarded youngsters are ill-equipped to explore the social nuances of sexual talk and behavior. They think they can compensate for their lack of understanding—although they rarely can—by following the prompting of peers. To get along, they think they have to go along. And it is this naiveté, fused with their hunger for acceptance, that can leave them open to sexual exploitation.

For the Fabers, isolating Leslie in a program for the retarded helped protect her, but only for the six hours of the school day. The rest of the time, they could only hope their child had enough judgment to stay out of trouble. No matter what precautions they took, parents could never be sure.

24

Something happened to Leslie Faber during her third year in high school that the Fabers knew nothing about. It was more than a year later that Leslie confided the story to Detective Sheila Byron. Once again Leslie had tried to be friendly, and once again events got beyond her control.

Leslie Faber always enjoyed belonging to organizations and institutions. The basketball team, the softball team, the church youth group, and the Girl Scouts—they all gave her a sense of significance. The uniforms she wore for the sports teams and the Girl Scouts conferred an official status, an attachment that the rest of her life sometimes seemed to lack.

On the day that Leslie told Detective Byron about, she was dressed in her Scout uniform and was selling cookies door-to-door to raise money for her organization, like any good sixteen-year-old Girl Scout.

She worked her way down Ridgewood Avenue, finally coming to a house she knew well. The home of Michaele and Douglas Archer.

She knocked a couple of times, the door opened, and standing there were her good friends Chris and Paul Archer. Wow! What luck! Who would have thought that in the middle of a weekday afternoon she would have stumbled into a party attended by some of the most popular guys in town? Looking past Chris and Paul, she could see Richie Corcoran, Kyle Scherzer, and others.

Chris invited her to join them, telling her that everything's cool, his parents aren't home. It seems she had interrupted a conversation about a movie some of the boys had seen recently—a porn flick about a girl who gets guys excited by putting all sorts of objects into her vagina.

It was Chris, Leslie said later, who remembered the hot dogs. A package of frozen hot dogs in the freezer section of the fridge. Leslie would tell the investigators: "Chris wanted me to put a hot dog up my vagina and I said 'no.'" But later in the investigation, she said: "Yes, they put the hot dog inside me."

When Richie Corcoran was interrogated by the police on June 29, 1989, he offered a different version: "About two years ago she went to the Archer house to sell Girl Scout cookies and she came in and we were eating hot dogs and she said that she wanted to have sex with us and she flashed her chest and she asked if she could insert a hot dog in her vagina."

Anything that happened was all Leslie's doing, Richie seemed to be saying. He did not explain how it would have occurred to this retarded young woman selling Girl Scout cookies to offer to insert a frozen hot dog into her vagina.

Richie didn't need to explain. No one found out about what happened until long afterward. It was one time when protective parents and sheltered school programs couldn't help Leslie. It was a moment parents of a retarded daughter dread: their child out there on her own, drowning in the rough seas of male adolescent sexuality. Their child—whose idea of a friend is someone who would play with her nicely—trying to be friends with a bunch of guys whose idea of play is pornography and voyeurism. It wasn't an even match.

25

Although Leslie was vulnerable to manipulation and abuse, it didn't mean that she was an uncomplicated person. She maneuvered between two worlds: the world of her parents and the kid world. In the kid world, you could talk about boys and sex. But you didn't bring it home. Home was reserved for nice, polite conversation.

When the weather was warm, Leslie spent many evenings at the nearby Linden Avenue School playground. On the evenings when Leslie breezed over to Linden Avenue, carrying her tennis racquet and basketball, she seemed to be relaxed and untroubled. But there was something about these excursions that bothered Charlie and Ros as Leslie turned fifteen and sixteen. A few nights she came home just a little later than she was supposed to. And there were times that a couple of boys whom her parents didn't recognize would trail Leslie to the house and sit out on the steps just a few minutes too long for a purely platonic conversation. When Charlie and Ros questioned her, she'd say she didn't know their names or much else about them.

Charlie would walk his dog over to Linden several times on a single night, just to check out the scene, to make sure nothing funny was happening to Leslie. He didn't see anything that made him suspicious, but he kept thinking that maybe there was a connection between the strange phone calls Les was getting and her regular visits to the Linden playground. The link was another kid who was a regular over at Linden. The younger Archer boy—Chris. That kid made him nervous.

When you thought about it later, it was clear there was something fishy about the calls. Always a male voice on the other end, asking to speak to Leslie. The voice Ros heard was high-pitched, squeaky. Other times it was deep. The voices Charlie heard were hoarse or muffled. The conversations were always terse: "Hello, I want to talk to Leslie."

"Who is calling?" one of Leslie's parents would ask.

Then Ros or Charlie would hear a name they didn't recognize.

One night Charlie asked Les, "Who *was* that on the phone?"

"Oh, that's Chris Archer." Blithely tossing it off.

"Has he been calling, using different names and strange accents?"

"Oh, yeah, he does that all the time."

"Why is he doing that?" Charlie wanted to know.

"I don't know. He's just being dumb."

Leslie would later tell a friend (in a tape-recorded conversation): "Chris Archer used to call me up and say he was jerking off on the phone." But at the time Charlie Faber didn't know that and he wondered: Why would a friend of Leslie's call and hide his identity behind fake names and fake voices? Was it just some silly gag, as Leslie tried to pass it off? Or was something else going on?

The next time Chris called, Charlie told Les to take the call, but he stayed on the line.

What Charlie heard:

"Les, meet me over at Freeman Gardens,[1] by the shed."

"No, I can't."

"Aw, c'mon. Sure you can."

"No, I can't do it. I can't meet you."

Suddenly Charlie broke in. "I find it very strange, Chris, that you call our house, that you ask to speak to Leslie, and you don't use your own name. Do you feel that for some reason you can't use your name?"

---

1. Freeman Gardens, botanical gardens reserved for use by Glen Ridge residents, are located near the south end of town. A wooden shed used for storing gardening implements is located within the garden. A similar shed adjoins the Linden Avenue Elementary School.

"It's nothing, nothing much," Chris mumbled before hanging up.

Leslie was furious at her dad. How dare he listen in on her personal conversation? How dare he break in and scold one of her very best friends? Didn't he want her to have any friends?

Charlie's first instinct was to call the Archers and find out what the hell was going on. But as he tried to mollify Leslie, he changed his mind. It was not because he thought Chris's parents would be unresponsive. Charlie knew Doug Archer from meetings of the Civic Conference Committee. Ros knew Michaele from the planning for the Glen Ridge celebration of the United States bicentennial. Later on, Ros would say, "I identified with them very closely. They would be the types of people I would gravitate towards. Doug has a winning personality, gives you a grin and a smile, gives you a firm handshake, and I respond to that. He's a go-getter and he is involved."

The Fabers were sure that if Chris needed speaking to, Doug and Michaele would tend to that. But maybe it was enough that Charlie had spoken to Chris in his sternest voice. Chris was old enough, Charlie thought, that he'd get the message. Besides, Leslie had firmly rejected Chris's invitation to join him in the gardens. Charlie told himself, If she rejected him this time, she'll reject him if he asks again.

Charlie and Ros, positive-thinking folks, resolute optimists, placed great faith in Doug and Michaele Archer, in all the good people of Glen Ridge. The Fabers had close friends whose two sons were Leslie's age. These people had firmly instructed their boys that they were never to touch Leslie. The Archers knew about Leslie's handicap. Surely, they had told the same thing to their boys.

Later on, Charlie would berate himself, *Why didn't I call Doug? I can kick myself for not calling. Maybe I could have stopped everything right there.*

But there was so much that Charlie and Ros didn't know. They didn't know that Chris had made many phone calls to Leslie, asking her to meet him in the gardens and at the shed outside Linden Avenue School. They didn't know that there had been times when Leslie had met Chris. They didn't know, as Leslie would later tell the police, that Chris had "fooled around" with her in the shed.

Without knowing, Charlie could not bring himself to make that upsetting call to the Archers or to report Chris to the police. The Fabers wanted to believe they were part of a community that truly loved kids, as Doug Archer once put it. The disillusionment, the jaundice that might have enabled the Fabers to detect the forewarnings of danger to their child, hadn't set in yet. They weren't ready to draw the connection from the dog excrement fed to a five-year-old girl to the taunting at a tennis lesson to the crudely disguised voice cajoling Leslie on the telephone.

The most heartless acts of the Jocks hadn't been publicized in Glen Ridge. They hadn't been arrested for wrecking houses and trashing the country club. They hadn't been thrown out of school for exposing themselves or for assaulting girls. The boys' behavior had always been the town's best-kept secret. None of the institutions in Glen Ridge had said anything to alert the parents of vulnerable children. Their transgressions remained hidden from folks like the Fabers.

Wait, the Fabers told each other. Wait until they all grow out of adolescence. Leslie will go her way; they'll go theirs. A lot could happen before then, but the Fabers, decent and trusting people, didn't have the cynicism or the facts to foresee it.

26

The memory of Homecoming weekend during their freshman year held out great promise for the members of the sports clique. In that first autumn of their high school years, they seemed predestined to win the fame and adulation traditionally accorded to the sports stars of Glen Ridge.

But in their senior year they had to confront the reality that the seductive hype of Homecoming would never be fulfilled. On the athletic field, they didn't come close to equaling the triumphs of the town's glory years. The football team's record of two wins and seven losses was nothing to celebrate. But the school and the families of the players went ahead and celebrated anyway.

With two of her sons as co-captains of the football team, Geraldine Scherzer took the lead, organizing parties, special breakfasts, and other festivities for the players. Mrs. Scherzer coordinated the annual football team banquet. It would be held on Sunday evening, December 4, at the Fairmont Restaurant in Little Falls. Players, relatives, cheerleaders, and fans were welcome. The cost was seventeen dollars a person.

In the school Homecoming week was the main event of the year, if you didn't count graduation. It was something of a personal triumph for

Bryant Grober. He dominated the senior breakfast by eating the most pancakes—cooked by the female Jockettes—and then threw up. Grober managed to pull himself together. The next night at the Homecoming dance, he was crowned king.

At the beginning of the year, Principal Buonomo had already announced the most elaborate plans in years for the Homecoming football game. An entire week in October, which he called "Spirit Week," would be devoted to events leading up to Homecoming. One day would be pajama day, and all students would be required to show up in pj's and slippers. On the night before Homecoming, a huge bonfire would be held; it would be followed by the Homecoming dance. The class that showed the most spirit during this week would be awarded fifty dollars.

The vice-principal also announced the formation of a Booster club to promote and support the school's teams. The club's fifty-dollar membership fee would be used to buy new basketball and wrestling scoreboards and an ice machine for the school's fieldhouse. High school sports were bigger than ever in Glen Ridge. High school sports for boys, anyway.

The studious kids were looking ahead to life after high school. The Jocks, whose academic records didn't qualify them for admission to the top-drawer colleges their classmates planned to attend, were clinging to the vestiges of their declining authority. But their poor grades for the first time put them in a subordinate position to the more diligent students.

Bryant Grober was on his way to graduating with a four-year grade point average of 1.96 out of a possible 4, and he was ranked 78th in a class of 101 seniors. He applied to Widener College in Delaware, East Stroudsberg University in Pennsylvania, Rutgers, and the University of Bridgeport and Brandywine College in Maryland. He ultimately went on to attend Widener.

Paul Archer, who had a 2.91 GPA and ranked 33rd in the class, was applying to Wake Forest University, the University of Delaware, and the University of Colorado at Boulder among other schools. He was eventually admitted to Syracuse University.

Kevin stood 88th in the class; his 1.75 GPA was the minimum requirement for athletic eligibility. He had a short list of colleges: Jersey State, Fairleigh Dickinson University in New Jersey, and William Paterson College. He got into Morris County College, a two-year New Jersey state school. Kyle, with a GPA of 1.82, was ranked 85th in the class. He applied to Upsala College, William Paterson, and Ramapo College. Next fall he would join his brother at Morris County.

Richie Corcoran, 94th in the class, with a GPA of 1.41, would get a construction job after graduating.

Peter Quigley, who ranked 82nd in the class and had a GPA of 1.88, had only one college in mind: Marshall University in West Virginia. This university, which put a lot of emphasis on its football team, reportedly provided Quigley with a partial athletic scholarship.

Chris Archer, who was a junior and still had a year to go before graduating, made the high honor roll in the 1988–89 academic year. At the end of the year, he ranked 12th in his class of 93 students and had a grade point average of 3.65. After he graduated in June 1990, he went on to attend Boston College.

Most of the young women who were friends with the Jocks were accepted at good colleges: Tara went to Purdue, Angie was admitted to Boston University, another young woman went to Pepperdine in Los Angeles, and several were admitted to Rutgers. After so many years of living in the constant shadow of the boys, the girls in their crowd were finally moving on to something better. At last the girls were being rewarded on the basis of merit—for their brains, not for the ability to throw a block. This was one prize that was beyond the reach of their guys.

But until the school year ended, the guys could still pretend that they were in command. The yearbook helped them sustain that illusion. The class had selected Tara Timpanaro as editor of *Glenalog '89*—a good fit, since her father, Vincent, was faculty adviser. His printing firm also published the yearbook. And it was apparent that Tara still thought the Jock clique controlled the school.

Of course, all the seniors were pictured in headshots in the yearbook. Those who participated in clubs, teams, and other extracurricular activities were also shown in group photographs. But the yearbook included many informal photos of students in "candid" poses. The student most often pictured in the candid photographs was Tara Timpanaro. She appeared in seventeen of them. The student who finished second to Tara in the most-photographed category was Richie Corcoran with twelve. Third place went to Bryant Grober, who had ten candid photos. In one picture Grober is surrounded by three young women. Bryant and his female admirers appeared to be a major photographic theme of the yearbook. On a different page he was pictured with five girls, on another with two girls.

Tara did not overlook her boyfriend, Peter Quigley. He got nine candid shots, including four with Tara. Kyle and Kevin each got eight candids. One shot of them together, arms around each other's shoulders, took up an entire page. Paul Archer appeared in only five photos, but, perhaps to compensate for this slight, he was shown with his arms around two girls.

By contrast, Michael Connolly, the valedictorian, soon to attend Princeton, voted the most intelligent and most likely to succeed, got the absolute minimum—one photograph on the same page as his headshot.

In their photographs the Jocks were almost always shown frolicking with other Jocks. They were rarely shown in the company of teachers or non-Jocks. When girls were permitted to appear with them, the girls looked like star-struck acolytes.

The yearbook reserved twenty-three pages for athletes and athletics. All the other clubs, excluding the cheerleaders, got six pages. Four full pages were devoted solely to the cheerleader squads, composed of twenty-five members. But there were only two pages of photos for the prize-winning high school band, with forty-four members. All non-sports organizations got only a quarter of a page each and no candid shots. No one could say that the yearbook lacked a point of view.

Leslie Faber appeared once in the yearbook, in a team photo. She was a microdot in Tara's tribute to the athletic giants of Glen Ridge High.

Must-read material in the yearbook was each senior's list of personal memories, which would be printed below each of their photographs. Some seniors in the class of '89 needed twenty or more lines to recapitulate all their experiences in a shorthand that was readily decipherable to most of the Jocks. This compilation of memories included some of their most excessive out-of-school behavior, particularly drinking, fighting, and sexual escapades. Of the students' memories, Tara said, "They're more like fun than they are like serious. I put things in, like little abbreviated things, that I wouldn't want my children to know."

Bryant Grober needed seventeen lines. He began, as all the seniors did, by listing his activities: football, wrestling, Key Club, Varsity Club, and Ski Club. Then he acknowledged his parents, "Mom and Dad ILY [I love you]." Next came some of his vivid adventures: "Train bombing. . . . Stole bus. . . . Arrest w/——, Copeman's brawl. . . . 7-11 brawls." The stolen bus was an apparent reference to the time a group of wrestlers got tired of waiting for their coach and drove off in the team bus without him. Tara Timpanaro, who was present for "Copeman's brawl," said it was a fight that started when the Jocks tried to crash a party held by an older boy, resulting in a wrestling match on the host's lawn. "Words were thrown and fists were thrown," Tara said. "It was probably like the biggest thing to all those kids because they were so much younger and they beat the shit out of these older guys."

The "7-11 brawls" were small-time scuffles, according to editor Timpanaro. "They go to the 7-11 and fight with the Guidos from Bloomfield— that's all it is. It's not like a brawl, like there were knives and guns. It's yelling, and that's it."

After that came Grober's more conventional activities: "Beach Boys Concert. . . . Hunter Mtn trip." Then he recalled events that stood out in the memories of many of the guys—the deck parties of Kyle and Kevin Scherzer. Grober listed the initials of his best friends (all guys): RC, PQ, PA, KS2 (Kyle and Kevin). He ended his memories with this quote: "If you're walking on thin ice, you might as well dance."

Paul Archer listed the same activities as Bryant had, mentioned his good times with good friends, and recalled parties he had attended, including the Scherzer deck party and Ryan's Wreck, the three-day house trashing in 1987. He remembered "Mr. G.R. nt.," referring to the male beauty contest held during the junior year. At that event Peter Quigley paraded across the school stage and dropped his shorts to moon the audience. (He was wearing a G-string under the shorts.) In Paul's memories the purchase and consumption of beer was a significant theme. There was "Gr Un=20 hrs," referring to the community service he performed after being arrested for trying to buy beer from Richie Corcoran at the Grand Union. (Paul did not mention the obscene messages on the dog licenses.) He recalled "runs . . . to No. Nwk"—to buy beer.

Paul left the word "Voyeurs" dangling, without elaboration, among his memories. Then four lines later, he recalled "Saranac"—the Christian camp he attended. He concluded with: "Mom & Dad Thanks." His end quote was: "Be at your best when your best is needed."

Kyle Scherzer's memories began with his sports activities: "Football, 9-12 Capt. . . . Baseball 9-12 Capt. . . . Varsity Club 10,11,12." Then he listed his fifteen good friends, which included one female, Angie. He didn't forget his "deck party" that was busted by the police. Then came his sexual activities. He used the vernacular "Hoover" to reportedly describe oral sex with a woman, and gave the initials of a male friend who was present. This reference was followed by a parenthetical expression of appreciation to the woman: "(thanx ——)."

Kyle also recalled his "7-11 Brawls" and then went on to describe various events soaked in beer: "Finals at Glen. . . . Eagle Rock (keg). . . . Funnels. . . . Piels (quantity not quality)." Then he returned to sex: "My Voyeur w/——." He included the initials of two guys, including "CA." He, like the other Jocks, did not omit his memorable brawls: "F-ball brawl. . . . Copeman's Brawl." On to other leisure activities: playing Nintendo, chewing tobacco with Richie Corcoran and Bryant Grober, ski trips, Cartaret Park days. He ended his memories: "Mom & Dad Thanks!"

Kyle's signature quote was: "You can't put a price tag on fun!"

After describing his athletic interests, Kevin Scherzer recalled his friendship with "THE BREW CREW" and then gave the initials of the familiar assortment of wrestlers, football players, and baseball players. Kevin went one better than his brother in the oral sex and voyeurism category. He included three references in his memories. The first was "voy-R w/[initials of three Jocks omitted] and the Seal." Some of Kevin's friends said the woman was called the "Seal" because they thought she performed like a trained seal.

Later in his memories Kevin included "Hoover." And then he brought up voyeurism again: "Voy-R down by the river." In addition to oral sex and voyeurism, the usual brawls, drinking parties, and deck parties were mentioned. He recalled a "PIG-nic." Some of his friends said he may have been referring to parties where the girls had to call themselves "pigs" to gain admission. Kevin ended by mentioning "Mom, Dad, Eric, Paul & Kyle . . . and all other memories I forgot!"

Kevin ended his memories with the quote: "Knowledge is good."

Richie Corcoran was a prolix writer. He needed twenty-two lines to recount his experiences. He began with his three years playing football and two years wrestling. He listed the members of the Jock clique as his good friends. He talked about his shore weekends with Paul and Chris Archer and other guys, remembered when Peter Quigley backed into a car, and recalled "Ryan's Wreck," noting parenthetically "Bud King." Apparently, not all Jocks drank the same brand of beer.

There were recollections of various brawls—"Brawl at McLaughlins. . . . 7-11 Brawls. . . . Copeman's Brawl"—and the Grand Union bust. Richie recalled the time Mrs. Scherzer spotted him trying to buy beer: "Mrs. Scherzer snags me $ Buds."

Like Kyle, Richie expressed his appreciation for oral sex: "Hoover w/ —— (Thanx ——)." He ended his memories by thanking his parents. His signature quote: "Is that the light I see at the end of the tunnel, or is it just another train coming?"

Although Tara recalled that in her senior year her romance with Peter

Quigley ran into rocky stretches, Peter began his yearbook memories with: "Tara ILU [I Love You]." His best buddies included Paul and Chris Archer, Richie Corcoran, Kyle and Kevin, and Bryant Grober. He recalled how one of the Jocks slugged a girl when she annoyed him at a dance.

Among his memories were the Grand Union bust, Ryan's Wreck, and beer parties with his friends ("Funls/w fellas"; "Mlr Drft Wkend"). Peter remembered his fishing, skiing, and camping trips and his shore weekends. He also recalled mooning the students at the high school beauty contest, the "Lawn Drive Brawl," and, in the next sentence, his stay at the Christian camp. His memories concluded with the quote "Failure comes after you stop trying."

One leading member of the gang did not have his memories in the yearbook. Chris Archer was still a junior in the 1988–89 school year. His memories would appear in the 1990 yearbook, and he would present them in much more circumspect language. In 1990 the school administration informed the students that their submissions to the yearbook would be carefully reviewed and that they should not include references to sexual experiences—even in code.

But that was in the future. When the Jocks of 1989 submitted their memories to Tara Timpanaro, they were in the full flush of senioritis. They could have hardly anticipated that in the coming summer and fall their recollections would be scrutinized, word by word, by the prosecutors of Essex County, New Jersey. Among other matters, the prosecutors would be interested in who hung out together in this crowd; the guys' sexual experiences would also be of interest. *Glenalog '89* proved to be a real page-turner.

The selection of good friends for inclusion in the yearbook was interesting for another reason. When the guys listed their buddies, the name of a girl was rarely included. The Little Mothers might cook their meals. Jockettes might do their homework and compose their athletic appeals letters. But, except perhaps for the individual girl who was a guy's immediate romantic interest, the girls weren't important enough to warrant a mention as friends in the yearbook. The Jockettes, by contrast, almost all mentioned "our guys" or "the guys" in their memories and sometimes cited them by name.

Later, high school officials would argue that the out-of-school experiences listed in the Jocks' yearbook memories should not have—and did not—affect their eligibility. Ben Tantillo, the vice-principal, said, "All that stuff that's in the yearbook is innuendo. That's all their own personal life that happens outside of school." The only outside-of-school behavior that could disqualify them was drinking; everything else the school considered irrelevant.

27

As graduation approached, Phil Grant was looking forward to life after Glen Ridge. The wildness of the Jocks made him nervous, and he was getting tired of the pressure to go along with every stunt they could dream up. One kid who really made him edgy was Chris Archer.

Chris was welcome at many senior events, accompanying his popular brother to parties and dances. By the spring of 1989, Chris had emerged as one of the most charismatic leaders of the Jocks and certainly the top dog among the junior athletes.

Friends of the Archer family thought the parents were doing a good job of raising Paul and Chris. "The boys were in church every Sunday," said one mother whose son was Chris's teammate. "Michaele had this little book where she wrote down everything the boys spent every week. And when she thought they weren't behaving right, she'd ground them. She had a great belief in the power of religion. That's why she thought sending them to a Christian camp would be good for them." Another of the Archers' friends recalled that Doug and Michaele believed in "talking out problems with their boys. But when the talking was over, the boys went out and did what they wanted to."

Chris was originally accepted into the Jock crowd because of his older brother Paul. Paul was one of the preppiest and most reserved guys in the Jock clique (if you didn't count Phil Grant). If he wasn't as outgoing as some of his teammates, he didn't have any trouble attracting friends, especially girlfriends. He had wavy blond hair, soft brown eyes, and thick eyelashes—the kind of looks you can find in a J. Crew catalogue or in a guide to Phillips Exeter Academy.

Paul was classically handsome. Chris was reasonably good-looking. People might describe Chris's appearance as "arresting." He, like his brother, was of medium height and stocky. But whereas Paul had regular, symmetrical features, Chris had angular cheekbones, straight light-brown hair, and piercing pale-blue eyes. Perhaps it was the cheekbones or the slight slant of his eyes, but his face had almost an oriental cast. It led his friends to call him "Gookie." But it was the eyes, the freezing intensity, that could stop you dead. His eyes could read your soul.

Where Paul took life in an easy lope, Chris galloped. He was everywhere at once, never backing down from a dare, always coming up with a fresh idea to turn a dull, boring outing into an electric adventure. Phil Grant thought, "When you're with Chris, there's always a surprise; you never know what's coming next."

This made some of his friends twitchy. "If I got into a car when he was driving, I would feel real uncomfortable," Phil Grant said. "Not that he'd drive too fast, but maybe he'd drive up somebody's driveway and do something crazy—or drive across a lawn for kicks. I remember going to McDonald's late at night after a party, and there'd be thirty kids and Chris in the middle of them, and I wanted to get the fuck out of there because I knew these guys were going to get in trouble. I can just picture somebody pushing Chris into somebody else and that starting a fight. Chris and all of them were always looking for somebody to be pissed at them."

During Chris's high school years, the hottest white rap-rock group in the country was the Beastie Boys. Their album *License to Kill* topped the charts. One of the most popular songs in the album was "Paul Revere." Critics described their songs as "nasty, loud, and lewd." Chris Archer seemed to love them. On the way to parties, one of his teammates recalled, Chris would pound the dashboard of the car and chant lines from "Paul Revere" about being hunted by the sheriff. Why was the sheriff after him? Because he "did it" to the sheriff's daughter "with a wiffleball bat."

"He'd sing it over and over again," Chris's teammate said. "He'd sing it and laugh—like it was the funniest thing."

Penetrating a girl with a bat. Big joke to Chris Archer. Big joke to many of his friends. But there were kids in Glen Ridge who were fed up with the Jocks' brand of humor. Phil Grant, for one, was anticipating the changes that would come after graduation. But, at the same time, Phil was still hanging on to the tail of the Jock comet. Sometimes he told his mom and his sister Sarah that the Jocks made him especially uncomfortable with the way they treated girls.

When Linda could, she tried to draw him out. The whole family went to see the movie *The Accused*, a dramatized account of a young woman who was raped in a New Bedford, Massachusetts, bar while a bunch of men stood by and cheered on the rapists. When they were discussing the movie afterward, Linda said, Phil had some difficulty understanding the concept of silent complicity: Why was it a crime to stand by and watch?

Linda started to explain the distinction between legal and moral guilt. "Legally, maybe the silent ones weren't guilty—." Before she could finish, Sarah broke in, "Don't you get it, Phil? It's not enough to stay silent. You have to do something to stop it. Or at least tell somebody who *will* stop it. That's everybody's responsibility." Phil nodded, as if he agreed.

Meanwhile, Phil was feeling a sense of foreboding when he got together with the guys. It was hard to pin down. "Somehow, somewhere, along the way," Phil said later, "all the years, I knew something could happen, something terrible, but I denied it to myself."

The seniors were looking forward to March. The regional wrestling finals started on the night of March 1. Chris Archer was scheduled to compete. On the morning of March 1, Phil Grant began to round up the guys on the baseball team for a practice session in the afternoon at Cartaret Park.

Early on the evening of March 1, Sam Wright,* a seventeen-year-old boy who was attending another high school during his junior year, was hanging out at the back of Glen Ridge High with a bunch of guys. Wright had played on the Glen Ridge football team and was friendly with many of the Jocks. Somebody mentioned a party that had been held that afternoon. Another kid said it had happened in the Scherzer basement. Both Scherzer twins had been in the basement. A lot of other high school Jocks had been there, and also this one retarded girl. What retarded girl? Sam asked. Oh, you know, Leslie Faber, he was told. Then the guys told him what happened at the "party."

Wright listened and went home for dinner. When he went to bed, he had trouble falling asleep. He often had trouble falling asleep. Sam was a special ed student, and he suffered from emotional problems. He took medication for his illness.

Like many of the kids who were on the margins in Glen Ridge, he idealized the police. Sam would talk to them every chance he got. He'd often sit on the steps of the municipal building hoping for a word with a cop. The cops considered him harmless, a lonely, unhappy youngster who wanted some attention from his heroes. He could get to be a nuisance, but usually they tolerated him.

That night at about 1:30 A.M., Sam got up, dressed, and walked down to the parking lot of a large liquor outlet called Brewer's World, located on the outskirts of Glen Ridge. He went there because he knew that it was the cop "hole." Cops on patrol often parked there, to shmooze, to grab a doughnut and a cup of coffee, or even to nod off for a few minutes.

Sam later recalled that he saw a couple of cops he knew parked in a police car. He tapped on the window. A cop rolled the window down. Wright said he told the cops, "You know about the gang rape today? In the Scherzer basement by Cartaret."

The cop smiled at him, Sam recalled, and said, "You always have a story, don't you? Get some sleep, son, it's late for you to be out. There's school tomorrow." Then the cop rolled up the window.

Sam went home disappointed. "I don't know why they didn't believe me," he would say later. "Every time I gave them information it was good information. It was good this time, too."

PART IV

Accusation and Denial

28

The topic of the day was yesterday. Everywhere he went in school on Thursday, March 2, 1989, Charlie Figueroa heard fragments of rumors about the Scherzers' basement yesterday afternoon. The words "blow job," "baseball bat," "broomstick," and "drumstick" became a kind of mantra in these conversations. The words were always clustered around the same name: Leslie Faber.

Many of his friends were asking the same question: Can we get Leslie to do it again? But it was mainly Kevin Scherzer who pushed the idea of staging a repeat performance, Charlie would say later, and capturing it on film. "Kevin . . . told me what happened and he said they were going to do it again at his house." Kevin wanted Charlie to film the next basement performance because he was the student manager of the school's audiovisual room and could borrow a video camera. Charlie said later that he told Kevin he wouldn't do it.

All through the day Charlie couldn't decide whether Kevin's stories were true. But Charlie started taking him more seriously when he hooked up with the Jocks clustered in the smoking patio at the end of the school day. They were all waiting to go to the same two places—the Scherzer house and the adjoining Cartaret playground.

One senior, football co-captain James Litvany, whom everybody called "Tucker," was providing a kind of shuttle service, according to Charlie. Figueroa and a bunch of other guys, including a couple of juniors, piled into Litvany's Buick LeSabre for the five-minute drive to Lorraine Street. Among the passengers was another football player, John Maher. He had been present when the cops busted the Jocks for trying to buy beer at the Grand Union in Bloomfield; he had been there for Ryan's Wreck; he had been tagged for the Candy Cane thefts in 1987, along with Kevin. John had been there for lots of important events in the last four years, but he had not been present in the basement on March 1.

Months later Litvany told investigators that during the car ride to the park the Jocks talked about getting a video camera to tape Leslie's sexual activity. Figueroa recalled that after depositing the guys Tucker said he would return to the school to pick up another carload of Jocks. In the park, as other Jocks waited, Kevin and Kyle went to their house and returned a few minutes later with a bat and a broomstick, Charlie said. Then they passed the two objects around to the boys who had gathered in the park. They mentioned that the day before, they had put a plastic bag over the head of the bat. Then someone said—Charlie wasn't sure whether they were talking about what happened on Wednesday or what might happen later that afternoon—"You don't have to be mean about it." The boy who said that ripped a splinter off the end of the bat, Charlie said.

Charlie's doubts dissolved. He no longer thought that Kevin had been boasting. What convinced him was the size of the bat. It wasn't a miniature bat, as some kids in school had said. "It was a full-size wooden bat," Charlie said. "It was, like, a Louisville Slugger, a regulation bat you used for baseball."

Charlie decided that people wouldn't say they had put a regulation-size bat into a girl if they hadn't. He looked around at the boys who were hanging out on the playing fields of Cartaret, his fellow Jocks. Peter Quigley, Bryant Grober, Chris Archer, Paul Archer, Kevin and Kyle Scherzer, Tucker Litvany, John Maher, and others—they were all there, he said later. And not one of them denied that a baseball bat and a broomstick had been used on Leslie Faber. Everybody treated the Scherzers' story seriously—so seriously, Charlie says, that he told his friends: "You shouldn't be messing with her because she's not in control of herself."

After a while Charlie got a lift home from Litvany. Charlie would say later that he never saw Leslie Faber at the park that Thursday afternoon.

But others did see her. Leslie came to Cartaret Park Thursday afternoon to play basketball, as she had the day before. Later Leslie told law enforcement officials that she was approached by members of the Jock group, as she had been on Wednesday. This time, however, it was not Chris Archer who invited her to a party in the basement. It was John Maher and Tucker Litvany, Leslie said. She knew that the two boys played sports, football probably. But she didn't know much else about them.

Leslie wasn't aware of any plans to videotape her. But she did know that she wasn't going to be tricked twice into going to the basement. Leslie said later that Litvany and Maher told her that "Paul [Archer] would be there and he'd go out with you," but she said she couldn't accompany them to the house because she was waiting for a friend.

All these Jocks who were staring at her in the park—many of them hadn't been in the basement yesterday. Leslie remembered just who had been there—and she knew that these kids had not been at the Scherzer house. Leslie also remembered very clearly what the boys had told her in the basement: "We're not going to tell anybody. This is our little secret." But the presence of all these new faces in the park proved that the Jocks hadn't kept their promise; what happened in the basement was no longer a secret, because the Jocks were telling all their friends.

If everybody was finding out, soon everybody was going to want her to repeat Wednesday's experience. She needed advice.

It made sense that Leslie would select Margaret Savage as her confidante. Savage was thirty years old, but she looked much younger. She was a tall, slender woman, strikingly attractive, with long fiery red hair. She was also athletic. Her job was to teach adaptive physical education to special ed students at West Orange High School. Leslie regarded her as a fellow athlete.

Savage had known Leslie for a year and a half. In the spring 1989 term at the school, Savage met with Les and other retarded youngsters every Friday morning at the swimming pool in the West Orange Young Men's Hebrew Association. On Friday, March 3, Les approached her teacher after the swimming lesson was over. She told her that she had gone to a party and "there were ten guys there."

"Well, how was the party?" Savage asked her.

"I don't want to talk about it," Leslie said and walked away.

Savage followed her. "Well, would you like to tell me tomorrow?" Leslie was planning to compete tomorrow, Saturday, in a Special Olympics swim competition at the Y pool. "Okay," she said.

The next day Les competed in the Special Olympics, and her freestyle crawl was strong enough to win her a medal. When Savage entered the locker room after the meet, Leslie at first seemed not to want to look at her. She stared down at the floor and spoke softly. "Remember the party that I told you about? Well, something happened at that party," Leslie said. "We were in someone's basement and the boys asked me to suck their dicks."

Savage didn't say anything. She waited for Leslie to continue. And waited.

"It really hurt me," she said. "They stuck something really big up my butt and it really hurt." Savage's mouth was paper-dry. She didn't dare breathe. "It hurt," Leslie said. "It did hurt."

"What did they stick up you?" Savage whispered.

Leslie wrinkled her forehead. She cupped her chin in her hands. "I forget what they call it."

"And then?" Savage asked.

"They also asked how many fingers that I could put up myself. I told them I didn't do that. That kept saying, 'Yes you do. Yes you do. We know you do these things. Show us how you do it.'"

Leslie said the boys made her promise to keep what happened in the basement secret. "They said, 'If you tell, you'll have to leave West Orange like you left the other school.'" She turned her head away from Savage and murmured, "I like West Orange. I don't want to leave."

The coach read the expression on her face as one of confusion, puzzlement. "I want them to be my friends," the teenager said. "But I don't want—I don't want this to happen again. So how can I say 'no' if they try it again?"

How do you say "no"? Savage thought back to her own life, back to what she had been taught in graduate school when she was getting her master's degree in counseling psychology. "First of all," she told Leslie, "it's your body. You have the right to say 'no,' and no one has the right to touch you if you don't want them to. The second thing is: Once you say 'no,' you leave; you get to a safe place. And the next thing is to tell someone you can trust."

Leslie took the words in, but it was difficult for Savage to know whether she really understood. Leslie seemed torn. If she said "no," the Jocks wouldn't be her friends anymore and she would get in trouble. If she acquiesced, the scene in the basement could be reenacted again and again.

Before they left the locker room, Leslie pleaded with Savage not to tell her classroom teacher about the party in the basement. Savage told her that she wouldn't tell her classroom teacher, but that she had to talk to someone who was expert in dealing with this kind of problem, like the social worker from the West Orange school district. Leslie said that was okay.

But before she boarded the bus, Savage repeated to Leslie's classroom teacher what the youngster had told her. Savage also asked the teacher to inform the school social worker first thing Monday morning.

Savage sat a couple of seats in front of Leslie on the school bus. As it pulled away from the Y building, Leslie got up and made her way down the aisle. When she reached Savage's seat, she leaned over and whispered, "The thing they put up—I remember, it's called a drumstick. The guys found it in the field in the park."

Savage had advised her to confide in someone she trusted. Perhaps the person she trusted most was Jennifer Lipinski, her best buddy, her closest friend. On Sunday, March 5, Leslie visited Jennifer at her house in Bloomfield. "I'm sooo excited, I had to show you this," Les told her. Then she held up the medal she had won at the swimming meet the day before. Jennifer thought Les was acting strangely today. She was pleased about the medal, but then she would look away, as if she had something else on her mind. "The way she was acting, I knew something was wrong," Jennifer said later.

Slowly, piece by piece, Leslie told her best friend about her experience in the Scherzer basement. She told Jennifer that a "little bat was used and Vaseline was used and they stuck it up me." Lipinski would recall later that Leslie told her, "I was forced into doing it."

Now Leslie had told two people. But she still hadn't said anything to the two people who cared most about her—her parents.

Monday, March 6, 1989. Leslie's classroom teacher spoke to the West Orange school social worker about what Margaret Savage had told him. The social worker, Gregory Clarke, decided he had to confirm what he had been told by talking to the source—Savage. And he did so. After talking to Savage, Clarke summoned Leslie to his office. Clarke later said: "She avoided my questions initially, but finally stated that she had been involved with some boys in a park on Wednesday, March first, in the afternoon, and that one of them had put a drumstick in her panties. She refused to give me any further information and asked to leave."

Then, Clarke said, he called Elizabeth Portuese, the Glen Ridge school social worker, and described to her what he had learned. He also informed his boss, the West Orange High School principal. By Monday, then, four members of the West Orange school staff—the social worker, Leslie's classroom teacher, her swimming coach, and the principal—knew the general outlines of what Leslie had experienced on March 1. But it was the fifth person, Portuese, who would have the most direct responsibility for taking further action, because Leslie was officially enrolled as a student in the Glen Ridge school system, although she was attending the special education class in West Orange.

On Monday afternoon Clarke phoned Charlie Faber at his office and recounted what Leslie had told Margaret Savage at the swimming meet. Faber said he and his wife would talk to Leslie that night and call Clarke back the next day.

As he drove home from work Monday night, Charlie Faber's head was swimming. His daughter at a party with a group of boys who wanted her to have oral sex with them? Boys inserting a "drumstick" into her rectum? Incredible. Unbelievable. Charlie did remember that last week Leslie was acting strangely, coming in late for dinner, moaning in her sleep, avoiding looking at him and Ros when they asked her if anything was wrong. But there had been no hint of something so bizarre.

That evening Ros and Charlie told Leslie that they had got a call from the social worker. Les had supposedly told her swimming coach about a party where something had happened.

"That's not true," Leslie said. "I never said that. No, no, no—there wasn't any party. I don't know where that story could come from. It's ridiculous. I didn't do anything."

"Well, Leslie, why would they call us for no reason at all?" Ros persisted. "Would they make it up?"

Charlie, exasperated, trying to keep his temper in check, finally asked, "Well, what did happen, Leslie?"

"I was in the park last week and there was a boy there."

"You don't have to tell us exactly who it was," her dad said. "But did something happen? What did he do to you?"

"He put his hand down my pants. He put his hand in my panties." She would give them that much and no more.

The call from the social worker. Leslie's response. The two accounts didn't agree. As Leslie's parents discussed what they had heard, they were inclined to favor their daughter's version. In the past few months different students would get up in front of Leslie's class in school and tell stories about their lives. When Leslie told them about her classmates' stories, the Fabers dismissed them as the outlandish boasting of teenagers, a classroom version of Can You Top This? Maybe, Charlie thought, Leslie was trying to one-up her classmates when she had been talking to Margaret Savage. Ros thought, This is something that couldn't possibly happen here in Glen Ridge; if Leslie is telling us it didn't, it makes sense to believe her.

Why didn't Leslie tell her parents what she had told Margaret Savage and Jennifer Lipinski? She had her reasons. Some had to do with her particular circumstances as a retarded adolescent in her family and the community of Glen Ridge. Others were more generic, common to many victims of sexual assault.

From the start, Leslie was adamant that the young men in the basement were her friends and that she didn't want to get them into trouble. She surely suspected that telling her parents the full story of what happened would have serious repercussions for the Jocks.

Then there was the forbidden subject of sex. She opened up to Savage and Lipinski, whom she regarded more as peers and friends. But she knew that her parents were socially conservative and proper. She shared with many other teenagers the certain belief that her parents would never understand if she talked to them about her sexual life. Motherhood, to her, was proximate to sainthood, and you didn't whisper dirty words to saints. Leslie's sanctification of The Mother was so absolute that she would never speak candidly to a therapist or counselor if she found out that she was a mother.

It was hard enough to discuss private matters with her parents. How about opening up your life to strangers? Leslie knew that if she told her parents, they might bring in the police or other school officials. Leslie would be required to discuss her personal life with them. She remembered when she was sexually molested six years before how embarrassing it was to describe the incident to the investigating Glen Ridge police officer. She had blamed her parents then for making her tell about this terrible experience to a strange man. She didn't want to go through *that* again.

She also had to consider the effect on her social life, which was already severely limited. Because she was retarded, Leslie may have been more fearful of being ostracized than other teenage girls would be. But it was really only a matter of degree. Many nonretarded young women in Glen Ridge also silently endured sexual misconduct and harassment by the Jocks because they were afraid they would be shunned by their most popular schoolmates, who idolized the athletes.

It just wasn't cool for female students to tell anyone in authority that Kevin was exposing himself or that Kyle was out "voyeuring." Besides, it was always your word—in Leslie's case, the word of a "retarded" young woman—against the word of the Jocks and their fans. Who would believe you?

Leslie's response to her parents, her denial that anything had happened to her, was no different from that of thousands of other women who have been sexually assaulted. One national study concluded that 85 percent of rapes are never reported to the police. Other national surveys found that more than 70 percent of rape victims expressed concern that their families might find out they had been victimized, and 65 percent feared that they might be blamed for being raped.

By remaining silent when she was questioned by her parents, Leslie placed herself right in the mainstream of rape victims.

Leslie hadn't even told the whole story and she was already feeling the first sting of betrayal. Her swimming coach had promised her that she wouldn't tell her classroom teacher—and the first thing she did was tell him. Already, the West Orange principal, the swimming coach, the teacher, the Glen Ridge social worker, and her parents knew something. Who was next? The kids in her class? All the kids in Glen Ridge?

That week, when Les met Margaret Savage at the Y for swimming practice, she was very angry at her for telling. But Leslie couldn't stay mad at someone she liked for very long, Savage said. "The next week she gave me a big hug, and said I did the right thing."

At home Leslie stuck to her story: one boy briefly fondled her in the park. The two social workers, Portuese from Glen Ridge and Clarke from West Orange, called the Fabers on Wednesday and Thursday, March 8 and 9. The Fabers would later recall that the social workers urged them to take Leslie to a doctor for a physical examination and told them that they should consider reporting the "incident" to the police. Charlie Faber, according to Clarke, asked for a few days to think over what to do.

Reflecting back on these first conversations with the social workers, the Fabers would recall that they appeared "concerned that we hadn't jumped on it and done anything about it." The Fabers believed that Portuese defined her responsibility as reporting to the parents what Leslie had told her swimming coach. Then it was up to the Fabers to check with their daughter. When Leslie denied the main elements of her revelations to Savage, the Fabers believed her. Ros thought that Leslie's supposed comments about attending a party with a group of boys might have been an attempt to exaggerate her popularity.

Although the Fabers were reluctant to make this an official police matter, they thought it was probably a good idea to check with Leslie's gynecologist. On March 14, two full weeks after her experience in the Scherzer basement, Leslie visited her doctor. The physician found no sign of injury or trauma in her pelvis area. This appeared to bolster what Leslie had told her mom and dad—that it was all "no big deal."

But that wasn't what she was telling people her age. In the second week of March, the Glen Ridge girls' softball team held a practice. Leslie started talking to a sophomore at Glen Ridge High—Susan Clark.* A couple of other players stood near them.

"You know about the party I went to?" Leslie said.

Susan, hardly paying attention, said, "Oh, yeah, did you have a good time?"

"There were all guys there," Leslie went on, in a monotone, "and they did things I didn't want them to."

Susan was more attentive. "What did they do to you, Les?"

Leslie didn't look at Susan. She didn't look at the other girls who had gathered around them. "They did things with a bat and a broom."

Susan tapped Leslie on the shoulder. "Look, Les, you've got to tell someone. It's important for you to tell."

"No, no, I can't tell," Leslie said. "I don't want people to know. I don't want to get the boys in trouble."

"Well, what did they do to you?" another player asked. "Leslie, what are you talking about?"

"They put the broom and the bat into me," Leslie said. "It was at the Scherzer party."

Now there were five or six girls standing in a circle around her. "You've got to go home and tell your parents," one girl said. "You've got to let them know so they can do something. It can happen again."

And Leslie answered, "I don't want them to not be my friends. I don't want them to not like me."

Susan fairly shouted, "Leslie, they don't like you anyway. Just tell someone. They're playing with your mind."

What Leslie had told them alarmed her teammates to the extent that they wouldn't let her walk home alone from the practice field. Just before they reached her house, the group stopped. "Now, Les, I want you to go inside and tell your parents what you just told us," Susan said in a stern voice. The other girls nodded in agreement. Leslie said she would do that.

She didn't.

If March was a tense and painful month for Leslie, the Jocks pretty much took it in stride. They behaved as they had during the last four years: They bragged about their sexual exploits, showed off for their fans in the student body, got busted by the cops for driving around with booze, and made life miserable for kids who tried to stand up to them.

Kevin was overheard bragging about "fucking Leslie" and "making a porno movie." Then, on March 3, two days after Les went to the basement with the Jocks, some of the athletes who were attending the wrestling finals in Kearney were picked up by police and charged with having alcohol in their car. Among those in the car were Phil Grant, Paul Archer, Richie Corcoran, and Stephen Grober. Stephen, Bryant's younger brother, was a member of the Glen Ridge wrestling team. He was fifteen years old and a sophomore.

The next night a gang of Jocks broke into a party to which they had not been invited and vandalized the house and uprooted a tree in the backyard. When the school yearbook came out later, the disrupted party was listed as one of the highlights of the senior year: "Attack of the killer Jocks."

On Wednesday, March 15, the Glen Ridge athletes paraded across the stage of the gym during the Winter Sports Assembly. The wrestlers, Bryant Grober, Paul Archer, and Chris Archer, drew the biggest cheers because they wore '70s-style clothes, plaid bell-bottom jeans and wide ties. There were so many awards, so many athletes to be honored, that the assembly had to be carried over to the next day. "I don't understand the school's priorities," one teacher said. "There's two hours for the athletic awards and fifteen minutes for the academic honors."

29

By mid-March a number of people reportedly had heard, directly or indirectly, that Leslie Faber had been at a party with neighborhood boys where objects had been put into her body. These included:

Ros and Charlie Faber
The West Orange swimming coach
The West Orange school social worker
The West Orange school principal
Leslie's classroom teacher
The Glen Ridge school social worker
Leslie's friend, Jennifer Lipinski
Susan Clark and several of her teammates on the softball team
Thirty or more athletes and their friends at Glen Ridge High School

The issue that would trouble educators, parents, and students in Glen Ridge for years to come was this: Why would it take more than three weeks before anyone reported Leslie's experience to the police?

The passage of time was important because it could make it harder to build a case against potential defendants. A lot could happen in three weeks, or even in a week, in a criminal case. Evidence could disappear: a baseball bat, a broomstick, a Vaseline-smeared plastic bag, semen stains, vaginal secretions. The cardinal rule of criminal investigations is: The sooner the better. The longer it takes to begin an investigation, the colder the trail gets.

A long delay also made it easier for possible suspects to get their stories together, to consult with lawyers, to develop alibis. This, apparently, was already taking place. Charlie Figueroa said Kevin told him: "The guys are going to get into trouble about the thing with Leslie. If anybody asks you about it, just deny it; don't give them any names."

A few days later, Figueroa said, Kevin phoned him to ask if the police had called him. Charlie said they had not, and Kevin responded, "Cheer up, you weren't there anyway. If the police ask me, I'm going to say I was lifting and when I came home she was there with other people."

Teachers and social workers and school administrators were expected to be concerned about the safety and welfare of their pupils. On March 4, when Leslie spoke to her swimming coach, Margaret Savage, she expressed anxiety. "I don't want this to happen again," Leslie told Savage. "So how can I say 'no' if they try it again?"

If any of the school personnel had felt the slightest twinge of alarm, they had several alternatives open to them. They could have picked up the phone and dialed 911—the police—and reported what Leslie said. Or they could have dialed (609) 292-0617, the phone number of New Jersey's Division of Youth and Family Services (DYFS). The state agency was responsible for investigating reports of abuse that occurred at home or in school by a "parent, guardian, or other person having custody and control" of a child under the age of eighteen.

Technically, school staff members were not required to report the alleged abuse of Leslie Faber, because it occurred outside of the school after school hours. And it was allegedly committed by a group of high school students, who were not Leslie's guardians or custodians. However, a DYFS official later observed, "Sure, technically, this isn't a DYFS case, but I'd fire one of our workers who took such a call and didn't say: 'You must report this to the police, and if you don't want to, I will.'"

But no one called the police or DYFS in that first three weeks. They all had reasons for their silence. The West Orange and Glen Ridge social workers, in particular, believed they had fulfilled their responsibilities by leaving the decision of how to proceed up to Leslie's parents.

Charlie and Ros Faber were concerned and loving parents, but they could not read her mind and discover what she had not told them. They were in no position to determine whether a crime had been committed.

Only one student crossed the boundaries and confided in a member of the Glen Ridge faculty. This student hadn't heard the story from Leslie. He had heard the story from Kevin and Kyle and other Jocks. Charlie Figueroa told what he had heard. He told his teacher.

Charlie was in study hall with his special ed class. The last class of the day had just ended, and Charlie was talking to a friend about the gossip swirling around Leslie and the Glen Ridge High School athletes.

At that moment Ariel Riviera, Charlie's special education teacher, heard only a few sentences of the boys' conversation, but what he heard provoked his curiosity.

Charlie's friend was repeating a part of an exchange between some of the boys in the basement and Leslie Faber. Riviera heard him say, "No, we want to keep doing it till you come."

Charlie added, "But she said, 'I already came.'"

Riviera asked them what they were talking about.

Charlie liked Riviera. He had a relaxed, casual manner with the special ed students. (Charlie was in the special ed class because he was dyslexic.) And he was Hispanic as Charlie's dad was. Charlie hesitated; then he took the plunge.

He told his teacher that he had heard about a "sexual gang-bang kind of situation," as Riviera later put it, involving a girl who played on the Glen Ridge basketball team but went to high school in West Orange.

What did Charlie mean when he said, "We want to keep doing it till you come"? Doing what? "Masturbating her with a baseball bat," Charlie said.

In twenty years of teaching, this had to be one of the strangest things Riviera had ever heard. "I couldn't understand how you could masturbate somebody with a baseball bat and that she would say, 'I already came.' It just sounded so bizarre," Riviera said later.

The teacher was wary of asking too much too soon. He didn't want Charlie clamming up. What he wanted to know was, Who was doing this? But that question would have to wait until the next school day.

The next time he saw Charlie, Riviera asked him the question. Charlie told him, "A bunch of the guys from the football team."

"Well, like who?"

"The co-captains of the team," Charlie said. "The twins."

Figueroa also said later that he told his teacher that the Jocks had planned to repeat what they had done to Leslie—and to videotape it. So Riviera knew one thing more than the other educators who had learned about March 1. He knew that Leslie could be a continuing target.

Charlie never felt that telling Riviera was an act of bravery. "People make me out as some kind of hero," Charlie said later, "but I'm not really. More or less Mr. Riviera overheard these things and I didn't come right out and tell him."

In fact, even while Charlie was providing some details, he was also pleading with Riviera to keep his name out of it. Charlie says Riviera agreed not to identify him as the source of his information. But if the police started investigating, that promise would be hard to keep.

As it turned out, Figueroa and Riviera would disagree on one important point. Figueroa insisted that he talked to the teacher on Friday, March 3, the day after he heard about Leslie's experience in the basement. At the very latest, he said, he spoke to Riviera the following Monday, March 6. Riviera said the conversation took place during the week of March 15.

Riviera didn't immediately report what Charlie had told him. Recalling his thinking at the time, Riviera said, "I couldn't imagine that thirteen guys in Glen Ridge would stand around and hold somebody down and force them. These kids were too—they were pussies, really." He said later that he also was deterred by the belief that Charlie often came to him with dramatic stories of misbehavior by kids. When Charlie told him about Leslie, Riviera said he couldn't make up his mind whether to believe him.

Besides, he didn't want to "snitch" on a student who trusted him. An added consideration was the teacher's overall assessment of the situation. "I didn't think it was going to be a big deal," he said. "I figured it was going to be some girl got caught in a compromising situation. You hear that shit all the time."

The result was that Riviera kept quiet, as did all the other school people who had heard about it, as did the dozens of students in the school who were hearing more and more about the "rape" of Leslie Faber.

March 8. A week after it happened. Silence.

March 15. Two weeks after it happened. Silence.

March 22. Three weeks after it happened. At 1 P.M. that Wednesday afternoon the silence was finally broken. Shattered.

The meeting of the Glen Ridge Child Study Team took place on Wednesday, March 22. A half-dozen or more members of the team attended, including a social worker, several special education teachers, a guidance counselor, a school psychologist, and a specialist on children with learning disabilities.

Several members of the team were talking about drinking by Glen

Ridge teenagers. "Yeah," said Al Riviera, "some kids talk about it in class like it's nothing." Others began trading stories about parties they had heard about. Riviera interrupted, "Charlie Figueroa's telling me about this party. I don't know if it was a drinking party or what. But he's telling me about this outplacement girl. She's from West Orange."

Around the room people were nodding "yes." They knew who he was talking about, Riviera realized, although he didn't know the name of the young woman. "Charlie's saying she was in a sexual gang-bang kind of situation with a bunch of guys from the football team," he went on.

Suddenly, the room was filled with language not normally used by educators. "Those fucking bastards," Riviera remembered one of his colleagues shouting. Another team member bellowed, "Goddamn those motherfuckers."

Then everybody around the table was shouting the same thing: Well, who were the guys?

"The only guys I got are that two of them are co-captains of the football team," Riviera said.

And in one voice the other team members roared, "The Scherzers!"

Some of those present later recalled that Elizabeth Portuese, the Glen Ridge social worker, interjected, "Oh, this was with a bunch of football players? Yeah, I heard something about this. They were using a stick. It was with a drumstick."

"Well, I heard it was a baseball bat," Riviera said.

The room was deathly silent. "We have to deal with it," a team member said in a whisper that pierced the hush.

"Yes, we have to report it," said another. "We must call DYFS."

"Oh, you have to tell Buonomo [the high school principal] right away," a teacher told Riviera and Portuese. "You can't wait another minute."

The unanimity of the study team bestirred Portuese. She went downstairs to her principal and vice-principal and told them what she had learned two weeks before about Leslie and the Jocks.

The principal's first call was to Dr. Richard Greco. Greco, a psychologist, was supervisor of the Child Study Team and head of special services in the Glen Ridge school system. Greco later recalled that he and the principal had the same response: "That's the kind of thing you call the police about."

Portuese took Charlie Figueroa down to the principal's office. As Charlie walked in, he almost collided with two men. He recognized one of them right away: a tall, heavy figure that was familiar to many of the Jocks in town—Detective Lieutenant Richard Corcoran, the father of Richie Corcoran. The other police officer was Detective Robert Griffin, an experienced investigator.

When the two policemen started questioning him, Charlie told them about his first conversation with his special ed teacher. Then he told them about how a group of Jocks had gathered at Cartaret Park and were talking about what had happened to Leslie Faber. Detective Griffin would note in this official report that in the park "oral sex was mentioned."

As he responded to their questions, Charlie was conducting an internal debate with himself. Should he say the name? Should he tell Detective Richard Corcoran that his son Richie may have been one of the boys in the basement? The two detectives leaned back against the edge of the principal's desk. Charlie sat in a straight-backed wooden chair. This is how Charlie remembered the questioning:

"Mr. Corcoran didn't do that much delving into anything that first day. I told him about Bryant Grober getting a blow job and Chris Archer and a baseball bat and I think a drumstick. He's like, 'Okay, okay, just give me the names.' He was writing them down. He's like, 'Are you sure about this?'

"I say, 'Kevin, Kyle.' And he's like, 'Last names, I want last names.' I also said a couple of names of kids who were there [in the park] the second day. But I didn't say Richie. I wasn't positive he was there [in the basement]. I wasn't about to say Richie. I don't want to get on his bad side."

Charlie apparently did not volunteer and the cops did not ask him about any plans the Jocks might have discussed to videotape a repeat of the experience with Leslie. As Charlie recalled the questioning, the matter of a videotape was never brought up; and the official police report of the interview with Charlie that was written by Detective Griffin contains no mention of it. If the police had learned of the plans to videotape Leslie and the boys during the questioning on March 22, that might have imparted a sense of urgency to the investigation; they might have concluded that Leslie was still the target of a group of predatory boys and that to ensure her safety they had to move swiftly.

The detectives told Charlie he could go. At 4:40 Detective Griffin called the state Division of Youth and Family Services. An official with the state agency told the detective that according to their regulations this was not a DYFS case. The two detectives might not be delighted by the fact, but there was no escaping it. This was now a police matter.

30

The next morning Detective Griffin and Elizabeth Portuese went to see Margaret Savage, Leslie's swimming coach. Savage reconstructed the conversation she had had with Leslie on March 4 at the Special Olympics swimming meet. Nothing Griffin heard from Savage was significantly inconsistent with what he had learned at the Glen Ridge High School the previous afternoon.

Thomas Dugan, the police chief, told Griffin to report the investigation to the Essex County Prosecutor's Office in Newark. The Glen Ridge Police Department did not have the experience, resources, and expertise to carry on an extensive felony investigation without assistance from the county prosecutor.

Griffin called Robert Laurino, the head of the county prosecutor's Sexual Assault and Rape Analysis Unit (SARA), or, as it was commonly called, the Rape Squad. The squad often assisted in felony investigations in small towns where the police force was not equipped to investigate a complex case on its own. But most of the time this unit did not run the investigation; the local police department did.

Laurino listened to what the Glen Ridge police had learned; he offered no suggestions. "You're doing the right thing, Bob," Laurino told the detective. "Go in, do the investigation, and contact us when you need something."

Griffin said he would get back to him four days later, on March 27, the following Monday. Police work in Glen Ridge proceeded with deliberate speed. The detective had one more step to take before he could go forward with the investigation. He had to talk to the Fabers and arrange for Leslie to talk to the police.

Griffin described what he had learned to Rosalind. He and the social worker, Portuese, reconstructed their conversations with the swimming coach and Charlie Figueroa. Now that phrase—"something really big"— that Leslie had used in her talk with Savage took concrete form. Leslie had been talking about a baseball bat! Glen Ridge kids had put a baseball bat into Rosalind Faber's retarded daughter?

It seemed to Rosalind that all these appalling stories, all these different people—Charlie Figueroa, Al Riviera, Liz Portuese, Margaret Savage— were converging here in her living room. The entire nightmare tossed in her lap.

Griffin looked straight at her and asked *the* question: What are you going to do?

What could she do? "I don't know, I have to talk to my husband," she said. "But it's basically out of our hands. This sounds like it's going to be a case of the state or the county versus whoever. It's beyond us now."

Griffin asked Ros to call him after she had talked with her husband. Then he left.

Ros and Charlie braced themselves for what they dreaded most—prying the truth out of Leslie.

"We can't be emotional," Ros told Charles as she wiped tears from her eyes. "We have to stay calm."

"If she sees we're upset, she'll try to protect us," Charles said. "It'll be, 'I don't know and I can't remember.' She'll put up all her defenses."

Leslie sensed that her parents knew more. She scrunched up her face and covered her mouth with her hand when her mom said, "Well now, Les, tell us a little more about what happened with these boys."

"I don't remember. I told you. Nothing happened."

Leslie tried to find out exactly how much her parents knew, and to repeat what they said without adding anything new.

"Why would the policeman say you went to a house?" Charlie asked her.

"It was a party. They invited me to a party."

"Well, what happened at this party, Les?" Ros said.

"I made friends. I made five new friends."

Back and forth, testing, probing. Then Ros said. "Enough of this nonsense. This is serious. The police said this and you said that. Now tell us the whole story."

Leslie didn't tell the whole story. Not nearly. But enough to confirm the essence of what the Fabers had been hearing: a group of boys, a basement of a neighborhood house. But nothing about a baseball bat. Nothing about a broomstick.

Leslie prefaced each precious detail with a plea: "Please don't get the boys in trouble. These are my friends. Don't get them mad at me."

Ros didn't want Leslie to feel that she was blaming her. But she had to ask: "Why didn't you tell us?" When the answer was only silence, she clenched her fists in her lap and said, "You told me you were going to the park. You know you are not supposed to go to somebody's house."

Leslie staring down. Leslie staring up at the ceiling. Leslie looking longingly at the stairway to her room. Oh, God, get me out of here.

Her parents had to tell her that this would not end here. "The policeman wants you to talk to somebody," Charles said, a catch in his voice. Griffin had suggested to Ros that Leslie might feel relatively comfortable talking to Sheila Byron. Charles had been introduced to Sheila at a high school graduation and remembered her as being friendly. "Her name is Sheila and she's a really nice lady."

Les thought for a moment. She didn't know Sheila, but maybe she would be as nice as her swimming coach. "Sure, I'll talk to her," she said.

31

When Leslie Faber spoke to Detective Byron on March 27, 1989, at the Glen Ridge police station, she confirmed generally what the police had learned from the teachers and Charlie Figueroa. The next step was for her to provide a fuller account of her experience for the county prosecutors.

The detective set up a second interview on Friday, April 7. Why wait eleven days? A member of the prosecutor's staff recalled that several considerations may have slowed down the investigation in its first phase: Who the victim was. Who the suspects were.

The victim. Could Leslie be believed? Could she describe accurately what had happened to her? Would she stick to her basic story? The reliability of a victim at a trial was always a concern. A member of the prosecutor's staff said, "The bottom line is, Is this ever gonna ever go to trial and what will the victim say on the stand? We needed to find out how firm her story was."

The suspects. "I had just handled a case where a carrot was inserted into a woman," one staff prosecutor recalled. "The facts that implements were used did not make this case more unusual. The fact that there was more than one person involved—not really unusual. The fact that star athletes were involved—yeah, that kind of threw me for a loop. That wasn't our usual clientele. Glen Ridge—now that stood out. Glen Ridge, where nothing ever happens. All we knew about it, it was a very white-bread town. There was just a feeling we had to go carefully. That we needed more before we moved."

On Friday morning, April 7, Byron and Lieutenant Corcoran picked Leslie up at her house and drove her to the Essex County courthouse in Newark. As she went up in the elevator to the prosecutor's office on the third floor,

Leslie could glimpse many of the stock players that made up the court-house cast: lawyers lugging accordion folders; detectives with their holsters clipped to their belts; and a boy, just about her age, his stocking cap pulled down over his forehead, his hands manacled behind his back. This was nothing like the homey police station in Glen Ridge, where most of the conversation was about traffic tickets and burglarized silverware.

She was led past the glass partition that bore the blue emblem of the county prosecutor into an office where a young woman looked up and said, "And you're—?"

"I'm Leslie Faber," Leslie said, extending her hand. "How you doin'."

A couple of other women smiled at her. "So, are you all my lawyers?" Les asked, flashing her own polite smile.

One of the women in the office, a junior staff member, recalled of that first meeting, "She was nervous, visibly nervous. She was overaccommodating, telling everybody how pretty they looked. Oh, she was such a people pleaser. I immediately hated these boys. I looked at her and I hated their guts because you just knew what they did. You just knew."

Now a middle-aged man introduced himself. He was of medium height, with square shoulders and a square jaw. Even in a dark business suit, he looked as if his body had been molded from poured concrete. His name was Giulio Cavallaro. Before joining the SARA unit as an investigator, he had worked for eighteen years for the Newark Police Department investigating sex crimes.

Cavallaro and Byron walked Leslie to a small room used for interviews. Before they even sat down, Leslie had to know, "Your knuckle, how did it get so big?" In a voice that sounded like a rock slide, Cavallaro explained that he was a master of martial arts, a Black Belt *sensei*, that he often did a "few" push-ups balanced on one knuckle. After years of hard use, the knuckle had developed muscles of its own. "Could I see one push-up?" Leslie asked. Nothing awed her more than athletic heroics. Cavallaro took off his glasses and obliged her. Boy! He might look old—older than *thirty* even—but she didn't know any kids her age who could do that. "If it's okay, I'm going to call you 'Knuckles,'" Leslie decided.

Leslie was very deferential. Would she like something to eat? A candy bar? Coffee perhaps? Oh, she wasn't hungry, but if Sheila wanted something, she'd have a bite. She displayed her good manners with the fierce concentration of the first-grader writing her name on the blackboard.

At about noon the conversation turned to March 1. Now that she was away from Glen Ridge, now that she was in her "lawyers'" office, her account seemed more clearly delineated—and it contained more damaging implications for the Jocks. At their previous meeting, Byron thought Leslie had seemed protective of the boys, never directly saying she had been co-erced. Today she was different. She began by recalling that she saw at least nine boys in the basement when she was walking down the stairs.

Then she said: "I sat on the sofa with—I think his name is 'Bryan.' He asked me to suck his dick. I said 'no.' He forced me, by grabbing the back of my head and forcing it down on him, on his dick. He made me suck him." She said that Grober did not ejaculate.

The phrases that she applied to her experience with Bryant Grober sug-gested coercion: I said "no." . . . He forced me . . . grabbing the back of my head and forcing it down. . . . He made me . . .

Leslie went on to say that Kevin had announced that he wanted to play a joke on her and "he then got a bat and broom. He then put a plastic bag and Vaseline around the handle of the bat and the broom. First, Chris put the broomstick up my vagina. It was scary. Then Kevin put the bat up my vagina. It hurt."

From a paper bag Byron took out the stick Leslie had found in Cartaret Park on March 1, which Mrs. Faber had brought to the police station when Leslie first met the Glen Ridge detective on March 27. "Was the stick used in the basement?" Byron asked.

"No. I just found the stick at the park," Leslie said.

Cavallaro asked Leslie whether "they" had taken her clothes off in the basement.

"Yes," she said. "Kevin and Chris took my clothes off. I was naked. . . . The rest of the boys were sitting around watching. Some were yelling, 'Put it up further.' 'Do it more.'"

The sex crimes investigator wanted to know whether all the boys had stayed in the basement while she was there. "No. Some left while Kevin and Chris were putting the bat and broomstick up my vagina," she said.

The six boys who left would insist that they were heading for the door at the moment when Leslie was preparing to have oral sex with Bryant Grober. But Leslie said they stayed a lot longer, and did nothing about what was going on.

Leslie went on to provide a detailed description of the Scherzer base-ment: six chairs, a reddish rug, a brown sofa, a bar with bar seats, and "on the wall were photos of the Scherzer family."

She was asked whether any other members of the Scherzer family were at home. "The grandmother," Leslie said. "She came halfway down the stairs and looked for Kevin because he had a phone call. This was before anything happened to me. Kevin went upstairs and came back down in a couple of minutes."

What did the grandmother look like?

"She's old, has white hair, sort of going bald. She's skinny and has a cane, a silver metal cane with a green handle."

Did Leslie tell her parents what happened?

"No, I was embarrassed," she said. "I was too scared to tell them. They wouldn't understand."

The questioning was over at 1:20 P.M. Although it is possible to read the seven-and-a-half page statement in five minutes, it took the investigators an hour and a half before they were done. In a jagged script Leslie then signed her name at the bottom of each page, showing that she agreed with it.

As the investigator and the detective walked Leslie down a corridor of the prosecutor's office toward the reception area, Robert Laurino, the director of the Sexual Assault Unit, wheeled around the corner and almost collided with them. "Oh, Bob, I want you to meet Leslie Faber," Cavallaro said.

Laurino had purposely absented himself from the questioning of Leslie. Investigators who question victims and witnesses to a crime may be called themselves as witnesses by the defense lawyers in a trial. Since Laurino could well be trying the Leslie Faber case for the prosecution, if it ever came to trial, he didn't want to become a potential witness.

Sensing, perhaps, that Laurino was the boss, or, at least, the supervisor of "Knuckles," Leslie was a little more formal with him. "Oh, hi, I'm pleased to meet you," she said, shaking hands with the prosecutor.

Laurino saw, standing before him, a teenager about five feet, eight inches tall, weighing about 160 pounds. She was dressed in a baggy T-shirt, gym shorts, and high-topped sneakers. She wore long dangling earrings of gold globes within a gold circle.

His first impression: "A really young kid. Very, very sweet, very respectful, a very, very friendly girl." Laurino saw something else: the extravagant effort to be agreeable and likeable undermined by the uncertainty of her status and significance. He saw the look in her eye, the way she held herself, and it was very familiar to him, as familiar to him as his own adolescence. He knew Leslie as he knew his own brother.

On her way out, Byron asked an assistant prosecutor, "What's next? Do I bring the boys in for questioning?"

"No, absolutely not," the assistant prosecutor told her. "You are not to speak to or take statements from any of the males involved. Under no circumstances—understood?"

More waiting. But for how long? the detective wondered. How much more do we need?

After Leslie and Byron had left, Laurino called his investigator over to his desk. Laurino leaned back in his swivel chair and rested one foot on an open drawer. "How did it go?" he asked Cavallaro.

"Excruciating," he said. "It took forever. Her attention span was short. She found a million distractions."

"So, what've we got here?"

Cavallaro, who had interviewed hundreds and hundreds of rape victims over the year, said, "I'm totally sold on it. What she says happened really happened to her. This is a legitimate case."

A legitimate case—maybe. But a case that would have to be handled very delicately.

As the Glen Ridge detective drove Leslie back to town, she reflected on the change in Leslie since their first meeting, when Leslie had projected the image of a kid who had been compliant during her time in the basement. Conned, manipulated perhaps—but not someone who had actively resisted. But today another Leslie had emerged: Someone who had said "no," someone who had been "forced," someone who had been "hurt." Today she much more closely fit the conventional profile of the rape victim.

Ros Faber never asked the question Sheila expected her to ask after her daughter visited the prosecutor's office: What happened? Throughout the lengthy investigation and years of pretrial proceedings, the Fabers always believed that what Leslie did over in that building in Newark was not their business. If something important came up, Sheila would tell them: That was their attitude.

Sheila was getting up to leave when Ros said in a barely audible voice, "One more thing. My husband and I think we'd like to have the charges pressed against the boys."

"You want to go ahead?"

"Yes, I think so."

Byron suspected that Ros had a lot more questions about the future than she was verbalizing. For example: Would there be reprisals against

Leslie in town, now that the Fabers were pressing charges? Would Leslie's continuing involvement in the case damage her psychologically?

The Fabers were earnest citizens. They lived in the world of business and culture and civic betterment. They were not streetwise and savvy about the law, the media, and the popular culture. But they did know they had certain responsibilities as citizens. As citizens they would do the right thing; they would seek justice.

"Before you leave, I was just wondering—I was wondering, What's happening with the boys?" Ros asked.

The detective didn't hesitate. "So am I," she said.

32

April 10. Still waiting. Detective Byron was going over the paperwork piling up on case number 52527. She was looking at the list of thirteen names culled from the interviews with Leslie and the school people. The first name on the list was Charles Figueroa, the last was Peter Quigley. Only Figueroa had been questioned by the police—and he wasn't a suspect. When was she going to get the okay to talk to the others? She left the station that night feeling irritable. We can't sit on this forever, she told herself.

When Byron came to work the next day at 3 P.M., her boss, Lieutenant Corcoran, said, "I spoke to Laurino and he gave us the okay to start calling the kids in." She checked to make sure the aspirins were in the bottom drawer, and started dialing the phone number of juvenile number 1 on her list, Charles Figueroa.

Charlie's mother, Mary, took the call from the detective. "Do we need a lawyer?" she asked.

Mary Figueroa said the detective reassured her, "You don't need a lawyer because he's not going to be involved. Nobody will know he's given us any information. His name is not going to come up."

After she talked to Sheila, Figueroa asked her son, "You committed yourself to this. Can you handle it?"

Charlie said, "Mom, what could they do to me? They're promising they're not gonna say anything. Sure, I'll do it."

Sheila began interviewing Charlie at about 3:15. Charlie recalled that as Sheila was questioning him Detective Corcoran entered the room. "My tongue dropped," Charlie said, "I thought, 'Oh, God, Mr. Corcoran is here.'"

The reason for his surprise, Charlie said later, was that he didn't want the lieutenant there, because he had been told by Kevin Scherzer that young Richie Corcoran had definitely been in the basement on March 1 and he didn't want to be the one to break the news to Richie's father.

The dry police report, according to Figueroa, does not reflect all that went on during his questioning. "All through the statement Corcoran is saying, 'Kevin did everything, didn't he?' I'm like, 'I don't really know. All I'm telling you is what I know.' But he's like, 'Kevin did it all, didn't Kevin do it all?'"

The seventeen-year-old high school senior said Corcoran's questioning then turned to the detective's three sons who attended the high school. "He asked, 'Was my boys involved?' I said, 'No.' He said, 'It's a wonder, all these boys are there and my boys weren't there.' I wasn't going to tell him, 'Oh, yeah, Richie was there watching.' I wasn't about to say that. He's handling the case. He has, more or less, my life in his hands."

So, Charlie says, he kept silent about Richie through the hour and a half he spent with Byron and Corcoran. His entire statement on April 11 was five pages long. Charlie thought that what he had said would remain confidential. "I didn't want the Jocks to know," he said, "because if these guys did this to a girl who's retarded, you can imagine them doing something to my mother or sister."

Charlie had been a relatively willing witness. Now Sheila had to approach the boys who might not be so willing—the boys who had been in the basement. The images of a lifetime working and living in a small town flooded her mind. The high school dances. Babysitting these kids. Handling security at the graduation. Oh, shit, do it, the voice in her head said, just do it. And she did. She dialed the phone number of Doug and Michaele Archer. The Archers were first because Sheila thought Michaele Archer "would cooperate."

Mrs. Archer answered. "Michaele, this is Sheila Byron. I'm calling because there have been some serious allegations made. I need to speak to Chris."

"Should my husband be there?" Michaele asked.

"I think it's a good idea," the detective said.

"Does it need to be right now?"

"It needs to be immediately."

Michaele said that Chris and Paul were at Hurrell Field, the school's athletic field.

"Could you get them and come here?" Sheila said.

"This sounds serious."

"It is serious."

The detective could hear her crying on the phone and thought: She's crying already and she has no idea how serious this is. When she would speak to the parents of other boys involved in the case, Sheila always used the phrase "allegations of sexual abuse." But she couldn't bear to speak those cold words to Mrs. Archer. "A person that's very, very upset, like she was, I could tell probably was going to have a heart attack on the other end of the phone," Byron said later. "Her, I didn't tell a thing to, except it was serious."

Twenty minutes after Figueroa left, Michaele arrived at police headquarters, accompanied by Chris and Paul. She was wearing, Byron recalled, a high-necked blouse and a long skirt. She was dressed as if she were going to her nursing work. Paul and Chris, coming off the practice field, wore their sweats.

They walked up one flight to the detective squad room. Sheila took Michaele aside. "She had to understand that we're going to read the boys their rights." Michaele listened, her lips set in a tight line. And she appeared to the detective at that moment to be more angry than sorrowful. Sheila recalled her saying, "They *will* talk to you and they *will* tell you what happened." As she heard Mrs. Archer's declaration, the cop thought: *She has no idea. She has no idea what she's opening the boys to.*

When they were buzzed that the Archers had arrived, Byron and Detective Corcoran had quickly decided how to divide up the questioning. Corcoran would talk to Paul Archer alone in an office. This was because Paul was eighteen, legally an adult, and the detectives didn't feel it was necessary to have a parent there. They decided that Sheila would question Chris with his mother present because he was only seventeen years old. (He had celebrated his birthday just three days before.)

Chris sat down on a chair near Sheila's desk. Michaele sat on a chair a few feet away. Byron recited to Chris his Miranda rights: You have a right to remain silent . . . At 5:25 Archer signed a waiver of his rights.

With each phrase Byron felt her police instincts clashing with the Glen Ridge way of doing things. She wanted Archer to talk and felt little sympathy for him. But she knew the practice of the Glen Ridge police in a minor case would be to warn a prominent town resident to get a lawyer before talking. But this wasn't a minor case.

As Sheila began talking to Chris, two things were happening at once. Chris was staring down at the floor, refusing, absolutely refusing, to look at Sheila. And his mother, it seemed to the detective, was recoiling as though each new disclosure from the detective was opening a fresh wound. This is a mother, Byron knew, who liked Leslie, who was protective of Leslie.

Sheila, empathizing with the mother, imagining what was going through her mind, was tempted to say, "Do you really want Chris to talk to me?" She pictured Michaele out of her chair, grabbing Chris by the collar, running into the other room, grabbing Paul, and running out of the police station. But Sheila didn't say that "because now you have to act more like the cop, and I really want to know what he's going to say."

Now the questioning begins in earnest. This is what Sheila remembers happening in the next few minutes:

Byron starts to tell Chris, "The victim alleges . . ."

Chris says, "Yeah, it did happen, but not that way."

Chris says Leslie approached Bryant Grober and touched him, and the next thing you know she's down in the basement and she's kissing Bryant Grober on the penis.

Chris says that a "small bat" and a broomstick were inserted into Leslie. He says, "Well, I'm not sure who put them into her and I'm not sure who was there," according to the detective.

As the detective recalled, Michaele Archer is up off her chair, saying, "No way. This is not what happened." She turns toward Byron and says, "I'm telling you that he's lying to you." And sits back down.

The detective is thinking: "This is great. Now he's going to tell us everything."

The kid's eyes are fixed on his shoes. He is not looking at his mother. He is not looking at the detective. He starts all over, "Well, it's . . ." Again, Mrs. Archer is standing up. She beckons to the cop and walks out of the room into the hallway. According to the detective, Mrs. Archer says, "I'll tell you right now, I know that kid, he's lying to you." Ahead of Sheila she marches back into the room and says to her son: "You're going to tell her what happened."

In the other interview room, Detective Corcoran was giving Paul Archer his Miranda warning. Paul signed the waiver. He was ready to answer Corcoran's questions.

Paul told the detective that Leslie approached him and his friends in Cartaret Park and "started talking sexually towards them and touching them." And he added, "She does this all the time to me and my friends."

The handsome blond football player told the former anchor of the Glen Ridge High School offensive line that he got to the Scherzers' house before Leslie and believed that the young woman entered alone. Reading Archer's statement later, Sheila Byron would observe that "Paul's clearly trying to separate everybody else from this."

Corcoran asked him about what went on in the basement. "I saw Leslie sucking on Bryant Grober's penis, but I don't know how that got started," Paul said.

Corcoran went to the heart of the matter. He asked Paul, "What about the baseball bat and the broomstick?"

Paul said there was a baseball bat there—a "small type given out at professional ballparks."

And what was going on with the bat?

"She was doing it to herself without the help of anyone," Archer said.

"Who gave her these objects, Paul?" the detective asked. In his official report Corcoran said Paul answered that "he wasn't sure, but he thought it was Chris and Kevin."

But Paul quickly interjected, "No one forced her to do anything. She did it on her own." That was his version, but he couldn't take back what he had said. At this point Paul Archer became the only eyewitness to link his brother, Chris, and Kevin Scherzer to the bat and broomstick—the only kid during a two-month police investigation to put faces and names together with the broomstick and bat.

Corcoran asked him how many kids were in the basement. "A lot, around fifteen kids, 'cause a lot of the baseball players came over."

Suddenly, striding through the second-floor detective bureau was a tall, balding man in a business suit—Douglas Archer. Detective Corcoran was already standing outside the office where he had been questioning Paul. Byron was surprised. Not that Doug Archer was standing there. She assumed that Michaele had called her husband at work before bringing the boys in. She was surprised that Archer had entered the Detective Bureau without being buzzed in, without warning the detectives that he had arrived.

Through the open door, Archer could see his wife and his son Chris. Michaele looked very upset. Chris hadn't said anything more yet. Doug held up one hand, like a traffic cop, and said: "Whoa, hold it right there. What's going on?"

Doug Archer and Corcoran talked for a couple of minutes. "Stop, knock it off right now," Archer told the cops. "I want to talk to a lawyer before my sons give a statement."

With a wave of his hand, Doug Archer summoned his family—Michaele, Chris, and Paul—and led them down the stairs and out of the Glen Ridge police station.

In a way, Byron recalled, she felt relieved that Doug Archer had intervened. The relief of a parent with a kid in deep trouble, not the relief of a cop trying to crack a tough case. "If it was my kid and somebody was accusing him, I'd know very clearly that I don't care what they did, we're not going to give a statement on the first day to the cops because then you have no chance of ever taking it back."

But mixed with Byron's relief was also disappointment. She and Corcoran had come so close. "If Mr. Archer hadn't come in, we would have had Mrs. Archer eating out of the palm of our hand," she told Corcoran. "Five more minutes and I would have had the kids. We would have had them, *absolutely*."

Keep the flow going. Keep making the calls. At 6:30 Byron called Peter Quigley and asked him to come to the police station. The detective knew that Quigley was eighteen and she didn't have to ask his parents' permission to talk to him.

At the police station, Quigley at first asserted his Miranda rights. As Sheila talked to Peter, Detective Corcoran was sitting in a corner of the room, listening. Byron recalled that Quigley interrupted her to say, "But you know we were all down there." Then turning toward Lieutenant Corcoran, he began describing where the boys were sitting and standing in the Scherzers' basement.

"You know, I'm there and Richie's over in the corner," he said.

And the lieutenant said, "Richie!"

To Byron, the look on Corcoran's face reflected shock. The look on Quigley's face, Sheila remembered, was—"Oh shit, what did I say?" Realizing what he had done, Peter implored Corcoran, "Oh my God, don't tell Richie I said he was there."

Quigley added, "I don't think I should talk about this any further. Maybe I should talk to my parents."

"Okay," Sheila said, as Peter picked up his jacket and headed downstairs. End of Quigley interview. Beginning of a new chapter in Sheila Byron's career as a Glen Ridge detective.

Quigley had barely left the detective bureau when Corcoran told Byron, "I'm going home to get my kid." He did not look pleased.

Before she made her next call Sheila sat by her desk, thinking about her relationship with her boss, Lieutenant Richard Corcoran, "Corky." Thinking about how he treated her, the first woman to become a detective in Glen Ridge's history—how he took her under his wing. Corky made her feel a part of the gang: going out on a target-shooting competition with the other detectives, low score buying dinner for the rest; barbecues in the summer; and in the winter a pop at the Town Pub, where Corky was a regular. He was a friend. He was her boss. Now this. Now, who, in the tight, clannish work of the small-town detective bureau, would protect her? In police work, you didn't make it as a loner. You needed a rabbi. Sheila had the distinct feeling that she was no longer part of the congregation.

But tonight she had to put these thoughts aside, immerse herself in the job: more phone calls, more people to bring in. While she was waiting for the Richard Corcorans, father and son, to show up, there was another call she could have made, but she decided not to. Earlier in the day she had called the Scherzers, but there was no answer. She could have tried again, but she didn't think it would be productive. "The Scherzers, I guarantee, they never would have brought their kids in," she said later. "Some parents, you call them on the phone and tell them it's very serious, they'll race up here to tell you what's going on. I don't think I would have gotten that far with the Scherzers."

Now the lieutenant was leading his son into the Detective Bureau. Sheila thought, Why is he bringing his kid back in here? Why doesn't he call it a night and say, "That's it. My kid is not talking to you." Sheila did not do what she did with the other boys: She did not read Richie his rights. "It's not like I made a conscious decision not to do it, I just never did," Byron recalled. "I never thought that his father was going to come back with him. It was the most uncomfortable situation I've ever been in."

Richie sat down and Byron described what she had learned about the case. Sheila recalled that Richie said: "No way. That's not what happened at all."

"What happened, Richie?"

"I was sitting in the corner playing Nintendo."

"You've got to be kidding me. You were sitting in the corner playing Nintendo?"

Then, Sheila remembered, Richie said, "What Leslie said happened did happen, but not the way she said it happened. She wanted everything to happen. She took part in everything that happened."

Right then, according to Byron, Detective Corcoran broke in with "All right, that's enough." It was clear to Sheila that her boss was calling an end to the interview of his son. She had no chance to ask Richie about baseball bats and broomsticks.

The last thing Byron did that night was tell the police chief that Lieutenant Corcoran's son had been identified by Peter Quigley as one of the boys who was present in the basement.

The next morning Chief Dugan told the sex crimes prosecutor, Robert Laurino, that there was a new wrinkle in the case—one of the Jocks had said that Corcoran's son had been in the Scherzer basement. Laurino's response was unequivocal: Corcoran must be taken off the case. From now on, the prosecutor's office would not play a support role; it had to be a combined investigation by the Glen Ridge Police Department and the prosecutor. The only local police officer authorized to work on the case would be Sheila Byron. All interviews would be conducted in Newark. The only local police official Byron could discuss the case with was Chief Dugan, and all the records of the case would be locked in Dugan's office. Sheila Byron had become the keeper of the secrets in Glen Ridge.

33

The morning after. On Wednesday morning, April 12, Charlie Figueroa walked into the school cafeteria and approached the table where the Jocks sat. No one said hello. The only kid who said anything to him was his football teammate, Kevin Scherzer. What he said was "Nice five-page report there, Charlie."

Charlie knew what Kevin was talking about: the statement Charlie had given the night before to Lieutenant Corcoran and Detective Byron. How did Kevin know about it? Charlie would never learn the answer. But there was no question what he was feeling there in the school cafeteria. He was feeling betrayed. All he could think of was what the cops had told him: Your name is going to be kept out of this, Charlie.

Charlie went to his special ed class, which was taught by Al Riviera, the first person he had told about the guys and Leslie Faber. "Charlie had a nervous breakdown, practically, in my classroom," Riviera recalled. "He freaked out. He was yelling, 'I'm going to kill them. If they fuck with my sister, I'll kill them.' He was all out of breath, tears coming out of his eyes, and just walking around in circles."

A few minutes later, Charlie was at home, telling the story to his mother. "All the kids know I'm the one that told on them," he said to her.

Mrs. Figueroa told the superintendent of schools, Rose McCaffery, to take him out of the high school and let him complete his schoolwork at home. The next day Charlie began his home instruction. That was when the phone calls started.

"Is the traitor there?"

"Is this where the niggers live?"

The Figueroas took their phone off the hook. And they never let Charlie return to Glen Ridge High School.

The afternoon after. Sheila Byron was back in her office typing up the reports of the interviews she had conducted the night before. The phone rang. It was Jack Scherzer. He told the detective that he had heard something about this investigation going on. She asked him whether he would bring the twins into the police station. No, said Jack Scherzer, he didn't want his boys speaking to anybody right now. But, Jack asked her, will you call me back tomorrow and tell me what's going on?

After I do that, Sheila asked, can I speak to the boys?

No, Jack said, I don't want you to speak to the kids.

There was a message on her desk that Mr. Archer had called. His response was similar to Jack Scherzer's response. Archer told her that his attorney had advised him against letting his sons make any statements. He told her one other thing. Doug told Sheila that he and his wife had apologized to the Fabers.

Charlie Faber opened the door. Standing there on the welcome mat was Doug Archer, in slacks and a sports shirt. Michaele was next to him. As Charlie remembered the moment, Michaele said, "We're sorry to hear about what happened. I'm just horrified to hear what happened."

The Fabers backed up a few feet. The Archers followed them into the vestibule. Ros would recall that Michaele said they knew Chris had some problems, but they were really very surprised to hear that Paul was involved.

After a while, Charlie said later, the Archers conceded that "our boys have been in trouble before and they have done some things."

Charlie recalled that Doug Archer then said, "Well, there's community service.The boys could do some community service."

Charlie didn't respond. Doug sent out a feeler. "What are you looking for on this? Do you think it'll be the same kind of thing—community service." Charlie thought, What do I want on this? If he's thinking about negotiating, he's got the wrong fellow.

Charlie told Doug and Michaele Archer: "No. It's much more serious than that. And it's out of our hands."

34

On April 14 Byron and county investigator Cavallaro interviewed seven of the boys who had left the basement or who had shown up in the park the next day. Some brought lawyers. Some came with parents.

A couple would not make statements. A few said they would talk to the Glen Ridge detective, but only on the condition that they would not be charged with a crime. Those who did talk recalled hearing snatches of conversations in the park or in the basement, but they could never remember who said what. They couldn't recall why they went to the Scherzers' house in the first place. Somebody was thirsty. Somebody wanted to make a phone call. Somebody wanted to line up a car ride for that evening.

The kids all left the basement before the main event. And they never did see what was going on on the couch. That was their story. Somebody tall was standing in front of them. Or they were distracted by the Nintendo game. They didn't recall anybody cheering or laughing or urging Leslie to perform sex acts. And even though they couldn't see or hear much, something told them, some inner voice, that they better get out of there. That was their story.

After so much delay, all the kids were prepared. "We are not going to get much out of the boys in this town," Sheila told Cavallaro. "I have a feeling that that part of the investigation is done."

They were coming back to what they had fought to escape: the stinking exhaust fumes; the half-deserted housing projects; the huge speakers blaring rap music on the pavement outside discount stores, and up the hill of Market Street the three stolid buildings that constituted the stony face of the justice system. Rosalind and Charles Faber were coming back to the city, not the New York of their childhoods, but Newark now, to hear the full story of how their younger daughter, Leslie, was used in the community of their dreams.

At the prosecutor's office, a man in a business suit led them to a small office where they could talk privately.

The man was Robert Laurino, thirty-six years old, a career assistant prosecutor, who for the past four years had directed the Sexual Assault Unit of the county prosecutor's office. He had prematurely gray hair cut long enough—or not often enough—so that it fell over his ears and just over the back of his shirt collar. He was slender and of medium height. He had sharp features that were softened by his brown eyes. Some people who worked with him said his eyes were gentle. Others, who knew him better, said they were sad. His complexion was pale, not the sallow color of the ex-con but the courthouse gray of a man who went for years without taking a vacation.

To the Fabers, Laurino seemed less a law enforcement professional than a neighbor in Glen Ridge—a college teacher, perhaps, or a doctor—who had come to them, awkwardly, tentatively, to break the news of a terrible tragedy. For almost two months the Fabers had been hearing various accounts of what happened from the school people and the cops and from Leslie. Now Laurino told them all he had learned. A few times, when it got too hard, he would lapse into the language of law enforcement—"the perpetrators," "digital penetration"—but most of what he had to tell he told without understatement or varnish. In his dealings with the families of victims—and, indeed, with the victims themselves—Laurino adhered to a single principle: If they have to go through this ordeal, they must understand why they are doing it.

For a while, the Fabers listened without comment or question. Charles's face was tight; he looked as though he could erupt at any second. Ros's eyes were moist, but when she felt she couldn't control herself, she'd whisper a word or a phrase to get by: "I see." "So that's what happened." They tried to maintain their composure, but, as he described what had been revealed in the investigation, their faces registered surprise first, then shock.

There was a long silence as they took it in. Then Charles Faber asked, What will these boys be charged with?

Laurino explained that the main suspects, the boys who allegedly penetrated Leslie with the objects and the boy who had oral sex with her, would probably be charged with using force and coercion against her.

What, exactly, would the charges be?

Aggravated sexual assault and probably other charges as well.

Aggravated sexual assault—how serious is that?

That was a legal term, Laurino said. Under New Jersey law it was equivalent to rape.

And what about the other boys who were in the basement, the ones who stayed and the ones who supposedly left?

We haven't yet reached a decision on those boys, he said.

Would Leslie have to testify?

We usually do ask the victim to testify. Not always, but usually, Laurino said.

Will her name get out? Will she be identified?

We will do everything we can to keep her identity secret, he said.

But would they be besieged by the press, and would reporters reveal her identity?

Usually the press will not identify a rape victim. But I can't speak for the press, he said. All we can do is ask for their cooperation.

Will the defense go after her personal life? That's what they try to do to rape victims, isn't it; pry into her sexual life, turn up every rock?

They do try to do that, Laurino explained, but in New Jersey there was a rape shield law to protect victims. But, you know, if this ever comes to trial, the question of whether Leslie was mentally capable of giving consent to sexual acts will probably come up and the defense will argue that they have to know about her past behavior. It's hard to know what will happen, he said carefully, but we'll fight to keep her personal life out of this.

When they were done with their questions, Laurino said he would like to know a little more about Leslie's mental ability, especially how she functioned in the community.

"One day we may not be around," Ros said. "Leslie is going to have to fend for herself."

Charlie said, "They used to lock kids like Leslie in a room and throw the key away. We didn't want to do that. This is a young girl we're trying to make part of the community."

"You don't send a girl out with the idea that somebody's going to jump her and rape her," Ros said. "We live in Glen Ridge. We thought she'd be safe in our town. You know, a town like that. Where did you grow up, Mr. Laurino?"

"Not that far from Glen Ridge. In Millburn."

"Then you know, Mr. Laurino."

He knew. Millburn was a fifteen-minute drive from Glen Ridge, a bigger town, but also, supposedly, a safe place. A line ran through the township. On one side of it was Millburn proper. On the other side was Short Hills. Most of the residents of Millburn were middle class. In Short Hills they were, for the most part, rich. The Laurinos, a second-generation Italian family, lived over in Millburn. Bob's father worked as a traffic manager for the Allied Chemical Corporation in Morristown, overseeing shipments around the world. Bob's mother was at home, raising the three kids in the family. Maria Laurino, Bob's sister, said, "We were very much an Italian-American family. My mother would talk about, This is Italian food and this is American food. Most of Millburn was a very WASPy town and I felt very Italian. I wanted to be American."

Millburn High School had almost three times as many students as Glen Ridge High, but there were similarities. The parking lot had a substantial representation of Mercedes, Firebirds, and Corvettes. The Jocks and the cheerleaders were the "popular kids." Bob played football, although he spent more time on the bench than he did on the field. "The cheerleaders would decorate the locker room with cutout paper dolls and scribble your number on them, but that's about as far as it went," he remembered.

The school had more Jews and more kids that came from poorer families than Glen Ridge did. "Basically, though, the school was like Glen Ridge. You get into the college track and move on to college," Laurino said. He was on the college track, but his favorite part-time job was working on a garbage truck. "I like hanging around with real people," he told his sister.

The Laurinos were Hubert Humphrey Democrats, strong believers in a government that protected and elevated the poor and the striving. Bob was eight years older than his sister, Maria, and she remembered that when she was a kid, eight, nine years old, he'd lecture her on social justice, explaining how a massive housing project in Newark would ultimately be abandoned because it failed to give the people who lived there a sense of home. If Bob had a childhood hero, it was Robert Kennedy. She never forgot Bob shaking her out of a deep sleep to tell her that Bobby Kennedy had been murdered.

But that was his serious side. He played another role in the family. "His job in the house was to make us all laugh," Maria said. "He had this subtle, dry wit—funny but basically shy like my father." Laurino went to college at Villanova, where in 1972 he was the head of Students for Mc-Govern. "He'd bring me home like thirty-two McGovern buttons," she said, "but I would never say Bob was a radical. But he did have this feeling for the underdog. Certainly, living with Louis was part of that."

Louis* was Bob's older brother, five years older than Bob. Louis was re-tarded. From his first meeting with Leslie, Laurino would gauge that she functioned on a slightly higher level than Louis did, but there wasn't much of a difference. Both of them had roughly the mental ability of a seven- or eight-year-old kid. "They are both educable retarded," he said. "That creates its own kind of problems. Both Les and Louis want to be nor-mal but know enough to realize that there's something different between them and others. And because of that it's more anguishing for her—and for him."

When Laurino was young, his family lived near a park as the Fabers did. He saw the kids there taunt his brother as the guys in Glen Ridge taunted Leslie. "Yeah, I think I had a better understanding of what Les went through than most people," he said. "I could see things in my own childhood, how Louis went through the taunting, teasing, how he would be striving to be normal like other kids, as Leslie was. Some people may have difficulty understanding why someone would do what they did to Leslie. But I knew the kind of kids these Glen Ridge kids were. They are the kind of bastards that don't care about anybody."

One afternoon when he was home from college, Bob took Louis out for a drive in the family car. They hadn't gone very far when Louis began clamoring to drive. He was the older brother, why couldn't he drive? Why couldn't he have fun, the way Bob did? It was not something Bob could ex-plain to Louis, who believed, who *knew*, that he was a normal male and that it was a normal thing for males in the suburbs to drive cars. Bob took Louis back home and resolved then not to drive ever again in Louis's presence.

Bob Laurino had a driver's license, but he never bought a car. If he had owned a car, Louis would have wanted to drive it, and what reason could Bob invent to deny him this simple pleasure? So, at the end of long winter days and sometimes late at night, when the cops and prosecutors and lawyers hurriedly scrambled to the parking lot outside the courthouse, Bob Laurino walked a mile, through the not-so-safe streets of Newark, to the commuter train station. When he was asked why he didn't drive, his stock answer was, "I like the exercise."

Laurino got a master's degree in political science from Rutgers and a law degree from Seton Hall University. From there, he took a job in the trials division of the Essex County Prosecutor's Office. His sister, Maria, didn't do badly either. After college she became a reporter for the *Village Voice*, a weekly paper in New York, and then was hired as chief speech writer for New York mayor David Dinkins. Meanwhile, Louis stayed home. For one brief period he worked at a department store through a program for the disabled. But he lost the job and was so deeply hurt by what he took as personal rejection that he never went to work again.

By the time Laurino finished law school, his brother was in his mid-thirties and his parents were in their early sixties. It was getting more difficult for Mom and Dad to take care of Louis.

In his adolescence Bob had begun to appreciate, with the guidance of two priests he was close to, the complex character and personality of his brother, a complexity that was often misunderstood or overlooked by those who didn't have anything to do with the retarded. He was learning that Louis could be generous and selfish, manipulative and innocent, joyous and depressed. But, above all, he was dependent. Louis needed his family. And so Bob decided to continue to live at home. "For my brother, the sense of obligation and duty is very strong," said Maria. "If anybody has been there for me and my parents, it's been Bob. And in the same way, Bob takes care of Louis, worries about Louis. My brother takes care of people."

Laurino litigated many different kinds of criminal cases when he was in the trial division, but he found a special fulfillment representing victims of sexual abuse. "In the Sexual Assault Unit, you're always dealing with a victim. Maybe that's what he likes the most: protecting the victim," Maria Laurino said. "What really motivates him is the idea that social justice should be extended to the weakest people. The idea he's always fought against is that if you are not *acceptable*, by society's standards, you have to suffer. It was impossible for Bob to accept that idea when he spent his life with Louis."

When they met with Laurino that April afternoon, the Fabers could not help noticing the awards from organizations representing the disabled. What impressed them was that he would hang them in a prominent place in a law enforcement office. Bob had not told them about Louis, but they felt that Laurino was a man who would try to protect Leslie. "Do you have any idea when the boys will be arrested?" Charles Faber asked Laurino.

"I guess it'll be pretty soon. Probably," he said.

35

Laurino did not control the pace of the Glen Ridge investigation. Herbert H. Tate, Jr., chief prosecutor of Essex County, did. One of Tate's distinctions was that at the age of thirty-six, with limited experience as an administrator, he now managed the largest prosecutor's office in the state, with some 30,000 indictments a year and a caseload of nearly 30 percent of all the violent crimes committed in New Jersey.

Tate's other principal distinction was that when he was appointed in 1986 by Republican governor Thomas Kean, he became the first black prosecutor of Essex County. The office was a weighty responsibility in Newark, one of the most heavily black and Democratic cities in the nation.

When Tate was appointed, he entered a bastion of white male power. Most of the 122 assistant prosecutors and 166 detectives and investigators on his staff were white, and they owed their allegiance to Tate's white predecessors. The majority of the suspects investigated and prosecuted by the office were blacks. This inherent duality made a normally cautious man even more cautious in handling politically sensitive cases. And few cases were more politically sensitive than the case of a group of white young men, from an affluent, conservative suburb, who had been accused of rape.

Tate's instinctive cautiousness was accentuated by his relative inexperience. He had a total of four and a half years of prosecutorial experience. Many in the courthouse suspected that his selection as prosecutor might have had something to do with the prominence of his father. Herbert Tate, Senior, had been a leader in the civil rights movement and had been appointed a Superior Court judge in Newark in 1969. But Tate was not the legend his father was. In 1990 a national organization of judges and court administrators would find that his office was one of the slowest and least efficient in the United States.

If Laurino made one misstep in his handling of the case, his colleagues said later, it was to alert the highest echelons of the office to its sensitive nature early in the investigation. "Tate was a politician first and a lawyer second," an official in the office said. "He didn't want something to blow up in his face." Tate's involvement in the investigation was driven, at first, by concerns about Lieutenant Corcoran's role and questions that might arise later in the press about a possible cover-up by the school or the police department. These anxieties were heightened when Peter Quigley confirmed on April 11 that Corcoran's son Richie was present in the basement.

It was also becoming apparent, after some of the young men who had been in the basement appeared at the prosecutor's office, that their parents had the money—or could find it—to hire expensive, politically wired legal talent. These lawyers knew how to fight in the courtroom and in the press.

Other issues to be resolved: What should be done with the boys who stayed in the basement but didn't have sexual contact with Leslie? And what about those who supposedly left? "People were divided," Laurino said. "Some thought, hell, everybody could be charged. Others thought that, legally, we'd have to go after those who actually did some overt act. I was saying we have to concentrate on those who really did some act. I couldn't see making a sweep and arresting thirteen kids. No jury, I think, would ever convict somebody who was there and just took off—and there were six who left."

And there was the age factor. Some of the kids potentially facing the most serious charges were under eighteen on March 1, 1989. They would have to be tried separately in Family Court, unless a judge ruled that they should be tried as adults. Usually that didn't happen unless defendants had a long record of serious crimes—and none of these boys did. The alternative was separate and lengthy proceedings for the adults and the juveniles. Lengthy as in *years*.

Ordinarily, these issues might take a few weeks to thrash out. But the pace was much slower in the prosecutor's office in the spring of 1989. The delay in making arrests did not go unnoticed in the Sexual Assault Unit. "The kids were handled with kid gloves," said one assistant prosecutor assigned to the unit. Every day when Laurino walked into the SARA office the women working there would chant: "When, Bob, when?"

The continuing delays were even more puzzling because by the end of the first week in May the prosecutor's office had received several detailed descriptions of the alleged rape from Leslie. On May 5 she gave yet another statement to "Knuckles" Cavallaro and Detective Byron, describing what each boy was saying and doing in the basement.

Of Bryant Grober, she said: "He forced me to perform oral sex on him." Of Kevin Scherzer, she said, "He put the bat into my vagina. *It was a regular-size bat.* He forced my legs open." Chris Archer, she said, was laughing when he put the broomstick into her vagina. Kyle, she said, put the plastic bag over the bat and later threw the plastic bag out and washed the bat and broomstick. But, she said, it was Kyle and Kyle alone who suggested that something improper was going on when he said: "Stop, you're hurting her." Peter Quigley was "cheering Kevin and Chris on," she said.

For the first time, Leslie said that Richie Corcoran was present in the basement. But she did not ascribe any actions or comments to him. He was just one of the boys who was there.

Two weeks later Leslie recalled that Chris Archer had tried to talk her into inserting a hot dog into her vagina, an incident that foreshadowed the experience in the basement.

Now Tate had three written and one verbal statement from Leslie. He had past IQ scores and evaluations. He had Charlie Figueroa's statement. He had partial confirmation from Paul and Chris themselves, during the time they talked to Sheila Byron in the Glen Ridge police station before their father had jumped in. The prosecutor had all that and still hadn't acted.

Unlike Laurino, Tate and his associates were emotionally distant from Leslie. In fact, staff members in the SARA unit recalled that on the few occasions when Tate met Leslie, he appeared uncomfortable in her presence, not with her account of the crime but with her disability and her personality. Was justice for this retarded young woman—a so-called "victim" who herself didn't want her persecutors to go to jail—worth risking the reputation of the office for? In a broader context, observers wondered whether the male policymakers in the office considered rape a serious enough offense to warrant such a high-stakes gamble. For these men rape was defined by an act of physical violence. By social background and professional experience, they did not completely understand and were made uneasy by a complainant who had not vigorously resisted the advances of the young men in the basement.

Laurino was different. He could add up the odds against him, just as the men in the command structure could. But he was also a believer. He believed that those who are discounted and marginalized in society deserve justice. Laurino thought he understood Leslie and what had happened to her—not only on March 1 but long before then—and this understanding committed him to a cause that would consume much of the next four years of his life. Laurino was different.

No one knows how long the investigation would have remained in limbo if Laurino hadn't picked up the phone and heard a vaguely familiar voice saying: "Mr. Laurino, I don't know if you remember me, but I'm a reporter. Are you guys investigating some incident in the town of Glen Ridge?"

The press had arrived. And time was running out on the chief prosecutor of Essex County.

36

As word of the investigation spread through Glen Ridge, the most important question for townspeople was: Will the story ever come out?

Some local residents thought that whatever had happened should be kept secret, because they feared that the town would never recover from the scandal. As a counterbalance, some people worried that a terrible crime might be covered up by the town. This fear was heightened by the passage of time—one month, two months, almost three months. People began to voice their anxieties.

When the local paper ran a picture of Kyle Scherzer playing with a preschool child on May 11, an anonymous caller told a reporter, "Now I see you're running a picture of a rapist on your front page."

The prosecutor's office got a number of calls. A few of the callers pressed the prosecutors to make an arrest. But most of the calls were not about the boys but about Leslie's character. Stories about her relations with boys. These callers never wanted to leave their names. They just wanted the prosecutor to know what kind of girl Leslie was.

So there the town hung in May 1989, swinging between suspicion and knowledge, rumor and fact. It took a skinny sixteen-year-old high school kid to force an end to the suspense.

In the spring of 1989 John Tierney* had two great passions: He loved his skateboard, and he hated the Jocks. It wasn't absolutely clear what he despised more: their arrogant manner or what he took to be the subservience of the school and town toward them.

John was a "Gigger"; he wore his hair long and liked to ask teachers questions they couldn't answer. He was a smart, vinegary kid who never shut up. In fact, when he was a runty freshman, he would follow the school principal down the hall badgering him about the "Jockocracy" in Glen Ridge High.

This spring John had a couple of concrete goals: Finish his junior year, and make sure that the Jocks didn't get away with what they did to Leslie Faber. Like most of the other students, John had heard about Leslie and the Jocks in April. But unlike most of the other students, what he had heard infuriated him. John and a couple of his closest friends dedicated themselves to ensuring that there would be no cover-up.

At night John would print up stickers: BRAINWASH EDUCATION LEADS TO

MOLESTATION. Then he would paste them on the bathroom walls. Sometimes he wrote on classroom desks: ARREST THE RAPIST JOCKS. In May John said to hell with anonymity. He painted a sentence along one side of his car. It read: YOU'LL SEE WHAT IT FEELS LIKE WHEN YOU GET RAPED IN JAIL. Still, that wasn't enough. The Jocks were in school. Everybody was talking about graduation-night parties and the baseball team and college. It seemed to John that Leslie Faber and the Jocks were rapidly becoming history. "It was like a bubble was over Glen Ridge and you'd never get the real story out," John said later.

That's when he and his buddies began making phone calls. Not to the police or the prosecutors—they didn't trust them. They called the media. John called the *Newark Star-Ledger*. Then one of his buddies called WNBC-TV in New York and, with John at his elbow, told a news clerk, "You hear about the Glen Ridge rape?"

Michael Callahan, the managing editor of the WNBC news department, got an anonymous phone message on May 4 about a possible sexual assault of a retarded teenager by a group of high school athletes in Glen Ridge. But municipal officials and the cops would not comment. Callahan assigned one of his high-profile reporters, John Miller, to the story. Miller specialized in organized-crime stories, but he was intrigued by this tip because he had grown up in Montclair, near Glen Ridge. Miller reportedly called an attorney who had worked in the prosecutor's office. The lawyer confirmed that the prosecutor was investigating a rape case in Glen Ridge. Miller and his crew were scheduled to visit the town on Tuesday, May 23.

After Laurino concluded that the suspects in the case would not talk to investigators, he tried to get approval for a warrant to search the "crime scene." The top brass refused, and the case seemed stalled. But if John Miller couldn't get confirmation from the prosecutor, he might go with a story anyway. The combination of a top crime reporter and a story that involved a rich suburb, thirteen Jocks, and a retarded victim spelled national news.

Besides, there wasn't justification for further delays. The investigators had got all they were going to get before an arrest. On Friday, May 19, Laurino said, arrest warrants—formally known as "complaints"—had been filled out for five Glen Ridge students: Christopher Archer, Bryant Grober, Kyle Scherzer, Kevin Scherzer, and Peter Quigley. The SARA unit was also drawing up a search warrant for the Scherzers' house. But there was a standing order in the case: All warrants had to be reviewed and approved by Herbert Tate, the chief prosecutor. But where was Tate? From Friday through Monday Laurino couldn't find his boss. Was Tate taking a long weekend off? Or was he just not taking calls?

In the late morning of Tuesday, May 23, someone phoned in a bomb threat to Glen Ridge High School. As the students marched out of the building, they were met by cameramen and a magisterial John Miller. Johnny Tierney was more than willing to be interviewed. After he was done, Kyle and some of his friends surrounded him, demanding to know what he had told the TV people. Johnny said he told them about what kids in school had been talking about for the last two months.

The cameras found a tall, muscular senior, a guy who could have been on the football team. Richard Corcoran, Jr., was asked about the Jocks and Leslie Faber. On camera Richie said, "She wanted it." And then he gave the finger to the camera. There was also film of him making gestures that suggested jerking off. Corcoran led the six o'clock news, and plunged real estate brokers in the area into acute depression.

Officials at the prosecutor's office watched the video of Richie Corcoran and the other high school kids, including Johnny Tierney. They heard Miller describe an alleged gang rape that was reported to Leslie's swimming teacher almost three months before; they heard about rich kids in a rich suburb and a retarded girl; they heard a high school football player confirm that the "incident" had taken place. The football player was the son of the local police lieutenant. The likely spin on the story was obvious—cover-up! The phone rang in the SARA unit. It was Herb Tate. "Arrest them," he said.

37

Wednesday, May 24, 6:15 A.M. In a light mist four unmarked cars left the garage of the Essex County courthouse. Each contained two or three detectives and investigators from the prosecutor's office. Their destination: Glen Ridge. In town the cars split up, each going to a different address:

34 Lorraine Street: the home of Jack and Geraldine Scherzer.
47 Ridgewood Avenue: the home of Douglas and Michaele Archer.

221 Forest Avenue: the home of Dr. Nathan Grober and Rosemary Grober.

8 Sommer Avenue: the home of Michael and Myra Quigley.

The police were going to these houses to arrest Kyle and Kevin Scherzer, Bryant Grober, Peter Quigley, and Christopher Archer.

Except for the police chief, Tom Dugan, no one in Glen Ridge knew it was coming. The surprise was right there in Jack Scherzer's eyes when he answered the knock on his door. Sheila Byron explained that they were there to search the house. Almost as an afterthought, she added that they had a warrant for the arrest of Kyle and Kevin Scherzer.

"I can't believe you're doing this, Sheila," Jack said, suddenly very wide awake. "Why? Why?"

The detective was going to answer "Why not?" but she caught herself in time.

"I have to call my lawyer," Scherzer said.

"You have a few minutes, Jack," Byron said. "But get the boys ready."

Geraldine Scherzer stood in the dining room, watching, not saying a word.

Now both parents were going upstairs. And it wasn't five minutes before Kyle and Kevin were coming down. To Sheila they looked less frightened than stunned: Is this really happening? Am I going to jail?

Kyle wore white sweatpants and a T-shirt that said: "Property of the Boston Red Sox." Kevin wore a white-and-tan pullover and blue sweatpants. Draped over their shoulders were their red-and-white Ridger team jackets. The Scherzers' lawyer, Donald Merkelbach, had arrived. It was then that Giulio Cavallaro stepped forward and snapped the handcuffs shut on the wrists of Kyle and Kevin Scherzer.

Similar scenes, with slight variations, were played out at the houses of the other boys: Peter Quigley rolling up the wrinkled sleeves of his blue-and-white striped shirt so he could be cuffed; Chris Archer, crisp and clear-eyed, tucking in his ironed blue oxford button-down; and Bryant Grober, head down, scurrying to the police car parked in front of the doctor's house.

The detective who picked up Grober would remember for years the look of both amazement and horror when Rosemary opened the door and called her husband, realizing that Bryant was about to be arrested. "She was so astonished it looked to me as if she was about to say, Bryant Grober, there's no Bryant Grober living here. But all she said was, 'Can I get you a cup of coffee while Bryant gets ready?'"

Laurino would later describe the procedure as among the most discreet and courteous in his years of arresting rape suspects in Essex County. But Allen Marra, Bryant Grober's lawyer, disagreed. "How would you like it? They come to your house, your kid is going to school that morning, three detectives at every house, hit it like a John Gotti raid. All at the same time, can you imagine? Tate pulls the kids down; the parents are crying. Unbelievable."

By 11 A.M. Byron had filled a garbage bag with articles she found in the Scherzers' house: three brooms with black wooden handles; a broom with a metal handle; one wooden broom handle; a tube of Vaseline; a tube of petroleum jelly; two baseball bats, one wooden, one aluminum; four boxes of plastic bags; and a fireplace broom. As it turned out, all the household items she collected were worthless as trial evidence. If Leslie's recollection had been accurate, the bat and broom had been washed on March 1, and the plastic bag that had been used to cover the bat had been tossed into the garbage. The search was about three months too late. Moreover, there was no police technician present trained in collecting semen and blood specimens. For Byron the search of the house was useful in one respect. What she found there—the couch, the bar in the basement, the chairs, the plaques on the wall, the refrigerator—were much as Leslie had recalled them in her statements to the police.

In the afternoon Quigley and the Scherzer twins were taken to the Newark courthouse to be arraigned. They entered Judge Sidney Reiss's courtroom with their wrists manacled in front of them. They had placed their team jackets over their hands to hide the handcuffs. What left an impression with onlookers was their deer-caught-in-the-headlights look. They seemed not to understand why a judge was looking down at them, why all these "media" people were interested in *them*.

Judge Reiss read the charges. All three were charged with "aggravated sexual assault"—in other words, rape in the first degree. They were also charged with conspiracy to commit sexual assault. Kevin, Kyle, and Peter pleaded not guilty. Judge Reiss set bail in a relatively modest amount for a rape charge: $25,000 for Kevin, $20,000 for Kyle, and $15,000 for Peter. To free their sons, the parents had to put up 10 percent of the bail amount, which they did on the spot.

Meanwhile, a couple of hundred yards down Market Street, Chris and Bryant were brought into Newark's Family Court building, where reporters were banned from the courtrooms and criminal cases involving juveniles were heard in secret. Chris and Bryant appeared before Family Court judge Julio Fuentes. (Grober was actually eighteen now and Archer seventeen.) Both Chris and Bryant were formally charged with conspiracy to commit sexual assault, aggravated sexual assault, and aggravated criminal sexual contact. They pleaded not guilty.

The judge sent Grober home under house arrest, which, essentially, meant that he would be confined to 221 Forest Avenue. Chris was sent to the city's Youth House, Newark's juvenile detention center, where he would be held for three days for psychiatric tests.

In the juvenile justice system, Grober and Archer could receive up to twenty years in prison if they were convicted on all the charges. Kyle, Kevin, and Peter, who were in the adult criminal justice system, faced a maximum thirty-year prison term if they were convicted. Or so the criminal statutes said.

Herbert Tate held a press conference to announce the arrests. It was not a flawless performance.

The prosecutor told reporters that the victim was "mentally impaired." Then later in the conference Tate said that Leslie was "mentally retarded." He said that the objects used to penetrate the vagina of the young woman were a "miniature baseball bat" and a broomstick handle.

After the conference some reporters lingered with Tate. He told them something else, something that he hadn't disclosed before: The victim had been sexually assaulted previously, in 1983. That fact was reported on national television before the day was over.

But there were other things that the reporters couldn't have known about then. First, they couldn't have known about the actual size of the bat. In her statements to the police, Leslie Faber had repeatedly described the bat as "regulation size" and "regular size." The only people to mention a "small bat" were Paul and Chris Archer during their brief interrogation at the Glen Ridge police station. One official in the prosecutor's office tried to explain Tate's acceptance of the Archers' version by saying, "I don't think Herb believed that anybody would put a real baseball bat into a girl's vagina. So it became a miniature bat."

Reporters during the next three years would describe it in their stories as a "mini-bat," a plastic souvenir bat, a small bat, a toy bat. It wasn't until the Glen Ridge case came to trial that they realized that a real baseball bat had been jammed into Leslie Faber's vagina.

Then there was Tate's disclosure of the 1983 sexual assault on Leslie.

Advocates for the rights of victims of sexual abuse would be troubled by the sight of the *prosecutor* publicizing this victim's past. Tate's purpose may have been to show how vulnerable Leslie Faber was to sexual exploitation. But by disclosing the earlier offense without elaboration or explanation, he served to fuel unfounded speculation. Were Leslie and her parents chronic complainers? Since there was no mention of a guilty verdict or jail time in the 1983 case, had the defendant been exonerated? Had Leslie been exaggerating or lying when she was eleven, and was she doing that again, six years later?

Defense lawyers were quick to exploit the opening Tate left them. Only nine days later, on June 2, Allen Marra, attorney for Bryant Grober, appeared on the Phil Donahue television talk show. "The reason that the school and police authorities were so cautious and careful was that the young gal had a prior problem in 1983," Marra said. "A sexual problem." Marra said that he had represented the eighteen-year-old man accused in the 1983 case. "It was resolved satisfactorily to both sides," he observed.

Leslie's identity was another problem. A lot of specific information about her was seeping out of the press conference. Many Glen Ridge residents and many of Leslie's classmates at West Orange High would recognize her instantly.

Actually, it seemed that more was coming out about Leslie than about the suspects. The prosecutor wasn't saying anything about voyeurism, or about the money that was stolen at the Candy Cane Ball, or about obscene phone calls or frozen hot dogs that were put into the vagina of the victim. In the press conference the victim's past got the attention; the boys' past was ignored.

Doubts about Leslie's truthfulness were amplified by the ambiguous description of her mental condition as "mentally impaired" and "retarded." Laurino knew that in an investigation that had lasted more than two months, the prosecutor had never approved an independent evaluation of her intellectual and social development.

The last time she had been evaluated by the Glen Ridge system was in December 1987—nearly a year and a half ago. Then she had been classified as "educable mentally retarded" with an IQ of 49 to 51. The school had found that she functioned at the level of a second-grader.

Tate's failure to order an evaluation before the arrests was regarded by some law enforcement officials as a critical lapse. They considered it an indispensable building block in a case where the victim's mental condition was certain to be disputed.

The ambiguity surrounding Leslie left the reporters—and, eventually, the defense lawyers—free to put their own spin on Leslie's mental state. As time passed, Leslie would be identified in most stories about the Glen

Ridge case as "marginally retarded," even though she actually functioned, at the age of seventeen, on the level of a second-grade student.

A "miniature" bat. A "marginally retarded" victim. A young woman who had been involved in a previous "sexual" incident. If you didn't know better, you might think that on the day the arrests in a sensational case were announced, the prosecutor was underplaying the enormity of the allegations and the significance of the victim's vulnerability.

38

Glen Ridge High School was trying, not very successfully, to cope with the fallout from the arrests. The most visible sign of the fallout was the overbearing presence of the media. From all over the country they came— newspaper and magazine reporters, columnists, TV reporters, producers and camera crews, talk show reps. They encircled the high school, inundated the town.

In the school, officials thought that the students needed to air their feelings at class meetings. The meetings were held in the school cafeteria, and the seniors were the first to meet. Some students remembered Rose McCaffery, the superintendent of schools, saying at the meeting that the seniors needed to demonstrate their "solidarity," that they should not be judgmental toward the rape suspects. Seniors recalled that she said: "We should stand by our boys." Principal Buonomo, looking to the future, urged: "Let's just go on."

One female student jumped to her feet and shouted, "How can we go on with rapists in our class?" Another girl yelled, "How do I know they're not going to rape me?" She was standing a few feet away from Paul Archer. One of the Jocks' friends said, "You're too ugly to get raped."

When the meeting was over, two groups of young women squared off in the locker room, the Jockettes versus the Gigger-Freaks. One teacher who was passing by tried to restore peace. "The first thing I heard was 'We're all in danger if we let them get away with this.' Then the girls are pushing and shoving. It was like a rumble from *West Side Story*. I told them to go to the bathroom and wash their faces. Their makeup was running."

Later McCaffery was heard repeating to the juniors what she had said to the seniors; John Tierney was on his feet, screaming, "You're out of your mind. You want us to support *them*?" Kids started throwing books, fruit, slide rules, and whatever else they could grab, including each other. Teachers ducked, Jocks and Freaks rolled on the floor pummeling each other, and a bunch of noncombatants raced for the exits.

The night after the arrests, Ros Faber and her daughter Leslie returned home from spending the afternoon with Ros's mother-in-law. At the front door, they found baskets of fruit, covered dishes of food, and bouquets of flowers. The Fabers' friends wanted them to know they had support in Glen Ridge. But Leslie misunderstood. "Why did they do this?" she asked her mother. "It looks like a funeral." But they had hardly started making supper when they heard a car horn blaring, someone shouting an obscenity, followed by a splat against their window. When they pulled the curtain to the side, they saw egg yolk dripping down the pane. It was not how the Fabers wanted to celebrate their daughter's eighteenth birthday.

The shock of the arrests had left many of the defenders of the accused in disarray. But after a day, they found a common theme in their remarks to journalists. The theme was the repackaging of an old idea in Glen Ridge: that it was the responsibility of young women to curb the cruder instincts of males. The way the friends of the Jocks saw it, a boy was helpless against the wiles of the seductress, and it was unfair to blame the guys for the consequences of her lust. That was how they portrayed the "incident" to the press.

For example, Damian DeVito, Chris Archer's wrestling and football teammate, said to reporters that Leslie was "very flirtatious and open." He said he knew his teammates "wouldn't make anyone do something against their will." Similarly, Steven Lackey, a 1988 graduate, didn't think the Jocks should be blamed. "These guys aren't criminals," he said. "I grew up with them and know they are good guys."

Among the reporters who were interviewing students was Lisa Marie Petersen, who worked for *The Record* of New Jersey. The first two people she met in Glen Ridge were cheerleaders. "I could hardly identify myself before they started ranting and raving about the victim," Petersen says; "You wouldn't believe the things they were saying."

Petersen recalls that she and another *Record* reporter talked to about twenty students that day. "Every one of them said the same thing: The victim was a slut. I couldn't believe what I was hearing."

She found only one person with a different view. Nick Salerno, a 1988 graduate of the school, had got to know Leslie when she was tutored by his mother. He described Leslie as an "angel," adding, "She was very nice— not someone who deserved to be taken advantage of like she was." When his comment appeared in the newspaper story the next day, he received an anonymous phone call from someone who threatened "to get him," the police reported.

Carol Ann Campbell, a columnist for *The Record*, wrote about the sentiments of many students in Glen Ridge: "A group of girls cried and yelled for the television cameras to leave and stop destroying their school. But they were not crying for the victim. . . . The sympathy most often went to the defendants. . . . The feelings of a retarded female victim are a footnote. They're not as important as the future of the popular college-bound athletes."

Adults didn't express much support or sympathy for Leslie either. For example, Ben Tantillo, the vice-principal, commented to the press, "We're trying to have the students not be judgmental" about the young men who had been arrested. Tantillo did not explain why it was desirable to be non-judgmental about what had happened in the basement. Was putting a baseball bat into the vagina of a retarded young woman debatable behavior? School officials could have used the time after the arrests to raise important questions for discussion by their students: What were so many of your classmates doing in the basement with Leslie Faber? What led up to this? What does it say about us as a school and community? But these provocative issues were not explored. Instead, the spokesmen for the school ducked behind the façade of "neutrality."

Some might even interpret the comments of various educators and school officials as an attempt to diminish the seriousness of the charges against the suspects. The school board, for example, described what they did as an act of "alleged sexual misconduct." Not alleged rape. Not alleged sexual assault. But *misconduct*.

School principal Buonomo emphasized the need for students to put this distasteful matter behind them. In his view, apparently, the main problem was the sensational media coverage of Glen Ridge, not the alleged rape of a retarded student. In press comments he accused news organizations of "not having a conscience. I am shocked at their willingness to embarrass the students just to get a story." The media attention had diverted the school system from its important work—the budget process and final exams. "The main focus now is . . . getting the kids back to doing what they normally do," he said. "We need to steer them away from dwelling on it."

One step toward restoring a normal school environment, Buonomo said, was suspending the five students for the balance of the academic year. This action was not intended to punish them or even to cast judgment on what they had done, he said. Evidently, it also was not done to safeguard other students, other young women, against the accused rapists. "They're suspended so their presence in school will not add to the current disruption," the principal explained. His goal was tranquility.

Another measure to reestablish "normalcy" would be the exclusion from graduation of the four seniors who had been arrested. But Buonomo did not use the word *exclusion*. "The parents of the boys have indicated their wish that they not impact or disrupt the rest of the students, and we fully support that," he said. In other words, it was all the parents' idea.

With educators urging the students to maintain "solidarity" with the accused and to be open-minded about what they had done, most of the seniors naturally thought that the four senior athletes should be allowed to attend graduation. Eighty-five out of the 103 seniors signed a petition that would have given their four classmates the "choice" of taking part in the graduation. The school disregarded the petition, but a parents' committee permitted the four to attend the post-graduation parties officially sponsored by the town. The committee members didn't have a choice; parents who were friends of the four seniors threatened to withdraw their funding of the parties.

While the Glen Ridge principal advocated neutrality and longed for a return to school routine, another administrator did offer an opinion. She seemed to be questioning the reliability of Charlie Figueroa, the one student who had spoken to his teacher and the police about what happened on March 1. Rose McCaffery, the superintendent of schools, in an interview with reporters, discussed Figueroa's account of how the Jocks had asked him to videotape a second encounter with Leslie Faber.

McCaffery said that Figueroa had received counseling and "was often seen" in the school's "resource room." She said that his statements were suspect because he "likes to fantasize."

"Charlie has a knack of fantasizing and takes off and starts discussing things," the town's top school official said.

Realizing, perhaps, that she had misspoken, McCaffery added, "I'm not saying this is not true at all. Because of the statements he made, we immediately notified the police."

One effect of McCaffery's remark was to raise doubts about the prosecutor's case against the five students. Figueroa was the only person who had independently confirmed part of Leslie's story. That's all the prosecution had. Everyone else who knew about it was as silent as a mummy.

McCaffery was also dishing out ammunition to those in Glen Ridge who believed the boys were innocent of wrongdoing or who wanted to deny that anything serious had taken place. On the opposite side, those who believed that the suspects had raped Leslie interpreted the superintendent's remarks as one more attempt by the town to cover up a devastating scandal. Whatever one made of her public comments, it was difficult for town residents to overlook the apparent inequity: Figueroa's school history and personal behavior had been made public, but not a word had been said to the public about the school records and behavior of Chris Archer, Kevin and Kyle Scherzer, Bryant Grober, and Peter Quigley.

A year and a half later, Charlie Figueroa and his family brought a $25 million defamation-of-character suit against the township of Glen Ridge, Rose McCaffery, Policeman Richard Corcoran, the Glen Ridge Police Department, and the board of education. In September 1993 Figueroa settled the suit out of court for a reported $21,000.

But in May 1989 McCaffery and the president of the board of education were insisting that the school had acted properly. At the same time, McCaffery announced that a retired appellate judge, eighty-year-old Samuel Larner, had been hired for $5,000 to study whether school system employees "properly and promptly" reported information about the case to the police.

The town government agreed with school officials that it was important to be impartial and nonjudgmental, that equal concern should be expressed for the accused and the victim.

Five days after the arrests, Glen Ridge held its Memorial Day parade under a sparkling sky. Doug Archer, dressed in his Navy uniform, marched briskly down Ridgewood Avenue to the municipal building, where Mayor Edward Callahan, Jr., told some five hundred Ridgers: "We have all experienced a range of emotions which include repulsion, anger, deep concern for the victim of this alleged act and her family as well as a similar concern for the parties who have been charged and their families." He implored his constituents to show "deep and mature compassion for the victim of these alleged acts, for the accused, and for all persons who are directly or indirectly involved in this tragedy."

The mayor emphasized that everyone in the town had acted properly. Not only public officials. Just about everybody who lived there had done the right thing and was blameless for what had happened—if anything really did happen. "We have . . . seen the name of our town unfairly treated as being part of this horrendous alleged act," he said. "We, the thinking people of this community, categorically reject the concept of universal guilt."

When there is a moral void at the top, you find cheap cynicism down below. Unable or unwilling to make moral distinctions, Glen Ridge's leaders left a vacuum for cynicism. And so it was that a few days after the arrests, a teacher in the middle school heard some sounds, punctuated by giggles, coming from the back of her classroom. As she eased toward the back, she could make out grunts and moans and a few muffled words. "Do it to me. More, more, oooh."

Five seventh-grade girls were making the sounds. "What is going on here?" the teacher asked. "That's the way a retard sounds when she's being raped," one girl answered, her words choked by laughter.

39

The reporters walked the base path and outfield of Cartaret Park. They focused their telescopic lenses on the entrance to 34 Lorraine Street. At night the camera crews carried their lamps onto the porches of the town's quotables, bathing the rattan furniture in a fierce white light that cast fretwork shadows across lush emerald lawns. Under flickering gas lamps they patrolled the streets. After a few days the reporters and the technicians moved on, but they left their imprint on Glen Ridge.

Their stories played heavily on the theme of race and class. In journalistic shorthand, the accused were "boys who had everything": nice teenage clothes, nice well-kept houses, and nice, respectable, responsible parents. The implicit assumption of their stories was: You didn't expect boys who looked like this to do bad things. You didn't expect gang rapes in Glen Ridge. The unexpected was news.

The *New York Daily News*, for example, described the boys as the "privileged sons" of a "picture book" suburb. The *New York Times* compared the alleged sexual assault in "this well-off Essex County suburb" with the gang rape of a jogger in Central Park in New York. The New York case involved a white victim and black suspects. But the kids arrested in Glen Ridge were white and middle and upper-middle class, which led the *Times* to ponder whether there was something about "teen-age group behavior" in general that was potentially destructive. "The Glen Ridge arrests seem likely to intensify public rage and agony over teen-age crime and its causes," the *Times* said in its theme paragraph. The media were making their contrast in black and white, in rich and poor. Central Park and Glen Ridge: a blend that had legs.

The headline with the most painful sting ran on the front page of the *New York Post*, a tabloid known for its jackhammer approach to journalism. It read: "TOWN OF SHAME." Inside the paper, another headline said: "A town's dirty little secret that wouldn't go away." The *Post*, in contradistinction to Mayor Callahan, believed in universal responsibility—or, at the least, complicity.

The editorial comments were still more unsparing. Ridgers were startled when the normally boosterish hometown weekly, the *Glen Ridge Paper*, said in an editorial that young people who criticized the athletes "are being persecuted." The editorial continued:

> Parents are begging their children not to say anything for fear they'll find their house spraypainted, or their tires slashed. People are speaking to the press, but anonymously, in order to avoid harassment. And by whom? Teenagers. It's more than frightening, it's absolutely terrifying.

The *North Jersey Herald and News*, a nearby daily, described Glen Ridge as the "town without pity" and found that adulation of athletes in the community created an "ethic of favoritism" that almost resulted in "sweeping an unspeakable and brutal crime under the rug."

In an editorial entitled "Brutality in Glen Ridge," *The Record*, one of New Jersey's most influential papers, said that "the victim, unfortunately, is as much on trial as those accused of assaulting her." However the case was resolved, the paper said, "one thing is clear: Something terribly wrong did happen in Glen Ridge. It went on for an hour, and it was brutal, humiliating, and degrading. Even if the young men believed she was consenting, how could they do such things to her?"

The town held several meetings during which residents got a chance to vent their anger and frustration, but they never did a reexamination of their values that could have led to reconstruction. Instead, they cast themselves as blameless victims of the callous sensation-mongering of the media. Ben Tantillo, the vice-principal, agreed with many town residents when he later said, "Why did the Glen Ridge story take off? Because, I think, it had everything: a poor, mentally handicapped girl, athletes, a black informer in a high-class white neighborhood. You couldn't have written a better script."

To some extent, he had a point. One might compare the Glen Ridge story with the rape of a thirteen-year-old girl in the blue-collar Jersey city of Bordentown by five teenagers in October 1988. This crime got scant news coverage. Bordentown was not Glen Ridge.

The media, as Tantillo justifiably complained, exploited the theme of evil in Eden. But that didn't change the essence of what had happened in Glen Ridge. It didn't change the fact that the incident opened to scrutiny how adults in a privileged community went about raising, socializing, and teaching children. Reverend Clayton Nelson, the pastor of Christ Church in Glen Ridge, found his fellow townspeople mired in "denial, and anger at the media. Our first reaction is to deny it has happened. Our second is to be angry and blaming."

Often, the person who got the blame was Leslie. Ben Tantillo later speculated that the "town had a hard time being sensitive to [Leslie] because they viewed her—I don't even know this for a fact—as sexually active." People considered Leslie's experience in the basement, Tantillo said, less significant than protecting the town's image: "It's Valhalla out here, Glen Ridge, whatever you want to call it."

In the weeks that followed the arrest, there were many stories criticizing "the town without pity" for denying responsibility, blaming the victim, and defending the alleged rapists. But Glen Ridge's reaction wasn't all that unusual. Although the press and the town didn't recognize it, almost everything involved with March 1—from the economic and social status of victim and victimizers, to the reaction of the town, to the delays in reporting the incident and making arrests, to the "neutrality" of school and town officials—fit the increasingly common pattern of gang rape and its aftershocks.

40

Many Ridgers denied that the alleged crime could have happened, as it was depicted by the media, because it didn't conform to their idea of a typical gang rape. The suspects were popular and handsome and didn't have any problem attracting girls. How could they be gang rapists? But experts who studied the case reached just the opposite conclusion: that what happened in Glen Ridge wasn't exceptional at all. It had all the elements of a classic gang rape. In fact, the very questions raised by some of the townspeople highlight the similarities between this case and other gang rapes.

For example, one response voiced by many people in the town was: *Why would boys who had so much do something like this?*

The question implies that money inoculates against evil. However, the recent research into sexual violence does not support that conclusion: Sex crimes are not limited to any economic class. It's just harder for some people to believe that a bunch of well-off, well-groomed kids would do something like this. That is why it's tough to get a jury to convict them. Judith Becker, director of the sex behavior clinic of the New York State Psychiatric Institute, said when she heard about the Glen Ridge case: "Most people think only minority kids commit these crimes. The fact is there's an equal number, but mostly minority cases are reported and go through the system. The other cases are covered up."

Another characteristic response: *Why would the most popular boys, leaders in the school and town, do something like this?*

To answer that question, it's useful to imagine another privileged community and its leaders—for instance, a community composed of college students. Like Glen Ridge, many college communities adhere to fairly homogeneous, traditional values and share common goals and expectations. And they select as some of their leaders young men who act the way the Glen Ridge young men did.

When the psychologist Chris O'Sullivan studied twenty-four documented cases of alleged gang rape on college campuses from 1981 to 1991, she found that it was the elite group at the colleges that were more likely to be involved. These included football and basketball players and members of prestigious fraternities. Not only were these young men regarded as above suspicion on campus, but their elevated status also discouraged them from moral reflection; it made them feel entitled, she said. In a similar fashion, the respect the Ridger Jocks received at the preppie high school they attended did not motivate them to think twice about their behavior.

Anthropologist Peggy Reeves Sanday writes that counselors report that "gang rape is a regular event on every college campus." In fact, some classmates of the Glen Ridge suspects said that they learned about "pulling train" and other practices associated with gang rape from older friends and brothers and sisters in college. A psychologist, Bernice Sandler, studied 110 cases of gang rapes on college campuses during the 1980s for the Association of American Colleges. Comparing these rapes to the Glen Ridge case, she told the *New York Times*, "I thought, No difference. Same scenario."

Why do people assume that athletes are going to go out and commit sex crimes?

Because in disproportionate numbers they do. That was another characteristic of the Glen Ridge case that was consistent with studies of gang rape. For the Glen Ridge suspects and their friends, life had always been centered around The Team. They played sports in which force and aggressiveness are prized. Bernice Sandler, who found striking similarities in the Glen Ridge allegations to the rape cases she studied in universities, said of these college males: "If they are not involved in a fraternity, they are members of sports teams. And it is team sports—football and basketball. It's never the golfers or swimmers." In 1986 an FBI survey found that football and basketball players were reported to police for sexual assault 38 percent more often than the average male college student.

Around the time of the Glen Ridge case, athletes at a number of universities—including St. John's in New York, the University of Oklahoma, Kentucky State University, the University of Wyoming, and the University of Minnesota—were charged with some former sexual misconduct.

Researchers disagree over whether the force and aggressiveness required to succeed in some sports nurture a tendency toward the abuse of women who are physically weaker than the athletes. But there isn't any argument that athletes form a special, distinct, and often protected class of adolescents and young men in high school and college, and that some of these men think their status entitles them to do whatever they want to women.

A former football lineman for the New York Giants told the author, "In my sophomore year of college, I never got out of bed. While my roommate went to class, I was sleeping off fucking all night. There were girls we treated like property. They were our 'whores' and the jocks shared them. We could do whatever we wanted with them. Lots of people in the school knew about it, but nobody said a word. We were the jocks and we got what we wanted."

In this athletic hothouse, jocks make friends, shape common values, and circulate their tales of sexual exploits. Dr. Mary Koss, who directed a pioneering study of sexual assault on campus for the National Institutes of Health, found that athletes were involved in approximately one-third of the cases she studied. "My gut feeling about gang rape is that it takes place in front of guys who know each other," she told the *New York Times*. "They live together, have a way that they become bonded together. They need a culture that supports treating women this way."

In Glen Ridge, as in many other American communities, belligerence, physical strength, competitiveness, a sense of superiority, winning above all—these qualities dominated all realms of these boys' childhoods from the nursery school to high school graduation. Males who demonstrated such traits were cherished.

In a more heterogeneous community, youngsters like the Glen Ridge boys might have found alternative models of masculinity—regular guys who enjoyed watching a tightly pitched baseball game but who also demonstrated compassion, fairness, and thoughtfulness. Guys who took more pleasure in appreciating females than in humiliating them. But in Glen Ridge the few public dissenters from the Jock ethic were treated as social pariahs.

Many members of the Jock clique grew up in isolation from girls, and that is often a characteristic of young men who rape in groups. Their families were primarily male: Of the defendants actually charged with first-degree rape, only Bryant Grober had sisters. The rest had only brothers. Their immediate environment did not cultivate great empathy for women. Also, apart from athletics, the Glen Ridge guys engaged in few organized activities in the school and the community—such as the band or volunteer social service efforts—where boys and girls participated together, on an equal footing, where they might have got to know members of the opposite sex as human beings worthy of caring and respect.

The psychologist Chris O'Sullivan reviewed literature about rape in different cultures around the world, and found that rape was more prevalent where the sexes were separated. "In rape-prone societies, the sexes are separated not only physically but also by rigid sex-role differentiation in which the male role is more valued. Thus, we might expect gang rapes to be most common among men who not only live apart from women but also perform roles closed to women (e.g., football players and fraternity members)."

As so many young men are, these Ridgers were taught that women's main purpose was to be decorative and to please and praise men. (Who were the young women in their lives but cheerleaders and wannabe cheer-leaders?) A girl who resisted this role was treated as one more opponent to be dominated or bullied into submission, the way an opposing team would be treated. Everywhere they looked—at school, in sports, at parties—the Jocks saw evidence that boys were entitled to take what they wanted from girls. It was the norm, not the exception, for the guys to assume the girls would feel honored to be included in the company of the town's exalted males, even if the price of inclusion was abuse.

It doesn't make sense—why would you do something like this in front of a dozen witnesses?

The power that gang rapists feel individually is multiplied many times when they are in their group. The presence of the group heightens the "thrill." Robin Warshaw writes:

> Gang rape also carries with it an added dose of humiliation. . . . Even when members of the group do not all participate directly, some may watch the rapes or take photographs or simply know "what's going on in the other room," and do nothing to stop it. . . . Indeed, members usually don't want to stop the rape because it enhances the group's good opinion of itself. The hu-miliation of the victim continues after a gang acquaintance rape as the group members brag to others who know the woman about their "achievement." And the woman feels horribly betrayed by men she may have to continue to see in her everday life.

Psychologist Chris O'Sullivan points out that in a group, even fringe members who otherwise would be repelled by their leaders' conduct may lose their sense of compassion for a potential victim. Another group char-acteristic is the loss of individuality. "Nice guys" are able to forget they are nice. "Wimps" are able to shed their "wimpishness."

These guys were just good buddies; don't make anything more out of their friendship.

The devotion to activities such as circle-jerks, "voyeuring," oral sex performed by one girl on a number of guys, humiliating girls, and watch-ing pornography together may suggest a homoerotic tendency among members of adolescent male groups that become involved in sexual as-saults. And in the Glen Ridge group, homoeroticism may have been a fac-tor. But some analysts interpret such adolescent behavior not as homoerotic but as an effort to prove heterosexual dominance and to establish masculine authority within the group. The real goal is overcoming your own insecurities about sex by impressing your friends with your sexual prowess. To achieve that goal, a guy needs an audience to witness his dominating performance. A group of appreciative and responsive buddies is essential to build a reputation for sexual control and domination.

Why would guys who had all these girls fawning after them get pleasure out of sticking a baseball bat into a neighbor's vagina?

Someone who knew the guys well might respond: Because they got a kick out of it. The social philosopher Myriam Miedzian, author of the book *Boys Will Be Boys,* said to *Time* magazine, "Why do a bunch of boys in Glen Ridge . . . think it is fun to shove baseball bats and broom handles into the vagina of a retarded girl? This isn't sex. It is violence." Dr. Miedzian was speaking before the case came to trial, but the ultimate verdict by a jury seemed less important to her than the values of the guys in the basement. "It really doesn't matter what is ultimately decided. What bothers me is why they think that is fun."

Yes, that is troubling, but not very unusual. Gang rapes more often involve elements of humiliation than one-on-one rapes. Robin Warshaw, the author of a book on acquaintance rape, cites a number of studies that find that certain abusive behavior is twice as likely to occur in gang rapes as in individual assaults: urinating on the victim; forced fellatio; pulling, burning, and biting the breasts; demanding that the woman masturbate herself while the rapists masturbate as they watch their victim. In her statements to police, Leslie described being forced to provide oral sex; she said that the boys asked her to put her fingers in her vagina and masturbate herself, and that they asked her to masturbate them.

Susan Brownmiller found in her study of wartime rape that "the ramming of a stick, a bottle, or some other object into a woman's vagina is a not uncommon *coup de grace.*" Citing one study of rapes in Philadelphia, Brownmiller says that in one-quarter of the cases "the victim was subject to some form of extra insult beyond the simple rape. Sexual humiliation ran higher in group rapes than in individual rapes."

Bragging about what they have done completes the ritual of gang rape. It's one more chance to humiliate the victim and demonstrate the victimizer's contempt for the rules and principles that apply to mere mortals. For the Glen Ridge guys, sex was more of a public than a private act. It was a coup to get sexual release while your buddies watched. But it doubled the satisfaction when you could sit in the school lunchroom the next day, as Kevin Scherzer did, and brag about it.

Peggy Reeves Sanday writes that fraternity brothers will refer to women they spent the night with as "gashes," "hosebags," and "heifers." To be accepted within the inner circle of the Jock clique in Glen Ridge, you had to be willing to tell your buddies about your sexual experiences, spicing your stories with lots of humiliating put-downs of the girl. For years the boys bragged about "voyeuring," and "Hoovering." They talked of girls as "pigs" and "animals." They boasted about their Saturday-night "blow jobs" within the hearing of the girl who had submitted to their demands, as well as any other teenager who was interested.

Compare their contempt for women to the comments made by frat members. Boasting about their latest degradation, the frat brothers describe *their* target as an "animal" or a "cunt" or "just disgusting." Because they regard her as barely human, it is one short step to treating her as subhuman.

What was "voyeuring" but a way of advertising sexual conquests and demeaning young women? In her study of fraternity gang rape, Peggy Reeves Sanday describes the practice of "beaching" by frat brothers, in which—by looking through windows from a nearby terrace—they watch another frat member having sex with a young woman. "The girls involved do not know they are being watched," Sanday says. "Usually the male knows that he is being watched, indeed he may communicate his intention to the brothers and leave the light on so as to make it easier for brothers to watch."

Why would they pick on someone who knew them so well and could tell their parents and identify them to the police?

The classic target of the rapist is someone the predator knows. A Justice Department report, studying the years 1992 and 1993, found that 80 percent of the 310,000 rapes occurring each year were committed by someone familiar to the victim. The pattern of "acquaintance rape" is quite distinct: The woman chosen for humiliation is someone the rapists know but is rarely an intimate friend or girlfriend of a group member. Most often she is regarded as an "outsider"—somebody who looks or seems different, who doesn't meet the standards the group sets for female attractiveness or sensuality. That is, they pick somebody like Leslie Faber.

And they pick her just because it's unlikely that she will tell anybody about what happened. She's too ashamed; she's scared that these popular guys will ostracize her; or she just doesn't understand what rape is. To would-be abusers, she seems like a safe bet.

Even if they were looking for someone who would submit to them, why would they pick a retarded woman whom they ridiculed as unattractive?

Maybe they wouldn't have if the issue had been sex. But, of course, it wasn't. The Jocks wanted to experiment, to test their power. Leslie was there for their amusement.

Anthropologist Peggy Reeves Sanday and other analysts have noted that the victim in sexual assault cases is often incapacitated—high on drugs or alcohol or, as in Leslie's case, mentally retarded. As Robin Warshaw notes, "The victim may be unpopular, unattractive, or simply naive and therefore easily flattered by the attention suddenly lavished on her before the assault begins." Leslie Faber got a lot of attention from her "heroes" in Cartaret Park and even more attention when she went with them to the basement.

Is it worth ruining so many lives to punish guys who got carried away for an hour?

Many powerful people in and out of Glen Ridge seem to think it is not. On campuses youths accused of group sexual assaults are rarely punished, researchers have found, and prosecutors are unlikely to prosecute. Often, the first response is not to build a case against the suspects but to cover up the allegations. In colleges or in municipalities, governing bodies and law enforcement agencies often believe that the shame disclosure would bring to the community far outweighs the value of prosecuting the accused.

That's because those who are in charge, in the courtroom or in the town or on the campus, tend to buy into certain myths about rape. For example, in the Bordentown case friends of the Bordentown boys said that the victim "asked to be raped" because she got drunk at a party. In Glen Ridge the guys' friends said Leslie asked for it because she was "flirtatious." Researchers working in different disciplines and in different settings throughout the United States have found that when adolescents and young men are accused of rape, many community members leap to the conclusion that it was up to the victim to regulate and control both her behavior *and* the behavior of her assailants. Blaming the rape victim is a common response—and not only in Glen Ridge.

There are other common responses:

When a girl enters a frat house or a basement with a group of guys, she is seen as complicitous in her own assault. "What was she doing there if she didn't want it?" the boys' friends and family members ask.

Many males, and not always young males, and a substantial number of females—*42 percent*—say they believe that if guys are aroused by the victim, it's legitimate and acceptable behavior to force sex on her, according to a survey by the National Clearinghouse on Marital and Date Rape. In some frat houses and jock dormitories, girls wearing low-cut or tight dresses are considered "fair game" for all the brothers or male residents.

Female friends of the accused rally to their defense, as the Jockettes did in Glen Ridge. What better way to win acceptance in the most popular clique in college or in Glen Ridge High than by defending the suspects against a young woman considered socially unacceptable?

In its rationalizations, excuses, and obfuscations; its willingness to blame and demonize the victim; its attempts to bury the charges, Glen Ridge was typical. It was special in only one respect: What happened there, what happened to Leslie Faber, could not be hidden. Not this time.

"I would not have said those boys could have done such a thing in a million years. What's happening in the world?" said a neighbor of the Scherzer family.

In this woman's mind, "those boys" were the least likely rapists she could imagine—not because they had such stellar characters but because the town had a stellar character. But the boys didn't live only in Glen Ridge. They also lived in a larger, malignant world. What was happening in that world also formed them.

Since their early teens, and maybe before that, they reveled in reading and watching pornography, activities favored by others who engage in gang rape, according to experts. Like the Glen Ridge clique members, some of the frat brothers Peggy Reeves Sanday interviewed would watch pornography before a party started. Sanday notes that pornography may often constitute a primer on gang rape, because the two main ingredients are "shared titillation and a certain distance between the viewer and the sex. . . . There is a thin line between getting off by proxy on the screen and getting off on a surrogate in the house."

One Glen Ridge senior told a writer for *Rolling Stone*, "They'd all get together [to watch pornographic movies] and they'd just start cheering. They just started fucking going, 'Yeah! Yeah! Yeah, look at that.'" Another student recalled that the Jocks would shout as they watched the movie, "Excellent! Fuck her!"

Some porn movies provide a how-to guide for guys who later commit gang rape: the woman/victim is insatiable in her need for sex; she may resist rape, but once it happens, she loves it; providing blow jobs is an ecstatic experience; the more guys she can have sex with at once, and the more orifices in her body that are penetrated by human parts or fabricated objects, the more exciting and fulfilling the sex is.

The point many analysts make is that a movie doesn't have to have an "X" rating or be labeled as "pornography" to contain themes that depict sexual violence and group rape. Mainstream culture is full of such references. Sociologist Gail Dines-Levy says, "Sex and violence have become inextricably confused in the minds of young people." And psychologist Daniel Linz observes, "The first sexual experience for many boys is a slasher movie."

It's no secret that the blending of sex and violence has become commonplace in American popular culture. A study published in *Ms.* magazine in 1990 found that one out of eight Hollywood movies depicts a rape theme. By the age of eighteen, the average youth has watched 250,000 acts of violence and 40,000 attempted murders on television, according to a study by the U.S. Bureau of Justice Statistics in 1990.

This study did not consider the impact of lyrics of popular rock songs, not to speak of the savage treatment of women in "gangsta" rap or in the misogynistic shticks of comedians like Andrew Dice Clay. The world the Glen Ridge boys moved in was saturated with this stuff. On his drives around town, Chris Archer would chant the rap lyrics from a song about sexual violence committed with a bat. The Beastie Boys' song "Paul Revere" came from the group's album *Licensed to Kill*. In March 1987 the album was number one on *Billboard's* "Top Pop Albums" chart, and the top-selling LP for CBS records.

In the community where they grew up and which celebrated their athletic achievements; in their isolation from women and their evolving attitudes toward girls; in their fascination with voyeurism and pornography and in their actual treatment of young women; and, finally, in their choice of victim—in all these respects, the Glen Ridge Jocks resembled the contemporary profile of other privileged and popular male groups that were accused of committing sexual assaults of women. That's not something most Ridgers, who were unaware of the research into group rapes, would have realized or would have been willing to accept.

41

In the eye of the hurricane, the Fabers tried to keep their lives as normal as possible. When the phone rang, they didn't pick it up. If they had to leave the house, they took their car. They adopted a policy of silence. Above all, they wanted to protect Leslie. They didn't go shopping with her in the Glen Ridge area, and they didn't let her go anywhere near Cartaret Park.

But the Fabers couldn't be with her every minute of the day.

On Friday, May 26, two days after the arrest, Lisa Marie Petersen, *The Record* reporter who had interviewed Glen Ridge students the day before, had a new assignment: to gather information for a profile of the victim. Early in the afternoon, the reporter entered West Orange High School and walked over to where special ed classes were held. She saw a young woman standing near a locker in the corridor. The reporter asked her, "Do you know the girl in the Glen Ridge case?" The young woman answered, "Yes, that's me." Lisa Marie asked Leslie if she would go outside and talk to her. Leslie said, Oh, sure.

Lisa Marie looked like the kind of young woman Leslie always wanted to make friends with. She was athletic and attractive. She wore a bright pink jumpsuit and lots of silver jewelry. She had a deep tan. It appeared to the reporter that Leslie "felt really uncomfortable" talking about her experience. But Lisa Marie persisted. She spent only twenty minutes sitting under the shade tree with Leslie.

Then Leslie excused herself to catch her ride home. Lisa Marie Petersen went looking for a phone. "What have you got?" her editor asked.

"I got her," Petersen said.

"You what—?"

"Her. I got the victim."

The story ran on Sunday, May 28, on the paper's front page. The headline over the story worked on several levels: "A Victim's Story: A Painful Act, Followed by a Deeper Hurt."

Petersen's story began with a quote from Leslie, referring to the Jocks:

"I thought I did trust them." It went on to describe how she was invited to the Scherzer basement. Lisa Marie wrote that Leslie "doesn't want to talk much about what happened next. Her lip quivers, her eyes mist over, and she turns her head away." That's when Petersen's one kernel of news appears in the story. Leslie is quoted as saying of the encounter at the Scherzers' house: "Some of it was force, some of it I allowed . . . because they wouldn't think I'd like them [if I didn't]."

The story went on to say that Leslie was upset by the way the press had depicted her as retarded. As a result of all the media attention, Leslie supposedly told *The Record* reporter, students at her high school were "teasing" her, saying, "Oh, that's you, the girl with the broomstick and the bat."

Petersen's story also provided a number of descriptive details: Leslie's jewelry, her hairstyle, her clothes, even the lettering on her T-shirt. If some kids knew about her before, the story made her even more identifiable.

It had a profound effect. Now more kids knew who Leslie was. They started calling her the "bat girl." Petersen's story demonstrated to the Fabers and to the school that if they let her move about the school and the town on her own, it could invite more stories, more occasions where Leslie would say anything and do anything to accommodate a new friend.

The school changed the times when she would be picked up by bus and left off in Glen Ridge. She wasn't allowed to leave her classroom unless she was accompanied by an adult. She couldn't go to the bathroom without an adult present. In Glen Ridge Leslie was more isolated than ever. Her parents wouldn't let her play by herself; she couldn't ride around town alone on her bike.

But Leslie didn't understand that it was *The Record* story that changed things. She thought her parents were punishing her. She thought it was the prosecutors' idea to keep her from her favorite activity—playing sports. She was angry at all of them for not letting her be herself. Leslie had no idea of how journalism worked.

42

Friday, June 23, Graduation. The four seniors who had been excluded were not forgotten by their admirers. A few hours before graduation, some students had spray-painted the driveway in front of the school: CONGRATS PETE, KYLE, KEVIN . . . WE LOVE YOU.

Regardless of the circumstances, the school and town wanted to give the Class of '89 an elegant send-off. Ordinarily, graduation night in Glen Ridge resembled a fancy-dress village party, a town fiesta in formal wear. This year there was less gaiety. This was the year of the "incident." Each graduate's family was given six tickets, and every ticket was checked before the guests were permitted to find their seats. Private security guards and most of the town's fourteen uniformed policemen patrolled the sidelines, eyeing the crowd and whispering into their transmitters. Reporters and camera crews prowled near the edge of the field.

For a moment, though, the 450 people sitting on the plastic chairs on the athletic field could shut out the distractions on the street and imagine that nothing had changed—or would ever change. The homogeneity of the audience was apparent—the men in their tropical-weight suits, the women in their feathery summer dresses. The similarities among the spectators momentarily disguised the divisions the case had created.

That same surface homogeneity was apparent among the graduates lining up in the back of the field. Their parents and friends would be reassured by the smooth succession from one generation to another, a transition that promised that the future would resemble the past. In the faces of these kids, the parents could conjure their own origins. Among the 105 graduates, there were four blacks; Glen Ridge was 97 percent white. There were eleven Jewish kids in the senior class; Glen Ridge was more than 85 percent Christian. Seventy-five percent of the graduates had been accepted in four-year colleges, and another 10 percent were entering two-year colleges; 65 percent of their parents had attended college. Unless the progeny deserted Glen Ridge in droves, the town would remain predominantly white, Christian, reasonably affluent, and relatively well educated.

Although the four seniors who had been charged with rape were missing, three of them would be there for the town-sponsored parties that would take place later in the evening. Only Bryant Grober would choose not to attend the festivities.

But the Jockettes would not let the absence of their guys from commencement go unnoticed. A dozen of the most loyal among them, the Little Mothers, deviated from the customary graduation attire and pinned small yellow bows to their gowns at the waist or shoulder. This was a full decade after yellow ribbons signified the absence of Americans held hostage in Iran, but the purpose tonight was roughly the same: to recognize those who couldn't be there. The yellow ribbons were the Jockettes' way of saying: We miss our guys.

It had rained earlier, and the students tiptoed through the mud, proceeding two by two toward their seats in the temporary bleachers behind the makeshift stage. In New York or in adjacent Bloomfield, high school kids would rent identical black caps and gowns for $10. Not here. In Glen Ridge the boys paid $60 to Starlight Tuxedos to rent their white dinner jackets, red bow ties, matching carnations, and black tuxedo pants with satin stripes. The girls would spend from $200 to $700 on the white formal gowns they bought from specialty shops in the malls or from Vera Plumb Sample Bridals in Montclair. That was appropriate, since many of the young women looked as if they could be attending a wedding: As brides would, some carried the trains of their gowns and clutched a spray of spring flowers. Their dresses were high style, 1989: see-through lace panels across the bodice, asymmetrical hemlines, off-the-shoulder necklines. Some had spent hours that morning getting their hair done at Exposé Hair and Nail or Who Cut Your Hair? in Bloomfield.

As each speaker mounted the stage, the crowd stirred expectantly. Would any of the speakers be so crude as to mention what had happened on March 1 at 34 Lorraine Street? The answer was: They would and they wouldn't. You might find hints or inferences in their bromides, but no forthright discussion.

Reverend Leisey, minister of the Congregational Church, talked about the need of youngsters "to belong to a specific group of their peers." But he reassured the audience that intimacy between parents and children could counteract the influence and pressure of peers. "The power of parenting still prevails over the power of peers in the arena of human values."

The Glen Ridge High School chorus sang a Billy Joel song. The sweet child voices, cracking a little on the high notes, brought an understanding titter from the audience that greeted Josh Golin as he took his place at the microphone.

Joshua Golin, the speaker of the Class of 1989, decided to make his statement by omission. Before he began his speech, he ran off the list of all those who were supposed to be recognized at such events. Members of the board of education. The principal. Teachers. Parents. The Class of '89. One name was conspicuous by its absence: Rose McCaffery, superintendent of schools, who had said of Charlie Figueroa, "Charlie has a knack of fantasizing." Golin never acknowledged her presence, but it was a slight of less than crushing impact. It happened so fast that hardly anybody noticed.

In a squeaky, thin voice, Josh went on to recount the past few months obliquely, but more explicitly than any of the other speakers. "Our class is a class which has certainly been maligned in the past few weeks. We have been threatened with everything from bombs to bodily harm. All one had to do was pick up a newspaper to read what a terrible class we were." But Josh praised students who had striven to "achieve great academic success" and he gave equal time to the school teams that had won championships. It was a diplomatic speech.

Michael Connolly kept his valedictorian address brief. Turning toward his fellow students, he said, "We've certainly been through a lot together. . . . Looking back ten or twenty years from today we can remember how we've loved these days." The class stood and cheered him. Michael's serious expression melted into a smile.

The principal was the last speaker. "Perhaps more than anything, I've learned that adversity when faced rightly and bluntly builds character and makes you stronger and stronger," Buonomo said. "The Class of '89 is a very strong class. They faced adversity and they're stronger for it."

The climactic moment had arrived. It was time to award the diplomas to the Class of '89. Buonomo turned the mike over to Kathryn Kahn, president of the board of education. Mrs. Kahn, a slender woman with angular features, always conducted the board's business in a brisk, terse manner. Tonight's business was no different. She was there to award the diplomas—and she did that without flourishes.

One unconventional practice at Glen Ridge graduations was to permit the graduates to pick adults of their choosing to present them with their diplomas. It was strange the way it worked out. If a parent (in Glen Ridge, most likely a dad) held public office or was prominent in local politics, he would give the diploma to his son or daughter. The children of carpenters and accountants had their diplomas presented by Mrs. Kahn.

"Charles Figueroa," Mrs. Kahn read from her list. As Charlie's name was called, someone hissed, someone booed, a couple of people applauded and cheered, and one person called out, *Snitch*. Charlie, who had attended military school in his junior year, marched stiffly toward Mrs. Kahn without turning his head, took his diploma, wheeled around, and marched back to his seat. Kahn called the next name without missing a beat.

After she presented a diploma to the last of the graduates, the audience erupted with applause and cheers. For the seniors who were present, Glen Ridge High was history.

With friends and family members, they drifted away from the athletic field and toward their homes to get ready for the parties to come. Elaine Monacelli, a member of the school board, told a reporter, "We just wanted to give the students one really good night, because they've really been under a lot of stress for the last month."

The celebrations began with a dinner at the country club. This was the first of three parties that the town would hold for the graduates tonight. A second party, held under a tent and built around a theme selected by the students, would begin at 1 A.M. The last of the celebrations was a poolside breakfast that ended around 7 A.M.

After the dinner the graduates went to a party held in the grandest of the mansions on Ridgewood Avenue. The theme tonight was Roman Times. The boys wore their bedsheet togas ankle-length, the girls wore theirs mid-calf. A few of the more ambitious boys had designed gladiator costumes. Hours before the kids arrived, the parents had trucked in mock columns, a mini-amphitheater, a "Roman" fountain from the showroom of the local utility company, and plastic flowers from the window displays of a nearby department store.

The kids, happily jammed seven or eight to a car, parked in the torch-lined driveway. They gathered beneath the yellow-and-white striped tent to consume mass quantities of popcorn and Swedish meatballs and hot dogs. They tested their aim with the Cleopatra Grape Toss and provoked snickers as they tossed rings at cardboard cutouts of Buonomo and assorted teachers attired in Roman costumes. ("Hang One on a Teacher. (Or Principal.)") When they circled around the keno and poker tables, some of the kids seemed extra-animated. Their eyes gleamed with an alcohol shine. They had loaded up in the cars on the way to the party; a few had tossed back beers or sipped champagne at home. In the morning parents assigned to the clean-up crew would find in the bushes beer cans and a couple of empty booze bottles.

Then *they* arrived. First, Richie Corcoran, sporting a little brush mustache these days. Richie didn't always exercise iron self-control, and his provocative gestures and comments before the TV cameras had agitated the town, but tonight Richie was greeted by the Jocks and their friends as a swell guy and great buddy.

Kyle and Kevin Scherzer arrived at the party soon after Richie. They were quickly surrounded by their friends and fans. Tonight Kyle didn't look any different than he had most days at school: hair combed neatly to the side, a tentative smile, skin tanned after days of dogging the surf down on the shore. Kyle, absent captain of the divisional champion baseball team, co-captain of the football team. Kyle, as always, acting a little bashful at all the attention he was getting.

"Kyle, baby, howya doin'."

"Kyle, you look mahvelous. Never better. Fan-tastic."

Kyle shrugging it off, eyes studying the grass. Mumbling: "Hey, well, you know. . . . Think I'll get a soda."

His brother, Kevin, was doing Kevin. Slapping palms. Putting an arm-lock around a buddy's neck. Yelling across the tent at a girl who had worn shorts and a T-shirt instead of a toga: "Pat, what's wrong with ya? Don't you want to be a good Roman? C'mon, catch the spirit."

Although Peter Quigley also got a warm greeting from all his buddies, only one person really counted: Tara. While he had been suspended from school and had received home tutoring, Tara had visited him almost every day. Now they were together again—in public.

It seemed like a millisecond ago that they were all freshmen, trying to live up to the legend of their brothers and other past Jocks. Now the old gang was busting up.

Peter and Tara acting love-struck. Kevin eating. Richie telling jokes. Kyle talking quietly with his friends. And the Giggers taking it all in, but never saying a provocative word. No battles tonight. Despite the fears that the different factions in the school might square off with each other, it was turning out to be a normal Glen Ridge graduation night. Games and music and food for a price of $5,000. Not even a reporter trying to crash the party. The chaperones and the cops and the security guards began to relax. Reverend Leisey, a member of the food committee, stood next to the hot dog stand and watched the guys mingling with their friends. True to his religious calling, his first reaction emphasized the power of healing. *Isn't this neat, the way the kids are still ministering to each other.* His second impression was a little more earthy: *Cheez, these guys have balls coming here, acting like nothing's changed.*

Bryant Grober's parents wanted him to keep a low profile. Bryant was spending graduation night at the family house on the Jersey shore, the house where he had spent so much of his childhood and adolescence. His friends had heard that he was severely depressed. Of all the families the Grobers seemed to friends the most stunned and saddened by what had happened.

As dawn broke, the graduates went off to a pool party. The kids were re-ally letting loose by now. Off with the togas, on with the swimming suits. Cannonballing into the pool, screaming, splashing. Kyle and Kevin and Peter playing blackjack. The sounds of good times, echoing down Forest Avenue into the dawn.

It was hard for one young woman to get into the fun and games.

Irene had gone out with Kyle Scherzer for a couple of months. She had known his brother, Kevin, had known all the kids, for seven, eight years, ever since middle school. But she couldn't defend them. She couldn't stand up for them the way Tara and the others did. Acting as if it had been all Leslie's fault. Pretending nothing bad had happened. *Vile* was the word she used when she talked to her friends about them. *Vile* and *heartless*.

She watched Kevin sitting at a poolside table, dealing cards on the red tablecloth. She watched him get up, exaggerating every step as he sneaked up behind the girl standing at the edge of the pool. She watched him unsnap the top of the girl's bathing suit, watched as he pushed her into the pool. The girl shrieked as she came up to the surface, sputtering, "Kevin, why don't you behave yourself? Kevin, people are watching."

Irene saw the girl reaching behind her to hook the top of her suit, acting as if everything was cool. If it happened to me, she thought, I would have said: What's your problem? What-is-wrong-with-you? But no one wanted to challenge them, even after all that had happened. Not tonight, not ever.

The sun was shining. It looked as though it would be a hot, clear day. Steam rose from the slate pavement, and all along Forest Avenue the lawn sprinklers were clicking. The girls and their guys finished off their sausages and scrambled eggs and piled into their cars. They would go home to take a quick shower and pack their bags. Then they would head south to the beach for a few weeks of rest and recreation

Charlie Figueroa didn't go to any of the parties. He wasn't going to a vacation on the beach. Charlie was Public Enemy Number One. Charlie the snitch, they were calling him now. Charlie had wanted to avoid a fight with the Jocks at the party. That would have ruined things for all the kids. So Charlie had gone home right after the graduation ceremonies. When he walked into his house on Essex Avenue, he felt as if a thousand pounds had been lifted from his chest. He looked into the kitchen. His little sister was holding a plate with a slice of chocolate cake on it. "Your graduation cake," she said. He reached for it, but it seemed to slip away. The plate shattered; the cake slid along the linoleum floor. Charlie started to cry. The sobs rippled through his massive body. "Have some coffee," his mother, Mary, said. She tried to lead him to the sofa in the living room. Charlie couldn't move. He felt as if all the strength was seeping out of his body. The tears streamed down his face and soaked his collar. His shirt was sticking to his chest. Charlie didn't stop crying for a long time.

PART V

Justice and Injustice

43

On television the suspects in a sensational case are arrested, and a commercial later the jury is bringing in a verdict. In real life it's usually a little more complicated. In the Glen Ridge case there were lots of complications, and they took a long time to resolve.

Richie Corcoran was one complication. He certainly attracted the interest of the prosecutor's office; yet not one of the twenty or more kids the investigators spoke to ever implicated Richie in the alleged rape. They confirmed that Richie had been in the basement with his friends, but no one said that he did anything to Leslie. Most important, Leslie didn't say he did anything to her.

On June 29 an investigator named Nicholas Guarino questioned young Corcoran. He was treated only as a witness, just as the other spectators had been. Richie insisted that what happened in the basement was Leslie's idea. Bryant didn't drop his pants, according to Richie; Leslie took them down. "And she gave him a blow for about fifteen seconds." Guarino asked him why Bryant told Leslie to stop. "She was biting his dick and he didn't want to do it anymore," Corcoran said.

During the oral sex between Grober and Leslie, Corcoran said, "Some people were laughing and others were saying that she was disgusting and [should] get out of the house." He went on to say, "She was asking people to fuck her and nobody would. Then she was asking people to get an object, and I think she asked for a bottle and they said 'no' and then she asked for a broomstick and they gave it to her. Then she put it in herself."

While all this was going on, Richie said, he was standing in the background, tossing a baseball from one hand to another.

Corcoran was articulating what would become the core argument of the defendants: that Leslie wanted to put objects into her body, that she asked for a broomstick and put one in her vagina.

Richie did say something that didn't help two of his buddies. Guarino asked Richie, "Who gave her the broomstick?"

"I think either Kevin Scherzer or Chris Archer."

"Did you observe anyone holding the broomstick besides Leslie Faber?"

"I think Kevin Scherzer and Chris Archer were holding the end of it."

Although Richie was saying that it was all Leslie's idea, he did confirm her account that Chris and Kevin were the ones who gave her the broomstick and that they *held* it while it was being inserted into her body. This information, coming from one of the two boys' closest friends, dispelled any doubts about who played the lead roles in the basement.

Corcoran also said that he didn't see a baseball bat being inserted into Leslie's body, but he did notice on a table when he entered the basement "a little one that you can get at Yankee Stadium."

The incident was essentially over, Richie said, after the broomstick was inserted. That's when some of the baseball players left the basement, he said.

If Richie felt a great sense of relief, it was understandable. He had given his statement and he had been assured by the people in the prosecutor's office that he was not a suspect and would not be charged with a crime. It appeared, for the moment, that Richie Corcoran was out of the woods.

At one of the long dining tables in the courthouse cafeteria, Leslie and Detective Byron were finishing a couple of slices of pizza. It was Wednesday, August 2, and Leslie chose that moment to share a confidence of monumental significance with Byron.

"I think I have everything figured out about what happened," Sheila began. "The only thing I don't understand is how the stick fits in."

The *stick*. The excellent throwing stick that Leslie had picked up in Cartaret Park before she ran into the Jocks. The stick that Roe Faber had put on the top of her refrigerator and then had given to Sheila before Leslie was questioned at the police station. Leslie looked at Sheila as if she were asking a question that Leslie had answered a thousand times before. "The stick, that's what Richie put into me," Leslie said.

"Excuse me."

"That's what Richie did," Leslie said.

Was it the astonished look on Sheila's face? Was Sheila thinking, Just when it's settling down, just when Lieutenant Corcoran and I are getting back to normal, and all the cover-up headlines are fading away—now she drops the bomb. Leslie read something in Sheila's eyes, and suddenly she seemed frightened. "Are we going now? Are we going home?"

"We're going to go upstairs and talk about this."

"No, I don't want to go."

"I'll tell them, Leslie," the detective said. "You don't have to tell them."

Upstairs in the SARA office, Byron told them what Leslie had just said about the stick and Corcoran. And just about everybody was yelling the same thing. "Leslie, why did you wait? Why didn't you tell us? Leslie, this isn't funny."

Bob Laurino walked into the office, picking up the drift in about ten seconds. Laurino, Mr. Let's-stay-calm Laurino, was visibly angry. "Why didn't you tell us before, Leslie?"

Leslie, backing toward the door, thinking, maybe this is a good time to go to the bathroom *alone*. Leslie said in front of a half-dozen or so witnesses, "I was afraid Sheila would get in trouble. He's her boss, Mr. Corcoran."

For two hours, as long as they could hold Leslie's attention, they went over it, Richie and the stick, the stick and Richie. Finally, with Leslie fading fast, they decided to stop and bring her in the next day to take a statement.

Leslie's statement: "After they used the bat and broomstick, Richard Corcoran put a stick up my vagina. It hurt. I told him that it hurt, but he didn't stop. He was asking me if it made me feel good. Everyone was laughing. It hurt. I was upset. I was crying to myself, but I had tears coming out of my eyes. The stick hurt because it went up me further than the bat and the broomstick."

When Leslie first told her swimming coach about what had happened to her in the basement she had said a "drumstick" had been inserted into her body by the boys in the basement. Later, Charlie Figueroa told the police that the Jocks had described how a "drumstick" was put into Leslie's vagina. But law enforcement officials had only been able to confirm the use of the bat and the broomstick. They didn't understand these references to a drumstick. Now, they surmised that the drumstick really referred to the red throwing stick Leslie had picked up in the park—the stick that she was now saying Corcoran had put into her body. In fact, the dowel-shaped stick could be mistaken for a drumstick, if you didn't look at it closely.

Previously, Leslie had not attributed any of the sexual acts to Paul Archer; now she did. "Paul had also asked me to play with him. I did." When she was asked why she hadn't said this about Paul before, she answered, "Because I really like him. He was my hero. He's cute. He's handsome."

Paul Archer was arrested on Friday, August 18, and charged with conspiracy to commit sexual assault and aggravated sexual contact. Because he was seventeen on March 1, Paul—like his brother Chris and Bryant Grober—would be treated as a juvenile and arraigned in private in Family Court.

As an adult at the time of the alleged assault on Leslie, Corcoran was arrested and charged with aggravated sexual assault—rape—and aggravated sexual contact and conspiracy.

Richie's attorney, Anthony Mautone, said that it was "preposterous" that Richie had been arrested three months after the first five youths were picked up. He said, "Suppose she changes her story next week and names two more people? I think it just leaves suspect everything she has said to date."

Now there were seven defendants, and no one knew when, if ever, judgment would be passed on them.

44

Leslie's parents got her a part-time job working for a local animal kennel. The puppies were cute, but they seemed unhappy cooped up in their cages. So Leslie did with them what she wished people would do with her: She let them all loose. That afternoon she was fired.

Leslie felt isolated. She had been labeled the "bat girl" by her schoolmates, called retarded in the newspapers and on TV. Her every move was watched by her parents and the school people; she was shunned by other Glen Ridge teenagers. Leslie was blaming herself for screwing up the lives of the boys every girl in town seemed to adore; when she didn't blame herself, she blamed the prosecutors and her parents.

Through the summer and fall of 1989 and intermittently through the next two years, Leslie spent many hours revealing her intimate thoughts to investigators and psychologists, psychiatrists, and other therapists. These therapists were employed by the prosecution and the defense to determine whether she understood sex and had the mental ability to consent to it. They asked her questions about her experience in the basement, her sex life, her emotional state, and the aftereffects of March 1. They probed her friendships with various boys, including the Jocks, and girls in and out of Glen Ridge and in her schools.

Leslie didn't realize that what she said to these strangers would be used later in open court—or how they would be interpreted by the defense lawyers and journalists. Did she ever know—Was the distinction ever made?—what would remain confidential and what would find its way into the public realm? She had no idea that discrete phrases, expressions she used but didn't fully understand, boasts that she hoped would impress all these adult listeners would ultimately be recycled as arrows to pierce her reputation. Leslie's priorities were not those of the people in the criminal justice system any more than they were the priority of the people who lived in Glen Ridge.

More than anything, Leslie wished for a good friend her own age. Suddenly her wish was granted.

It wasn't a friend from Leslie's special ed class or from the teen social group of retarded youngsters that Les sometimes socialized with. Her new friend was one of the more popular students in the Class of '89. She had been voted best "girl athlete" by the seniors, played on Leslie's basketball team, and was a star runner on the track team. She was now preparing for a career in nursing. Her name was Mari Carmen Ferraez.

A pretty, popular, athletic young woman—and she was taking an interest in Leslie. She certainly seemed to enjoy Leslie's company, calling her frequently, inviting her out for rides in her car, talking "girl talk" for hours. And what pleased the Fabers most was Mari Carmen's family: Her dad was a high-ranking national official in the Salvation Army; her parents were moral, churchgoing people, an ideal family for Leslie to make friends with.

"Charlie, do you know who Les is seeing?" Ros said to her husband. "Mari Carmen, that girl Les played with on the basketball team. Look at the nice kid she's turning out to be. She's so giving of herself."

There were a few things the Fabers didn't know about this nice girl Mari Carmen.

They didn't know that she had spent a lot of her time in high school trying to work her way into the Jock clique.

They didn't know that she had gone out with Kyle Scherzer.

They didn't know that Mari Carmen had been one of the student leaders of the petition drive to permit the suspects to attend graduation.

One other thing: They didn't know that she was something of a mechanical klutz and that she was concentrating really hard these days on learning how to operate a hidden tape recorder.

Mari Carmen invited Leslie out for a drive and maybe some ice cream on Tuesday night, November 14. They drove to Holstein's, a pleasantly old-fashioned ice cream parlor in Bloomfield. On their way, they talked.

After a while, Mari Carmen said, "I was gonna go home because I have homework to do."

Leslie didn't want to leave her friend just yet. "Just a little bit more," she pleaded.

Their conversation turned to Chris Archer. "Chris Archer is one of the sexiest . . . I ever went with," Les volunteered.

"So why are you saying all this stuff about him then?" Mari Carmen wanted to know. "Why don't you just—?"

"I don't know, they're making me say it."

"Are they making you say it?" Mari Carmen wanted to know. "Or do you want to say it, or what?"

"No, I don't wanna. I don't. I hate going down there."

"Well, who makes you say all this stuff?"

"Sheila, the lawyer. I have the stupidest lawyer."

"Why, like what kind of sick things do they make you say?" Mari Carmen asked.

"You have to tell the truth. You have to do this. You have to do that." Leslie responded.

"But why don't you just say—I mean, why don't you tell them exactly how you feel?" Mari Carmen asked, as she drove toward the ice cream parlor. "That way maybe it wouldn't go this far and you wouldn't have to deal with any of this stuff."

"I, I don't know."

"I mean, have you ever thought about doing that?" Mari Carmen pressed her.

"What do you mean, like not testifying?"

Then referring to the scene in the basement, Mari Carmen answered, "Yeah. Just being like, 'I had fun and that's all there is'—ya know."

When they got to the ice cream parlor, Mari Carmen didn't seem anxious to be seen in Leslie's company. "Do you wanna like get your ice cream to go? Like, I'll wait out front for you?"

"Whatever's good for you," Leslie said, trying to please her friend.

Leslie went in and bought her cone of peach ice cream. When she got back into Mari Carmen's car, she said, "Not too many people like me no more."

"That's because of all the stuff that's going on," Mari Carmen suggested.

"It doesn't bother me," Les said.

"It doesn't bother me," Mari Carmen reassured her.

As they turned on to Leslie's street, Mari Carmen asked Leslie whether her sister knew about "your sexual habits."

"No, no," Leslie said.

"Well, I guess this is yours and my secret," Mari Carmen said.

Before they separated, Leslie wanted to say something more to her friend. "You're very special. . . . I never met anybody like you. I mean, no like, I never met anybody as nice as you. I'm not just saying that. I mean, you're so nice. A lot of people, you know, couldn't care less about me. I mean, I don't have that many friends."

"Really?"

"I like to talk to Sheila."

"Yeah, but you don't tell Sheila everything."

"No, I didn't . . . no."

Mari Carmen said, "Maybe we can get together again tomorrow night or something."

"Okay, and I promise, I won't tell anybody."

"I won't tell anybody either, okay, Les," Mari Carmen Ferraez said. And then Mari Carmen drove away. But she left Leslie with much to think about on the eve of her appearance before the grand jury.

Did Mari Carmen's "secret" intimate conversation with Leslie influence Leslie's grand jury testimony the next day, Wednesday, November 15? Leslie was the first witness. Her account was lucid and straightforward at moments, hedging and reticent at others, and, occasionally, fractured and jumbled. Was she trying to please whoever was questioning her? Or was she responding to someone who had talked to her last night or last month?

Her testimony took a little more than two hours. The most intelligent rape victims don't always give a sequential, coherent account of how they were raped. Under gentle questioning by Laurino, Leslie, however, was able to present a rational and credible account of her entire experience. "That was the main thing we learned from her grand jury appearance— what a great witness she was," said one law enforcement official.

There were times, especially in her second hour, when she apparently got confused and couldn't accurately recall what she had said earlier to investigators. One example is that she reportedly identified Chris Archer as the boy who put both the broomstick and the bat in her vagina. It's noteworthy that she reportedly testified that Richie Corcoran put a stick into her vagina and that it was inserted deeper than the bat and the broomstick had been.

Leslie reportedly ended her grand jury testimony by describing how two Jock hangers-on, John Maher and Tucker Litvany, approached her on March 2 and asked her to return to the basement. And how she had to say "no" because she was waiting for a friend. She didn't mean to hurt their feelings, Leslie said; she really did plan something for that afternoon.

45

Early in January 1990, while the grand jury was still in session, the defense lawyers told the prosecutor that they had important new evidence. The fresh material had been developed by two attorneys who worked closely together. They were Michael Querques, who represented Kevin, and Louis Esposito, who represented Kyle.

At a meeting with the prosecutors, Esposito and Querques explained that they had asked the twins to draw up a list of people they knew in Glen Ridge who might be helpful to their cases. The lawyers then assigned their investigator, a man named Richard Childs, a former Newark cop, to talk to the people on the list. That's how they found Mari Carmen Ferraez, the lawyers said later.

Mari wanted to help. Mari told Childs that she had been on the high school basketball team with Leslie. She was sure Leslie would be glad to talk to her. Mari Carmen was told: Get it on tape. So Mari Carmen went to Radio Shack and bought a tape recorder and audiotapes. Then she started calling Leslie. Mari Carmen explained to her that she needed a mentor, a woman wise in the ways of the world, who could explain the mysteries of sex to her, who could guide her if she wanted to duplicate Leslie's experience with the Jocks in the basement. Mari Carmen said this was something she really wanted to do, go to the basement with the guys, experience the thrills that Leslie had experienced. They arranged a code so that they could have their phone conversations in private.

That's how Leslie was set up.

Now the defense lawyers were ready to display the fruits of Mari Carmen's labor. They had put together a fifteen-minute "highlights" audiotape of what they considered the most significant remarks secretly taped during three conversations between Mari Carmen and Leslie from September 10, 1989, to November 14, 1989. Then they turned on the tape recorder and watched the expressions on the faces of the men and women prosecuting the Glen Ridge case.

The "highlights" tape consisted mainly of Leslie's comments on three subjects:

Her sexual experience, with emphasis on her experience at the
    Scherzers' house
Her feelings about the prosecutors
Her observations about Richie Corcoran's behavior in the basement

About March 1, 1989:

MARI: Did it feel like you were having sex? . . .

LESLIE: It felt like I was, you know, coming, but I wasn't coming really. . . .

MARI: But you've done this stuff before, haven't you?

LESLIE: Oh yeah, with a lotta guys.

MARI: Oh, you do?

LESLIE: I'm experienced, you gotta be an experienced person. I've been doing it since I was like really little.

MARI: Oh, good. . . . Now you can tell me, you know.

LESLIE: I'll teach you the ropes.

MARI: Oh, you will? Good.

More about March 1:

LESLIE: So after I went down there, I, um, blew Bryant Grober.

MARI: Yeah.

LESLIE: That was exciting.

MARI: Oh, was it?

MARI: So, why were you down there?

LESLIE: Because I like Paul. It was fun, Mari, let me tell you it was so exciting, it was perfect [*inaudible*].

MARI: Really? Would you do it again, though?

LESLIE: Yeah.

The tape played back what Leslie had told Mari Carmen about the prosecutors, whom she said she now "hated."

LESLIE: These, these bitches and bastards won't get off my . . . I mean, I don't need these stupid lawyers, I don't need these stupid people to tell me what to do.

MARI: Right. Well, you just do what you think is best for yourself, and for the guys.

And now Richie Corcoran:

MARI: Have you ever lied to the lawyers, though, about—

LESLIE: Yeah, one person. . . .

MARI: What did you say to them that was a lie?

LESLIE: Well, actually, if, if I tell you, you can't tell nobody.

MARI: I promise.

LESLIE: Richie Corcoran really didn't do anything to me. I just said that
            because they wouldn't get off my back with Corcoran. I didn't
            mean to lie about it, though, but he never did anything to me,
            and I lied.

MARI: Yeah, now, but did you lie about anyone else?

LESLIE: No, not really.

Laurino thought the "highlights" tape was a shattering blow to the case. "I was devastated," Laurino recalled. "After just that first hearing, we thought the case will be essentially impossible to win if that kind of information is throughout the tapes. We just thought, Major, major problem."

The defense lawyers were driving home their points. Listen to the tape: She says she had fun, she enjoyed it. Listen to the tape: She says she hates her "lawyers." She says the prosecutors are always on her back. Listen to the tape: She says she lied about Corcoran; she says he didn't do anything.

All of it hurt, but what hurt the most was Leslie's remarks about hating her lawyers. Don't take it personally, Laurino told himself. But he did take it personally. He had no way of knowing that Leslie deeply resented her isolation after the newspaper story about her appeared, and that she thought her parents and the prosecutor were to blame for her being confined in her house a lot of the time.

But, substantively, it was her other remarks that were potentially lethal to the prosecution's case. Her boasts about sexual experiences. Her admission that she had lied about Corcoran. How would the prosecution ever recover from that?

Laurino called Sheila Byron after he heard the excerpts from the tapes. For a small-town cop, the tapings came as something of a revelation. Much of the routine police work in Glen Ridge involved negotiations and compromises. Give a kid a break and he'll straighten himself out. Secretly taping a retarded young woman sharply raised the stakes. "I realized that this is definitely hardball," she said later. "My God, the lawyers are going to do anything they have to do."

Then she started worrying about Leslie. God, who's going to tell her?

Leslie got the news on Tuesday, January 9, when she came to the prosecutor's office. Laurino and an assistant prosecutor who had been assigned to the case recently were excluded from the meeting because of Leslie's critical remarks about her "lawyers" on the tapes. Two top officials in the prosecutor's office were present, as was a psychologist who had evaluated Leslie during the summer. Her purpose was "to minimize any potential mental or emotional trauma."

Leslie was unprepared for their first question: Had she spoken to a girl named Mari about the case?

"I can't tell what I told Mari," Leslie said. "I promised not to tell, and Mari also promised. She's being very good about keeping the promise. Mari's my good friend and I don't want to lose a friendship."

The prosecutors asked her how she would feel if she knew that Mari had revealed their conversations. "I'd be mad, but I know she didn't tell. She's very good. You might think she did tell, but she didn't. Me and her are like best friends."

The prosecutors said they knew that Mari had disclosed her conversations with Leslie because they had been given a tape recording of the conversations. "You're kidding me," Leslie said. "She couldn't of."

Suddenly Leslie began to believe that she could of. "Does Sheila know?" she asked, perhaps thinking of her many promises not to discuss the case. "I got to see Sheila. She's the only one I can talk to. Can you promise you won't tell my mother?"

"I can't believe that," Leslie continued. "Mari wanted to be like me. She wanted to go down to the Scherzer basement and do what I did." She looked shocked by the revelation. Clinging still to the rubble of her disbelief.

Leslie asked, "Where did she tape it—down here?" No, the prosecutors said, Mari taped the conversations when she was on the phone with Leslie or when they went driving to an ice cream parlor or to a park where they could see the skyline of New York.

"Oh, my God, I feel like she's a reporter," Leslie said.

For the first time, she showed anger. "She was my friend. She promised and now she's laughing at me—sort of. She made me look bad."

The prosecutors asked her about two segments of the tapes. One had to do with Leslie saying that she had lied to her lawyers. The other concerned her remark that she had lied about Richie Corcoran's putting the stick into her body. "I might have said it, but I was sticking up for my friend," Leslie explained. "Mari is good friends with Richie."

But what's the truth? the prosecutors wanted to know. Did Richie do anything? *"I'm not sure if Richie did anything,"* Leslie said. *"It's been so long."*

Leslie had told Mari that she lied about Richie because the prosecutors "were on my back." Was that really true? "That wasn't true," Leslie said. "I was just saying that because Mari got on my nerves—she'd get on my back."

Now Leslie began to understand: Perhaps Mari had an ulterior motive in cultivating a friendship with her. "Maybe she was trying to protect the boys," Leslie said. This insight led to a suggestion: "I think her parents should know what she did to me. She could do this to someone else and they'd beat her up. But I won't because I'm nice."

How did Mari persuade Leslie to talk to her? the prosecutors asked. "She made me talk to her," she said. "She made me—it's hard to explain." She added, "Well, I kept my promise." She thought about that for a moment and said, "It just seems you can trust boys more than girls."

The prosecutors asked Leslie whether she would like to listen to the tapes.

Leslie said, "Yes."

Then she was silent.

Then she said, "No."

Anthony Mautone, Richie Corcoran's lawyer, told a reporter, "Based upon my interpretation of the tapes, the case is over." Vincent Nuzzi, a former prosecutor who was now representing Peter Quigley, said, "If you listen to the tapes, you'll hear the girl herself describe her previous sexual escapades and her experiences after the incident. She was capable of consenting."

Laurino wasn't so sure. Night after night, he sat alone in his office listening to every word on the tapes. Compared to the "highlights" tape, which he considered an unmitigated disaster, the unedited recordings were more of a mixture, some helpful to the defense, some clearly unhelpful.

Laurino thought a jury could well interpret the back-and-forth of the girls as a not very elaborate cat-and-mouse game, orchestrated by Mari, who pretended she needed the tutelage of the sexually experienced Leslie, who, of course, was eager to guide her protégée, eager to prove just how experienced she was.

Occasionally, the game didn't work as Mari hoped it would. On the tape of the September 10 phone conversation, Mari wanted to know how the broomstick was used. "Did you do the broomstick at all yourself? Like, if I wanted to, could I do it?"

Leslie laughed nervously. "You want to do that to yourself?" she said. On the tape she sounds surprised.

Leaning back in his chair, his feet up on the desk, Laurino marveled at Mari's relentlessness. Whenever Leslie wanted to talk about something else—basketball practice drills, vacationing in the Bahamas—Mari Carmen rerouted Leslie back to sex, the ultimate destination being March 1, 1989. To keep Mari as a friend, Leslie had to generate more and more sexual juice. When Leslie ran out of sexual anecdotes—truth or fable was anybody's guess—Mari would yawn audibly and end the conversation.

Infrequently, their conversation would veer away from sexual braggadocio, and then the other Leslie would emerge—the passive, fearful, vulnerable Leslie. For example, Leslie says she had "fun" in the basement, that it was an "exciting" experience; but almost in the same breath she tells her friend that the Jocks "conned" her into going with them and that the experience was frightening.

MARI: If you had to do it all over again, would you go down again?

LESLIE: I'd be scareder, I don't know.

MARI: Would you do it again?

LESLIE: Yeah, if you went down with me.

MARI: If I went down with you, and the two of us were down there and we were gonna do it . . . would you do it again?

LESLIE: Yeah.

MARI: So you had fun?

LESLIE: Yeah.

MARI: I see. Maybe when it's all over, I'll do it and then we could compare notes [*inaudible*] about the bat. (*Laughs.*)

Laurino thought, The tapes cut both ways, they really did. If you were on the jury and you listened hard, you might get the idea that Leslie was a pawn in a fairly transparent scheme to vindicate the defendants.

46

Even in a complex criminal case, a determined prosecutor can get an indictment in a week or less by presenting a couple of cops and the victim as witnesses. But it took the Essex County prosecutor, Herbert Tate, almost six months just to convene a "special" grand jury that would be restricted to hearing testimony only about this case. Then he threw his whole case into the grand jury room, leaving it up to the jurors to decide what was important.

Deliberation lasted from November 1989 to May 1990. During these six months the grand jurors heard thirty-two witnesses, several of them appearing more than once. Among the witnesses were former students at Glen Ridge High School, the boys who had been in the basement and left, the boys who gathered in Cartaret Park the next day, girlfriends of the accused, and teammates and buddies of the Jocks. The common theme that ran through all of their testimony was: We're not going to say anything that will incriminate our guys.

When one of Chris's friends said he couldn't remember whether Chris had mentioned that he had put a baseball bat into Leslie, the frustration of some grand jurors surfaced. One juror reportedly said: "Lying in here is starting to piss me off, and I'm not going to let it keep going. It's against the law."

One of the Jocks who testified before the grand jury said later that the experience only strengthened his bond with the boys who had been arrested. "They tried to make me spill but I didn't," he told the author. "I wouldn't ever point a finger at a friend. They had been my friends forever. I wanted to show them I loved them. Anything they need, I'll always be there for them."

The grand jury also heard from Leslie and her mother, from her swimming coach, and from Charlie Figueroa. There was testimony from police investigators and Detective Byron, from psychologists and experts on the effects of rape. It took months to improve the sound quality of Mari Carmen's tapes and then play the tapes for the grand jury.

Laurino thought the tell-all approach was a terrible idea. To parade a long line of witnesses before the grand jury would reveal your case, tip off your theory and strategy to the defense. The delays and interruptions, most observers agreed, would make it harder to win a conviction. As time passed, the recollections of the youths in the basement, never exact to begin with, would continue to fade. There was no physical evidence in the case, so the prosecution would hinge to a great extent on the testimony of a victim who was clearly ambivalent about, if not sympathetic to, the defendants. Watching the case drag on, many blacks in the courthouse thought Tate was bending over backward to be fair to the white defendants from the affluent suburbs.

Finally, on May 22, almost a year after the first wave of arrests, the grand jury returned indictments of Kyle and Kevin Scherzer, Peter Quigley, and Richard Corcoran, Jr. They were indicted on charges of aggravated sexual assault, aggravated sexual contact, and conspiracy. A fifth young man, John Maher, was indicted on charges of conspiring to bring Leslie to the Scherzer house the next day.

But it was the sixth person indicted who got most of the media attention—Mari Carmen Ferraez. She was indicted on charges of witness tampering and obstruction of justice. The indictment accused her of "attempting to . . . cause the victim to testify falsely and/or withhold information." In other words, Mari Carmen was being indicted for what she had said to Leslie the night before Leslie's grand jury appearance. She faced a maximum of five years in prison if she were convicted.

According to New Jersey law, surreptitious taping is not illegal as long as one party, and not necessarily the target, knows about the taping. In the arena of public opinion, however, the defense lawyers were heavily criticized. Sidney Schanberg, a columnist for *Newsday*, a New York newspaper, contended that the two defense lawyers had "entrapped" Leslie and wrote that "their scheme was legal but truly scummy."

Almost overlooked in the furor over Ferraez's indictment were the indictments of Richie Corcoran and Peter Quigley. The indictment of Corcoran alleged that he "inserted a dirty stick into [Leslie's] vagina." The only physical act attributed to Quigley was the allegation that "Peter Quigley asked [Leslie] to masturbate him and she did." Otherwise, the grand jury charged, Quigley's participation was verbal: He allegedly laughed when the bat was inserted; he allegedly said, "Put it up further"; he allegedly cheered Kevin and Chris while they were inserting objects, saying "Come on, come on."

Herb Tate had left everything up to the grand jury. Now the grand jury left the prosecutors with more defendants than they had ever expected.

A few days after the indictments were returned, Leslie and her mother were having dinner and Leslie said, "I didn't tell the truth about Richie Corcoran."

"What do you mean?" Ros asked her.

"About the stick," Leslie said. "He didn't use it."

Ros admonished her about telling the truth.

"Oh, he can say anything about me, but I can't say anything about him," Les said petulantly. Perhaps she thought that Corcoran was spreading untrue rumors about her, so she felt she could do the same to him.

When the Fabers told Prosecutor Tate, he scheduled a rare Saturday meeting with Leslie and Ros Faber. Before the meeting started on June 9,

Detective Byron noticed that Leslie's face was flushed and she looked upset. Byron, sitting next to her, said, "How are you?"

"I did a really bad thing," Leslie began, forgetting her customary niceties. "I told my mom I lied about Richie Corcoran and the stick, and she was mad at me."

"Did you lie about Richie?" Byron asked.

"Yes," said Leslie.

"Did Richie do anything in the basement?"

"No."

As Byron and Leslie were leaving the prosecutor's office, out of nowhere Leslie asked the detective: "So how's Mari?"

"Mari Carmen? I don't know. Do *you* know?"

"Oh, yeah. I talked to Mari on the phone last week, and Mari said she was sorry about taping me and she's my friend and she'll never do it again."

Byron had cautioned Leslie not to talk to anyone about the case and especially not to talk to Mari Carmen—the Mari Carmen who had just been indicted for witness tampering. But Byron stayed on the subject of Corcoran. "Now, Les, what did you say to your mother about Richie Corcoran?"

Leslie replied that Richie had put the stick into her, Byron later wrote in a report to the prosecutor.

Why did you change your story? Byron asked Leslie.

"Well, it could have been Mari Carmen who told me to say Richie didn't do anything."

Byron responded angrily, "Don't tell me who it could have been. Tell me who it was." In her report Byron noted that Leslie became evasive. "Well, everybody is behind him," Leslie said. "All the girls say he is going to get in a lot of trouble, and they're all his friends."

Then Leslie mentioned the names of a couple of girls who were friendly with Corcoran and were telling her that she was making Richie's life miserable by pursuing the case.

During the drive home, Sheila asked Leslie whether Mari Carmen had called her or she had called Mari. "I called her," Leslie said.

Leslie's contradictory stories about Corcoran's role were creating a legal nightmare. Should the prosecutors continue to pursue the case against Richie? Should they drop it now—and how would that affect their case against the other defendants?

Richie Corcoran had one big problem: He was the perfect fall guy. A made-to-order villain. Loud—"obnoxious," his classmates called him. In trouble when he was in school. Filmed making crude gestures. He was the kind of kid who arouses suspicion. Many times officials in the prosecutor's office would say, "I can't believe that Richie Corcoran was in the basement and he didn't do anything." What's more, his dad's role in the investigation had been clouded when rumors of a cover-up swirled around the case. To drop the charges against Richie would generate a media tirade against the prosecutor. For the prosecutor and the press, Richie was the kid you loved to hate. But that didn't mean he was guilty of rape.

47

The grand jury indicted only some of the young men who had been arrested. Three others were under the jurisdiction of the Family Court because they were under the age of eighteen on March 1, 1989.

In June 1989 Tate had asked the Family Court judge, Julio Fuentes, to "waive" the rules and permit him to bring Paul, Chris, and Bryant to trial as adults, given the seriousness of the charges.

Some so-called "waiver" hearings take a few hours or a few days at the most. Not in the Glen Ridge case. There was a blizzard of paper: psychological assessments, school records (1,200 pages), statements taken by the police and the prosecutor's investigators.

Sheila Byron was one of the few witnesses at the hearing. She was on the stand for four days, and her experience foreshadowed the gender wars that would later dominate the actual trial. When she was cross-examined by Thomas Ford, the lawyer for Chris Archer, he asked her, "So, what is it that you do all day besides sitting there trying to look pretty?" Byron looked up at the judge, with an expression that said: Do I have to answer this?

One afternoon, during a break in her testimony, Byron dropped her lipstick into the drain of the bathroom sink. "It's brand new, like fourteen dollars," she recalled later. "So I ask Bob Laurino for pliers. So Bob goes back into the courtroom and tells the defense lawyers that Detective Byron dropped her lipstick down the sink. That's all they needed. I was the laughingstock of the courtroom for days."

Three middle-aged defense lawyers implying that the testimony of a female police officer was inherently unreliable because she was preoccupied with physical appearance, with emotions, with feminine concerns. They weren't asking male witnesses whether they shaved once or twice a day or which brand of after-shave lotion they used. "Four days on the stand felt like four weeks," Byron said later. "I never felt the defense treated me like a professional."

The waiver hearings were prolonged by lengthy arguments by defense lawyers. Mari Carmen's tapes had to be analyzed. Then, when the grand jury proceedings were delayed for months, Fuentes waited to see what would happen there.

Finally, on September 24, 1990, almost a year after Fuentes had held his first hearing on Tate's request, he ruled that the three defendants should be tried as adults. The defense lawyers appealed. That, of course, took some time—about seven months. On April 19, 1991, a panel of three appellate judges agreed with the decision to try the juveniles as adults. The decision was a serious setback for all the defendants, because it expanded Judge Fuentes's ruling.

Fuentes had found that the three boys could be tried for rape because, in his view, Leslie was incapable of giving consent. He did not find that force and coercion were used against Leslie. The appellate judges disagreed. They cited the guys' threats to tell Leslie's mother and school officials; they noted the presence of thirteen boys in the basement and the use of Paul Archer as an enticement. All of which, the judges said, "represented an express and implied threat."

After two years, the identities of the Archers and Grober were made public. Their appeals exhausted, Chris, Paul, and Bryant were publicly arraigned as adults and freed on bail. Their pictures ran in the newspapers, and now they faced the same penalties as did their slightly older friends, who had already been indicted.

On Friday, September 27, 1991, the grand jury in the Glen Ridge case finally completed the remainder of its work, a month short of two years after it began its deliberations. The grand jury indicted Chris, Paul, and Bryant, adding them to the five defendants who had been indicted earlier.

By this time, most of the defendants had resumed their normal lives. They were all out on bail. They were working, attending college, playing football, dating girls, and, for at least a few months in the year, enjoying home cooking. It wasn't pleasant, being accused of being a gang rapist, having your picture published in national magazines, along with pictures of convicted sexual offenders. But as media coverage of the case receded and then virtually disappeared, they could resume the nearly quotidian rhythm of their lives.

Of the principal defendants, only Chris Archer, who was finishing his senior year of high school, was constantly visible in town. He played for the high school football team, and although another boy was chosen as captain, some teammates recalled that Chris was recognized by most of the players as the unofficial captain; he got the loudest cheers at the school's sports assemblies. The student poll in 1990 said that Chris had the nicest eyes.

In his high school memories, published in the yearbook, Chris included Ryan's Wreck, the legendary party that had left Mary Ryan's house in ruins. But he didn't say anything about "Hoovering" and "voyeuring." And there was not a word about March 1, 1989.

Academically, Chris finished the year near the top of his class. Then he began preparing for his freshman year at Boston College, a Catholic institution.

48

As time passed, some residents of the town interpreted the delays as an effort by the prosecutor to bury the case. They thought he was trying to avoid a trial that he couldn't win. These Ridgers tried to offer him a way out.

Friends of the boys sent politically wired lawyers to speak to Laurino. C'mon, Bob, they told him, can't we fix this so everybody's happy? When Laurino said "no," they shook their heads and told their colleagues, He used to be a reasonable guy; now he's gone nuts over this case.

One town resident thought he had an idea that would restore reason and good sense. He called his idea "A Better Solution." It took the form of an unsigned computer-printed one-page message that had been left in the mailboxes of members and clergy of Christ Episcopal Church in Glen Ridge.

This was the church attended by the Archer family, and the message seemed calculated to influence the minister, Clayton Nelson, to deliver a sermon on the rape case. The anonymous author wrote: "The law says that if found guilty the boys must pay for what they did. The solution is let them pay. One Million Dollars. Sounds like a lot? Sounds impossible? It really isn't."

The author went on: "If a fine of One Million Dollars is paid, reasonable people can be convinced that justice may have been done. One hundred thousand dollars could be paid to the prosecutor's office for the cost of the investigation. Nine hundred thousand dollars will be paid to the victim. With that amount of money she will have an endowment that should enable her to live a more normal life."

What followed was a precise description of how the money would be raised and disbursed. The parents of the defendants would put in a total of $250,000. Each of the defendants would pay the balance of the million dollars over time, beginning when they completed college or got a job. "If they miss *one* payment they could be picked up and brought to jail. Maybe there should even be a life insurance policy to insure payment to the victim in the event of an accidental death. In addition to the fine, they should do community service in Glen Ridge."

The author argued that "this is *not* about buying off the law. This is *not* to further prove the theory that laws are only meant for the poor. It is about putting a crime in the proper perspective with a proper and equitable settlement for all involved." The message ended with a capitalized plea: "THINK ABOUT IT!!!!!!"

The minister of Christ Church did not deliver a sermon based on this proposal.

March 1, 1991, was the second anniversary of the "incident," as people in Glen Ridge liked to call it. At about this time, the police department received a call from Boston. The caller asked for the detective who was investigating the Glen Ridge rape case.

Sheila Byron dialed the number on the message slip. This is what she said happened next:

A woman answered. She identified herself as a security guard on the campus of Boston College. "This isn't a college matter," she said, hesitantly. "I mean, this didn't happen on campus."

"What didn't happen?"

"Well, this is a little strange. Do you have a guy named Chris Archer in the rape that happened in your town?"

Now she had Sheila's attention. "We have this female student," the security guard reportedly told Byron. "She was real broken up, and she went to talk to her dorm adviser. I mean, she couldn't stop crying and wouldn't go to classes. She doesn't want to leave her room."

"And—?"

"The girl says she was assaulted by this guy Archer, sexually assaulted, violently assaulted."

"Violently?"

"The girl says he ripped her clothes off and shoved his fist into her vagina. Punched her in the vagina."

"Where did you say this happened?"

"Right on a public street. Dragged her down behind some bushes."

"And when was this supposed to happen?"

"Last October. October tenth. Late at night."

"Let me call the prosecutor's office," Byron said. "I'm sure they'll want to talk to you."

The young woman, who was a student at Boston College, came to Newark to tell the prosecutors her story. She told them that she had grown up in a town near Glen Ridge. She said she had been introduced to Archer by a girlfriend who knew one of Archer's former classmates at Glen Ridge High School. Archer and his high school buddy were freshmen at Boston College.

On the night of October 10, 1990, the young woman said, the four of them had gone out to a local pub. At the end of the evening, Archer and the young woman said goodbye to the other couple and were walking toward her residence, she said, when Chris grabbed her and pulled her down behind some bushes. "Right here, right now," Archer ordered her. This was on a public street, not on campus grounds. When she resisted, she said, Archer tore off her clothes and panties. When she screamed, "No," Archer began punching her in her vagina, the young woman told the prosecutors. She said Archer penetrated her vagina and her anus with his fingers.

When he was finished with her, she said, Chris Archer jumped up and proclaimed: "I'm a rapist."

For months she did not file a criminal complaint against Archer because her friends had told her, "Your name'll be dragged through the mud." During most of that time, she stayed in her room, spending days in bed. She cried frequently. Finally, she confided in her dorm counselor, who told a campus security officer, who eventually called the Glen Ridge police.

This young woman, who would begin her junior year in September, was very different from Leslie. She was physically attractive, highly intelligent, and very articulate. Unlike Leslie, this young woman wasn't worried that Archer might not like her anymore if she testified against him. What did make her anxious was that her identity would be disclosed if she pressed charges. She was also afraid of reprisals by Archer or his friends, not only on campus but also in her hometown. The prosecutors said they would try to keep her identity secret, but they could not promise that it wouldn't become known.

She signed an affidavit that described what she said Archer did to her. The affidavit was sealed. It was given to the judge before the start of the Glen Ridge trial. Legal restrictions would prevent the prosecution from calling her as a witness or disclosing her affidavit unless Chris Archer testified in his own defense, which was unlikely. But the young woman could testify at Archer's sentencing if he were found guilty. At that time prosecutors could introduce evidence of past crimes by the defendants. But charges related to his actions in Boston were never brought against Archer, and he was never tried or convicted in connection with the woman's allegations.

49

The town's self-esteem was boosted by a report written by Judge Samuel Larner. The retired judge had been asked by the school board to investigate how the "incident" had been handled by the school. The judge completed his ten-page report in a year and promptly billed the board for his fee of $5,000. He exonerated the school social worker, Elizabeth Portuese, and other school system employees of any possible wrongdoing in failing to report what they had heard to the police. "Portuese did not feel obligated to take any further action in view of hesitancy about the reliability of the victim's description of the event," Larner said.

Since the alleged abuses had been committed by a group of high school students off school grounds, the school had no responsibility to alert the police or the state Division of Youth and Family Services, Larner said. He thought it was "manifestly preposterous to place the blame at the footsteps of the school house. It is just as preposterous to imply a cover-up on the part of the social worker." The judge didn't find it inconsistent that the Glen Ridge High School principal had called the police the moment *he* heard about it.

Any delay was the Fabers' fault, Larner concluded. "The mother expressed doubts that her daughter was involved in the alleged incident and demonstrated no interest in following up with any complaint or official action," the judge said. Predictably, the headline in the *Glen Ridge Paper* read: "School Officials Cleared: Judge's Report Faults Victim's Parents." When Ros Faber read this headline, she said to her husband, "Why didn't he ever talk to us?" He never had.

50

As the conflicts in the prosecutor's office deepened over Tate's strategy and tactics, the chief prosecutor moved Laurino out of the picture. He put two new people, whom he regarded as allies, in charge of the pretrial prosecution. Neither had extensive experience trying rape cases. Then Tate announced that three other prosecutors would try the case. Laurino was not one of them.

The day the grand jury returned all the indictments, September 27, 1991, was Tate's last day in office. He was leaving his job to take a position with the Bush administration in Washington. Deputy Attorney General James Mulvihill was Tate's successor. Mulvihill had twenty years' experience in state law enforcement. A few weeks after he assumed his new post, Mulvihill announced that he had assembled a new no-nonsense team to prosecute the Glen Ridge case: Glenn Goldberg, the chief trial attorney in the office, who in the past eighteen years had prosecuted many famous and difficult cases; Elizabeth Miller-Hall, a specialist in appeals litigation; and Robert Laurino. Laurino's exile was over.

With the new prosecution team in place, the pace of the Glen Ridge case accelerated. First priority: winnowing out the defendants who had played a lesser role in the case. "We decided [that], to get the best shot at conviction, we had to just focus on the guys who actually did some type of penetration," Laurino said. "And that's how we narrowed it down to the four of them."

Mari Carmen Ferraez was the first to be cut loose. She was admitted into the Pre-Trial Intervention (PTI) program, in which she would be required to do forty days of community service. After six months the witness-tampering and obstruction charges against her would be expunged from the record.

Next in line was Peter Quigley. This deal was more complicated. Quigley had been in the basement from start to finish. He had been indicted on a charge of aggravated sexual assault. Before admitting him into the program, the prosecutors wanted a sworn statement from him about what he saw and heard on March 1.

Quigley gave his statement to the prosecutors on April 3, 1992, more than three years after he was present in the Scherzers' basement. He said Leslie told the boys that "she wanted to get laid . . . and everybody looked around and said, 'I don't want to do it.'" Then, Peter said, Kevin "just walked around the other end of the basement and picked up a broom and he brought it over to her and he asked if this was okay, and she said, 'Yes.'"

What did Kevin do with the broom?

"He was kind of like sticking it in and out of her, and she was guiding it with her hand, making sure it wouldn't go in too far." While Kevin was inserting the broomstick, Peter said, Kevin "was in front of her, kneeling or squatting on the floor."

After Kevin got tired of pushing the broomstick in and out, what happened?

"He [Kevin] stopped and gets up and looks for something else, and Chris takes over and basically does the same thing."

Was Chris also inserting the broomstick in and out?

"In the same position, yes, doing the same thing; she is guiding it with her hand so it doesn't go in too deep."

Peter said that Chris was pushing the broomstick in and out for about "a minute and a half, two minutes." Kevin had pushed the broomstick into Leslie for "two and a half, three minutes, "Quigley said.

Next: the bat. Quigley said it was Kevin or Kyle who got the bat. It was a wood "fungo" bat; "[it] has . . . a handle like a regular baseball bat, but the barrel is a lot skinnier." Peter said, "Kevin then took the bat and Chris or Kevin told Leslie to sit up and lay on the table next to the couch. , , , Her back was flush against the table and her legs were up in the air and that's when Chris came over and just held her legs up so they wouldn't fall down, and Kevin inserted the bat."

Was Kevin able to get the bat inside her vagina?

"Maybe for a brief moment," Peter Quigley said.

Did he make several attempts?

"About two or three," he said. "He realized it just wasn't working, and he just stopped."

Quigley said that after someone—he couldn't remember who—told Leslie to "keep her mouth shut," Richie Corcoran turned to Peter and said, "If my girlfriend finds out, forget it, it's through. It will be over with."

Quigley said he turned to Paul Archer and said, "You know, maybe we should get out of here; we might get in trouble." Quigley said Paul answered, "Why? We really didn't do anything wrong."

Peter said he wished he had acted differently in the basement. "I realize Leslie had a learning disability. . . . I think maybe I should have just left, but . . . I didn't want my friends talking bad about me, calling me a wimp. . . . Maybe people would have followed me out if they just saw someone do it first. . . . If I left and other people followed me, she might have stopped doing it."

That's what Peter Quigley told the prosecutor. Like Richie Corcoran before him and like Paul and Chris in the police station, Quigley tried to attribute the responsibility for what occurred to Leslie: "*She* might have stopped doing it." He was trying to exonerate his friends, but in the process he was providing more eyewitness details than the investigators had been able to gather in three years from anyone other than Leslie. If the defense lawyers called Quigley as a witness, as the prosecutors expected, his statement could yield a bountiful harvest for a prosecutor skilled in the art of cross-examination.

The statement, nineteen pages long, achieved Quigley's purpose. It got him admitted into the program; he was required to perform sixty hours of community service. After six months all charges against him would be wiped clean from his record.

Should Paul Archer be admitted into the pretrial program? Leslie had said that Chris's promise to get her a date with Paul had drawn her to the basement. Long ago investigators had begun referring to Paul as "the bait."

Letting "the bait" walk was wrong, some staff members in the prosecutor's office argued. Paul's long experience with her, dating back to childhood, made him aware of how easy it was to manipulate Leslie. Let Paul go free? It wasn't right, they protested.

But other prosecutors pointed out that it wasn't Paul who got the bat and broomstick; it wasn't Paul who inserted them into her vagina. During the hour the Jocks spent with Leslie, she said she had masturbated him, but there didn't seem to be a way to corroborate that. He was no more involved, they argued, than Peter Quigley had been—and Peter had been given a pass.

There was also a strategic consideration. If they made a deal with Paul and he gave a statement to the prosecutors that implicated his brother, it could have great force if he testified at the trial. Brother turning on brother. Cain and Abel. They finally reached a consensus: Let's bring Paul in. Let's see what he has to say.

They talked to him on Monday, June 22, 1992. A few hours with him persuaded Laurino that, as a defendant, he would not enhance the prosecution's case. Paul with the wavy blond hair. Paul with those soft brown eyes that could melt a stone. "He's like this Paul Newman type. This dashing, handsome, baby-faced kid who's giving us this rather bullshit but rather pathetic story," Laurino said. "Paul Archer sitting there day after day looking sorrowful—I just couldn't see that helping us."

The next morning Paul Archer, accompanied by his lawyer, Willard Byer, gave a statement to Laurino. Paul began by saying he knew people treated Leslie differently from other kids. For example? "One incident I heard of, she was in the park one day and some boys told her that a piece of dog excrement was actually a Snickers bar and she should eat it, so she picked it up."

Turning to the scene in the basement, Paul said Leslie "asked for something to be inserted inside of her" and Kevin handed her a broomstick. Paul said this happened while "she's laying lengthwise across the couch" and Kevin was "standing in front of her."

Laurino asked: "And is Kevin doing anything with this broomstick when Leslie's holding it?"

Paul: "She takes the broomstick and inserts it inside of her. After she started to move it inside, Kevin takes the bristled end and moves it along with her."

Laurino: "Did Kevin pass the broomstick on to Leslie or is he continually holding it?"

Paul: "He had let go and he took it again."

Archer said that Kevin was holding the broom for two minutes. Now Laurino asked: "At the end of that two minutes, what does he then do to the broomstick?"

Paul Archer answered: "He hands it over to my brother Chris."

Laurino went on, "What does your brother do?"

Paul Archer answered: "He does the same thing just as Kevin did for about the same time, two minutes."

Laurino asked whether Kevin then got the bat.

"Yes," Archer said, "Leslie asked for something larger to be inserted inside of her, so my brother Chris was still holding on to the broomstick. Kevin got a fungo baseball bat."

Kevin gave the bat to Kyle, who wrapped a plastic bag around it, Paul said. Kevin then handed the bat to Leslie, he continued. "Leslie tried to take the bat inside of her like she'd done with the broomstick, and then Kevin got on the end but it didn't work. . . . He tried about two or three minutes, which lasted about approximately thirty seconds."

Paul said Leslie was told to keep her experiences in the basement secret "because we didn't want it to be leaked out . . . because it would be embarrassing. . . . We didn't want our parents or our teachers or our girlfriends to find out."

Were you concerned that what went on in the basement was wrong? the prosecutor asked him. "In a moral sense if that's what you mean," Paul said. "We didn't think we had committed any legal wrong."

Laurino asked him whether the guys were talking when the broom and the bat were inserted. "Just small talk between one or two people standing next to each other," Paul said. "But there wasn't any loud yelling or anything of that type. . . . No cheering or no high-fives."

Laurino asked him how he felt about the incident—now.

"At the time, we knew Leslie had a learning disability but we didn't understand how severely retarded she was and we didn't think what we were doing was legally wrong," Paul said. "[But] I now understand . . . how sick she really is, and I just feel a great feeling of guilt and shame and I wish nothing had ever happened."

Archer had given a confidential, sealed statement that would remain secret until he became a witness in the trial. But Paul Archer wasn't done. To get admitted into the pretrial program, he had to appear before a judge and say in public at least a little of what he had said in confidence to the prosecutors.

The next morning Paul Archer, his father, and his lawyer turned up in the courtroom of Burrell Ives Humphreys, perhaps the most powerful judge in the busiest court system in the state. Humphreys, a gray-haired, stoop-shouldered man with a quiet, weary demeanor, was considering all the pretrial arguments and motions in the case. After three years of delays and maneuvering, the judge was eager to move the case to a conclusion.

Judge Humphreys' courtroom was almost empty. There were only two spectators in the public gallery: Diane Curcio, a reporter for the *Newark Star-Ledger*, and the author. Other journalists had not been alerted. Neither the prosecution nor the defense was eager to publicize the fact that Paul Archer was going to walk out of the case—after describing his brother's treatment of Leslie Faber. Both sides were hoping to conduct this transaction in the shadows.

Judge Humphreys asked whether the prosecutor had agreed to Archer's admission into the pretrial program. Laurino said that he had.

Archer was pleading guilty to a misdemeanor charge of endangering the welfare of a mentally incompetent person. Judge Humphreys asked Archer to describe what he had done.

Archer stood. The twenty-one-year-old college student didn't seem to know what he should say. The judge asked him again to describe the crime to which he was pleading guilty. Again Archer tried to find words, but couldn't.

Paul's lawyer asked, "Could I do it by questioning him?"

"It would be helpful," Humphreys agreed.

Byer turned toward Archer, who was standing at his side. Laurino leaned forward, cupped his chin in his hand, and stared at Byer.

"Paul, how long have you known [Leslie Faber]?" Byer asked.

"Since I was ten, eleven years old," Archer answered.

"You knew she had a learning disability?"

"Yes." Archer spoke in a loud, clear voice.

"In the basement did you see an act of oral sex with Leslie Faber and Bryant Grober?"

As Paul said "Yes," Laurino leaned back and turned the chair so that he could look directly at Archer.

Byer continued the questioning. "Did you also see your brother, Christopher, and Kevin Scherzer put a broomstick into her vagina?"

Stop time. One beat. And Paul Archer answered, "Yes."

Archer looked back over his shoulder, saw the two reporters taking notes, and his cheeks turned pink. He had thought this was going to be kept confidential.

Byer just kept asking more questions. "Did you also see Kevin Scherzer attempt to put a fungo bat into her vagina?"

"Yes," Paul Archer said.

"Did you take any steps to stop this?"

"No, I did not," Paul said.

Archer achieved his goal: He was admitted into the pretrial program; he had to do sixty days of community service and report for six months to a probation officer. Then his record would be cleared. But he achieved this at a price—telling the world what his brother did to Leslie Faber.

Outside the courtroom, Laurino asked, "Did you hear what I heard?"

"He said his brother did it," Curcio said.

"He didn't have to say it," Laurino said. "It probably would have been enough to show the judge Paul's statement. But Byer asked the questions and Paul answered."

"In public," Curcio said.

"On the record," Laurino said. He was smiling.

51

In the spring and summer of 1992, Judge Humphreys took care of the final pretrial business: Which defendants would be tried together, which judge would preside, and what evidence could be admitted. When that was done, he set a date for the beginning of the trial: September 8.

First, in May the judge ordered a separate trial because of unspecified medical reasons for John Maher, who was accused of trying to entice Leslie back to the basement on March 2, 1989. The judge also agreed to a separate trial for Richie Corcoran because, in his statement to investigators in June 1989, Richie had referred to some of the other defendants. The rest would be tried together.

In August Humphreys made a ruling that would have a devastating effect on Leslie. In New Jersey the rape shield law sharply restricted trial testimony about the sexual history of a rape victim. But Judge Humphreys ruled that accounts of Leslie's previous sexual conduct could be admitted as evidence in the upcoming trial.

Two central issues in the case were whether Leslie understood the nature of sexual relations and whether she understood that she had a right to reject sexual advances.

How could you assess Leslie's knowledge of sexuality and her awareness of her right to say "no" without considering her past sexual behavior? Humphreys asked. He acknowledged that exploration of the victim's past conduct would be painful to her, but "to shroud the truth is to invite an unjust verdict."

The judge's ruling came at a time when a national debate was being waged over what constituted sexual harassment and rape. In the rape trials of a group of St. John's University frat members, fighter Mike Tyson, and William Kennedy Smith, defense lawyers had suggested that a woman's unaccompanied presence in a hotel room, on a beach, or in a frat house was evidence of her willingness to have sex. "The theme in all of these high-publicity cases is, 'What was the woman doing there in the first place?'" said Ruth Jones, a staff lawyer for the National Organization for Women's Legal Defense Fund.

The defense lawyers in the Glen Ridge case were trying to prove that Leslie's visit to the Scherzer basement was part of a larger pattern of sexual promiscuity, one more instance where she had made herself available for sex. Representatives of women's rights groups said that neither Leslie's presence nor her previous sexual activity proved that she understood she had a right to say "no" to the insertion of a bat and a broomstick into her vagina. They pointed out that a jury could determine her mental capacity by learning whether she was able to travel to school alone or take a phone message; and it could determine her history of mental impairment by examining the results of her psychological examinations and, finally, through her own testimony.

In ruling that the defense had a right to exhume Leslie's sexual past, the judge did set some limits. The "emphasis must be properly placed on what happened in the basement," he said. "The defendants shouldn't be able to forage at will [in] the private life of [Leslie]."

The defense lawyers were busy foraging. For openers, they wanted to review Leslie's gynecological records. The Fabers asked their private lawyer to fight the defense effort. But the state's appellate division ruled that the defense lawyers needed the records to defend their clients. Even before the trial started, the terrain had shifted from the basement to Leslie's sexual experiences.

Humphreys' ruling was general in scope. The actual trial judge would have to decide, issue by issue, whether to permit the defense lawyers to explore Leslie's childhood and adolescence. That was not something Humphreys would have to worry about. He designated another judge to preside over the trial: forty-eight-year-old R. Benjamin Cohen, a former assistant prosecutor and chief of that office's appellate section; onetime general counsel to the state's Casino Control Commission; and since 1984 a judge in the criminal court.

Cohen was often described by litigators as intelligent and sophisticated in his understanding of the law, and adept at explaining complicated rulings to a jury in clear English. In 1989 the *New Jersey Law Journal*'s annual judicial survey ranked Cohen fourth out of Essex County's forty-five judges on the basis of overall competence.

When the defendants were first indicted, in 1990, Judge Cohen reportedly approached Judge Humphreys, who assigned judges to upcoming cases, and told him, "This is a big case. Some day when this comes to trial, if you need somebody, if you need somebody good, keep me in mind."

Not long after, when he began to appreciate the complexity of the issues and the fierce controversies they aroused, friends said he began to regret what he had said. "Why did I tell him that?" he said on one occasion. "God, I hope he doesn't remember that."

Now Humphreys thought that Cohen was the man for the job. And now Cohen had to start living with the legacy of Humphreys' rulings.

52

When prosecutor Elizabeth Miller-Hall had prepared her legal briefs for pretrial arguments, she had not spent much time with Leslie. Neither had the chief trial attorney, Glenn Goldberg. Laurino wanted both of them to meet her informally, on her own turf, to encounter her as they would encounter his own retarded brother.

A couple of weeks before the start of the trial, in the late summer, the three prosecutors visited the Fabers at their home in Glen Ridge. They came straight from the office. Miller-Hall, an attractive thirty-three-year-old black woman, wore a white suit and high heels. Laurino had on a tan summer suit, and Goldberg, a somewhat formal man, wore a dark suit.

For a while they sat stiffly in the Fabers' living room. Leslie brought out iced tea. She didn't look happy. These were her "friends" and she didn't want to share them with her mother. Then Ros suggested that they could watch videos of Leslie competing in Special Olympics swimming matches.

The videos made Elizabeth think, She has no form at all, but boy, is she fast. "That's tremendous," Laurino said. "You're really terrific." For the first time that day, Leslie grinned. "Les, I think they would like to hear you play the piano," Ros said. Leslie frowned. If a parent prodded you to show off, it took all the fun out of it. But she sat down anyway and played the theme from *Cats*. Les couldn't read music, but she could play from memory.

"You really have a talent," Miller-Hall said.

A tentative smile played on Leslie's face. Miller-Hall thought, She has such a low sense of self-worth, she can never be sure if people mean the praise or if they're trying to get over on her.

As Leslie played, Liz Miller-Hall watched Mrs. Faber. She was beaming. She's so proud of Les, Miller-Hall thought. It's hard enough to adopt a child, but to adopt a child and find out she's mentally retarded—that would be hardest of all. Would I be able to create the bond that Ros has with Leslie? the prosecutor asked herself. Elizabeth, who was married but did not have children, thought: This is why people have kids—because they can give so much pleasure. Sometimes.

Laurino wanted to talk to Ros Faber alone about the upcoming trial. So Glenn suggested that Leslie show him and Miller-Hall a gazebo in the backyard. Eventually, Laurino came out to join them. At his side was the

Fabers' dog. "I taught him to go get the frisbee," Leslie boasted as she tossed it and the dog retrieved it.

Laurino teased Miller-Hall, "Bet you can't get the dog to do that."

"Oh, she can do that," Leslie said. "I'll show her how." Elizabeth thought, She doesn't understand that Bob's teasing me. She remembered when she had once introduced Leslie to James Mulvihill, the chief prosecutor, joking, "This is the big cheese." And Leslie later said, "He doesn't look like cheese to me." Everything was literal to Leslie.

Laurino said to Miller-Hall, "Liz, let me show you how to shoot a basket."

"No, no, I'll show her," Leslie said. But she couldn't verbalize her instructions. All she could do was shoot and hand the ball to Liz, who, in her suit and high heels, tried to copy her.

Goldberg, who was standing back by the gazebo, said, "Can I try?" Leslie tossed him the ball. Without taking off his suit jacket, Goldberg took a long, long shot. It went in. There were laugh lines behind his glasses. A meticulous man, he counted off the steps from where he had taken the shot to the basket. "Forty-two feet," he announced triumphantly.

Leslie wasn't all that pleased. This nerdy-looking guy in his boring suit who drives an old-fogey car canned one from forty-two feet away, a shot that Leslie couldn't make. "Oh, that's nice," she said, quietly. "When my father comes home, we'll see if he can do it."

She didn't pout for long. Soon they were all back playing: the reserved, avuncular chief trial attorney; an assistant prosecutor who goes after rapists; a thirty-three-year-old Princeton grad whose specialty is writing appeals briefs; and a twenty-one-year-old retarded woman. Dodging the berry bushes as they fired up shots at the hoop; throwing the frisbee to a dog who never got tired of retrieving; finally, all of them collapsing in a giggling heap in the grass. Well, there must be a dry cleaner somewhere who could get grass stains out of a white suit.

As Goldberg drove the other two to the train station, Miller-Hall said, "You know what made this so great? It wasn't about the case at all. We were just accepting her for herself."

But, inevitably, there was the case, and the extra-legal feelings of the three prosecutors about Leslie influenced their approach to the trial and their professional relationships with each other. These feelings mirrored in miniature the themes that made this trial a compelling national drama of conscience and morality, that charged it with a significance beyond conviction or acquittal.

Glenn Goldberg, a man of cool temperament, who was regarded as a tenacious advocate and a clever courtroom strategist, thought the trial was primarily about the abuse of a retarded young woman. "We will have to educate the jury about retardation," he said just before the trial began. "If we can do that, the jury will understand what happened to Leslie."

Elizabeth Miller-Hall, the appeals specialist and the only woman on the prosecution trial team, had a somewhat different interpretation. "Retardation is a big part of it," she said. "But all over the country women will be waiting to see what happens, because this is a definitive test of whether women can receive equal justice. Legalistically, this may be about protecting the retarded. But culturally, socially, this is also a battle for women's rights."

Miller-Hall was attuned to the sensibilities of women who for many years believed there was a separate, more lenient standard for men who raped—a standard that permitted many men, particularly white males, to escape punishment by crawling through the cracks in the law.

Laurino's job was to put rapists in jail. But this case got under his skin in a way that other rape cases—some more vicious in their details—rarely did. The fact was, he was emotionally bound to Leslie, but was she bound to him? He wanted Leslie to believe in him, to trust him to fight for her. But he couldn't rip apart that web of misplaced loyalties and unfulfilled needs that entangled her and the Jocks.

He saw himself not only as Leslie's defender but also—and more importantly for the case—as her interpreter to his more detached colleagues. He also saw himself as Leslie's messenger to the jurors, who might not understand the emotional, social, and sexual life of a retarded young woman. It was a responsibility that came more naturally to him than to the other prosecutors because of his relationship with his brother. But there was something else about this case, something that seemed to provoke him more than it provoked his fellow prosecutors: the values of the defendants. He discerned in their relatively brief lives a pattern of abuse of power, a corruption of decent intent, for which these young men and many of the adults who had guided them shared responsibility.

It was beyond his reach, but if he could have done so, Laurino would have convicted the values of Glen Ridge. "They believed themselves to be invincible," he said of the four men on trial. "They knew that problems that would arise would be taken care of out of the deep pockets of their parents or the compassion of a small-town police department or the compassion of a small-town school system or the compassion of small-town residents who knew each other and wanted to handle things among themselves. They've been getting free rides all their life."

He knew all that. He also knew that it was unlikely the judge would let him tell that to the jury. But sometimes jurors understand without hearing the words.

53

Labor Day came and went. The opening of the trial was a couple of weeks away. And the word *deal* floated in the breeze.

A deal that would avoid a trial held some appeal for both sides. After the prosecutors' visit to the Fabers' home, Elizabeth Miller-Hall had said she believed Leslie would make a strong witness for the prosecution. Laurino shook his head warily. "I don't know, Liz," he said. "I've known Leslie for three years, but I don't know what she'll say when she gets on the stand. The big unknown in the case is her. We're her friends today; the boys will be her friends tomorrow. The minute she starts to talk, the case could go up like a puff of smoke."

The defense lawyers didn't lack incentive, either. "When you let a case go to a jury, who knows what you'll get," said one of the defense lawyers. "You always have to remember that there's a smell around all the defendants. The baseball bat and the broomstick leaves a very big stink on everyone."

With a long, costly trial looming that would be as painful for Leslie and her family as it would be for the defendants, Judge Cohen brought the prosecutors, the defendants, their parents, and the defense lawyers together to discuss a deal. This wasn't the first attempt to settle the case out of public view. Back in July, after the two sides met to talk about a deal, the defense attorneys said that the prosecutors' terms were too harsh: maximum sentences of from five to nine years. The heavier sentences would go to Kevin and Chris, who allegedly wielded the bat and the broomstick. Kyle and Bryant would be at the lower end of the scale.

In the plea-bargaining process, "five to nine" were only negotiating numbers. It could turn out that the two defendants facing the most serious penalties might have to do, at the most, two to three years in state prison.

The two defendants contending with the lesser charges might wind up with a year behind bars.

The wrinkle in the prosecution's offer was that it had to be accepted by all the defendants. All or none. The defense lawyers rejected the offer, declaring that the families of the defendants and the defendants themselves would not accept any deal that included a day of jail time.

After Labor Day the prosecution sweetened its offer: Chris Archer and Kevin Scherzer would get sentenced to three or four years but would actually do a year behind bars; Kyle and Bryant might get sentenced to a year or so, which meant that they would actually do three or four months in the county jail, regarded by many in the criminal justice system as a much more hospitable place than the state prison. But one element of the plea offer had not changed: All the defendants had to agree to the plea, or the offer would be withdrawn.

All the other deals had been cut: Gone were Peter Quigley, Paul Archer, and Mari Carmen Ferraez. Richie Corcoran and John Maher had been severed from the trial and, ostensibly, would have separate trials later. The Glen Ridge rape case was down to the hard core of Kyle and Kevin Scherzer, Bryant Grober, and Christopher Archer.

Judge Cohen asked the families of the four defendants to come into his chambers. He laid out the offer that the prosecutors had made and reportedly said, "It's a fair offer. Consider it carefully." He would be overstepping his professional bounds had he urged them to accept it. Some of the defense lawyers were unequivocal when they discussed the offer with the parents. "Take it," one defense lawyer told the parents of the defendant he represented. "It's a very generous offer."

The families met separately with their lawyers; they also met as a group. Their decision: No deal. Sources close to the case said the offer was rejected by the Scherzers and the Archers. Jack Scherzer reportedly said, "I can't see Kevin doing a year for this."

This decision made some of the lawyers nervous. "Three months is three months," said one defense lawyer. He was referring to the jail time that Kyle and Bryant would be likely to serve.

There was nothing left but to go to trial. On September 21, 1992, three years and almost seven months after Leslie Faber and thirteen high school athletes met in a basement, jury selection would begin in the Glen Ridge rape trial.

PART VI

Moral Judgments

54

Now the reckoning. The jury had been sworn in, and the trial began on Thursday morning, October 15, 1992. The setting was the spare, 1950s-functional courtroom of Judge Cohen on the eighth floor of the Essex County courthouse in Newark.

The people who designed the courtroom may have imagined that the bare-bones furnishings—the back-breaking rows of the public gallery, the elevated jury box, the plain witness stand, and the stolid judge's bench—would encourage a businesslike atmosphere and suppress high-flying rhetoric and emotional outbursts. But it had the opposite effect. The blandness served to highlight the principals as the long narrative of the trial unfolded.

This morning, unexpectedly, belonged more to the parents than to the defendants or the lawyers. They were the first to enter the courtroom, at 9 A.M. Rosemary Grober wore a gray suit and a white blouse, a handbag slung over her shoulder as she walked briskly to her seat on the aisle in the third row. Directly in front of her, Michaele Archer sat staring at the vacant judge's bench. She mouthed a few inaudible words to herself. Geraldine Scherzer, hands clasped in her lap, hunched over as though she were meditating or trying to hide, sat silently next to her husband.

The mothers had appeared infrequently during the past two and a half years; but the fathers, Dr. Nathan Grober, Jack Scherzer, and Douglas Archer, had repeatedly visited the Newark courthouse. They had attended pretrial hearings and listened to hundreds of hours of arguments. Grober had rescheduled his office hours to attend each event; as soon as a recess ended, he was on his feet, buttoning the jacket of his blue or gray suit, nervously waiting to enter the courtroom.

Doug Archer was there almost as often as Grober. He always dressed in business suits, and he often greeted reporters with a bright morning smile that turned into more of a grimace as the hours passed. During breaks in the proceedings, he would dash to a phone to call his office. His apparent cheerfulness made it hard to believe that two of his sons had been indicted on a charge of rape.

Jack Scherzer had not attended as often as the other two fathers had (because his sons were not involved in the stretched-out juvenile "waiver" hearings). But he had managed to attend most of the important hearings, often wearing a leather jacket over a white shirt and tie. He was quiet and unsmiling, and he rarely talked to the other fathers.

The question that every person in the courtroom seemed to be asking the parents, the mothers especially, was, How can you bear to be here? And then: You who know them best, how can you explain what your sons did? And finally: Could any parent explain what must seem like the unexplainable?

As the trial began, the first three rows of the right side of the courtroom were reserved for parents, family members, and friends of the defendants. Many of the seats were filled with girlfriends, past and present, of the defendants and other female acquaintances and relatives. It was as if the defendants had brought their own, adult version of the Jockettes to provide moral support during the trial.

On the other side of the courtroom, the first two rows were reserved for the Faber family, their friends, and others who knew Leslie. But the Fabers would almost never attend the trial. Their seats were quickly claimed by the media. Represented were all the major networks, the newsmagazines, the big East Coast newspapers, and the important New York and New Jersey dailies.

Behind the reporters and courtroom artists, two women sat together. They were Christine McGoey and Carole Vasile, the only two salaried organizers for the New Jersey branch of the National Organization for Women. They would be present every day, offering a running commentary to the press.

The hard set of their jaws, their lips pressed into thin tight lines, could not conceal the parents' anguish, fear, bewilderment, and rage. Not even the most jaded reporters could bring themselves to question them. But the questions and judgments were voiced by others. And loudly.

When the parents and lawyers entered the courthouse, they could see and hear in the small plaza in front of the building dozens of women marching to express their opinions about the trial.

They chanted:

Two, five, seven, nine;
victims' rights are on the line.

They chanted:

We are women,
hear us wail.
Glen Ridge rapists
go to jail.

In the following weeks, demonstrators would wear T-shirts that located the trial in the international geography of sexual violence. The T-shirts read: "Rape Trial World Tour: Palm Beach, St. John's, Indianapolis, Glen Ridge, Bosnia."

But there was something that distinguished this from other urban protests. For the most part, the participants looked like average suburban-ites—white women wearing stylish suits and dresses, brightened by the occasional piece of gold jewelry—and were ardent subscribers to the principles of majoritarianism: careful, incremental social and political change.

Most of the women who demonstrated and the few men who joined them came from towns and villages that had more in common with Glen Ridge than with New York or Newark. And they brought with them their own hometown memories of experiences that evoked Glen Ridge. They were posing a challenge that would attract the interest of the American and international media, that would make Glen Ridge a hot-button case, that would place it at the intersection of law and morality. That challenge had to do with who the defendants were: clean-cut, middle-class, educated white guys, Glen Ridge's guys, the country's guys. "They lived their lives thinking they were special and their specialness would protect them," one demonstrator said. "Will it? We'll find out."

That's why the Glen Ridge story, dormant now for almost three years, was working its way toward the front page again. The attention it would receive in the next five and a half months would impress the prosecutors and defense lawyers, the victim's parents, the defendants and their families, and the judge, too. For a judge, it took no great courage to dispense justice to those you expected the least of. But it required a truly subversive impulse to punish the progeny of the country's heartland.

The four defendants walked singly down the middle aisle of the public section and then sat in chairs placed against the wall opposite the jury box. Today they had decided to emphasize their separateness—no gabbing, no supportive back slaps and shoulder squeezes. Each occupied his own florescent hell. Chris Archer—in his blue oxford button-down and blue-and-red striped tie, tan slacks, and blue blazer—had a notebook and pen to take notes and pass messages to his lawyer; Bryant Grober, in a gray blazer and white shirt with a plaid tie, chewed gum. His jaw muscles worked overtime, but otherwise his face was composed in an impassive block. Kyle Scherzer, in a gray suit and white shirt, also was unexpressive, except that he would lean forward from time to time as though he was tired of sitting in one place. His brother, Kevin, hair slicked back, spiked, and cut fairly short in front, twiddled his thumbs.

Three and a half years had changed the guys. In 1989, despite frequent visits to the weight-lifting room, they were still growing into their bodies. Since then their shoulders had broadened, their necks thickened; the features of Kevin and Bryant had coarsened. "When I took the case, I was defending boys," said Louis Esposito, Kyle's lawyer. "Now I'm defending men."

But appearances notwithstanding, the indictment manacled them together as surely as if they were on the same chain gang. The separate counts of the indictment ascribed different actions to different individuals: Chris and Kevin inserting the bat and broomstick; Kyle covering the bat head with a plastic bag; Bryant Grober engaging in fellatio with Leslie. But the emphasis in the indictment was on shared culpability. The very first count charged that each of them had conspired with the three others to commit "aggravated sexual assault"—to rape Leslie Faber. The indictment alleged that all of the four had "aided and abetted" one another in everything they did during the time they spent with Leslie in the Scherzers' basement.

Judge Cohen took his seat behind the bench and said: "Please bring in the jury." It had taken three weeks to select these twelve jurors and four alternates, who were now filing into the jury box. The twelve who would actually deliberate on a verdict would be chosen by lot from among the sixteen when testimony in the trial was completed. The jurors consisted of ten women and six men, eight blacks and eight whites. The majority of the jurors were in their thirties and forties, although a few were in their late fifties and early sixties. One woman was twenty-six years old.

The jury composition reflected the urban and suburban blend of Essex County. Most of the blacks came from Newark and other predominantly black towns and cities; most of the whites lived in suburban towns such as Maplewood and Cedar Grove. A wide variety of occupations were represented: a word processor, an administrative aide, a truck driver, a school bus driver, a guard at the Essex County jail that adjoined the courthouse.

Judge Cohen explained to the jury that to determine whether Leslie was capable of saying "no" and whether the defendants knew she was mentally defective, the lawyers would have to delve into her sexual history. "There will be testimony about sexual conduct by Leslie Faber on other occasions [in addition to March 1, 1989], but this is not an attack on her character," he told the sixteen jurors. "Leslie Faber is not on trial here."

After finishing his remarks to the jury, Cohen said, "The prosecutor may make his opening statement."

Assistant Prosecutor Glenn D. Goldberg stood up and faced the jury box, a sheaf of notes under his arm. Goldberg was the chief trial attorney in the prosecutor's office. In his seventeen years as a prosecutor, he had taken on some of the hardest cases; he won a lot of them, but he was not always successful. He had won a conviction against a woman accused of sexually abusing nineteen children at a day-care center; but that conviction was later overturned on appeal, and the defendant walked. And he had lost a bitter, racially charged case against a white police officer accused of wrongfully shooting a black youth. A fiercely competitive lawyer, he was not adverse to risk. If he had his way, he would have taken everybody to trial in the Glen Ridge case: Mari Carmen Ferraez, Richie Corcoran, Peter Quigley, Paul Archer, and John Maher. The more the better.

In this case Goldberg's mission was clear. He had to prove to the jury's satisfaction that the defendants raped Leslie by penetrating her vagina and by committing fellatio. Those were the most serious charges, the rape charges. He also had to establish that a conspiracy was under way in the basement and that the defendants aided and abetted each other.

To enable the jurors to reach that conclusion, the indictment advanced two theories. The first one: The defendants knew or should have known that Leslie was "mentally defective"—a legal term meaning that a person was incapable of consenting to sexual relations. The second theory: The defendants used force or coercion to violate Leslie. The jury members did not have to buy both propositions. If the prosecutor persuaded them that one of the theories was true, that was enough to convict the four.

The case did not conform to the stereotypical view of rape, in which a woman is beaten or held at knife point while someone sexually assaults her. When someone is in mortal danger, there is little question that sexual relations are taking place against the victim's will.

One of the prosecutors' biggest problems was that Leslie apparently had never said "no"—had never openly resisted the advances of her friends, the Jocks. The first task of the prosecution would be to persuade the jurors that Leslie was so mentally "defective" that she was incapable of consenting to these acts.

Toward this end, the prosecution was aided by a recent ruling by the New Jersey Supreme Court. The court said that a defendant could be found guilty of sexual assault even if the victim did not resist or audibly say "no." Conversely, to gain a verdict of acquittal for their clients, the defense lawyers had to show that Leslie gave permission freely.

The prosecutors could prove that Leslie was "mentally defective" in two ways. They could show that she did not understand what she was consenting to, that she was "innocent" about sex and did not realize what the Glen Ridge athletes were asking her to do. They could also demonstrate her incapacity by showing that she did not know she had the right to say "no"—or didn't know how to say it.

To make that case, the prosecutors planned to call experts, psychologists and psychiatrists, as well as Leslie's friends and family members. They would testify to her limited comprehension of social relations and sexual situations. The prosecutors also planned to emphasize how easily Leslie could be led by others.

It came down to this: The prosecution had to persuade the jurors that Leslie lacked the capacity to understand what the boys were doing to her, and that it went against her nature—her mental and emotional makeup—to resist, even if she could.

The most important witness of all would be Leslie Faber. Through her testimony, the jurors would be able to judge for themselves her level of understanding. Through her demeanor on the witness stand, the jury would decide whether Leslie Faber was "mentally defective" under the law.

But the prosecution had one additional test: It had to demonstrate not only that Leslie lacked the ability to consent but also that the males who had gathered around her were aware of her limitations, or, at least, should have been aware of them. To establish that element of their argument, the prosecutors would rely on testimony that showed how obvious Leslie's disabilities were to people in her school and community—to friends, teachers, and even casual acquaintances. But, again, Leslie's testimony and appearance on the stand would rule. If she seemed lucid and competent to the jurors, they might question how a group of teenagers, high school seniors and juniors, could have known of her disability. If, however, she appeared confused and childlike on the stand, the jury would be more likely to conclude that these young men—teenagers in 1989—should have been aware of her mental condition and purposely seized on her vulnerability.

The alternative path for the prosecution was to prove that the defendants had used force or coercion against her. The prosecution planned to argue that the entire environment in the basement was coercive: the presence of thirteen muscle-bound athletes intent on exploiting a lone girl in an enclosed space with only one exit. And the prosecutors would contend that what happened constituted acts of force, especially the penetration of

Leslie's body with the bat and broomstick. The prosecution would also interpret the oral sex between Leslie and Bryant Grober as force, using, the prosecutors hoped, Leslie's testimony that Bryant had pushed her head down onto his penis.

In his opening statement, Goldberg tried to introduce to the jurors the one woman missing from the courtroom—Leslie Faber. He spoke in a hard, steely voice, an unforgiving voice. The prosecutor said that in March 1989 Leslie still functioned at "the educational level approximately of an eight-year-old." Examples of Leslie's limitations: "Leslie couldn't cook. . . . Leslie couldn't take public transportation. . . . TV even was kind of puzzling to Leslie at age seventeen because sometimes you see people get shot and killed on the television and what Leslie was never able to understand [was] how could a character be shot and killed one day and be alive again on another day."

Goldberg then offered the jurors his version of what had occurred on March 1, 1989. When she was promised a date with Paul Archer, she followed Chris Archer and the twelve other boys down to the basement, he said. He turned toward the defendants who were seated in a row across the courtroom against a wall. "Bryant Grober began to engage Leslie Faber in an act of oral sex. That is to say, his penis into her mouth." Some of the young men in the basement "began to feel very, very uncomfortable and . . . began to leave. . . . They had the built-in sense and knowledge of what is right and what is wrong."

What happened next, Goldberg said, was that "Leslie was raped." He paused and repeated: "Raped." Rape, he said, involves the insertion of something into a woman's body. Rape, he said, was a penis thrust into Leslie's mouth. And rape was "wooden sticks" thrust into her body.

One of the early acts of sexual assault, Goldberg said, "was when Chris Archer took a broom and put it between Leslie Faber's legs, into her vagina." Again, he turned to point out a defendant—this time Archer. "He inserted the broom into Leslie Faber's body and pushed it in and out and in and out." The prosecutor motioned with his hands as though he were driving a stake into the ground. Goldberg pointed to Kevin Scherzer, who, he said, took the broom from Chris "so that he could insert the broom in and out, and in and out."

Next came the bat. "Kevin Scherzer took that bat and . . . did the best he could to try to insert the bat in the same place from where the broomstick had been withdrawn—into Leslie's vagina." Kyle Scherzer had "aided and abetted" Chris and Kevin by putting a Vaseline-smeared plastic bag "over some of these instruments," the prosecutor said. He said that it wasn't clear whether Kyle did this "to protect Leslie . . . [or] to protect the broom and the bat." Compared to Goldberg's dramatic description of what he said Chris and Kevin did, he seemed to gloss over Kyle's actions.

Goldberg said that while the charges would be depicted as sexual crimes, the underlying theme of the prosecution's case was that the defendants committed "certain acts of aggression, certain acts of cruelty, acts of humiliation and degradation to this young victim."

Then the prosecutor spoke the lines that would make their way into tomorrow's headlines: "This was not really what one considers when one thinks about sex. This was more in the nature of some sort of obscene science experiment that was going on in the basement of the Scherzers that day."

For a moment, but a telling moment, he seemed to be dissecting the values of Glen Ridge itself, perhaps the values of many Glen Ridges. "The reason they did it to Leslie Faber is because . . . they knew they could get away with it. . . . After all, after all, suppose she . . . did tell anybody. So what? Who would believe Leslie Faber, this defective, mentally retarded teenage girl?"

Goldberg did what he could to prepare the jurors for the uncertainty of Leslie's testimony. "Will she be able to tell you today what happened back then, so long ago? Will Leslie Faber be distracted by all you strangers sitting there, the defendants themselves sitting near her, looking at her?"

The prosecutors had decided that they couldn't wait passively for the defense lawyers to present Mari Carmen's tapes as evidence of Leslie's sexual practices or of her willingness to consent to the acts in the basement. The jurors, Goldberg said, would have a chance to hear Leslie as she was three years ago by listening to Mari Carmen's recording. He tried to prepare them for sections of the tapes where Leslie was presenting herself as a sexual virtuoso and as a romantic, willing intimate of the Jocks. To do that he decided to concede at the outset that Leslie understood what sexual conduct was. "She knew the mechanics of sex," he acknowledged.

The fifty-year-old prosecutor, whose voice had become raspy after almost three hours of talking, ended by reading the forty-four overt acts listed in the indictment, without inflection or emphasis. This wasn't legal argument so much as a story with a beginning, middle, and end. And the jurors seemed engrossed.

After Goldberg was done, the defendants and their relatives and supporters clustered at the entrance of the courtroom, talking softly. For the first time they looked frightened.

55

Tommy Ford, Chris Archer's lawyer, was the first defense lawyer to address the jury. Ford was a stocky man with thinning wavy hair and bushy eyebrows. He wore double-breasted pin-striped suits brightened by wide ties with floral patterns. There were heavy pouches under his eyes, and his prominent jowls quivered alarmingly when he got excited. He was sixty years old, and it had been twenty years since he had worked as first assistant in the prosecutor's office. In his earlier years, one lawyer said, "Tommy Ford could be one hell of a sarcastic guy." The years had sanded away some of the sarcasm, but no one would ever say that Ford was terse.

Ford, like the other three defense lawyers, had developed strategies to counter the prosecution's battle plan. But they all knew that any one of their possible strategies could backfire, with disastrous results for their four clients. The simplest strategy was to argue that the alleged rape never happened. After all, the prosecution had no eyewitnesses to corroborate all of Leslie's account. (Paul Archer and Peter Quigley had corroborated only certain elements.) So, theoretically, the defense could contend that it was her unreliable word against that of a group of hometown heroes.

Through the past year, Kyle Scherzer's lawyer, Louis Esposito, would ask, mockingly, "What bat, what broomstick?" as though the charges were the figments of Leslie's overheated imagination. But that was before Paul Archer and Peter Quigley gave their statements to the prosecution in return for entering the pretrial program. Now the defense was confronted by the inescapable fact that standing behind the curtain, awaiting their cue, were two members of the Jock clique who had been in the basement from start to finish and could testify that a bat and a broomstick had been used.

No longer able to deny the basic elements of Leslie's story, Ford and his colleagues had no choice but to argue that she was mentally capable of consenting or that the guys didn't realize she was incapable. To support that claim, the defense could call experts of their own, to counter the prosecution's experts. The trial could turn into a battle of experts.

Another potential weapon was Mari Carmen's tapes. But the defense didn't know whether the jurors would interpret Leslie's taped remarks as proof of her sexual awareness or as a calculated manipulation of Leslie by Mari Carmen to rescue her friends.

A third strategy was to show on cross-examination that Leslie was sexually experienced. That could be very dangerous, however—staking everything on Leslie. How could they show that she was experienced and knowledgeable about sex without seeming to attack the character of a sympathetic victim?

Then there was the road almost never traveled by the defense in a major criminal case. That was to put the defendants on the stand. Defense lawyers generally agree that a defendant is his own worst witness. So the core question for the defense lawyers was: How could they make a plausible argument that the four defendants didn't know Leslie well enough to assess her mental state without putting them on the stand and exposing them to a relentless cross-examination?

The heart of the defense strategy was to exploit the tapes, chip away at the qualifications of the prosecution's expert witnesses, possibly use Archer or Quigley as witnesses to shift the responsibility for the sexual activity to Leslie, and pray that she would make a poor witness.

There was also the down-and-dirty approach. That required the defense lawyers to assert explicitly or insinuate in every question and argument that Leslie had vast sexual experience, and that what happened to her in the basement was just one in a long series of sexual encounters. They were prepared to play this card.

But not right away. Ford began his opening not by attacking Leslie's reputation but by disapproving of his client's behavior. Ford told the jury, "Don't get the impression that anybody in this case deserves a medal or a commendation." But he urged the jurors to remain impartial "in spite of the word 'baseball bat,' in spite of the word 'broom,' in spite of the fact that Leslie Faber unfortunately is mildly retarded."

"Chris Archer was only sixteen years of age," Ford said. He argued that the prosecution would have to establish that the teenager knew what Leslie's understanding of sex was and that she was incapable of consenting. "The evidence is going to show . . . that's an impossible fact to establish."

Ford paced along the rail of the jury box as he shifted the discussion to Leslie. Now it was time to begin assaulting Leslie's reputation. The trial would show, he told the jurors, "some promiscuity on the part of Leslie Faber . . . that will make you painfully aware of her knowledge and her ability to say 'yes' and 'no.' . . . She went willingly because it was her desire, as it had been in the past, to perform these types of actions."

The medical reports by doctors who examined Leslie after the incident suggested that she had controlled the movement of the bat and broomstick, he said, because "Leslie never had any type of wound or injury to the vaginal area."

Ford repeated that he was not proud of what the defendants had done. "I am not condoning these boys. I would like to give them a slap, but that's all, not convict them of a crime they weren't guilty of."

When they would meet Leslie, Ford said, the jurors would say: "Gee, she doesn't sound like she's that retarded at all."

Ford said the Scherzer twins' grandmother entered the basement when Leslie was there. All Leslie had to do was say, "'Come on down. I don't like what is going on.' That would have been the end of it. There is nothing to show that Leslie couldn't have walked out of that room any time that she wanted."

One hand in his trouser jacket, the other bent at the wrist, Ford strolled in front of the jury box. He said that Archer was standing trial not because he had committed a crime but because people "didn't like" what he had done in the basement. "That's what this is all about," Thomas Ford told the jury in the Glen Ridge case.

The next morning Bryant Grober's lawyer, Alan Zegas, was scheduled to make his opening and he was nervous. He was thirty-nine years old and was good at writing appeals briefs and arguing points of law, but all his trial experience had been in the federal courts. This was his first case in state criminal court. And such a high-stakes case, too.

Zegas had replaced Grober's original lawyer, who had a scheduling conflict with another case. A warm relationship had developed between Zegas and the Grobers. Zegas's aunt and uncle had a summer home on Bradley Beach, a New Jersey resort town where the Grobers also had a house. Years before, when Zegas visited his relatives, he often found them on the beach chatting with the Grobers. The lawyer didn't become close friends with Nathan and Rosemary, but his aunt would give Zegas's family bundles of clothes that the Grobers' children had outgrown. "Nice clothing, in perfect condition," Zegas recalled later. "They were very thoughtful." This was long before Zegas became involved in the case.

Zegas was an intense man. He was intense when he ran in a marathon race. He was intense this morning as he waited to make his opening. Zegas had devised a theme that he thought might save Bryant. He had to separate his client from the other three defendants by persuading the jury that the oral sex between Bryant and Leslie was very different, in moral and legal terms, from the penetration of her body with a bat and a broom. And he had to show that Bryant was much less familiar with Leslie than the other three athletes and therefore could not be expected to gauge her mental defectiveness.

The trick was to plant this separation in the jurors' minds without damaging the co-defendants. "If you have the defense pointing fingers at each other, everybody is going to suffer," he said later. "I wanted to walk this fine line, to try to bring out Bryant's separateness without casting stones upon what the others might or might not have done."

Zegas, a short, fit man, advanced toward the jury like a charged field of energy. As he started talking, his hand shook. He was not noticeably ingratiating. He just went after the prosecution's case against Grober. Zegas suggested that retardation is not a severe impediment. "Retarded people are like us in just about every way except they might learn a little bit more slowly . . . retarded people can have sexual needs."

None of the defense lawyers would "demean this woman," he promised the jury, but Leslie did engage in "teasing and provocativeness . . . where she could verbally ask for sexual favors."

The defense lawyers argued that the people of Glen Ridge considered her basically normal. "She didn't walk around the school with an IQ sticker pinned on her head, you know, 67, or 49."

From Leslie's sexual behavior, Zegas turned to the behavior of Sheila Byron. The defense lawyer said the evidence would show that Leslie "would say what she thought Detective Byron wanted her to say." An example: Leslie's accusations against Richie Corcoran and her subsequent retraction.

Two-thirds of the way through his opening, Zegas mentioned Bryant Grober for the first time. Up to then, it had been all Leslie Faber. When Grober was in Cartaret Park on March 1, Zegas said, Leslie "grabbed his crotch [and said,] 'Nice dick you have there.'" He urged the jury to remember that Grober was only seventeen then.

Zegas said that Leslie asked Bryant: "Do you want a blow job?" The defense lawyer contended that the prosecution could not prove that Grober forced Leslie into an act of fellatio and that Bryant's hand on Leslie's head was "part of the act itself." Soon after the fellatio began, Grober "became greatly embarrassed and ashamed of what he was doing and he stopped it," the defense lawyer said.

That was the first degree of separation—Bryant's shame. Another way to separate him from the other defendants was the use of the bat and broomstick. In her conversation with Mari Carmen, Leslie had described the fellatio with Grober as something she "loved" and said it was "great."

"Do those sound like the words of a person who was forced into doing something that she didn't want to do?" Zegas asked rhetorically. A juror could infer that Leslie was less enthusiastic about the bat and broomstick, which were associated with the other three defendants.

A third degree of separation was to show that Bryant didn't know Leslie as well as she knew the other defendants. Zegas pointed out that she had identified him as "Bryan" rather than "Bryant" in a statement to police. The jury was left to conclude that Leslie knew the other boys in the base-ment—and they in turn knew her—much better than she knew Bryant. Zegas was pressing his theme on the jury: Bryant was separate, different, from the other Jocks.

Then Zegas told the jury: "Bryant Grober is not a criminal, is not a rapist, is not any of these evil, sinister things the prosecutor would have you believe. He was just a boy that probably did a thing he will regret more than anything he had ever done in his life."

Fifteen minutes after Zegas finished, every seat in the courtroom was filled. Behind the last row, lawyers, prosecutors, detectives, and court-house employees of all stations stood three deep. They had come to hear the Master Defense Lawyer. They had come to hear Michael Querques.

In a career of thirty-five years, Querques had earned the respect of his fellow practitioners by ably defending the most difficult clients to de-fend—members of organized crime, mob guys. But he had defended many others as well; his style and strategies were adaptable to the charges and the defendants. But his work habits never changed. When he was preparing for a case, he closeted himself in his office in Orange, New Jer-sey, and was rarely seen in public until he had to appear in court. Trials were work and he was confident of his work skills, but he was not senti-mental. When the case was over—win or lose—he moved on.

Querques was a short powerful man; at the age of sixty-three, he was proud to say that he weighed 150 pounds, twenty pounds lighter than when he threw the shotput and played football in high school. His grip clamped on your shoulder like a bear trap. He had been in poor health recently, but he still did his 100 sit-ups each morning. "Not so long ago it was 250," he said.

Lawyers came to see him open the Glen Ridge trial not so much to observe his tactics and strategy as to watch him perform. To watch him hitch up his pants. To watch him adjust his expression, from righteous rage to stunned amazement to profound sorrow to puckish mischievousness. Querques wasted nothing. His suit jacket, always buttoned up to the lapels, was his armor against the treachery of a prosecutor. Even his rumpled features and his gray, hospital pallor were converted into assets when he introduced himself to the Glen Ridge jury, with a sigh of resignation, as "this dead-tired little old guy."

But the tired old guy was full of juice today. Right from the start he shredded Leslie Faber's reputation in an opening statement to the jury that had courtroom spectators gasping at its ferocity. "The young lady, by reason of whatever experience . . . she had before March 1, 1989, was ready, willing, and able to do what she did. . . . She was anxious to do what she did . . . and would do it again. . . . Leslie Faber, like many, many people, discovered that it is pleasurable to give sex, to see the joy on a boy's face when he ejaculates, or to use her word, come."

Laurino, sitting at the prosecutor's table a few feet from the jury box, turned to look at the jurors. He was expressionless. Two women in the first row of jurors shifted in their seats.

"Did this young lady know what it felt like to touch skin, to caress it, the opposite sex's body?" Querques asked. "Did she know . . . the pleasure that comes from kissing?"

Querques compared Leslie's sexual urges to a basic need, like thirst. "Do you think Leslie Faber, because she is retarded, doesn't have feelings? . . . Let me tell you, . . . she had her feelings for sex, her drive, if you like, for sex. Her brain and her stomach and her genital signals are greater than normal. Obsession. One word—obsession."

It wasn't only her "obsession" that compelled Leslie to do what she did, Querques argued. The sex-obsessed American culture was also to blame. "What was considered perversion in 1940 is not considered perversion at all today to most people. . . . You can engage in what some call perversion and others say, Beauty, wonderful. . . . It's glorious. It's euphoric. It's ecstatic," he said.

Now he addressed one of the main legal issues in the case. "Did she understand she had the right to refuse to engage in sex? We say she absolutely did." Querques referred to words and phrases Leslie had used in her tape-recorded conversations. "Don't be offended. . . . She uses the word penis; as synonymous with penis she will use dick, she will use prick, she will use boner. For fellatio she will say blow job."

"She has knowledge that—that may end up shocking you." This was a young woman with cravings, he said. "She wanted affection, she thrived for affection. That is an absolute given. But she also thrived for the kissing, she craved the caressing, she craved the embracing, she craved that euphoria, that ecstasy . . . the pleasure of engaging in sex, because her brain functioned that way."

The sixty-three-year-old man painted a word-picture of the adolescent Leslie: "A full-breasted young lady, she is a full-blown young lady, was at 15, 16, 17 . . . and she is going to do like you and me. When the trigger goes off, when the feeling goes off, you have got a ladyfriend, you do it."

He stood there behind his lectern, his hands jammed into his jacket pockets. He took his hands out. He raised his palms in the air. He leaned toward the jury and whispered a confidence. "I am going to tell you something, I run a risk. . . . I think we have ten women here out of sixteen. I am going to tell all of you, all sixteen, including the ten women, girls will be girls. All girls are not the same. There are some girls who are Lolitas. Do you know Lolitas, 14, 15, and dress up like they are 18 and 19, to entice and attract?

"There are some girls who are like nerdy boys, very bashful. I have a daughter"—Querques drew his breath in—"big-breasted girl, walks this way to hide her breasts. Her sister is flat, she sticks it out"—he stuck his chest out—"she sticks it out, what little she has got, so I know what I am talking about. . . . You come in all shapes and sizes . . . and there are some that are very, very flirtatious. Huh?"

Goldberg stood up and walked to the end of the jury box closest to the spectator section of the courtroom. He clasped his hands behind his back and watched Querques, who gave no sign that he noticed Goldberg's presence. Querques said, "Now if I took a chance, at least I was honest . . . there are women who when they like a guy they will set out to get him in a devious way perhaps, perhaps in an aggressive way."

There came now, from the back rows in the courtroom, the sound of a woman muffling her crying. Querques continued, apparently undistracted. He said he was done talking about Leslie Faber. Now he wanted to discuss the "average boy." And you know how boys could act, Querques said. "Boys will be boys. Pranksters. Foolarounds. Do crazy things. Experiment with life and disregard their parents. Boys will be boys."

By his reasoning, it wasn't Leslie who had been victimized; it was the defenseless Jocks. Pretending to address Leslie's parents, he said, "You ought to do something to look after the young people she comes in contact with before you label them heinous criminals. . . . It's a two-way street here. Everybody, but everybody, needs protection."

Querques's voice was a gravelly whisper. Wiping his forehead with his handkerchief, he warned the jurors to watch out. "Everybody has a con game," he said. And he walked back to the lawyers' table, packed his briefcase, and left the courtroom.

During his hour and a quarter before the jury, Querques had touched on a number of subjects. But there was one subject he never discussed. Actually, two subjects. He never discussed the bat. He never discussed the broomstick. He never said that the evidence would not support the charge that Kevin Scherzer had penetrated Leslie Faber's vagina with a baseball bat.

It never came up.

Months before, a defense lawyer who was then associated with the case described a strategy that could be used at the trial. The lawyer spread his legs. He grasped his chest as if he were grasping a woman's breasts. He rested his head on the back of his chair and moaned as though he was about to have an orgasm. Then, pretending to mimic Leslie Faber, he cried out, "Please, please fuck me. Put something in me. I don't care if it's a baseball bat, I don't care if it's a broomstick. Just do it to me." That, the lawyer said, was one strategy the defense could adopt. "It's the argument that the boys were just being good fellows, helping Leslie out in her hour of need. Now, you might find that disgusting. But remember, the defense only needs one juror who thinks the same way. You get one juror and you have a hung jury."

Querques presented this argument with more polish and finesse than the lawyer had, but stripped down to its core, it was the insatiable female (or, alternatively, irresistibly seductive Lolita) defense. The defense that argued, The boys were helpless against the female aggressor/seductress who could not be denied.

Querques conceded to the jury that he was running a "risk" by making this argument. One risk was legal. Commenting on Querques's opening, the *New Jersey Law Journal* said later that he "laid out a defensive strategy that skirts the outer boundaries of the Rape Shield Law and—according to some critics—goes further than the law allows."

The other risk was alienating the jury. The jurors had been instructed not to read newspaper stories or watch television accounts of the trial, but they were not sequestered; and few lawyers believe that jury members truly insulate themselves against media discussion of a controversial case, especially in a long trial.

After the judge recessed the trial for lunch, the battle in the court of public opinion was joined. Just inside the entrance to the courthouse, in the glare of the strobe lights, Carole Vasile, the NOW representative, was describing her reaction to Querques's opening. "I almost fell out of my seat," she told a television reporter. "We haven't heard words like this in thirty years. We're hearing about 'big-breasted women' who are 'obsessed' by sex. We're hearing about a seventeen-year-old mentally defective young woman who turned into a 'Lolita,' who seduced a gang of boys at the tender age of seventeen. We heard about guys who can't help it 'when the trigger goes off.' Schools, condoms, TV, pornography—everything's to blame but the defendants. This is typical of gang rape trials. The girl gets the blame. The boys disappear in the crowd."

Louis Esposito, Kyle's lawyer, was the calm after the tempest. Esposito and Querques were not law partners, but they practiced out of the same building in Orange, New Jersey, and sometimes collaborated in cases. While Esposito, twenty years younger, considered Querques his mentor, he did not try to copy Querques's courtroom style. His manner before the jury was easy, relaxed, a couple of folks having a "commonsense" conversation, as he liked to call it. Esposito was not a powerful orator; when he exhibited emotion, his voice tended to squeak rather than thunder. Just an average working stiff, his tie hanging loose, scratching his head to show he was just as confused as the jurors must be. Just a little guy, wearing a suit off the rack, hanging out and schmoozing with the jury.

It could be argued that Esposito had more to work with than Querques and the other defense lawyers. Kyle Scherzer was accused of putting a plastic bag on the bat and coating the bag with Vasoline. The charge against him was that he aided and abetted the other defendants. But, according to Leslie, he was the only boy among the thirteen in the basement to show any compassion. When Kevin was inserting the bat, Kyle was the one, Leslie said, who cautioned: "Stop, stop, you're hurting her."

But the others didn't say that.

And that was Louis Esposito's big problem. If he highlighted Kyle's five words of compassion and sympathy, he also highlighted the indifference of the others in the basement, including Kevin. The strongest argument he could make for the acquittal of Kyle Scherzer could help to send Kevin Scherzer to prison for a long time.

But the defense lawyer didn't burden the jury with his problem. He told the jurors that he'd let them get away for the weekend as soon as he could. Esposito began by quoting Peter Quigley's pretrial statement: "Leslie wanted to get laid; she pulled down her pants by herself and did this at no request."

The fact that his client, Kyle Scherzer, came from Glen Ridge, an affluent community, didn't mean that he was affluent, Esposito went on. "He doesn't live in a mansion; he is a working stiff today."

The only involvement Kyle had in the basement was that he allegedly put "the plastic bag" over "either the broom or the bat." Esposito told the jurors: "That's what they say is . . . the horrendous act he supposedly did."

Esposito never told the jury in his opening argument that Kyle had urged the others to stop.

After the trial was over, Esposito explained why he left the words out. "The same person paid the check for Querques and me—the father," he said. "Jack Scherzer never consciously saw a great deal of difference between what the boys did. He never contemplated that they could be found guilty.

"Sure, I could have done a different defense. I could have said, 'Kyle is the only innocent one in the case, the only person who tried to save this girl from being defiled by these animals.' But where would that have left Kevin? My hands were pretty much tied. So my argument was that nobody did anything—and he was the least of the nobodies."

56

Among their first witnesses, the prosecutors called three eyewitnesses who had been at the scene on March 1, three former Glen Ridge High School students. All three said they had left before the bat and broom were used and before the oral sex began. But they had seen something, and they also knew a little about how Leslie was regarded by teenagers in Glen Ridge.

First up was Philip Grant. His parents, Schuyler and Linda, sat in the back row when he testified. For more than three years, they had urged him to tell what happened in the basement. They felt that their son, who was now a student at the University of Vermont, had a moral responsibility to disclose what he had seen.

Grant helped Laurino to establish that the Jocks were aware of Leslie's mental condition. "It was very hard for me and a lot of people to communicate with Leslie," he said. "It was hard to bring yourself to her level. . . . For me, I avoided Leslie."

He said he never saw any of these boys socialize with Leslie.

Did he see any of the Jocks chatting with Leslie in the park on March 1?

Yes, Grant said, he saw Paul, Peter Quigley, Chris, Richie, and Bryant approach her on the basketball court. A few minutes later, he added, he "received some sort of invitation" to go to the Scherzers' house.

When he reached the basement, he saw Grober and Leslie sitting side by side on the sofa, Grant said. "He [Grober] pulled his jeans down . . . and his underwear, too," Phil said. "His groin area was exposed."

And what happened next?

"Leslie leaned over toward Bryant's lap," Philip said. "To me, it was the motion of a female about to perform oral sex."

It was just at this moment, Grant said, that his view of the couple on the couch was blocked by the other guys.

How would he describe the scene?

"[It] is like a group of guys watching one of their friends feeding a tank of piranhas. You put some fish in the tank and wait for something to happen. . . . You get closer to the tank the way people in front of me were getting closer to the couch," Grant said.

Later Grant would say that all he was trying to do with the piranha analogy was illustrate how his view was blocked. But under these circumstances—a retarded juvenile and thirteen Jocks in a basement—headline writers seized on the word to describe what had been inflicted on Leslie. The next day, the front-page streamer in the New Jersey paper *The Record* read: *"Like 'feeding a tank of piranhas'— Glen Ridge eyewitness tells of sexual encounter."* Unintentionally (he said), the twenty-one-year-old junior had created one of the most striking images of the trial.

With Leslie's head in Bryant's lap, Grant said he thought it was a good time for him to leave. "I didn't feel comfortable being part of some sort of group sex. . . . It's hard for me to say to this day why I left. . . . I don't think I thought something wrong was going on. I didn't think I should be there."

Grant looked as uncomfortable on the stand as he sounded. A lot of what he had to say was qualified. The boys weren't piranhas feasting on an innocent victim; they were just watching piranhas being fed. Phil didn't think anything wrong was happening. He just felt uncomfortable. Nobody was being victimized; it was victimless group sex.

"I represent your old friend Bry," Alan Zegas said with a friendly smile. Just so the witnesses wouldn't forget their old friends, the defendants had rearranged their chairs. When the defense lawyers made their opening arguments to the jury, they had sat against the far wall, directly facing the jurors. Now they all sat behind the defense table, directly facing the witnesses—their old friends, teammates, and neighbors.

"You didn't see Bry take her head and pull her head over to his crotch?" Zegas asked Philip Grant.

"No."

"What you saw is that she voluntarily leaned over. Is that correct?"

"Correct," Grant said.

"Was it fair to say," Zegas inquired, "that Leslie Faber had a reputation for doing sexually aggressive kinds of things?"

Laurino jumped up and objected. Judge Cohen didn't hesitate. Even by the lenient standards of this trial, asking Grant to judge Leslie's character was out of bounds. "Sustained," the judge said.

The next morning Querques asked Philip whether he was concerned that Leslie would "reach for your crotch" when she met him on the street. Before he could answer, Laurino objected. Cohen sustained the objection. Cohen appeared annoyed with the defense's persistent emphasis on Leslie's reported sexual habits.

In his redirect questioning, Laurino asked Grant, "You didn't see Bryant Grober push Leslie away or say, 'Stop,' or get up to leave, like you did?" Laurino said.

"No," Philip said.

Laurino asked him what he was thinking as he left the basement. What Laurino hoped for was: I thought it was disgusting; I thought these guys were manipulating and abusing Leslie, who everybody knew was retarded. But the prosecutor didn't get that. "I didn't think it was wrong because I would then have to admit I was wrong by not stopping it or seeking out any other authorities," Philip said. Leaving Leslie and the boys back in the basement was "almost a cowardly act," he said, "but at the same time it was a brave act."

When he was done, Grant passed his old teammates as he made for the doors of the courtroom. His parents walked out into the corridor with him.

They looked sad and weary. "He did the best he could, considering—" his mother said.

Two other early-leavers, Bart Ciccolini and J. P. Bolen, supplemented Grant's testimony. Ciccolini, who had been a high school sophomore in 1989 and was nineteen years old now, began by describing Leslie as "slow, simple . . . the butt of jokes." He said that after a minute of conversation, "you would know she was slightly retarded. . . . Everybody knew she was slower. Everybody teased [her]."

In the basement, Ciccolini said, he saw Leslie reaching toward Grober's "groin area."

Laurino asked him whether any of the boys were talking to her.

"I couldn't hear what Chris Archer was saying to Leslie," Bart said. "I wasn't paying attention." But "I came to the conclusion he asked her to re- move her clothes because of the puzzled, skeptical look on her face—and she did."

When Leslie started undressing, Bart said, he thought it was time to split. "Something wasn't right there and I wasn't really friends with these guys and I had to get out of there," he said. He didn't say what wasn't right.

In his cross-examination Alan Zegas asked Bart to describe how Leslie looked three and a half years before. "Was she big-breasted?"

"Fairly," said Bart.

Then Zegas moved on to another theme: Leslie was compliant in the Scherzer basement.

"You didn't hear Leslie Faber say, 'I don't want to do this'?"

"No."

James Patrick Bolen—J. P. as the guys knew him—had been a high school senior in 1989; now he was a college senior. Bolen, like the two witnesses who preceded him, testified that Leslie was regarded as "slow" and was sometimes referred to as "retarded."

When he reached the basement, he saw Grober sitting alone on the couch with his pants down, Bolen said; and not long after that, Leslie sat down next to him. So: According to Bolen, Grober was undressed even before Leslie reached the couch, suggesting, perhaps, a degree of pre- meditation.

A bunch of guys in red-and-white varsity jackets clustered around the couple, he said. When Leslie leaned over toward Bryant, he testified, he decided it was time to leave. As he went up the stairs, he heard "voices and some laughing. There was a tone of 'C'mon, Les.'" The expression on Leslie's face, he said, was "contented . . . sort of smiling."

The defense lawyers asked questions suggesting that they thought Bolen had left because of what he had heard about Leslie's sexual history; they wanted to know what Bolen had heard about it.

Judge Cohen, usually mild-mannered and genial, seemed furious. He glared at the four defense lawyers. "You're trying to show that this is some kind of loose woman who consented to sexual acts in the past and probably did so on this occasion. You've been trying to do that since Day One, and I'm not going to permit it." Despite his admonition, the defense lawyers would continue to pound on the theme of what they called Leslie's "promiscuity."

One person was conspicuously absent from the lineup of former Glen Ridge high school students who had been called as witnesses by the prosecution: Charlie Figueroa. Charlie was a pivotal figure in the long history of this case. He was the only student to tell his teacher about what happened in the basement. His account buttressed what Leslie had told her swimming coach. What Charlie had told his teacher led the school to call the police. If it hadn't been for Charlie, Leslie's experience in the basement might have been disregarded and ultimately suppressed. If it hadn't been for Charlie, there might not have been a trial.

So why wasn't he called as a witness? There were several reasons, both procedural and tactical. What Kevin Scherzer told Charlie about the basement reportedly involved other people, including some of the co-defendants in the trial. This would have been considered "hearsay" testimony, prejudicial to the other defendants. To get around this obstacle, the prosecutors had asked the judge to convene two juries. One jury would hear the case as it applied to all the defendants. The other jury would hear Charlie's testimony as it applied only to Kevin. The judge rejected this request.

There was also a tactical consideration. The three young men who had just testified had been partial eyewitnesses to the activities in the basement. Other witnesses, who would be called later in the trial, would testify about what occurred before March 1, 1989, during Leslie's childhood and adolescence. Charlie's testimony would relate what he heard and saw the day after the alleged rape. The problem this presented for the prosecutors was that on March 2, Leslie reportedly rejected the entreaties of the Glen Ridge Jocks to repeat her experience in the basement. The prosecutors were concerned that the jury might infer from this that Leslie was capable of saying "no" to sexual overtures. If John Maher, who was accused of trying to induce Leslie to return to the basement, was tried later, Charlie could be called as a witness. But the prosecutors decided that it would be too risky to call him for the trial of the four defendants.

Also absent were twins who lived in a New Jersey town not far from Glen Ridge. These boys recalled meeting Kevin Scherzer on the day their high school baseball team played against Glen Ridge in the spring of 1989. Both boys told an Essex County investigator and Detective Byron that Kevin, referring to Charlie Figueroa, said: "I can't stand that nigger for telling on us for a rape we did." When the twins read in the newspapers about Kevin's arrest, they told their parents, who got in touch with the police.

Because Kevin had reportedly used the collective word *us*, the twins' testimony could have also violated the "hearsay" rule against one defendant incriminating co-defendants. For that reason, they were not offered as witnesses.

As he left the courtroom for lunch after J. P. Bolen testified, Doug Archer was chuckling. He seemed to enjoy it when the defense lawyers mixed it up with the judge and prosecutors. His wife, in a red jacket and black pants, a striped bow tied at the neck of her blouse, didn't appear to be amused. To her there was little about this trial that was funny. A month before the opening statements, they had circulated copies of a letter, signed by them, which said that they had spent about $75,000 in legal fees. "Paul is a free man. We have believed all along that good sense would prevail and the prosecutor would simply understand that he cannot win." Doug Archer said he was "writing to ask if you would know someone who might be able to lend us $1,000 to $5,000 or so. . . . We need $40,000 to pay Chris's legal fees through the trial. . . . We simply need to know names of people who may be willing to help."

Ciccolini and Grant had described Leslie as "slow, simple, not normal." While they corroborated that something had happened, nothing they saw or heard confirmed that a rape was in progress when they left. Grant said he left because he didn't find the scene "appealing." Ciccolini thought "something wasn't right." Bolen remembered a "jovial joking-around atmosphere."

Ciccolini thought there had been a "puzzled, skeptical" look on Leslie's face when Chris and Kevin had talked to her. Bolen didn't remember Leslie as puzzled; he thought she looked "pleased and contented."

The jurors could take what they wanted from the testimony of the three boys. There were no revelations here. More and more, it looked as though only one person would be able to provide substantive eyewitness testimony for the prosecution. That was Leslie Faber. The three young men from Glen Ridge had left Leslie on her own.

57

The practice of putting a rape victim's morality and sexuality on trial has a long history in rape cases. In the early 1930s, for example, lawyers representing nine black youths accused of raping two white women in Scottsboro, Alabama, based much of their defense on attacking the morality of the alleged victims. There was plenty of other evidence that those defendants had been unjustly accused, but the defense believed that the two women's "immorality" would be the most persuasive argument they could make before a Southern jury. Now the Glen Ridge defense lawyers were resurrecting the loose-woman strategy once again, but women's groups in 1992 were not nearly as quiescent as they had been in 1932.

Some three hundred demonstrators marched through Glen Ridge in a driving rain on Saturday, October 24. The marchers came from nearby suburban communities. They carried signs that read: "Rape Is Violence, Not Sex" and "Lolita Was an Abused Child." As they marched down Millionaires' Mile on Ridgewood Avenue, they chanted: "Boys will be boys, men will be men, that excuse won't work again." It was not his intention, but Michael Querques was providing the script for the demonstration.

Carrying bats and broomsticks, the marchers passed the football field on Bloomfield Avenue where the Ridgers were playing Cedar Grove in the annual Homecoming game. Some of the 1992 Jocks had forbidden their girlfriends to join the demonstration. They told the girls that they would not take them to the Homecoming dance if they supported the demonstrators. One of the girls told her boyfriend, "Screw you," and led half a dozen of her friends out to the line of marchers.

But other Ridgers expressed their disapproval. One resident, Ondine Bennett, told a reporter that she was friends with the parents of some of the defendants. "Something terrible happened," she said. "We are behind our friends because they are in trouble. These people are marching for hate. What we are trying to do here is unite for love."

Doug and Michaele Archer took note of this woman's sentiments. In a letter dated October 25 that was circulated to "family and friends," the Archers described Bennett as a "great friend" who "believes (as we do) that since the trial is in process, it should take place without interference."

The Archers said that the financial support by residents "has been unbelievable. You have lent us over $30,000 and letters keep coming in."

They wrote that two girls "who know the boys well have not only lent us money from their college funds, but one has joined us in court." One family gave the Archers a car, the letter said, and another offered to lease them a car for a dollar. "WOW!" the Archers exclaimed. That's what was good about living in Glen Ridge; your friends came through for you in a pinch.

58

The idea was to flank Leslie with witnesses who could explain and interpret her life. Most of the witnesses called by the prosecution were so-called experts, who formed two separate groups. One consisted of professionals who knew Leslie: teachers, counselors, psychologists, and psychiatrists. The second group was made up of laypeople who had a personal relationship with her: family, friends, schoolmates—experts from her private life.

Then the prosecutors would bring Leslie in to testify.

Interspersed among these witnesses would be a few law enforcement types—Sheila Byron, for sure, and perhaps one or two other investigators. That was the plan.

Jeanette DePalma was the first of the experts. She had been Leslie's special education teacher at West Orange High School for three years. DePalma said that although Leslie seemed to be powerfully built, she would never fight back when kids picked on her. She recalled seeing Leslie cowering against a locker while a smaller girl pummeled her. "Leslie couldn't defend herself," she testified.

However, under cross-examination the teacher acknowledged that she had written a report in which she said that Leslie "makes inappropriate and/or provocative remarks to peers which result in negative interaction."

Dr. Susan Esquilin followed DePalma to the witness stand. A clinical psychologist, she was the prosecution's first certified expert witness. She began her testimony on Monday, October 26, after the special education teacher had completed hers. She continued on the witness stand for almost two weeks; half of that time she was under severe cross-examination by the defense.

Esquilin was an experienced witness. She had testified in some twenty sexual abuse cases for the Essex County Prosecutor's Office alone. During her career she had examined more than one thousand children who might have been sexually abused. The first part of Esquilin's testimony concerned her examination of Leslie for the prosecutor's office in the summer of 1989. In her first afternoon on the stand, the psychologist described Leslie as a young woman who was distraught and possibly suicidal after her encounter with the Jocks.

During four meetings in June and early July 1989, Esquilin said, Leslie described her difficulty in sleeping, her nightmares, her loss of appetite, her dismay at being described as "retarded" in the press. She also exhibited "a tremendous feeling of guilt" about what could happen to the defendants if they were tried.

When she talked to Leslie's parents, Esquilin testified, the Fabers told her that Leslie had confided to them a few weeks after the investigation began that "she wanted to be dead" and had talked about "wanting to commit suicide."

Glancing at her notes, the psychologist said that Leslie had told her she didn't want to go to the basement when Chris Archer invited her. "They knew I was a nice girl," Leslie told the psychologist. When Esquilin asked Leslie what she meant by a "nice girl," she said, "I had never told on them before."

What was there to tell? Leslie told Esquilin that she had received phone calls from Chris Archer and a couple of other boys once a week since she was eight and nine years old, and that they had said "sexual things" to her. In person, Chris would also "talk dirty" to Leslie, the psychologist said. She also told the psychologist that she recalled two instances of sexual contact with Archer in a park and a schoolyard.

Were there "elements of coercion" involved, Laurino wanted to know, in getting Leslie to come to the basement? Esquilin said that, according to Leslie, Chris had threatened to tell her mother about these earlier experiences. But that wasn't the only thing that scared her. Esquilin said Leslie told her: "The way they looked at me, like I was supposed to do it—like a movie."

Again referring to her report, Esquilin described what Leslie had told her about the experience in the basement: "She said it was Chris's idea to pull her pants down," the psychologist said. "She said Bryant Grober asked her: 'Would you suck me?' Leslie said. 'I didn't want to and he pushed me down.'" Leslie told Esquilin having oral sex with Grober was "'gross. . . . But it didn't bother me at first. I just did it.'" Leslie also told Esquilin: "I didn't want to put him down. It would be putting him down not to do it."

Leslie told her about the plastic bags that had been placed on the bat and broomstick. Esquilin asked her whose idea that was. The psychologist said Leslie answered: "Theirs, not mine. . . . I would never do that." In her report Esquilin noted, "She then looked down sadly and said, 'You probably think I'm sick to let them do that.'" Esquilin added, "It was the use of the baseball bat and the broomstick that made this incident particularly bad in Leslie's eyes."

Laurino asked about the bottom line: What was Leslie's mental condition? Esquilin said, "I don't think she really understands she can refuse to consent. . . . [She] gives lip service to the right to say 'no' to having sex. But with people she has any familiarity [with], even momentary, she feels as though it were a friend and a friend is obligated to go along with whatever the friend asks. . . . She doesn't feel she has any autonomy, any sense of individuality. She takes whatever is stated at face value. She doesn't understand that something may be going on behind the scenes."

Laurino asked, "Does this open her up to manipulation?"

Esquilin replied, "Absolutely—she has a high risk of victimization."

Then Esquilin said the words that punctuated the first stage of her testimony: "I believe that she is mentally defective."

The defense tried to chip away at Esquilin's credibility. The lawyers learned that she had treated Leslie as a private patient after she had examined her for the prosecutor's office. They therefore questioned the psychologist's objectivity as a presumably impartial expert. They also closely scrutinized Esquilin's notes of her sessions with Leslie and asked pointed questions about any references Leslie purportedly made to sexual experiences with other boys. Didn't that substantiate their contention that she was profligate?

In the arguments about Leslie's morals and Esquilin's impartiality, a juror could easily lose sight of Leslie as a person who also had rights. Had she understood when she spoke to the psychologist that her words were going to be repeated in open court? Did she know which phrases, thoughts, and offhand comments would work their way into Esquilin's notebook and then into her testimony? Would the "real" Leslie—whoever that was—be rendered accurately by a psychologist talking in the courtroom? Wasn't she entitled to doctor-patient confidentiality? Nobody was making public the sexual history and private fantasies of the defendants; their rights were being zealously protected. But who was protecting Leslie?

When the jurors filed into the courtroom on Wednesday, October 28, they found a set of headphones on each of their seats. This marked the start of the second phase of Dr. Esquilin's testimony—her interpretation of the tape recordings that Mari Carmen Ferraez had made of Leslie Faber.

The tapes the jurors heard did not represent the exact conversations between Mari Carmen and Leslie; they represented Judge Cohen's edited version of the conversations. The judge had cut dozens of lines from the transcripts of the three recordings. For instance, the judge had deleted Leslie's description of past encounters with specific males who were not involved in the case; he also deleted some of the generalized chatter about sex and guys that was a staple of all the taped conversations. The final agreement on what would be retained and what would be left out was a product of tough negotiations between the judge and lawyers for both sides. The defense said that anything sexual in the conversations was essential to proving Leslie could consent; the prosecution said that leaving much of the tapes intact would shred Leslie's rights to privacy.

However, the judge left in lots of chitchat about Leslie's private life. Although it is not difficult to understand the reasons for the exclusions—mainly to protect the identity of people Leslie mentions—it is much harder to determine the rationale for inclusion.

For example, in a reference to kids from Bloomfield, Mari Carmen asks, "What kind of things did you do [with the kids from Bloomfield]?" Leslie answers, "Let's see, I gotta, I gotta think." Leslie never does answer, and the reason for including this part of the tapes is hard to understand.

In another section of the tapes, Mari Carmen asks why Leslie left Columbia High School in Maplewood. "Got kicked out," Leslie answers.

"Why?"

"I was making love with this one kid," Leslie says. And later she adds that she was "messing around" at the school. That may have been Leslie's perception, but it was not the perception of school officials. No educator would ever testify in the trial that Leslie was dismissed from Columbia for sexual misconduct. Nevertheless, the judge allowed Leslie's remarks to be played to the jury.

If the prosecution was still arguing that Leslie didn't understand the basics of sex, some of this questionable material might be pertinent. But Goldberg in his opening acknowledged that she was familiar with the "mechanics" of sexual relations.

Judge Cohen had cautioned the jury that the tapes and other testimony about Leslie's private life were hearsay and that the jurors should consider this testimony only to determine her "state of mind." In fact, the defense attorneys would never present a single witness who could substantiate Leslie's sexual experiences. What the jury heard was teen talk. Gossip. But who knew what the jury would make of it? If you threw enough stuff at them, some of it might stick.

William Glaberson, a *New York Times* reporter and a former lawyer who sat in for part of Esquilin's testimony, wrote: "Just two weeks after the start of the Glen Ridge sex-assault case, the mildly retarded young woman at its center has hardly any privacy left." Leslie's name was not publicized, Glaberson said, but "she has been portrayed as a sex-crazed teen-ager who delighted in seeing boys naked." The *Times* reporter noted that New Jersey and ten other states gave judges wide latitude to suspend all or part of the rape shield laws that are designed to protect the privacy of women who may have been sexually assaulted. Glaberson asked, "Can women lodge . . . rape charges without taking the chance that they will, in effect, be placed on trial?"

Esquilin took her seat in the witness box, the jurors and the defendants put on their headsets, and the prosecution began playing the tapes of the three conversations between Mari Carmen and Leslie recorded from September 10, 1989, through November 1989. The jury heard the tinny, quiet voice of a child and the more assured, confident words of her friend, Mari Carmen. As the tapes played, the defendants listened without showing any emotion, except for a short exchange between the two young women. While they talked, there was a wisp of a smile on Kyle's face.

LESLIE:	Kyle is so cute.
MARI:	Oh he is? I know he is, isn't he?
LESLIE:	Yeah, you guys [Kyle and Mari Carmen] go to the mall?
MARI:	Yeah, he took me to the mall the other night.

> LESLIE: Oh, wow, he did?
>
> MARI: Yeah, can you imagine that?
>
> LESLIE: What kind of car does he have, is it a BMW?
>
> MARI: It's an Audi.
>
> LESLIE: Oh, he's so rich.

Leslie had not been part of the Glen Ridge social scene, but she clearly had picked up what teenagers valued there.

When Leslie said, sadly, that sex made her feel like a "whore," Esquilin noted that Mari Carmen suggested that Leslie's experiences are "very interesting, exciting things she is doing, and wants more information."

Sometimes jurors could get the idea without Esquilin's commentary. Leslie spoke in glowing terms about her experience with the Jocks: She said it was "so exciting, it was perfect." The terms were glowing, but Leslie's voice—the voice the jurors heard—was flat, dull, fading to inaudible.

The prosecutor interrupted the tapes at those instances where Leslie expressed misgivings and anxiety about what happened with the guys.

He stopped the tape when Leslie said she was "conned" into going to the basement. He stopped the tape when Leslie said she would be "scareder" to repeat the encounter. He stopped the tape and stared pointedly at the defendants during the following exchange:

Mari Carmen asks, "Did you do the broomstick at all yourself? Like if I wanted to, could I do it? Like, did they let you do it yourself?"

On the tape Leslie sounds amazed at the thought. She laughs and answers, "You want to do that to yourself?" Laurino asked the psychologist about this part of the tapes. "Mari Carmen is priming the situation," Esquilin said. "She's saying she's trying to accomplish the thing that Leslie accomplished—to get into the house and into the basement. Leslie . . . follows that lead."

The prosecutor let the jury hear one part of the taped conversation without elaboration by Esquilin. The topic discussed was the day Leslie visited Chris and Paul Archer at their home. "We, I, they were like watching, like X-rated movies. . . . Those are good movies," Leslie tells Mari Carmen. "His little brother was watching and it was so cool."

The jury was learning that the relationship of Chris and Paul to Leslie went back quite a way.

Defense lawyers complained that not enough of Leslie's personal life had been exposed. Michael Querques tried to compensate for the deletions in the tapes. For five hours Querques fired questions at the psychologist to get her to concede that Leslie was a wanton woman. But Esquilin conceded little. She continued to depict her as a retarded child who tried to please anyone who showed interest in her.

The next morning Querques tacked a chart to the bulletin board in the courtroom. The name *Kyle Scherzer* was printed in large block letters in red ink. Below that in black ink was the sentence: "No, I didn't do Kyle because I didn't want to." It was an excerpt from Leslie's testimony before the grand jury. Querques shrugged and looked as though he were perplexed. "Isn't Leslie demonstrating for the world that I [Leslie] can say 'no'?" he asked.

Most of Querques's questions to the psychologist implied or stated outright that Leslie had lived a wanton life. "Did you know that her parents became aware of her flirtatious behavior and sexual episodes . . . including propositioning of boys? Did you know she was approaching boys . . . and was saying, 'Do you want to feel my boobs?'" Such supposed comments by Leslie had not appeared and would not appear in any firsthand testimony during the trial, except when the defense lawyers referred to them.

During a break in the testimony on Friday, November 6, Jack Scherzer wandered into the hallway where spectators at the trial would sneak a smoke. The air was stale with the smell of dead butts. "I used to smoke," Jack Scherzer said, "but I quit when I saw this sign in a hospital warning against smoking menthol cigarettes. That's the kind I smoked—so I just quit 'cause I'd always be seeing the sign in my mind."

How did he think the trial was going?

"I fought for my country," he said. "I never thought it could reach this."

His jaw muscles were working overtime. "Tate was behind all this. His personal vendetta—the race thing. That's why we're here." He looked as though he wanted a cigarette. "How much can you take? My wife's mother, she's eighty-one. She was hospitalized when the trial started. It never ends."

Scherzer looked out the window. "Look," he said to the author, "I'm not defending the morality of the situation. What happened was—but you're talking about sixteen-year-old kids with a hard-on. What would we do at that age?"

Court officers said the trial was about to resume. Jack Scherzer opened the door to the public corridor, but stopped and looked back. "I tell you, I'll never be the same," he said.

59

The prosecutors wanted the jury to hear about how Leslie was sexually molested on April 23, 1983, a week before her twelfth birthday, by an eighteen-year-old high school student in Cartaret Park. The young man, who was arrested, had entered a pretrial community service program. All three prosecutors, but Laurino particularly, thought that the jury could learn a lot about Leslie if they knew about the 1983 incident.

They could learn why Ros Faber had put Leslie on birth control pills, a reasonable precaution after she had been molested, but something the defense chose to interpret as proof of its theory of her sexual availability.

They could learn how a retarded child might come to believe that what she experienced when she was eleven years old was "normal" and "commonplace," how the experience might reinforce her sense of worthlessness, how it might make her more susceptible to the enticements of other Jocks on the same Cartaret playing fields six years later.

In his chambers on Friday, November 6, Judge Cohen reportedly said that bringing up the earlier case in this trial would violate Leslie's rights of privacy. This was the same judge who ruled that the defense lawyers could examine Leslie's gynecological records, who ruled that the jury could eavesdrop on the tape-recorded gossip of two teenage girls, who permitted defense attorneys to poke into virtually every corner of Leslie's life with unsupported and unverified speculation. Laurino argued that the prosecutors had the approval of Leslie's parents to discuss the earlier sexual abuse. No matter, the judge said; it invaded a rape victim's privacy.

Advocates for women's rights said: Ridiculous. "The rape shield law hasn't shielded the victim in this trial and now it's being used as a sword against her," said Christine McGoey of NOW as she left the courtroom Friday afternoon. Her face was pinched with anger and disappointment. "It's a terrible ruling."

On November 9, Susan Esquilin finally ended her testimony. The next day, Carol Manzi,* Leslie's older sister, took the stand. She was twenty-four, married, and the mother of two young sons. She wore a gray suit and a white blouse. Her expression had a bruised quality, as though she had hit a few bumps in the road; and when she testified, she spoke in a rough voice.

She recalled that when Leslie was five years old, a group of kids, including the Scherzer twins, had fed her dog feces. Gasps and hisses spilled from the spectator section. Kyle looked down at the defense table. Kevin stared straight ahead, tapping his fingers on the table.

Cross-examining her, Ford asked, "Did you ever hear Leslie use words of a sexual nature?"

"When she was about fifteen, she started saying, 'That guy's got a cute butt.' She said it about my husband." The jurors started to laugh, and many spectators joined in. For a moment the tension in the courtroom broke.

Zegas began where Ford left off—with insinuations about Leslie's sexual proclivities.

"Did she know the word 'coming'?" he asked. "Did she know what 'jerked him off' meant?"

"Not unless someone explained them to her. I wouldn't expect her to use those words with me," Carol said. "But if she heard words in a sentence, she'd parrot it back. She'd get attention like a young child using the word 'doo-doo.'"

Carol said that Leslie didn't realize she was taking birth control pills. "She thinks they're to regulate her period."

"Were you aware in 1989 that your sister needed watching with respect to her sexual behavior?" Zegas asked.

"Leslie would say a boy is cute," Carol said. "But she never expressed anything sexual. She kept her feelings private."

Querques, in his cross-examination, stuck to the subject of sex.

"Did she ever confide to you that her body was changing to that of a woman?" Querques said.

"She told me when she got her period, got her first bra. I knew she was shaving her legs and armpits."

"Did she confide her sexual urges and desires?"

"No."

"She never gave the slightest clue about sex, that she liked to enjoy sex?" Querques rubbed his chin, squared his shoulders.

"I never had any reason to believe that she has desires."

"Once she developed breasts, were boys magnetized to her?"

"No. I wouldn't say they were magnetized."

"Was she magnetized to them?"

"No," Carol said.

The next witness was Andrew Provost, who had tried to teach Leslie how to play tennis in 1982, when she was ten. He testified that Chris and Paul had ridiculed her during the summer tennis sessions, calling her "stupid" and "retarded."

Leslie's sister and Provost lent credence to the argument that Leslie had never known how to say "no." She might look disgusted when she had to eat dog feces, she might cry when the Archer brothers ridiculed her on the tennis court, but she had never stomped away in fury, never even tried to avoid her tormenters. Her entire life was an apprenticeship in submission.

Outside the courtroom, there was no armistice in the gender wars. Elizabeth Miller-Hall didn't have a major role in the day-to-day jousting of the trial, but she would often complain privately that whenever she made a motion or objection, she could hear some of the four male defense lawyers snickering at her.

For Miller-Hall this wasn't just another case. This was *the* case. There were *principles* at stake. After a long, contentious day, she would speak to journalists or to the women monitoring the trial for advocacy groups. As she talked, she would lean closer, her face a few inches away from the listener, her expression growing more animated as her indignation boiled over. "If you believe in anything, they treat you like you're stupid," she said of the defense lawyers during a break in the trial. "It's the boys' club, and if you're a woman you don't belong. If you're a woman, you're automatically inferior, you're automatically the enemy." When Tom Ford saw her talking to the NOW representatives, he said to a reporter, "What's the Bush"—a crude sexual expression—"bitching about now?"

The next witness, Dawn Lipinski, was one of the two sisters in a family that had been friendly to Leslie Faber. Under cross-examination by Tom Ford, Lipinski, a twenty-six-year-old nursing student, testified that Leslie had told her that the experience in the basement was "a terrible thing." Leslie told her the bat and broom "had hurt her," the witness said.

This was in direct conflict with what Leslie had said to Mari Carmen— that what had happened in the basement was "fun and exciting." When the prosecutors got their turn in redirect examination, Goldberg asked Dawn to describe how Leslie looked when she talked about being hurt. "She was very sad, very quiet, and she didn't maintain eye contact. She didn't know what to say afterward. When she realized what she was talking about, she was at a loss for words."

60

As Rosalind Faber entered the courtroom, she touched the gold pin on the lapel of her black suit jacket. The pin was in the shape of a guardian angel. She and Les had made this pact. They both would wear their pin when they testified, their amulet to ward off misfortune.

The courtroom was crowded. Ros saw a few of her friends, all women, sitting in the front row. On the other side of the aisle she saw Jack and Geraldine Scherzer, Doug and Michaele Archer, the old neighborhood people. Once everybody had seemed so normal, maybe even a little boring. She wished she could return to the boring days.

Passing the prosecutors, Ros saw the stick at the edge of their table, the fourteen-inch stick Leslie gave her when she came home on March 1, 1989, the dowel-shaped stick flecked with red paint that Richie Corcoran had supposedly inserted into Leslie's vagina. The stick jarred Ros back to reality.

She sat at the edge of the witness chair, attentive, alert. Laurino gently led her through the early years, let her explain how she adopted Leslie, how she learned that her daughter was retarded. In the first few minutes, Ros's eyes misted with tears but she did not cry.

Ros explained why Leslie left Columbia High School in Maplewood and transferred to West Orange. "I knew she couldn't hold her own academically." But her daughter also experienced "social problems. She'd do things to attract attention." School officials told her, she said, that "there was a potential rape situation. That was the most immediate thing that caused her to be removed." But Leslie had always imagined it was her fault, her mother said. "She felt she had been kicked out."

After her daughter left Columbia, Ros said, she put Leslie on birth control because of the "concern about rape," but stopped giving her the pills in January 1989. "We felt there was no further need." But two and a half months later, after the Fabers heard about what happened to Leslie at the Scherzers, Ros said, they put Leslie back on the pills. "We had been made aware that she had been raped." She said it softly, almost matter-of-factly.

On cross-examination, Ford asked, "Were you embarrassed by the fact that you put her on birth control pills?" There was loud hissing from the spectator section. "No," she said. "I don't think so."

That ended Ros Faber's first day on the stand. The family ate dinner that night without talking. Ros took seriously the judge's admonition not to discuss the case. Before Ros went to bed, she said to Charlie, "I feel so drained. I never want to testify again."

When Ford resumed his cross-examination of Ros Faber on Friday, November 20, he wanted to know whether Leslie's parents ever asked her what the police and prosecutor were questioning her about.

"I don't question my daughter on what she's asked," she said.

Did Ros change that policy after Leslie said she had lied about Richie Corcoran? Ford asked.

"We have talked a bit about telling the truth," Ros said. "But our home is a sanctuary. . . . We don't read the papers about the case. It's the ostrich syndrome. If we don't know, it won't hurt."

That last answer interested Alan Zegas, who was the next defense lawyer to cross-examine Leslie's mother. Did Ros Faber *really* know what her daughter was doing when she was away from home? Zegas wondered. For more than two hours, the defense lawyer was unrelenting in his questions about what Ros Faber knew of her daughter's sexual life.

In one series of questions, Zegas asked: "Are you aware that she made sexual advances to sports team members? Are you aware she lifted up her shirt and exposed her breasts in a classroom? Are you aware she made verbal sexual advances?"

Ros said she hadn't been informed about such instances, but added, "We are loving and concerned parents and we are concerned by her behavior. Her whole problem throughout has been socially inappropriate behavior."

Zegas's goal was to convince the jurors that Leslie had approached his client, Bryant Grober, and offered to have sex with him. Do you think, Zegas asked her, that Leslie "posed a danger to the welfare" of other students she met?

Faber looked at Zegas as if she couldn't believe that he had asked that question. Leslie: a danger to others? "We've never been told that, we've never been told that," she repeated.

Zegas said he was curious why Mrs. Faber had not followed up the first reports that Leslie may have been sexually assaulted by a group of Glen Ridge students.

"Unfortunately, it was such a bizarre incident, we really didn't believe such a thing happened," she said, wiping her eyes with a tissue. "We live in [the] town, we know the people—"

Something had always bothered Alan Zegas: There seemed to be a wide gulf between Leslie and her parents. The picture the tapes painted was very different from the Leslie depicted by her friends and her family, he believed. To him that spelled a dysfunctional family—not dysfunctional in the sense of abusive or uncaring, Zegas would hasten to add, but dysfunctional in the sense that Leslie's parents and sister would not acknowledge Leslie's sexuality.

"Definitely Leslie knew it was wrong, but she'd go ahead and participate," Zegas said after the trial was over. "Participate maybe because it gave her pleasure and maybe the pleasure came not from a physical feeling but because she felt that someone else liked her. That's an aspect of personality that explains a problem."

The defense lawyer believed that Ros Faber was aware of this aspect of her daughter's personality. "The term 'victimization' has been overused," he said. "You had Mrs. Faber saying, 'I took Leslie out of school because she was a target for victimization,' or whatever. I don't think it was because she was a victim. I think it was because she would make advances to boys that were inappropriate—and I believe her parents knew that."

When Zegas continued his cross-examination of Ros Faber on Monday, November 23, he wanted to find out whether Leslie's mother knew more about her daughter's personality than she had revealed up to then.

Standing a few feet away from the witness, Zegas asked her whether she had told a psychiatrist hired by the prosecution that Leslie had "propositioned" boys?

"I don't know," Ros said. "I don't recall, but I guess I did."

Was she aware that Leslie had engaged in "sexually aggressive" behavior? Zegas asked.

"Yes," she answered in a flat voice.

Since the age of sixteen? Zegas continued.

"Yes," Ros answered.

Was that why Leslie had received therapy long before the alleged rape on March 1, 1989? the defense lawyer said, standing on his toes, the psychiatrist's report pressed to his chest.

"Yes," she said.

That ended his cross-examination. Zegas thought he had made significant progress toward showing that Ros Faber knew that her daughter had been "sexually aggressive."

When she got home, Ros told her husband, "Oh, how they twist your words around." Ros said she couldn't even recall saying these things to the psychiatrist. "'Proposition'—does that sound like a word I would use about Les?" she said. "It was three years ago—I can't even remember what the psychiatrist asked me." Then she said, "Oh, God, do I have to go back there again?"

"One more day," Charlie said, grimly.

That day consisted of four more hours of cross-examination by Querques and Esposito. Querques rocked back and forth on his heels. "Your daughter knows how to say 'no'?" he asked.

"She's a teenager," Ros said. "Some teenagers say 'no' when you don't do what they want. Leslie is a very complex person."

"Just yesterday you said to the young lawyer"—pointing to Zegas—"that since she was sixteen she was aggressive and propositioned boys?"

"'Propositioned' in quotation marks," Ros responded sharply. "It was his [the psychiatrist's] phrasing, not ours. . . . She does not proposition. It's an inappropriate word. She doesn't know what that means, and I wouldn't use it myself."

Querques stepped closer to the witness box. "Does she have knowledge of how to perform intercourse?"

"I haven't taught her. I would say at this stage of her life she does [have knowledge]."

Querques was crouching. "Doesn't know fellatio, what a blow job is?"

Rosalind Faber, the embodiment of propriety, the personification of rectitude. This sixty-three-year-old man was quizzing her on blow jobs. Laurino scraped his chair against the floor as he turned toward the jury. He shook his head slowly. Sad eyes.

The defense lawyer stood in front of Ros, patiently waiting for her answer.

The mother fell back in her chair, looked up at the judge. "That's an expression I don't know," she said to Cohen. "I never would use words like that."

"When did your daughter Leslie develop breasts?" Querques wanted to know.

"Twelve, ten, eleven—I don't know."

"Ten? That strikes me as kind of young. . . . From the time she developed breasts, did she learn that boys were magnetized to her and she to them?"

"I know that the sex topic was starting in middle school. She has normal hormones."

Querques asked, "What did you do to protect young males in the event they touched her?"

"Nothing, sir," Ros said.

What concerned Laurino was not what Ros was saying under cross-examination, but how she was saying it. In any rape trial, a jury expects the close relatives of a victim to be upset. In a case involving bats and brooms, jurors would anticipate strong emotions from a distraught mother. Ros had generally kept her emotions under control. The Fabers just weren't a publicly emotional couple. Laurino wanted to ask a question that would allow Leslie's mother to express her feelings, to let go.

On redirect, Laurino asked her whether she remembered telling Zegas that when she heard about Leslie's experience in the basement, she "didn't believe such a thing could happen." Could she explain what she meant by that? the prosecutor asked.

Tears ran down her cheeks. Her shoulders shook. "It has many different aspects to it—" she started, but couldn't go on. Ford objected. He asked for a conference at the bench. It was a mistake. While the lawyers whispered among themselves, the jury and the spectators listened to Rosalind Faber sobbing.

Minutes passed. The judge said she could continue. "Who would believe anyone would do this to anyone?" she said, drying her eyes. Her voice breaking, she gasped, "The incident itself was unbelievable to me and the fact we lived in the small town where people know each other and the people involved have known each other for years. It's just unbelievable."

Laurino waited for her to collect herself. The lawyers had asked her why she waited to take action when she first heard from the social workers; now Laurino asked, What was she feeling, how did she react, when he, Laurino, finally told her what had happened to her daughter.

"I—I was totally horrified," she said.

A few minutes later, Ros Faber stepped down from the stand, her testimony done. She sighed deeply. Laurino sighed, too. A trial could be very painful to everyone, but the pain was nothing compared to the pain Rosalind Faber had felt three and a half years ago. The jury had the entire Thanksgiving Day weekend to think about that.

61

Detective Sheila Byron testified on December 2, three days after she returned from her honeymoon on the Caribbean island of Aruba. (She was married on November 14 to a New Jersey police officer. The wedding was attended by the Glen Ridge police chief, Tom Dugan; Ros and Leslie Faber; and Lieutenant Richard Corcoran, among others.) Actually, she had been scheduled to testify after Leslie took the stand, but the prosecutors decided they had better get her in there because the defense lawyers were portraying her as the mastermind who had turned Leslie against the defendants.

Before she took the stand, the prosecutors arrived in court with a 33-inch "fungo" baseball bat and a broom with a bright-red handle. Now the jury could see "the instruments," as they were called in testimony. The prosecutors said they planned to introduce the objects as "replica" evidence to replace the actual bat and broom, which had never been found by investigators.

Laurino led the Glen Ridge detective through testimony on Leslie's various statements to law enforcement officials, including her accusation against Richie Corcoran and her subsequent recantation. She went on to describe how Leslie told her that Corcoran actually had inserted the red stick into her. As she testified, she was aware of the defendants staring at her. "Chris never took his eyes off me," she said later. "He was glaring at me and then he'd draw these stick figures on his pad. And then Kevin'd take over, both of them going back and forth. And Mrs. Archer, too, she never took her eyes off me."

With her auburn hair and long gold earrings, Byron made an attractive witness, a fact that did not go unnoticed by some of the defense lawyers. Ford said during a break in her testimony, "See what a witch she is. Did you see the slit in her skirt? Did you see her blouse? She just used those looks to seduce that poor kid." Ford was not often heard expressing sympathy for Leslie Faber.

The detective told Ford that the first time she had heard of the Fabers was when she was working as a civilian dispatcher for the police department in 1983 and got a phone call from Ros. Sheila wanted to shout out: That's when the Fabers called the police to report that Leslie had been sexually molested the first time. But Laurino had warned her that if she talked about the 1983 incident, the judge could declare a mistrial. This was the last time in the trial that the jurors could have heard about the first sexual offense committed against Leslie—but the judge refused to let them hear about it.

Byron knew about Michael Querques's reputation as a fierce interrogator. In all his years as a lawyer in rackets cases, he had certainly learned how to go after a cop.

He began with questions about the relationship between Leslie and the detective. "Did she become attached to you?" Querques asked, inventorying her red-and-black checked jacket, her red skirt, and her white silk blouse.

"Like a little kid who looks up to you," Byron answered, evenly.

The lawyer cocked his head to the side. "Did she like you so much . . . she would try to do what you liked her to do?"

"No, I wouldn't say she did."

Querques moved to the subject of Leslie's sex life. He asked her whether Leslie had told her about previous sexual experiences.

Byron said that Leslie had mentioned two.

Querques said there was no reference to these in Byron's written reports of conversations she had with Leslie.

"It's not there," she said. "I chose not to put it in the report." Her voice got colder. "I never put in a police report a *rape victim*'s sexual history. I only wanted to find out if Leslie was a virgin, because it could make a big difference in a *rape case.*"

Despite her determination to keep her cool, Byron was getting angry. Querques's scratchy, wheedling voice was a fingernail against a blackboard. And putting Leslie's reputation on trial—she wasn't going to cooperate in that.

Referring to Leslie's remarks to Mari Carmen, Querques said, "You did not ask her whether it [the basement] was fun?"

Her voice rising, the detective said, "No, I did not. It was apparent it was not."

Querques had turned his back on her and was walking toward the defense table. Byron's eyes were burning. She was thinking: This asshole, I can't believe he said that. And then she said to herself: Sheila, you better calm down. Her heart was racing and all she could think of was: I want to punch him right in the face.

"You're not looking to be cute and clever?" Querques said, looking back over his shoulder.

"Absolutely not," said Byron.

A few minutes later, Querques ended his cross-examination, bowing slightly, courteously murmuring, "Thank you."

The next afternoon, Querques gripped the author's shoulder. "When I do a cross, you're always looking at me. You know why?"

The author started to say that it was interesting to watch him work in the courtroom, but the lawyer cut him off. "Tension," he said. "That's my job—to create tension. To make the jury listen to me. You feel the tension; that's why you're paying attention."

Well, the author said, he had certainly captured the jury's attention during his cross-examination of Sheila Byron.

"That bitch!" he snarled. "Who's gonna believe her?"

The next witness was Leslie's guidance counselor at Columbia High School in Maplewood, Carol "Penny" Bolden. She was the first significant witness who was black. After saying that Leslie was moved to another school because her safety was at risk in the building, Bolden left the jurors with one telling vignette from Leslie's life.

When the black students in the school's Martin Luther King Association threw a dance, Leslie was the only white student present. "She was by herself all night. . . . in her own corner dancing around by herself." Of all the accounts of Leslie's sad adolescence, none told more about her isolation.

Bolden was the prosecution's eighteenth witness in a trial that was now in its ninth week. Tomorrow morning, Wednesday, December 9, the prosecutors would call their nineteenth witness. Her name was Leslie Faber.

62

On a Sunday, a couple of weeks before Leslie was going to testify, Laurino asked her to come to the courthouse. They were standing by a window looking down on the county jail. "What's that building?" Leslie asked.

"That's the jail," Laurino responded, the next minute regretting that he uttered the word.

"Jail, is that where you go when you're bad? Is it bad in there?"

"It's like when you're grounded because you did something bad," Laurino answered, trying to think how he would answer if his own retarded brother asked the question. "It's a punishment. It's not forever."

Looking at her face, Laurino thought: She's absolutely tormented at the prospect of them doing time. Leslie bit her knuckles, concentrating hard. "I know you're my friend," she said, "and if I lie in the trial, I'll hurt you and I don't want to hurt you. But if I tell the truth, I'll hurt my friends."

A detective drove Leslie home, and Laurino made the long walk to the train station alone. The weather was getting cold, and he buried his hands in the pockets of his car coat, thinking, thinking, I'm getting too close. Too involved. I don't know what she'll do when she gets up there, and I can't do anything about it.

On Tuesday September 8, Judge Cohen excused a juror after learning that her husband had worked for a firm at which Charlie Faber was a personnel supervisor. Now twelve jurors and three alternates remained.

Leslie was scheduled to testify on Wednesday, December 9, starting at 11:30 because the late morning and early afternoon were the hours that she usually functioned at the highest level. But some reporters arrived at 8:30 to make sure they would get a seat. Folding chairs had been placed in the aisles to accommodate the overflow of spectators. Leslie's friends and relatives were packed together in the first row.

Among the recent arrivals were the media types. You could tell the media types from the reporters because they were the ones with the perfect makeup and clean nails. They weren't here to cover the story. They were here to size Leslie up as "talent"; they were here to snare the Fabers. They were the sensation mongers, the bookers and researchers for the TV talk shows. Their eyes never left Leslie's sister and Dawn Lipinski—the gatekeepers, they thought, to Ros and Les. The sister and Dawn were the prize catches, but the media types would tuck their cards into the jacket pockets of anyone who had the remotest connection to Leslie and her family. The jackpot was Ros and Les, sobbing for a half hour on air.

At home in the morning, Ros gave Leslie a glass of water and Ritalin, a medication she used to improve her concentration and diminish her hyperactivity. Ros brushed the lint off Leslie's red-and-blue top. She pinned a gold guardian angel pin on her blouse. Leslie wore her best gold earrings and a gold bracelet and necklace. "You look very nice," Ros said.

As the time for Leslie's appearance at the trial drew near, Leslie retreated deeper within herself. To her mother, she looked frightened. Ros wished she could be in the courtroom with her, but Leslie had insisted that she didn't want her parents to attend. But Dawn Lipinski would be there and so would Leslie's sister, and Jeanette DePalma, one of her former teachers.

They stood together, mother and daughter, near the front door. "Now remember—," Ros said.

"My doll," Leslie interrupted her. "Where is she?"

"She's right here." Ros picked up from the table the soft raggedy doll that Leslie had kept since she was two years old. Leslie smothered the doll against her chest.

Ros opened the door. She felt flushed. Her blood pressure must be going through the roof. "And remember, you have to tell the truth. Everything will be fine if you tell the truth."

During the past two weeks, the defendants had been seated against the wall, directly opposite the jury box. Now they moved behind the defense table, where they had a straight-ahead view of the witness. Most mornings, they talked to each other before the testimony began. Today they were silent, waiting.

Leslie entered the courtroom at 11:25 from a side door off the judge's chamber. Everyone in the courtroom saw the tall, plump young woman with dark close-cropped hair settle into the witness chair. From the front row to the back, spectators, after one look at her round scrubbed face, whispered to each other a one-word description of Leslie Faber: "plain." Before Leslie uttered a word, Judge Cohen realized that Leslie was not "Lolita" and he could see, as could almost everyone else, that the image the defense had painted of a calculating, seductive temptress was absurd.

With the jury out of the room, the judge began to question Leslie, to determine whether she was competent to testify. Leslie could be disqualified if she didn't understand that she had a duty to tell the truth, if she was unable to express herself, and if she had no idea of what was going on at the trial.

The judge wondered why the defense insisted on holding a competency hearing. If Leslie were found to be incompetent, wouldn't that be decisive evidence that she was incapable of saying "no" to the young men in the basement? If Leslie were found competent, that would only highlight the credibility of her testimony. Either way, the defense lost.

"Hi, I'm Judge Cohen," the judge said, leaning sideways toward the witness. He told her that it was very important to tell the truth. He pointed to his robe and said, "If I said this was red, would that be the truth?"

"Noooo," said Leslie. She sounded like a first-grader.

Did she know what would happen if she told a lie?

"Yes," Leslie said. "You would get in trouble."

Querques was the only defense lawyer to question her. He suggested that Leslie had heard about lying and telling the truth from the prosecutors many times before "the nice judge" questioned her today.

"I knew it on my own," Leslie answered. Firmly.

The hearing, with the jury absent, was over in fifteen minutes. The judge ruled that Leslie Faber was competent to testify.

At 12:45 Laurino stood up and said, "The State calls Leslie Faber."

The prosecutor knew that he had been granted greater latitude in questioning Leslie because she was retarded. He could ask questions that verged on leading the witness, and he could repeat the subject of a line of questions to keep her attention focused. Cohen gave him the same freedom to guide twenty-one-year-old Leslie that he would have given a lawyer questioning a child.

The prosecutor asked Leslie if she had gone to Cartaret Park before March 1, 1989.

"A couple of times," Leslie said.

Laurino felt the first pinprick of alarm. A couple of times? Leslie had spent half her childhood in the park. But maybe it was unintentional.

Leslie described the radio and basketball she brought to the park and the red stick she found there. She appeared surprised to see the pink portable radio in court.

She said there was a group of boys at the park: Richie Corcoran, Paul Archer, Chris Archer, a sophomore named Peter Ostello, and others. For some reason, she left out the Scherzer twins. "A couple of people . . . came over and talked to me," she said.

Who talked to her?

Leslie scrunched her face. "There was—there was—I can't remember."

Laurino thought, *She can't remember?* She could remember when she testified to the grand jury. She could remember when she talked to Byron and other investigators. Assuming the role of the brisk, somewhat stern teacher, Laurino urged her, "Think real hard, put on a little thinking cap. Who came over and talked to you?"

"Was it more than one boy?" Leslie asked *him.*

"Yes, there was."

She remembered: Peter Ostella, a sophomore baseball player. Ostella?

"Okay. And who else?"

"Chris."

"Okay. And who else?"

"Grover."

Esposito broke in. "I can't hear."

The judge said, "Who was the last name?"

Leslie corrected herself. "Grober."

"Anybody else, Les?"

"Not that I can remember."

Laurino knew that when she had testified to the grand jury, she had included Kyle and Kevin in the group of boys who had approached her.

"What were they talking about to you?"

"How you doing?"

"Okay. And what else did they say?"

"What's up?"

Leslie was trying not to look at the guys. But they were looking at her. She could see them.

"Okay, what else?" Laurino said.

"I don't know," Leslie answered.

Get her off this, he thought. Come back later. He asked her what Grober's first name was. Leslie said: "Brian."

Leslie repeated, "Brian."

Laurino returned to his earlier track. Was there anything else the boys had said to her? "Think real hard. . . . What if anything did Chris Archer say to you?" Laurino asked.

Leslie raised her eyebrows. She covered her face with one hand. "Oh, God. He might have said 'Hi.'"

Laurino rubbed his chin. "And what else?"

"What else did he say? Nothing else, I guess."

In a chilly voice, he asked, "Just 'Hi,' was it?"

"Yes," she said, quietly.

Did Grober say anything to her?

"No. . . . He said nothing."

How about Peter Quigley?

"He said nothing, either, too."

Suddenly Leslie remembered something. "They said if I—before we left, they said that . . . if I go down to the basement . . . I'd go out with Paul Archer."

Did she remember who told her that? the prosecutor asked.

"*Grover* said that," Leslie answered.

Laurino's heart went through the floor. From the first time she talked to Sheila Byron in March 1989, she had always said that it was Chris Archer who promised her a date with his brother. But Leslie wasn't saying that now.

Miller-Hall's eyes widened. She glanced at Goldberg, who was sitting next to her. He had on the bland expression he always assumed in the courtroom, but at that moment he looked somber. Leslie shot a look at the two prosecutors. Oh, no! Miller-Hall thought desperately. Oh, no, she's playing with us—and she knows it.

Leslie wasn't down on the third floor, amidst the warm, doting smiles of the prosecutor's staff. This was a courtroom in which Chris Archer sat a dozen feet away. Where Michaele Archer sat in the third row.

Abruptly Leslie's testimony took a detour. The prosecutor asked her whether she had walked with anybody to the house.

"I walked with Chris," Leslie said. "It was like—it was kind of romantic."

A murmur in the courtroom: The spectators knew how this particular romance would be consummated. If Leslie could still describe anything about her experience with Chris Archer as romantic, it suggested, at the least, stunted social development. Leslie didn't seem to notice the reaction. All she knew was that she was saying something nice about her friend Chris. "It was romantic because he had his arm around me and we walked down to the basement together."

Leslie's answers about Chris's romantic walk with her gave Laurino hope that she was picking up the threads of the story she had told all along since 1989. But he couldn't be sure.

"And did Chris say anything to you when he was walking with you?" Laurino asked.

"No," said Leslie. She wasn't looking at him. She was sliding her bracelet up and down her arm. She wasn't going to say anything more about the walk.

Leslie's memory was pretty good when it came to remembering the boys who were in the basement. She listed all of the boys, leaving out only Peter Quigley and Paul Archer.

In detail Leslie described the furnishings in the basement, from the refrigerator to "like lounge chairs" to "this big huge couch." What else did she recall about the basement?

"It was set up like a movie," she said.

"How was it set up like a movie?"

"Well, there were chairs there and like a big couch and stuff."

"Was it that way when you first got there, Les?"

"No, because no one—well, when I first got there, the chairs weren't set up yet."

And what happened when she arrived?

"People were setting them [the chairs] up . . . near the couch."

To Miller-Hall this was a clear suggestion of conspiracy by the males in the basement. What Leslie said might engender a series of other images for the jurors; the Jocks scuttling to the basement before Leslie arrived, the boys jockeying for a front-row seat.

Leslie said she sat on the couch and was joined a "little time" later by Bryant. She recalled that a middle-aged lady, whom she called the "grandmother," had come down to tell Kyle that he had a phone call. After a while, she said, "they [the Jocks] told me to do something."

"What did they tell you to do?"

"Finger myself," said Leslie.

"What does that mean?" the prosecutor said.

"Well, you put your hands in your vagina." Leslie's voice was as flat and unemotional as if she were describing a homework assignment. Leslie said she took her clothes off. Laurino asked whether anybody was saying anything to her.

"They're saying to put five fingers up your vagina." Again, she could have been reciting her homework.

Repeatedly, the prosecutor tried to get Leslie to identify the boys who were asking her to do these things. But her answer was always the same: "No, I don't remember."

"Tell us about Bryant Grober," Laurino said.

"Well, he told me to suck his dick," Leslie said. Zegas wrote furiously in his legal pad. He looked furious. Leslie's memory failed with respect to Chris, but she kept putting Grober into the action. "I did suck his dick," Leslie said.

The boys urged her to "go further, further, further," she said. "Chris was saying it." Laurino was surprised. An hour ago, she couldn't remember what Chris was doing; now she recalled what he said.

"Where were Bryant's hands?"

"On my head," Les said.

"And could you show me, Leslie, could you use my head?" Laurino asked.

Leslie threw her head back and breathed deeply. She flushed and rolled her eyes. "Oh, brother," she said.

"Show me with your hands."

Leslie put her hand on the back of Laurino's head and pushed down hard. She took a deep breath. She seemed glad that was over.

"Was something inside your mouth?" Laurino asked her.

"His balls," Leslie replied, with no evident embarrassment.

Where was her face then?

"It was on his balls."

"And where was his penis?"

"In my mouth," Leslie said.

While this was going on, she said, she was kneeling on the floor while Grober was sitting on the couch.

Back in a conversational tone, Laurino said, "What happened next?"

"Oh, then came the broomstick," she answered casually.

She said Kyle got the "fire-engine red" broomstick and put a plastic bag slicked with Vaseline over the broom handle and tied it with a rubber band. Laurino showed her the broomstick that Leslie and a detective had bought only a few weeks before. "That's the broomstick!" Les exclaimed. The judge had to explain to the jury that it was a "replica"—a broomstick that looked like the one in the basement.

Now, what had Kyle done with the broomstick he had covered in plastic? Laurino asked. Leslie said that Kyle gave the broom to his brother, Kevin.

Kevin Scherzer looked hard at Leslie.

"He stuck it in me," Leslie said. Kevin kept looking at her.

What was the position of her legs?

"They were spread out. . . . I was on the couch . . . laying down." Her hands, she said, were "behind my head."

"How did that make you feel when your legs were spread out?" Laurino asked.

"Okay, I guess," she said. She spoke in a dull, colorless tone.

Laurino wanted to make it as concrete as he could. "Where did he put the broomstick?"

"In my vagina," Leslie answered.

When the broomstick was in her vagina, Richie Corcoran was saying, Go further, go further, and calling her "Pigorskia," she testified.

"Did Richie ever call you that before?"

"Many of times," Leslie said. For the first time, her words were spoken with bite.

Leslie was saying, "Then came the bat."

She said that Kyle gave it to Chris. Laurino showed her the bat that was recently purchased by the prosecution at a sporting goods store. "That's the bat that was used in the basement," Leslie volunteered. The judge had to instruct the jury, again, that they were looking at a "replica" of the bat.

Was there something different about this bat?

"That's a fungo bat," she said. She pointed to it and said that's where Kyle had placed the plastic bag, which she called a "baggie."

When Kyle gave the bat to Chris, Laurino asked, what did Chris do with it?

"He stuck it up my vagina," she said. Chris Archer stared at his old hometown friend.

In the courtroom, the silence of the tomb. Laurino waited for her words to sink in. To make certain the jurors appreciated all they had heard in the last fifteen minutes, he recapitulated: "We've talked about the blow job, and we've talked about the broomstick, and we've talked about the bat. Could you tell us what happens next?"

"Then comes the little tiny stick," Leslie offered.

Leslie said Kyle didn't cover the stick because Richie thought "it would be easier to stick up than the others." Then Richie "stuck it up my vagina" while her legs were "wide out," she said.

After that, Leslie said, Grober, Kevin, Richie, and Peter Quigley sucked her breasts, which she called her "tits, boobs."

Laurino told the judge that he thought Leslie was getting tired after testifying for an hour and fifteen minutes. The judge called a fifteen-minute recess.

During the break, Leslie went to the bathroom with her sister and Dawn Lipinski. Leslie's sister and Dawn talked about which Caribbean island was the most fun to visit. Leslie stood next to them, listening silently. Her sister was carrying her coat, which had a fur collar. Tentatively, Leslie reached out and began to stroke the fur. Again and again, as if she were petting one of the dogs she'd let escape from the kennels.

When Leslie returned to the stand, she recalled that she had "jerked off" some of the guys in the basement. Laurino asked, "What did you do when you jerked somebody off?"

"What does that mean?" she said, seemingly surprised that somebody would ask a question with such a self-evident answer. "It means that you put your hand on their dick and you go up and down." Leslie was showing that she knew something about sexual practices.

After that, Leslie said, Kyle washed the bat and broomstick and threw both objects away. But, she added, "it wasn't time to go yet."

"Did anybody say anything?" Laurino asked.

"Not to tell anybody," she answered. "All of them, all of them said that."

What had the boys said would happen if she told?

"They said that if I told anybody I'd get in trouble . . . that they'd tell my mother."

What were the boys doing when they were swearing Leslie to secrecy?

"Everybody had their hands on everybody else. . . . Like a basketball, when you play basketball." Leslie demonstrated, putting one hand on top of the other, showing how she had become a member of the team.

And after they completed this sports ritual?

"Well, I waited around to see if I would go out with Paul. And then Kyle said I could go home by then."

"Why were you waiting around for Paul?"

"Because I thought he still might want to go out with me," she whispered.

"Did Paul go out with you that night?"

"No."

"Had Paul ever gone out with you before?"

"No."

Leslie seemed to have overcome her early nervousness. She even managed a smile at her sister and Dawn in the front row. She didn't appear to be distracted by the four defendants and she didn't look at them, though they stared hard at her. Laurino thought he would make one more attempt to nail Chris.

"And who told you that Paul would go out with you?"

"Chris," Leslie responded without hesitating.

Laurino asked her why she hadn't left before then. What Leslie said didn't have anything to do with sexual acts. But it had everything to do with who Leslie was and why the prosecutors were arguing that she was incapable of consenting to sex and could not reject any man who wanted to use her.

Leslie said: "'Cause I thought they weren't through, what they were doing."

"Now, Les, Leslie, the next day—could you tell us how you felt the next day?"

For most of her time on the stand, Leslie had answered Laurino's questions without long pauses; she had described sexual acts in street language without visible discomfort or evasion. But this time she buried her head in her hands. Looking at the prosecutor through the slits between her fingers, she mumbled, "That's an embarrassing question."

"How did your body feel?" he asked.

"Okay." Her voice was tiny.

"Okay, Les, how did you feel the next day?"

Judge Cohen asked, "You said, 'Okay'? . . . Is that how you felt the next day after this happened?" Judge Cohen was the teacher, the principal, the father. He was the one who told her that she had to tell the truth. "*No*," Leslie said.

"Tell us how you felt, Les," Laurino said.

She squirmed. She put her head down on her arms. She covered her face. She pulled at her lip. "It's embarrassing."

Laurino wouldn't be put off. "I know it's embarrassing, but we're all grown-ups, so you can tell us."

"It hurt," Leslie said, covering her face again. "It hurt when I went to the bathroom," she said. Talking about bodily functions were embarrassing to Leslie—and to many other very young children. But talking about sex didn't make her uncomfortable because that was what she heard teenagers talking about all the time.

The prosecutor asked her why she hadn't told the boys "to just leave you alone."

"I didn't want to hurt their feelings," she said.

Would she ever get any of her friends in trouble?

"No," she said, her voice rising.

"The boys in the basement that day, Leslie, do you consider them still your friends?"

"Sort of," she said, not looking at them.

Laurino asked her six times whether she understood the meaning of the word *force*; six times she said she didn't, although she had told the police that Grober had forced her to have oral sex.

Laurino gave up on force. He asked her if she had talked to Chris Archer before March 1. She said she talked to Chris "many a times" on the telephone. What had they talked about? "Life," said Les.

And what else? he asked.

"Sports."

And . . .

"Sex," she said, reluctantly.

And had she ever talked to him face to face?

"Yes," she said. Leslie squirmed, craned her neck to look at her sister. "Oh, God," she moaned.

Laurino wanted to ask one more question about Chris. He wanted to ask her about the time that she visited the Archers' house and—according to her statements to investigators—a hot dog was inserted into her vagina. But the judge had precluded him from asking that question unless Leslie specifically linked the act to watching porn movies with Paul and Chris, as she had in her police statement. But Leslie clearly wasn't going to be forthcoming about her relationship with Chris. Laurino didn't want to risk a mistrial. So he never asked her about the hot dog incident, and an act that seemed to foreshadow what happened in the basement was never disclosed to the jury.

The prosecutor played several excerpts from Leslie's taped conversations with Mari Carmen. The first excerpt consisted of Mari's expressed desire to duplicate Leslie's experience with the broomstick. Leslie had said to Mari: "You want to do that to yourself?" Laurino asked Leslie what she had meant by that.

Leslie said she had meant: "Why would anybody want to do that to themselves?"

Laurino then read to her the part of the tapes where Leslie said she would be "scareder" to return to the basement. "What did you mean by that?" he asked.

Suddenly, Leslie couldn't recall. "I don't remember saying that."

"Okay."

"I know it's on there, but I don't remember saying that."

The prosecutor hadn't felt it for a couple of hours, but his earlier sense of foreboding returned.

Then came the moment Leslie dreaded—and Laurino wasn't exactly looking forward to it, either. But it had to be done. "Are any of those boys that were in the basement in court today?" he asked.

Breathing deeply. "Yes."

"Could you point them out and tell me who is here?"

Hoarsely, Leslie pleaded with Laurino: "Do I have to?"

"Yes," he said.

Leslie stood up, holding onto the railing of the witness box.

"Which boys do you see?"

"Oh, boy, okay," Leslie groaned. "That's—this is going to be hard. They're twins."

Cohen interjected, "Can you tell us who you see here who you saw in the basement?"

"Okay. Oh, boy, there's a couple of them over there."

Laurino urged her, "Tell us which ones."

She pleaded, "Do I have to?" Long ago, Leslie had pledged to keep the secret. Now she had to give it up. Leslie tried once, twice. But she didn't get the names right.

The prosecutor walked around behind the defendants. He stopped at the first one, pointing to him. "This individual at the end is who?"

"This is Grover."

Zegas interjected, "*Grover*, your honor?"

"Yes," said Judge Cohen.

Laurino pointed to the next defendant.

"Chris," said Leslie.

The next one?

"Kyle."

And the last one?

"Kevin."

She said she had known "Grover" since high school. Chris she had known "a very, very long time," from the first grade. Kyle she had known when she was young.

"And how about his brother, Kevin Scherzer?"

Leslie volunteered, "He's a bodybuilder."

"And, Leslie, are those boys still your friends, the four boys?" The boys looked at her.

"Sort of," she said in a tiny voice.

"What do you mean, sort of?"

"I mean that I still care about them," Leslie said.

Laurino glanced at the clock on the wall. It was one minute to four. "Is there any one of them that you consider to be a better friend than the rest of them?"

"Chris," said Leslie Faber.

"I have no further questions, Judge," Laurino said.

Unless you were a true believer in the defendants' innocence, you could come to only one conclusion after Leslie's first day on the stand: Her testimony was devastating to the defense. Factually, she had put the bat and broomstick into Chris and Kevin's hands. She said she had oral sex with Grober after he pushed her head down. She said Kyle prepared and then threw away the bat and broomstick—actions that, if the jury believed her, amounted to aiding and abetting the rape.

Those were issues of fact. But there was the matter of Leslie's mental state. Perhaps 150 people had watched her grimace and groan. They had seen her shame when she had to talk about urinating. These strangers had listened to her uninflected recital of raw sexual activities, a description that was remarkable for its asexuality and lifelessness, a recitation that was completely lacking in affect. Who could doubt that Leslie Faber was retarded, and that her condition was apparent to anyone who had spent even a few minutes with her?

In many newspaper stories that ran the next day, the same word appeared: *childlike*. Despite her use of sexual terms, journalists saw her as the prosecution had depicted her: a child in the body of a mature woman.

Another way to assess the impact of her testimony was to talk to the defense lawyers. One of them told a reporter after Leslie finished her direct testimony, "The effect is horrible, if the jury believes it."

Tom Ford said, "If she's not damaging, who would be? This is certainly the high point of their case." Ford and Zegas said her testimony was "riddled with inconsistencies." However, Ford acknowledged that highlighting the inconsistencies wouldn't be easy because of Leslie's mental condition. He told a reporter for the *Washington Post*, "You can't handle her. I would love to have a Phi Beta Kappa graduate of Wellesley on the stand, someone that's very intelligent."

Downstairs in the prosecutor's office, Miller-Hall was rerunning Leslie's testimony for some of the representatives of NOW. She wasn't happy. Leslie had said it was Bryant, not Chris, who invited her to the basement. (Despite that, Leslie did say it was Chris who promised her a date with Paul.) She refused to define force, although she had used the word in a number of statements to the police, particularly with reference to Bryant Grober. "I'm demoralized," Miller-Hall said. "Over the weekend she told us force was when people held you down by your hands and legs. Now she says she doesn't know what force is. I could see the look she was giving us."

But the NOW members thought Leslie had made a strong witness for the prosecution. "She was fine," Christine McGoey reassured Miller-Hall.

"She said all the important things—the bat, the broom, the date with Paul Archer. She showed how Grober pushed her head down. She was *very* strong, and she was herself. The jury knows she's not Lolita. Now they know how vulnerable she is."

Laurino was cautious. He agreed with McGoey, but he knew that Miller-Hall was right, too. There were flaws in Leslie's testimony that shouldn't have been there. He hurried out of the office to watch the 5 o'clock TV news. He heard soundbites of the defense lawyers saying that Leslie was a compelling witness.

When he returned, Laurino was still nervous, but maybe he was missing the big picture, which everybody seemed to think was pretty good. Pretty good with Laurino questioning her. But how good would it be with the defense lawyers cross-examining her? After all, it was Leslie who said she'd do anything for a friend, and the defense lawyers, Laurino was sure, would try to persuade her that they, too, were her friends. Laurino knew that Leslie made friends fast.

63

Tom Ford's strategy was to treat the retarded young woman in her purple polyester pants and matching shirt as he would any other adult witness—a cop, for example, or a teacher. "As you think back, Chris never did anything to hurt you, did he?" He asked the question after Leslie had been on the stand for a minute. He asked the question before he could gauge how she would respond.

Leslie answered: "Yes, he did."

"Where?"

"He did the bat," Leslie said.

That was how Thursday, December 10, Leslie's second day as a witness, started out. And it continued in the same vein throughout Tom Ford's cross-examination. He didn't seem to realize that he should tamp down his flowery language so that Leslie could understand him. Leslie looked lost in the thickets of his syntax. His other problem was that he pressed too hard to sculpt her answers to conform to his version of what happened. But Leslie was no piece of clay; she couldn't be shaped by Tom Ford. She kept to her version and even reinforced it.

Ford took Leslie back to testimony she had given three years before to the grand jury or even earlier, to a statement she gave to an investigator.

Sometimes he would refer to Laurino's questions the day before and then in the same sentence would mention Laurino's questions before the grand jury in November 1989. It might have been confusing for a Harvard grad. It was very confusing to Leslie. She put her hands on her hips. "Well, I mean, what's your point?" she asked.

The jurors, who by now had sat through two months of Ford's windy and repetitive questions, empathized with Leslie, and laughed. Chris Archer also laughed. The other three defendants didn't crack a smile.

The defense lawyer tried to explore Leslie's understanding of "force." He reminded her that she had said to a police investigator that she wasn't forced by Chris Archer when he sucked her breasts.

"Yes I was . . . It was true," Leslie insisted.

"But . . . it wasn't done by somebody threatening you?"

"*No, they just did it,*" she said. She sounded as if she hadn't had much say in the matter.

Ford kept at her. "Nobody said . . . you have to do this?"

"They said they were going to tell my mother."

So far she was proving to be a tough witness.

Around and around Ford went on whether she had complained of pain and injury after the alleged rape. "Didn't Mr. Laurino ask you several questions relative to whether or not you were bothered the next day and you answered, 'No,' and then he kept asking you questions until you changed and said, 'Yes.'"

Leslie didn't seem to follow him. Ford pressed on. "You didn't say anything to the doctor about this problem?"

"No."

"You didn't take any medication, did you?"

"There wasn't any bleeding . . ."

"Any marks?" Ford asked.

"No marks," she said, heavily.

"And no bleeding?"

"No."

Ford asked whether Leslie made an attempt to leave the basement.

"No way," Leslie said emphatically.

"No one was holding you from leaving?"

"Right."

With these answers, Leslie enabled the defense lawyers to argue later that she remained voluntarily. Leslie's answers also made it much harder to prove that force was used against her, and that she had suffered injury and experienced pain. Laurino knew it was coming; Les had never said that she tried to flee the basement. Still, it hurt, Leslie sitting there, saying there was "no way" she would attempt to leave.

Ford wanted to establish another theme: that Leslie understood that what she was doing in the basement was not socially permissible behavior. "You wouldn't have done this in front of your parents?" he asked.

She sat up straight and moved back in the chair as if she were recoiling from the idea. Her eyes wide, she said, "Oh, no way."

"You wouldn't like them to know that you would do that type of thing?"

"Right." She was emphatic, but the word was also tinged with sadness.

Ford mentioned the "blow job" with Bryant Grober. "How did the act end, how did you stop? Did you just raise your head?"

"Yeah."

Ford could have left it there. But he wanted to drive the point home. He couldn't resist one more question.

"You raised your head up and stopped and the individual was sitting there on the couch next to you?"

"When he was holding the head," Leslie replied, holding the back of her head.

"But he wasn't holding—" Ford began, but was interrupted by Laurino, who pointed out for the record where Leslie had placed her hand.

"But the point was . . . you raised your head."

"No, no, no," Les said.

She pressed her knuckles against her temples. "Can you repeat that, please?"

Again Ford tried. "When you wanted to raise your head off his penis, you just raised your head up, didn't you?"

"When his hand was on there, yes," she said. It was one of the first things she had told Sheila Byron. No matter how hard Ford tried to wipe away that image, Leslie remembered Bryant Grober's hand on her hair, on her head.

After three more questions, Ford got Leslie to say no one was holding her after she had oral sex. But while she was saying that, she kept a hand on the back of her head. She wouldn't give that up.

She said she took off her sweatpants when "they mentioned the broom-stick." After that, she said, "I had to take my underwear down."

Judge Cohen asked, "What do you mean by that, you had to take your underwear off?"

"In order to do it," Leslie said.

Before the broomstick was used, she was lying on the couch in the basement with her legs spread, she said.

"Now, nobody, they didn't grab your legs and move them, did they?" Ford said, indulging his proclivity for asking that one extra question for which he didn't know the answer.

"They *told* me to spread my legs," Leslie said.

Ford strode across the courtroom, twirling the red broomstick as though he were a geriatric drum major. "Do you recall how the broom was being held?"

"When they were putting it in me?" Leslie asked. This was not helping the defense. Some lawyers might have bailed out then, moved on to another subject, but Ford stuck to it. "Yes," he prompted Leslie.

"It was up like you were holding it, it was up, but it was standing like that."

Ford was holding the broom with the handle slightly raised, pointed at Leslie.

Leslie was moving right along. "And then they're putting all this stuff on it."

"All right," Ford muttered, turning his back to her. "Now, fine. After that was put on, how was the broom held?"

Ford would have bought himself a bottle of champagne if she had started her answer with *I*. But she didn't. She said, "It was given to one of them."

The lawyer, still hoping for deliverance, asked, "Given to *you*."

"No, given to one of *them*," Leslie insisted.

"What did they do?" Another bad question.

"They stuck it up me," Leslie said.

Impatience beginning to build, Ford said, "Well, I'm asking you how were they holding it when this happened."

"How were they holding it?"

"Yes."

"Like you are holding it now—well, like this." Leslie motioned as if she were lining up a cue stick.

Ford slid his hands down toward the bristles. It would have helped Chris's defense if Leslie had testified that the boys had held the broom only by the bristles; that would have suggested to the jurors that Leslie voluntarily guided the broomstick into her vagina by holding the handle end.

But Leslie wouldn't contribute to Ford's strategy. Ford said, displaying his exasperation, "You show me, you take the broom and show me how they were holding it."

Laurino stood up to see. The jurors leaned forward in their seats. Chris Archer stared at Leslie, but the other three defendants looked at the judge or their lawyers or anything else but at Leslie. Esposito dropped his pen on the table. He slumped back in his chair, his hands dangling at his sides, his head lolling to the side. He looked as though he had just been shot.

Slowly, Leslie unfolded herself, stood up, took the broom from Ford. Leslie was going to show everyone in the jam-packed courtroom exactly how the boys penetrated her with the handle of the broom.

Leslie held the handle with both hands curled around it, knuckles pointing toward the floor. One hand was close to the bristles. The other was about a foot away—maybe a little more—toward the tip of the broom handle. One reporter later said it reminded him of someone shoveling snow.

Ford wanted details: "Now, when it was inserted, did it go straight in?"

"Yes," Leslie said.

Perhaps, Ford thought, if he helped her a little, she'd give the answer he wanted—that she guided the broom handle into her vagina. "Isn't it true . . . you were holding it near the end closest to . . . where it was being inserted into your body?"

"No, I wasn't," she said, politely but firmly. "I was holding my hands behind my head."

Ford showed her the fungo bat.

"How far would you say . . . this bat was inserted?" Ford asked.

"Pretty far," Leslie said.

Querques said he couldn't hear her answer.

Judge Cohen said, drily: " 'Pretty far' was the answer."

"Pretty far," Leslie repeated.

Before the lunch break, Ford asked her a few questions about why she had left Columbia High School in 1987. There was this incident, he said, where she approached varsity players in the cafeteria and, as the lawyer delicately phrased it, "indicated to them that you wanted to give them a blow job."

"Right," Leslie said.

Ford reminded her that one day her mother came to the school and took her away. "I was pretty ticked off because I liked it there," she said. Why did she like it? "Because I liked the popular people in my class. . . . They were nice people. . . . We were like buddies and partners."

As Leslie revealed her longings to be accepted by the "popular people," she also revealed two sides of her nature. She showed that her intellectual development had been arrested in the early grades of elementary school.

But the social side had been truncated at the most awful time, at about the time that the attention of the "popular people" means more than anything else in the world.

"And you never went back to Columbia for a minute after that, did you?" Ford asked.

"No, I wanted to, but I couldn't," Leslie said.

For months Zegas had been thinking about how he would cross-examine Leslie Faber. "My feeling was to use a conversational style, and at a more elementary level than with another witness, and to try to empathize with her," he recalled.

Zegas was much younger than Ford, had young children. He thought he could communicate with a child's mind. So here was Zegas standing, with one hand grasping Bryant Grober's shoulder. "You've seen him before, right?" Zegas asked Leslie.

"Yeah."

"What's his name?"

"Grover."

"Like in the 'Sesame Street' character?"

Breaking into a wide smile, Leslie said, "Noooo. He doesn't look anything like that." Zegas grinned.

"And his first name is what?"

"Brian."

"You didn't live in the same neighborhood as Brian when you grew up?"

"I don't know where he lived," said Leslie.

In a few seconds Zegas had tried to show that Leslie didn't know Bryant Grober as well as she knew the other three defendants. And he had shown that he could talk to her in a gentle, casual sing-song. ("The last thing in the world you want to do is to create an impression that you are taking advantage of this poor, mentally impaired person the same way that your clients in the basement purportedly took advantage of her," Zegas said later.)

Zegas moved right up to the witness box, talking head to head with her. Nice and easy. Zegas looked at her beseechingly and said, "I want you to think as hard as you can. Tell me when you've ever been to the home of Sheila Byron?" The attorney knew that when Ford questioned her she had testified that she had never visited the detective.

"Honestly?" Les said, just like she might with a good friend like Mari Carmen.

"Honestly."

"All right, yes, I was at her house once," Leslie said.

Now he wanted to drive the point home. "You knew that when Mr. Ford asked you the same question, you weren't really being honest then, were you?" he asked.

"No," Leslie said, looking down.

"But from now on, you promise that all your answers are going to be honest, right?"

"Yes," Leslie promised.

Alan Zegas had demonstrated that Leslie could be handled.

On March 1, she said, she went to the park and saw Richie Corcoran shooting baskets.

Anybody else?

"A couple of people, but I can't remember who they were," Leslie said. The day before, her first day on the stand, Leslie, at Laurino's prodding, had recalled a number of names.

Zegas stopped there. He told the judge that Leslie seemed to be getting a little tired. The judge recessed the trial until the next morning. Leslie's second day had ended with her unable to remember—except for Richie— who had been at the park. Maybe it was just the Ritalin wearing off. Maybe it was something else. Laurino didn't regard it as a favorable augury.

Before Leslie returned home, Goldberg saw her in the prosecutor's office. "Why are you looking so sad, Les?" Goldberg asked.

She hesitated for a long time before she answered. "Oh, it's a long story."

"I have lots of time," Goldberg said.

"I'm making you guys look bad," Leslie said.

During their first day of cross-examination, Ford and Zegas had got answers from Leslie that could be helpful to their case. They had caught Leslie in a few contradictions and in one lie about visiting Sheila Byron. They had got Leslie to say that she hadn't felt pain or suffered a physical injury as a result of what the defendants did to her. Most important, the defense now had Leslie on record saying she did not attempt to stop the Jocks, and did not try to leave until the boys were done with her.

But the day had not been an unqualified success for the defense. Responding to Tom Ford's incautious questions, Leslie had said that Chris had hurt her by using the bat on her. She said that the boys told her to undress. She repeatedly demonstrated how Bryant Grober had held her head during an act of oral sex. And she had physically shown to the jury how the broomstick was inserted into her body. Leslie had not changed her account of the central acts in the rape case: the oral sex and the insertion of the bat and the broomstick. After the trial was recessed for the day, Laurino said, "Considering she was being cross-examined, Leslie was still on a roll. I thought she did a great job on Ford, when he thought she was just going to fold after the first few questions. It was just great when Ford said, 'Did Christopher hurt you?' and she said, 'Yeah, when he put the bat in.' I know she was getting confused and they were confusing her, but she was not changing her basic story. This was the best I could ever expect Leslie to do on cross."

Robert Hanley, the reporter for the *New York Times*, was writing his daily story longhand on a bench in the courthouse corridor. "How do you report this damn thing?" he grumbled. "In this case you just can't report what people say in the courtroom and leave it at that. There's got to be more." That was the problem confronting reporters who had come to Newark from all over the country to cover Leslie's testimony. The convention that still ruled trial coverage was to report a literal account of what people said. But was what Leslie said the literal truth?

The reporting of rape trials had come under considerable criticism for lack of interpretation and for the absence of instructive context and background. Most of the major news organizations covering the Glen Ridge trial had tried to broaden the perspective by quoting experts on relevant legal issues, such as the question of consent. They also included analyses by women's advocacy groups, thereby reminding readers and viewers that the defense lawyers were trying to make Leslie's sexual history the dominant issue of the trial.

But the basic coverage still consisted of a literal rendering of what the witness had said. There had been little independent investigation of who the defendants were, how they behaved in Glen Ridge, and how they treated nonretarded girls, not to speak of a retarded one. Because most of the reporting stuck to what was said in the courtroom, the defense lawyers were able to turn the case into a trial of Leslie's past, while the defendants, individually and as a group, remained faceless stereotypes.

Another convention of trial coverage was to highlight the themes that were emphasized that day by the lawyers in their questioning of witnesses. The day before, when Laurino was questioning Leslie, the reporting focused on those parts of her testimony that supported the charges against the defendants. Today it was the defense's turn. Most of the stories about Leslie's cross-examination emphasized that her testimony supported the defense's contention that she had not been forced into the acts that took place in the basement. One New Jersey paper went so far as to report, "In testimony that could toll a death knell for the state's case, the alleged victim . . . yesterday admitted that no one forced her to stay." It was mainstream journalism's idea of balance and fairness. But fairness and balance didn't always advance the work of getting reasonably close to the truth.

Strangely, most of the papers and television stations buried far into their stories Leslie's demonstration in the courtroom of how the boys had inserted a broomstick into her vagina. Some left that out entirely. It didn't fit today's theme.

64

A powerful Nor'easter struck New York and New Jersey the next morning, Friday, and the trial was recessed until the following Tuesday. That gave Leslie four days to think about her testimony.

On Monday morning, December 14, the prosecutor heard from Leslie's minister. She told him that Leslie said she had lied when she testified she hadn't suffered any injury from the broomstick and bat. The minister said that Leslie told her she had seen blood in her urine the day after the alleged rape.

Leslie reportedly explained her lie by saying, "If I tell the truth, it'll send the boys to jail at Christmas time."

If Leslie hadn't told the truth about the blood, what else might she lie about to save the boys? Laurino got the feeling from the minister that Leslie was distressed about lying, but when she returned to the stand after the four-day break, she seemed buoyant.

"How are you?" Zegas asked.

"Fine. Nice tie," she responded brightly.

Leslie had spent an afternoon in court with Zegas that past Thursday, and now she was treating him like an old friend.

Zegas's first objective was to impress on Leslie the consequences of lying. "If you tell a lie and the jury thinks that your lie is really the truth . . . then the four boys back here could be getting into a lot of trouble, do you understand that," he told her.

"Really?" Leslie asked, eyes wide.

"Really."

Zegas added that if Leslie lied, the boys could be sent to jail. "Do you understand that?"

She lowered her head and said, "Yeah."

When the defense attorney asked her whether Detective Byron had ever said the boys could be sent to jail, Leslie seemed rattled. "Don't say that," she said loudly. "Wait a minute." But then she said Byron "never told me anything about that."

Leslie was reassured by the short, trim man. In Leslie's hierarchy of trustworthy adults, those who ranked highest were the people who were easiest to confide in. They were the least judgmental. They were the ones who understood that she had a life to live separate from her parents. In Leslie's words, those were the "really nice guys." And that's how Alan Zegas, soft-spoken and understanding, was coming across right now.

"There are certain things that you never say to your parents?" the nice man asked her.

"Oh, never, never, never," Leslie said, shaking her head in agreement.

Zegas's strategy was to use Leslie to demonstrate that the testimony of her mother and teachers was unreliable because they didn't really know about her secret life.

Buddy to buddy, Zegas asked her, "Do you get along with your parents?"

"Not really," said Leslie, joining the ranks of about thirty million teenagers in the country.

"Is it hard for you to talk about things with them that matter to you?"

"Yes, it's very hard," she said.

Laurino saw her slipping into the cozy psychospeak of analyst and analysand.

"And you would never talk with them about sex, right?" Zegas led her.

"No," Leslie said, shaking her head hard. "Never, never."

Was that because her parents didn't want her to tell them about her sex life?

"They wouldn't want to know, I wouldn't think," Leslie said, then qualified the thought: "Well, they would, but I wouldn't want to tell them."

Was that something she wanted to hide from them? the lawyer inquired, disarmingly.

"Right," said Leslie.

At lunch, Leslie seemed to Laurino to be cranky, tired. Or was it that she was bored and wanted this to be all over with? Leslie hadn't hurt the prosecution's case yet, Laurino thought. She was showing off as an authority on sex. But that was Leslie. If you encouraged her, she would try to do what you wanted of her. The prosecutor thought the jury would pick up on it. But then she looked up from her food and said something that scared him. "Can I tell the judge I don't want to get the boys in trouble?" she asked.

It was a smooth slide from the general idea that Leslie kept secrets from her parents to a specific secret, like her departure from Columbia High School.

Did she tell her parents what really caused her transfer?

"No, they found out on their own. That's how most of the things that happened, they find out on their own. I don't tell them. I'm not close with them." Leslie's answers to Ford and Zegas had been terse. Suddenly she was unwinding complete sentences, whole thoughts.

Zegas was running her now; he could get more. Did her guidance counselor, Carol Bolden, tell her parents about what Leslie was doing in school?

"Yes, she's the one that opened her big mouth, yeah."

Big-mouthed teachers: Leslie was showing another, unexpected facet of her personality. A retarded person could be just as rebellious and self-absorbed as any other teenager. But she lacked the self-restraint to hide it. The more she talked, the more she showed, and Zegas kept the questions coming in a smooth, easy flow. Yes, Leslie told him, she knew a lot about sex, she had a lot of sexual experience, the experiences went back to when she was eleven, twelve years old.

Wouldn't she approach lots of boys to ask for sex?

"Once in a while they asked; sometimes I would."

And she'd never tell her parents about that?

"No way, José," said Leslie, talking as she would to one of her classmates.

All of these questions were prelude. Setting the scene for Leslie and Bryant Grober.

"You know, when you give a boy a blow job, that's something that can make him real happy, right?"

"Yeah, I know," Leslie said. When someone approached her as an expert, an authority, she responded as an expert. Mari Carmen did that. Now Alan Zegas, who had an M.B.A. from Harvard, a law degree with honors from Rutgers University Law School, was doing that.

He asked Leslie, who five years before had an IQ of 49: "Now, you know from your experience that if you are too rough with a boy['s] penis, that could be painful to him, right?"

"Oh, yeah, you don't want to yank on it too much."

"And, also, a boy's balls are also very delicate?"

"Yeah, they're the size of a football field."

For a moment Zegas appeared flustered. In the crowded courtroom, people were asking their neighbors, What's she talking about? Zegas breezed past her answer. Without pausing, he said, "If you unravel the tissue . . . it would be the size of a football field?"

"Yeah," she readily agreed.

Zegas focused on Bryant. "He didn't tell you to rub his dick, right? This is something you wanted to do?"

"Yeah."

"And after you began rubbing his dick, you then asked him if he wanted a blow job, right?" he asked.

Leslie balked at that. "No, he asked me if I wanted to give him a blow job."

"You began to rub his dick and he didn't ask you to do that, that was your decision, right?"

"Yes, that was my decision," Leslie said.

What she was doing was clear to Laurino. "She was going down the toilet on us and we could see that, but there was nothing we could do to stop it," he said later.

Zegas continued, "Did you say words to him like, Bryant, do you want me to suck on you? . . . You weren't rubbing him for no reason, right?"

"Well, you have to make—never mind, I'm not going to admit that."

Zegas plowed ahead, talking faster, in short, sharp sentences. "You did get him excited, right, and then you gave him a blow job, which is what you wanted to do?"

"Yeah."

"Your teeth had touched his balls?"

"Yes," Leslie said. "Yes."

"And then he stood up. . . . Think carefully now."

"No, he couldn't have stood up. How could he stand up if my mouth is still on—"

Zegas didn't let her finish. "Did he push your head off him? Think about it, think real carefully about that."

"No, he didn't push his head off me." Leslie got her thoughts jumbled, but she still insisted that Grober hadn't pushed her away.

The lawyer asked her whether Grober hadn't pushed her away because she had her "teeth on his balls" and "he was in pain."

"He was in pain?" Leslie sounded alarmed.

"Was he hurting from your teeth?"

"No way. No."

"Do you remember being pretty strong on him with your mouth, do you know what I mean?"

"Oh, strong like—"

"Like sucking hard."

Leslie looked horrified. She half-raised herself out of her seat. The jurors watched her. "No, I wouldn't have sucked hard, no," she insisted. "You got to be easy, you know. No, no, no, I was easy with him."

Was she getting him excited? Zegas asked.

"He seemed to like it." That didn't conform to how Zegas was portraying Grober—as embarrassed, ashamed, contrite.

"This is something you were doing because you, Leslie Faber, enjoyed it?"

"Yeah."

"Like you enjoyed it before with others, right?"

Leslie nodded in agreement. "Um-hum, lots of people, yeah."

Laurino felt numb. He asked himself, We've been in this for four years, why is she doing this now? As she answered Zegas's questions, willingly, eagerly, Laurino thought: This is betrayal. At the last moment, she betrayed me.

Zegas was almost done. His voice was sweet. He looked kind, concerned. "And he's [Bryant] never been mean to you, has he?"

"No way," Leslie agreed. "He's a sweetheart."

"And he's never teased you or anything like that?" Zegas went on.

"No," she repeated. "He's a sweetheart."

65

Michael Querques had been unwell, and he looked worn down. When Zegas completed his cross-examination, Querques rose creakily and walked slowly toward the witness. He stopped a few feet away. His first words were so soft that the jurors strained to hear him. "Leslie, can you tell I'm nervous?" he whispered.

"You don't look it," Leslie said.

"I'm a little afraid to ask you some questions," he told her.

"Don't be afraid," she encouraged him.

Querques hitched up his pants. He pointed to the three prosecutors, whom he called her "friends"—"Bob" and "Liz" and "Glenn."

"I'm not your friend; is that correct?" he said, sadly.

"I don't even know you," Leslie said.

"That's right, but *they* are your friends."

Querques leaned toward her, reaching out. He clasped his hands and raised them to his chest, as if he were about to offer a prayer. He pleaded with her, "You think, Les, do you think if I ask you pretty please, pretty please, Les, to try to be my friend a couple of hours today and tomorrow."

"Yes." She sounded eager.

Querques walked back to the defense table and unrolled a chart he had prepared. On it, he had printed the names of all the people that the prosecution had employed in the case. Querques's pointer stopped at the name of a psychiatrist who had evaluated Leslie for the prosecution.

"He asked you a lot of questions?" Querques said.

"Is he from your side?" she asked.

Querques looked pained. "Is he from my side? You know, Les, you touched a sore spot now. . . . Some people told you this is the good side, that's the bad side. Is that what you think, Les?"

"Uh-huh."

"Be real nice to me, Les; who told you that side is the bad side?"

Leslie pointed to the table where the prosecutors sat motionless. Laurino, Goldberg, Miller-Hall.

"You are pointing to Mr. Laurino?" Querques asked softly, resigned.

"Them," Leslie summarized.

Querques seized the word. It was "them" that ruined her weekends by bringing her into the courthouse when "you normally might shoot baskets . . . visit your friends . . . go for ice cream."

Querques told her, "Les, they stopped it, didn't they, Les?"

"Yeah. I hate them for that," she said.

What little color was left had drained out of Laurino's face. He looked stricken. Some people in the spectator section snickered because Querques's tactics were so transparently manipulative. Michaele Archer herself seemed close to tears. Laurino understood that Leslie was being steered. That was his cerebral side working. But his emotions screamed at him, She's betraying you. Leslie was retarded, but she had learned how words could inflict pain. Laurino thought she knew that she was hurting him.

Querques stood beside Leslie, moving his pointer down the list of names. "Now, here's the one, Les, I'm really interested in."

"Susan Esquilin," she responded.

"Oh, yes," he said.

"I hate that woman," she said vehemently.

"I'm sorry, Les. I have to ask you why you hate that lady. What did she do?"

"She does things crazy, you know, the way she tests you and stuff. And it's like look up this, look this, this, that, that, you know." It was one of Leslie's longest answers.

"So you think she's a little—"

"—Wacky," she offered. There were titters among the spectators. She heard them and smiled, too. Leslie seemed to gain confidence from the laughter.

Querques said, "I've got to take a deep breath because I'm nervous. I'm beginning to get the feeling, Les, that you like to be your own person and you don't like people to order you around."

"Right," she said.

He returned quickly to Esquilin. "She was on your back, she was annoying you, Les?"

"Oh, she was a pain in the butt," Leslie said, again drawing a few laughs, but not as many as before.

"But isn't it odd, isn't it odd, Leslie, nobody on this side has been on your back?"

"Right."

"Until you came in here the other day. Now we've been on your back a little bit, right?"

"Not really."

"'Not really.' I love that. I appreciate that. We haven't been on your back, I appreciate that." He had a sweet, gentle smile on his face. Was he going to hug her?

"You are doing the best you can; that's all that counts," Leslie assured him.

Querques was rhapsodic. "Oh, you are wonderful, Les; you are wonderful, Les.

You are going to forgive me, Les, because I'm not saying it—"

"—Why?" she interjected.

"Some people, not *me*, Les, some people say that you are retarded. Now, that's not true, is it, Les?" Querques asked. Laurino clasped his hands behind his head and looked at the defense lawyer. This trial was getting very personal.

Every eye was on the two of them, Querques and Leslie, huddled in whispered intimacy at the witness box. Even the four defendants, whose attention often wandered, appeared transfixed.

"Well, a lot of people used to call me that in school," she answered softly.

"But you don't believe that, do you, Les?"

"No, I don't look retarded," she said.

"And you are proving to these people right now"—he swiveled toward the jurors—"because you can answer questions, that you are not retarded?"

"Right," she said. "If I was retarded, I couldn't answer these questions. I wouldn't know what I'm talking about."

"Perfect, Les," Querques said, grinning.

Pointing to the three prosecutors, he said, "And these are the same people that want the world to think you are retarded."

Goldberg had had enough. "I object to counsel making a completely untrue statement," he shouted.

Judge Cohen held his head and told Querques, "I must ask you to ask questions, not make statements or testify."

It was almost three o'clock. Leslie was tiring, the Ritalin wearing off. Querques wanted to end the day's testimony with an exclamation point.

"You are trying to do the best you can for us, aren't you?" he asked the witness.

Leslie looked over at the four defendants. "Yes," she said, "I don't want to hurt anybody."

Querques stroked his chin. "Why don't we talk about that, Les?" Still looking at her, he snapped his fingers. Kevin stood up. Querques pointed at him. Kevin came a few steps closer. Querques took him by the arm and walked him up to six feet from Leslie. The lawyer put his hand softly on Kevin's shoulder, a father-son pose.

"Les, who is this big guy, Les?" Querques asked her.

"Oh, he's a bodybuilder," she said.

"What's his name, Les?"

"Kyle—no, Kevin."

Kevin stood there, unsmiling, looking over Leslie's head to the chart tacked to the bulletin board.

"Now, you don't want to hurt him, do you?" he said.

"No," she answered fervently. "I don't want to see anybody hurt."

"You don't even want to see anybody hurt. And that's what you've been saying for almost four years, isn't that right?"

"*Yes. Yes.*"

"You don't want to hurt anybody?"

"Right. *I care about them.* I know they don't give a hoot about me, but I care about them." There were no words spoken in the trial with more feeling.

"Who told you they don't give a hoot about you?" Querques saw Leslie sneaking a look at the prosecutors. "You are looking over at them again?" he asked.

"No, they didn't say that," Leslie said. She looked wretched.

"Who said that?" he demanded. He wasn't the kind elderly grandfather anymore. He was showing steel. "Look at them. Who said it, Les?"

Leslie fidgeted. She couldn't look at Laurino. She put her face in her hands. After a while, she sighed and said, "Okay, they said it."

"They told you a lot of bad things, didn't they Les?"

"Yeah."

Querques tightened his grip on Kevin's shoulder. "You know him a long time, don't you? He was always considerate of you, wasn't he?"

"Yeah, he always—he never spent very much time with me because he was always busy with his other friends."

Querques nodded sympathetically. "He was busy building his body and learning how to be an athlete?"

"Yes, he's a good one, too."

Querques was moving in perfect rhythm with Leslie now. "And he's a good one, and you like him, don't you."

"Yes, he's very handsome."

"You more than like him?"

"Yes."

"You love him a little bit?"

"Uh-huh," she whispered.

"Maybe a lot?"

"A lot, yes." Les professing her love for Kevin Scherzer, the guy, she testified yesterday, who put a broom into her vagina.

"And you don't want to hurt him?"

"No."

Querques gave his client a little shove toward his seat. He said to Leslie, "But other people have told you to hurt him, is that it?"

Her lips barely moved as she whispered, "Yes."

Laurino felt the knife twisting into his gut.

"Go ahead," Querques urged her. "Leslie, are you proud of your lawyers?"

Her jaw dropped. Querques helped out. "Not really?" he said.

"I don't know," Leslie tried. "It's hard to say." Kevin, back in his chair, looked at her. Looked and looked.

"You want to be proud of them, but you are not?"

"No."

"Isn't that right, Les?"

"Yes," she said, looking at Kevin.

Querques was the preacher in the tent, exhorting her to shout to the heavens. "You are saying 'yes,' Les?"

"Yes."

"Say it out loud, Les."

"Yes."

He turned away from her. His shoulders slumped. He asked, like a ditchdigger or a bricklayer who has exhausted himself at hard labor, "May I quit for the day, Judge?"

The judge recessed the trial.

Querques collected his papers and put them into his briefcase, leaning over and whispering to his associate, Esposito. Querques allowed himself a faint, crooked smile.

He never lingered. Tonight, as he did every night, he pulled on his coat, said good night to Kevin and Esposito, and hurried to the elevator. Michael Querques didn't believe in holding end-of-day postmortems for reporters. His work in the courtroom spoke for itself.

66

Alan Zegas, with his chatty, just-buddies manner, had opened Leslie up. Querques took advantage of his opportunity. And they had done it, Zegas and Querques, without once mentioning those "instruments," the bat and broomstick that "stunk up" their case. For one day at least, the Zegas-Querques tandem had fumigated the trial.

As they left the courtroom, Laurino and Goldberg tried to divert the reporters from the red meat served up by the defense. "They led her by the nose," Laurino said. But the reporters wouldn't buy that. The prosecutors' slant, if it appeared at all in their stories, came near the bottom. This was the defense's day, and the prosecutors couldn't change that. Headline writers summarized Leslie's testimony:

"Jersey Woman: 'I Care About Them.'"

"'Victim' May Be Best Defense in N.J. Sex Case."

"I Love Sex, Glen Ridge Woman Tells Jury."

The *New York Times* was alone among papers in the area to suggest that Leslie's testimony might not have been entirely spontaneous. Under the main "'I Care About Them'" headline, the *Times* ran the subhead "Response Comes Under Defense Guidance."

After the trial was recessed, Leslie came down to Laurino's office. Laurino couldn't speak to her, couldn't even look at her. Leslie sat in a chair beside his desk. She waited for him to say something. Laurino was silent. Then he said to a detective, "Just take her home. It's enough."

After she left, Goldberg leaned against the half-open door to Laurino's office. "What annoys me most," he said, "was the way she'd come down here during the breaks and immediately say she lied. And then she'd express *remorse* for lying—and she looked like she meant it. And she'd go right back up to court and lie again. Her thrust was, clearly, 'I lied, I know I lied, I did it because I don't want to hurt the boys.'"

The room was crowded: investigators, detectives, Miller-Hall, people who knew the prosecutors from previous trials. They moved silently around the desk where Laurino was sitting, acting as if this were a wake for a dead case. The body they were viewing was Laurino's. He made a fist and pressed it against his chest—a dagger plunged into his heart. "She did it to us," he said. "Three years I thought I knew her, and she did it to *me*."

Colleagues tried to cheer him up: It was just one day; the jury couldn't help but see how Leslie was led by the defense lawyers; anybody looking at Leslie would see how vulnerable she was; when she had used words like "sweetheart," when she said she "loved" the defendants, it would explain how easily the Jocks were able to use her. All of what they said made sense, and none of it eased Laurino's ache.

His life had been intertwined with hers for so long. All that time, he'd known that there could be a day like this. Regardless of what the Ridgers had done to her, they were part of her history, her childhood, her world, while Bob remained a stranger, a distant figure at best—a grown-up. Slender, stoop-shouldered, prematurely gray—Bob Laurino wasn't tan and muscled and "cool," he wasn't a "dude" who drove an Audi, he wasn't an "awesome" Jock.

The first day in the prosecutor's office they taught you: Don't personalize the case. But Laurino broke the rule: In some subconscious semaphore he had communicated to Leslie: Choose me or choose them. And today she had chosen them. No, that was wrong. Leslie wasn't betraying him. She was only doing what made sense in her own world.

Most of the staff people had left the office when Laurino's sister, Maria, arrived. She found the mood funereal. She couldn't remember ever seeing him so discouraged. "Everybody said, Don't try this case, this case is a loser," he said angrily.

"You can't fault Leslie," Maria told her brother. "If anything, today showed what she's like. That was Leslie the jury saw." But he couldn't be consoled. Leslie was his witness. Goldberg had done the opening statement, and it was likely that Goldberg would do the summation. But the hub was Leslie, and today, he told Maria, "The case is going down. I can feel it. It's going down." Could he have done anything to prevent this? Had he missed something because he'd got too close? He looked up at his sister. "Maybe I need to put a little distance between her and me," he said.

Leslie walked into the house, and Ros Faber could tell she was upset. "What's wrong?" Ros asked before she could take off her coat.

"They're mad at me—Bob and all of them," she said, looking at the floor.

"Did you tell the people in the court what actually happened?" Charlie asked.

"Not quite," Leslie said in a whisper. "I didn't tell them what I should have said."

"You've got to tell the truth," Ros said. "If you tell the truth, nobody is going to be mad at you."

"You have got to tell them what actually happened," her father said.

Judge Cohen had issued a "sequestration" order, which meant that Leslie was not permitted to discuss the case while she was testifying. But that night Leslie talked to three people in addition to her parents: Molly Blythe, the minister of the Presbyterian Church in the Green in Bloomfield, the church attended by the Fabers; Jean Ahrens, a volunteer in the "big sister" program that Leslie participated in; and her friend, Dawn Lipinski. Leslie cried bitterly on the phone when she talked to them. As

Laurino learned the next morning, she told the three women the same thing: I lied in court because if I tell the truth the boys'll go to jail.

The next morning, the defendants were sitting on a bench in the corridor, waiting for the courtroom door to be unlocked. The Scherzers and Chris Archer were giggling, jostling each other. Tom Ford saw the defendants having fun, and he didn't like it. "This is serious business," he said, wagging his finger at them. "Everybody's watching you. You can lose a case by how you look." The Jocks put on a serious face. The minute Ford walked away, they cracked up.

With the jury out of the room, Laurino erupted before the judge. "We learned that when she was taken home last night, she was crying. She was crying this morning . . . because she knew she lied on the stand. The reason she lied was she didn't want the boys to go to jail." He pointed to Querques. Laurino said that Querques had "totally poisoned the mind of this girl" when he suggested she was not retarded, but that the prosecutor wanted the world to think that she was. "The defense did a very cruel thing," Laurino said.

Zegas said that Leslie had been "happy, elated" when she testified the day before. Why was she crying today? "Leslie Faber was made to feel that what she did in court wasn't good for the prosecutor," he said.

Before the court session began, the prosecution had informed Judge Cohen that Leslie had spoken to three people the night before. Cohen ruled that by talking to Dawn Lipinski, a witness at the trial, Leslie had technically violated his order not to discuss the case. But he concluded that the violation was not serious enough to warrant a mistrial or to warrant preventing the prosecutor from further questioning of Leslie, as the defense had requested. The "big sister" and Leslie's minister were people "she would ordinarily go to" in a crisis, the judge said. Cohen said he would inform the jurors that Leslie had spoken to several people the night before—and they could draw their own conclusions.

It was 11:30 when Leslie began her fourth and last day of testimony. Her eyes were puffy and red-rimmed. She hadn't slept much, and she looked unhappy. Querques took one glance at her and said, "I have no further questions, your honor."

Esposito was the last defense attorney expected to cross-examine her. There was a lot riding on her answers. Leslie was the one eyewitness who could say that Kyle, alone among the boys in the basement, had expressed concern that she was being hurt. But if she said that, Esposito knew, it could crush Kevin Scherzer's chances of being acquitted. Something else. Yesterday Leslie had appeared alert, helpful, eager to please. Today she appeared upset and volatile. She scared him. Zegas and Querques, he believed, had strengthened the defense position—without ever raising the bat and the broomstick—and he didn't want to undercut them with a "new" and perhaps less helpful Leslie on the stand.

Esposito said after the trial was completed, "I could just see she was set to go off that day. If I cross-examined her, I definitely would have blown myself up. By passing, I was trying to demonstrate that Kyle didn't need a vigorous defense."

In the courtroom Esposito got halfway out of his chair and said, "I represent Kyle Scherzer. I'm not going to ask you any questions. I'm going to wish you a happy Christmas from myself and from my client, Mr. Kyle Scherzer." The defense was done with its interrogation of Leslie Faber.

Laurino's last chance. The night before, he had settled on a strategy for his redirect questioning. First, his manner would be brisk and businesslike. He wanted her to appreciate how seriously he took her answers. Second, he planned to scramble the order of his questions. He didn't want to give her a chance to calculate whether she was helping the defendants. The last element of his strategy was to elicit full answers from her, to get her to reason through her replies, as much as that was possible with Leslie.

"What does the word *force* mean to you, Leslie?" he began.

"When somebody does something without—of—of your will."

"Explain how somebody would do that against your will."

"If, like, if somebody sticks a broomstick up you."

"And how does somebody force you?" he asked.

"They make—they make you do—." She stopped and pulled at her bottom lip. "I mean, not make you do it, but they do it to you and—."

"Do you want to do it?" Laurino asked before she got swallowed up in her ambivalence.

"No," she said.

Laurino asked why she hadn't been able to define *force* when he first asked her last week. "Because I was embarrassed," she said. "Because it's a strong word."

"You concerned about anybody getting in trouble?" he asked sharply.

Before Leslie could answer, the four defense lawyers objected that it was a leading question, and Cohen sustained their objections.

Then, under further questioning by Laurino, Leslie said she had lied when she told Zegas that she had made sexual advances to Bryant Grober in Cartaret Park.

One juror was apparently disgusted over Leslie's conflicting—and con-flicted—testimony. "That's it," she muttered.

Laurino asked Leslie why she had lied.

"Because I was afraid . . . [of] hurting people."

"Who would you be hurting?" Laurino thought she might answer: the boys. But, instead, she blurted out, "You guys."

How would she hurt them? he asked.

"Not being honest."

Leslie wasn't answering Laurino's questions. She was venting her anxieties.

"Was Mr. Zegas being nice to you yesterday?" Laurino asked.

"No, he was being an airhead."

The jurors and the spectators laughed. It was a dry laugh, though. Leslie was plucking a phrase out of her experience or memory—perhaps some-thing that unkind kids had called her—and dropping it into her testimony.

It was an opportunity to demonstrate that Leslie didn't understand many of the words the defense lawyers had used in their questions. So Laurino gave her what amounted to a vocabulary test.

Intercourse?

"It's sex—it's like—like how you make babies," she answered.

What is sex? he asked.

"That's when two people who get together and they do it when they're married and not when they're—they do it when they're married and not when not married, and they have *passionate* love."

He asked her to define another word: pressuring.

"Pressuring," she answered, just as she would in a classroom. "When somebody pressures you to do anything against your will."

"Did I ever pressure you to do anything against your will?"

"No, no," she said.

"And how about Sheila?"

"No, of course she wouldn't do that."

Continuing his strategy of posing questions out of sequence, Laurino asked her, What happened with the stick she found in Cartaret Park?

"Richie is the one that stuck it up me."

In the basement, Laurino asked, why was she kneeling on the floor when she was having oral sex with Grober?

"Because he forced it on me. . . . I got on the floor when I was down on my knees doing it."

He asked why she thought it was a "hard question" when Ford had asked her whether anyone threatened her in the basement.

"Because he was holding my head. . . . Bryant when he was doing—when I was giving him a blow job—holding me down."

"Did anybody tell you to spread your legs open when you were in the basement?"

"Well, that was Chris and that was Richie—"

"Do you remember anyone else?"

"No."

In a conference at the bench, Zegas voiced his suspicion that she had been coached by the prosecutors: "If they did not meet with her directly, then they did it through her sister. . . . I cannot accept that the prosecutor is relying upon Leslie Faber's memory to suddenly change every single answer she's given on cross-examination."

Cohen appeared incensed by Zegas's allegations. "If you're going to make those kind of accusations, you better have something more to back it up. . . . You're accusing these prosecutors of something that goes beyond the grossly unethical—it verges on the criminal."

After the lunch recess Laurino said: "Les, yesterday . . . you said that Bryant Grober was a sweetheart."

"He wasn't a sweetheart," she responded.

Laurino pushed harder: So why did she say it in the first place.

Leslie pressed her knuckles into her cheeks. "Because, um, I thought so, I thought he was, and then he's not because he never cared about me."

Once again: So why did she call him a sweetheart?

"Because—'cause ever since this situation he's never done anything to me except make fun of me."

Judge Cohen tried: "Do you know why you said that yesterday, Leslie?"

She bit her lip. She thought. "Yesterday I was feeling bad," she told the judge.

Laurino asked, "What were you feeling bad about?"

She wiped tears from her eyes. She rubbed her head. She looked down at her lap. "I was feeling bad from—what did I do," she began. "I was concerned that—." She just couldn't say the words Laurino wanted to hear. "This is a hard question," she said.

Cohen asked: "Do you know the answer to it?"

"No," she said.

Leslie wouldn't say that she had lied to protect the defendants.

Laurino went back to the subject of the defendants' presence in the courtroom. "Has it been difficult for you to testify with the boys sitting here?" All the defendants stared at her, as they had ever since she first took the stand. But Archer was the most intent.

"It's hard to say this." She rested her head on her arms. "Some—I'm having a hard time. To some extent, yes."

What made it difficult?

"They're too close," she said, crying. "I get nervous up here, I guess." Leslie said she was nervous about "hurting people."

Who would she be hurting?

"You," she said to Bob Laurino. Then she changed to: "I would."

Why would she be hurt by telling what happened?

"By not telling everybody how I really feel."

"And how do you really feel, Les?"

"Confused."

"Why are you confused, Les?"

She looked over to where Miller-Hall and Goldberg were sitting. Then she looked at the four faces of the defendants. "Because—here's one side, and here's the other side, and it's hard to choose between one side to another."

Leslie's loyalties were still divided.

Time passing. Leslie's voice becoming fainter and fainter. Laurino had to move quickly. He reminded Leslie that Ford had asked her whether she sustained any injuries from the bat and broomstick. "Okay, Les, the next day did you have any pain, any marks or scratches or any blood?"

"*I had blood*," she said. It was what she had reportedly told her minister over the weekend, but Laurino could never be sure what her answer in court would be.

"Where was the blood, Leslie?"

"When I went to the bathroom," she said, squinting to hold back her tears.

"And, Leslie, why didn't you tell us last week when I asked you that?"

Leslie threw her head back. "Because I was embarrassed . . . saying that in front of all these people."

Laurino pointed to Louis Esposito and said, "He didn't have any questions to ask—he wished you a Merry Christmas. Les, are you concerned with it being Christmas time . . . and the trial is going on?"

"Yes, yes," Leslie said.

"Could you tell us why you're concerned, Les?"

Leslie said: "My concern is that everybody should be out shopping . . . and not being here."

Laurino shook his head. "Nothing further," he told the judge. "Thank you very much," he told Leslie.

The defense attorneys said they had no more questions to ask Leslie Faber. At 2:05 P.M. on Wednesday, December 16, 1992, Leslie stepped down and left the courtroom through the door adjoining the judge's chambers. The jurors and the defendants and the lawyers watched her go. At last, she could return to her life, whatever remained of it, in Glen Ridge.

The prosecution had succeeded to the extent that Leslie said she had lied to the defense lawyers. In her last day on the stand, she said that she had seen blood in her urine, that she had been forced to the floor by Bryant Grober during oral sex, and that force had been used when the bat and broomstick were put into her body. Was that enough to counterbalance her testimony under cross-examination—when she professed her affection and love for the defendants?

The defense lawyers were less jubilant than they had been before; Laurino was less glum, although he was still disappointed that Leslie hadn't said she was lying to prevent the defendants from doing jail time.

In the end, maybe the conflicting testimony didn't matter that much to the jury. Maybe what mattered most was *how* Leslie had responded to the questions. She had demonstrated that if you struck the right tone, you could ask Leslie Faber almost anything and she would try to comply. Many of those who watched her testify came to the same conclusion: She just didn't know how to say "no."

67

Unsure whether Leslie's testimony spoke for itself, the prosecution called other witnesses to bolster its argument that she was unable to give consent to sexual acts. One of these was Dr. Gerald Meyerhoff, a former chief of child psychiatry at a New Jersey hospital. He said Leslie became "more and more bewildered" as time passed in the basement. "She didn't grasp she could refuse to participate," he testified.

Meyerhoff recalled that he had asked Leslie during his two interviews with her whether she took pleasure from sexual experiences. "She didn't seem to understand. I had a feeling she was quite asexual," he said. "She engaged in sexual activity without gratification or great joy or considerable pleasure."

Referring to Querques's opening statement, Goldberg asked the psychiatrist whether he thought Leslie Faber resembled Vladimir Nabokov's fictional "Lolita."

"Lolita was an eleven-, twelve-, thirteen-year-old girl, a quite brilliant, attractive, clever girl who was able to think about sex in a conniving way," he replied. "She was the very opposite of what this young woman looked like. And this young woman was certainly not the type of wonderchild who was interested in exotic, intellectual variations of sexuality."

Cross-examining the psychiatrist, Querques established that he was not the author of the theory that "once she [Leslie] developed breasts, she was magnetized to boys and they to her." Meyerhoff testified that that insight was contained in one of his own reports about Leslie. It was one more demonstration of how Leslie's words, uttered in trusting innocence three years before, were interpreted by an expert and were used later to bludgeon her reputation in the courtroom.

The defense lawyers hoped the jurors would be alienated by Meyerhoff's consulting fees—$2,000 for a day on the witness stand—and his officious manner. At least one juror seemed to share their mistrust of the psychiatrist. She rolled her eyes and laughed audibly when the defense lawyers made sarcastic remarks about the psychiatrist. Putting her hand up to her mouth, she would whisper to the jurors on either side; often, they would swivel their chairs away from her. The judge, of course, had instructed the jurors not to discuss the case.

In fact, she was but one of a number of jurors who had exhibited unusual behavior for some time. Others had the habit of nodding off after lunch. A few jurors broke out in laughter during the most somber testimony by key witnesses, including Leslie. It wasn't surprising that their attention wandered. When the jurors had been selected, the judge had estimated the length of the trial at six to eight weeks. By now, the jury had been sitting nearly two and a half months, with the end not yet in sight. The jobs of some jurors were in jeopardy because of their prolonged absence. There were family illnesses and child-care problems. The trial was taking a big chunk out of their lives.

On December 23 Judge Cohen recessed the trial for the holidays. It would resume in eleven days, on January 4, 1993. At least the jurors could celebrate Christmas without thinking about rape.

Margaret Savage, Leslie's former swimming instructor, was one of the last prosecution witnesses. She recalled Leslie's asking her "How do I say 'no' if this happens again?" It was one of the defining moments in the trial. Savage's testimony clearly supported the prosecution's argument that Leslie didn't know how to reject sexual demands.

The way she looked and the way she testified made Savage a compelling witness. She was a young, attractive woman with red hair that framed her pale, freckled face. She spoke plainly and earnestly. Although she had told her story before to police and to the grand jury, her voice was choked with emotion as she answered Goldberg's questions.

The defense attorneys didn't want to waste a second getting Savage off the stand. Zegas and Esposito both frowned when Ford got up to cross-examine her. The message must have got through to him. He took less than fifteen minutes, something of a record for him. The other three attorneys passed.

Zegas later recalled that Bryant Grober said to him after Savage stepped down, "She hurt us, didn't she?"

Another witness, Ann Burgess, was a psychiatric nurse whose research in the 1970s developed the concept of "rape trauma syndrome." Burgess, a professor of psychiatric nursing at the University of Pennsylvania, was a middle-aged woman with a kindly face and a soft voice. She wore a conservative blue suit and a white blouse and frequently polished her glasses when she answered questions. She explained the psychological and emotional aftereffects of rape patiently, in plain language. She appeared motherly.

She said that victims she had treated often blamed themselves for being sexually assaulted. Also, youngsters were reluctant to disclose what happened to them when "they are told not to tell. They fear retaliation," Burgess testified, and it wasn't an unreasonable fear when victims were warned that "something was going to happen to them or to their family" if they didn't keep the rape secret. She noted that the friends and relatives of abusers often visited victims and urged them to keep the rape a secret. "That's one of the reasons you get a recantation," she said.

Answering a question by Judge Cohen, she said that Leslie's delay in reporting what happened and changes she made in her description of the activities in the basement were consistent with the conduct of someone suffering from the trauma of rape.

But Burgess did more than talk. She showed. What she showed were drawings made by Leslie in October 1989, when she was eighteen. Burgess said it was standard practice for her to ask rape victims to draw pictures during psychological evaluations. They could be useful when the victim was young or impaired. Burgess asked Leslie to draw a picture of herself as she appeared when she was younger, a picture of herself today, a picture of her family, and a picture or series of pictures depicting the alleged sexual assault.

The drawings were made on plain paper with colored pencils or markers. Burgess said she was silent while Leslie drew the pictures. After each drawing was completed, the psychiatric nurse asked Leslie to tell her what the people in the picture were "thinking, feeling, and doing."

In the courtroom the drawings were displayed on two twenty-four-inch monitors. One of Leslie's drawings showed her when she was five years old. Watching the monitors, the jurors saw a picture of a little girl at the top of the page. The girl is wearing a dress, and her arms are spread wide. She is smiling, and her thick dark hair seems to be flying in the wind. Leslie told Burgess that the little girl "wants to have friends. She is happy and she is playing with her friends."

Burgess compared that "clearly female" portrait with the next drawing in the series: Leslie at the age of eighteen, after the alleged rape. In this picture a slender, small, sticklike figure has short spiky hair and wears a dull green outfit. There is little in the drawing to suggest that the figure is that of a female. Her clothes cover her body from her shoes to her chin. The psychiatric nurse said that Leslie told her that the girl in the picture is thinking "how life turns around in different places."

Another drawing was supposed to be a family scene. Leslie drew a table set with plates and silverware. At each end is a stick figure with the letters *M* and *D* over their heads to denote her mother and father; Leslie is absent from the picture. When Burgess asked Leslie what her parents were thinking about, she said, "They're thinking about me and how many problems I had all these years and how I get myself into these things."

The next picture was the first in a sequence of five that depicted the sexual activities. The first drawing showed an act of fellatio between her and a boy, who are positioned side by side on a couch. Six human figures are shown in front of the couch, and four others are watching from a flight of steps. The boy's penis is exposed, and lines are drawn from the girl's head to the penis. The boy appears to be smiling. The girl's face has no features, except for a dot that suggests her mouth.

Just before the day's testimony ended, Laurino asked the witness, "Did she say what she depicted in the drawing was fun?" Burgess's answer sliced through the defense lawyers' objections. "No, she did not," Burgess said.

The next morning the witness showed the four other pictures in the basement sequence. The first depicted a boy holding a long object that is being inserted into the body of a female lying on a couch. Leslie told Burgess that the picture showed "either Chris or Kevin with the bat." The end of the bat that is being inserted and the stomach and vaginal area of the female are completely shaded in thick black strokes. The male figure appears to be smiling slightly. The mouth of the female is downturned. The arms and legs of the female are not shown. This, Burgess said, showed the woman to be in a "helpless state." The dark shading where the bat is being inserted suggests "intensity," the psychiatric nurse said. Five stick figures are shown standing at the back and five at the front of the couch. Next to one group of five figures Leslie had written: "LEAVE."

As that picture disappeared from the monitor screen, the four defendants did not display a flicker of emotion. The third drawing in the sequence showed a figure prone on the couch, arms spread. Her trunk is rendered as one single line. A male is standing at the end of the couch, holding a long object aimed at the woman's body. At the end of the object, depicted in thick black strokes, are the bristles of the broomstick, Leslie told Burgess. The male holding the broom is Kevin, Leslie said. Four figures are watching the insertion of the broom.

The fourth sketch in the basement series showed a male holding a thick, dark object pointed toward the woman's vagina. Three boys are watching. Burgess noted that there are no features on the woman's face. "In her mind she [Leslie] is faceless and is not appearing as a person," Burgess said. The witness testified that Leslie identified the male as Richard Corcoran. Leslie said the drawing showed him "inserting a thick stick," according to the witness.

The fifth and last drawing in the sequence consisted of two scenes. One showed two males with a line drawn from their faces to a woman's exposed breasts. Leslie told Burgess that this drawing represented two boys sucking her breasts. The female figure does not have arms. The second sketch, drawn on the same sheet of paper, depicted a female touching the penis of a male figure, Leslie told Burgess.

The entire sequence, Burgess said, showed Leslie "deteriorating" and reflected her heightened "distress." She testified that Leslie's plummeting self-esteem could be seen in her sketches of herself, in which she appears as an anonymous and virtually featureless figure.

From these drawings Burgess concluded that Leslie exhibited symptoms of rape trauma syndrome.

Leslie's last picture for the psychiatric nurse could depict any subject. She drew a picture of herself and Burgess. Both figures are animated and are clearly feminine, and they contrast sharply with the earlier androgynous self-portraits. Under one of the figures she wrote: Les. Under the other one: Dr. Ann B. Pointing to her drawing of Burgess, Leslie had said: "This is you who always loves kids." Pointing to the picture of herself, Leslie had said to Burgess: "This is me talking about my problems in Glen Ridge."

Copies of Leslie's drawings were displayed soon afterward in a Manhattan art gallery. They were reportedly provided to the gallery, exhibiting "feminist" art, by a member of a women's advocacy organization. No one had asked Leslie for permission to exhibit the drawings of her being raped with a bat and a broomstick.

68

When Professor Burgess ended her testimony on Tuesday morning, January 12, it was also the end of the twelfth week of the trial. Ann Burgess was the state's twenty-fourth witness—and its last.

The defense spent the next day, Wednesday, January 13, arguing that all the charges against the defendants should be dismissed by the judge; Cohen denied the defense's motion. Then, suddenly, on Thursday, January 14, he halted the proceedings. All day he questioned individual jurors. He spent more than an hour with one woman juror, Avis Thomas. She was the jury member who sometimes whispered to other jurors while witnesses testified, and had expressed skepticism about Leslie's testimony and the answers of the state's experts.

Another juror closely questioned by the judge was Ronald Simpson, a corrections officer assigned to the Essex County jail. After these meetings Cohen disclosed that he had learned that Simpson, who aspired to become a minister, had led prayer meetings in the jury room almost from the beginning of the trial on October 14. The judge said most of the prayers were sympathetic toward Leslie Faber, but when some jurors complained, Simpson included the defendants in the prayers.

Cohen also said that Simpson told jurors that he was "sick and tired of women being raped and having their whole histories exposed in court." According to the judge, Simpson reportedly said to his fellow jurors, "Soon these boys will be close to me," an apparent allusion to the fact that he worked in the county jail.

Meanwhile, Cohen said that he had learned that Avis Thomas had expressed a "general disbelief" in the opinions of psychiatrists and psychologists called as expert witnesses by the prosecution. Thomas's views about therapists were shaped by her belief that her son had been misdiagnosed by a school psychologist, the judge said.

Cohen dismissed the two jurors, although he said that for the most part Simpson's "prayers have not been inappropriate." With their departure, twelve jurors and one alternate remained. If more problems developed in the jury room, the judge could wind up without enough jurors to reach a verdict.

69

Now it was time for the defense to present its star witness: Paul Archer. The story of one brother managing the fate of the other should have commanded the attention of all the journalists attending the trial. But it was very difficult for them to keep their minds on that story. The defense lawyers were too distracting. As the trial drew toward a conclusion, it appeared that the case had become as much a cause for the lawyers as it was for the families and the feminists.

Here was Michael Querques, outside the courtroom, during a break in the arguments just before the prosecution rested. "This girl is a pig," he said about Leslie. "She's just a plain pig. If she wasn't retarded, everybody'd say, She's a pig. She's somebody I'd keep my kids away from. I'd make sure I protected them from *her.*"

And here was Michael Querques in the courtroom, cross-examining the psychiatrist Gerald Meyerhoff. The lawyer leaned back in his chair at the defense table and clasped his hands behind his head. He uncrossed his legs and spread them. During a recess in the testimony, Querques explained to the author what he was doing: "I wanted to show the jury what Leslie was like when the baseball bat and broomstick was used." Querques grinned. "I just wanted to open my legs to show the jurors how she was enjoying it."

One New York columnist said that some of the defense lawyers were using the courthouse corridors as their "own makeshift locker" in which they railed against women who were sympathetic to Leslie. In her column in the *New York Daily News*, Amy Pagnozzi said that some of the lawyers described the two NOW representatives as "The Twin C—s." After the column appeared, Zegas, who had not made such remarks, came up to reporters and said pointedly, "My wife is a member of NOW."

Among Tom Ford's favorite subjects were the members of women's advocacy groups. One morning, before the judge came into the courtroom, Ford saw a reporter talking to the NOW representatives. He waited until they finished; then he grasped the reporter's arm and said, "So what are the two bitches saying now? These cunts never shut up."

But it wasn't only the comments in the corridor that attracted attention. What happened inside the courtroom also generated a lot of discussion. Even the relatively reserved Zegas impressed some as overzealous in his take-no-prisoners cross-examination of Ros Faber and in his speculation about the "dysfunctional" Faber family. Only Kyle's lawyer, Louis Esposito, who adopted a kinder, gentler defense in the courtroom, displayed a measure of ironic detachment during the courtroom proceedings and in his informal comments.

But the world outside didn't always see the issues as the more vociferous lawyers did. For some teenagers especially, the prime issue was unequal and unjust treatment of female adolescents. Already, young women in these Jersey suburbs, catalyzed by Leslie's experience and organized by NOW, were petitioning their schools for a new code governing how they were being treated by their male classmates and by male faculty members. Already, other cases that alleged sexual harassment by male students against female high school students were working their way through the federal courts toward judgment by the U.S. Supreme Court.

Leslie's rights versus the well-being of a group of decent, good people— the defendants and their supporters. For these lawyers the scales didn't balance. Go out and ruin everything these three lovely families had struggled to build, families like their own, and for what? For Leslie Faber?

But the lawyers weren't alone. The grief and anger they saw every day on the faces of the defendants' families and friends affected the judge also. When Judge Cohen took his seat and looked down to his left, he saw a familiar, comforting tableau of suburban life: There was the Scherzer twins' sister-in-law, already visibly pregnant; there was Linda Grober, Bryant's older sister, whose pregnancy was not yet visible, and her doting, protective husband; there was Kyle's girlfriend, slender, blond, not yet twenty years old, her eyes never leaving him; and there, next to Doug and Michaele Archer, was the Archers' spiritual adviser, Reverend William S. Gannon, minister of Christ Episcopal Church in Glen Ridge. He was wearing his cleric's collar. God and motherhood were arrayed on the defendants' side.

Seated behind the parents were the pumped-up athletes who were friends of the defendants and their younger brothers. And more: grandparents, parents, teenagers, friends, ministers. Breathe deeply and you could imagine the smell of fresh-cut grass and backyard barbecues in the courtroom. Judge Cohen—who lived in Maplewood, an attractive upper-middle-class New Jersey suburb, who drove a red convertible sports car, who had a son who wrestled in school—recognized these faces. They looked like the faces he had spent much of his life with. Hardworking, churchgoing people. People who sent their kids to the Little League, who belonged to the Civic Association.

And what did he see when he looked to the right? He saw strangers, outsiders—the tiny rabble of reporters and feminists. Even the people you thought would attend the trial to show their concern for Leslie were usually absent—notably, advocates for the mentally retarded. Many of them were concerned that a guilty verdict might send the wrong message—that all retarded citizens are incapable of consenting to sex. Such a message could further isolate and stigmatize these citizens. (The jury *could* decide that Leslie was temporarily incapable of consenting because of the situation she found herself in, suggesting that in unpressured circumstances a person at her stage of mental development did have the capacity to give consent to sex. That would be the most reassuring judgment for those who fought for acceptance of retarded people by the mainstream population.)

The only Glen Ridge resident to sit regularly on this side of the courtroom was Cherry Provost, whose son had been a witness for the prosecution. She was the only one from the whole town whose frequent presence in the courtroom reminded the judge of the wrongs Leslie had suffered. A woman who never stopped saying, "Leslie Faber was raped." From the judge's vantage point, she represented a minuscule, anomalous minority in the courtroom.

70

Paul Archer's moment. The defense lawyers made him the centerpiece of their case. They did not call any experts to refute the contention that Leslie was "mentally defective." While they had hired experts, many observers speculated that they did not use them as witnesses because their conclusions might not stand up to the prosecution's cross-examination. That left them with the witness whose soft, sad eyes could melt a cheerleader's—or maybe a juror's—heart at thirty feet. Paul Warren Archer II, everybody's son, everybody's sweetheart.

Paul wore what had become his standard-issue outfit for court appearances: blue blazer, rep tie, khakis; Doug wore his gray businessman's suit; and Michaele wore a green-and-pink blouse, gold necklace, and long skirt.

Tom Ford had disagreed with his colleagues' decision to call Paul. After reading Archer's statement to the prosecutors seven months earlier, Ford argued that even if Paul described March 1, 1989, in the light most favorable to the defense, his testimony about the bat and broom couldn't help Chris—and might hurt. But the other lawyers contended that Paul's slant could favorably influence the jury. "Leslie Faber was their eyewitness and Paul Archer was our eyewitness," Esposito said later. "We wanted to demonstrate we weren't afraid to call an eyewitness."

Technically, Archer was Alan Zegas's witness. (Ford had rested his case right after the prosecution was done.) The other three defense lawyers were permitted to "cross-examine" Paul. Hands clasped in front of him, Paul Archer spoke softly, deliberately. He introduced himself as a twenty-one-year-old college senior who had been seventeen in March 1989, a year older than Chris. After school on March 1, he had gone to lift weights with his friend Peter Quigley, he said, and then he and Peter went to Cartaret Park, where they were joined by Bryant and Chris and their other friends. Zegas asked whether Bryant had been a consistent member of this group of guys. Archer said he hadn't seen Bryant at Cartaret when he was growing up and that "Bry" lived "two miles" from the park.

Paul said he was ten feet away when Leslie started speaking to Bryant. "She said things like 'Bryant Grober, you're really hot, you're really sexy, I like your bod.'" Archer uttered these suggestive remarks in such a toneless voice that they seemed expurgated.

He said Leslie reached for Grober's crotch and said, "Nice package," which "startled" and "shocked" Bryant. Archer said he heard Leslie tell Bryant, "I'd like to give you a blow job."

"Were you surprised by how Leslie Faber was talking to Bryant Grober?" Zegas asked.

"Not at all," Paul said, smoothing his tie, looking down at his hands.

"Did you ever hear Leslie Faber say 'no' to sex?" Zegas asked.

Archer nodded "yes" and offered: "In front of the high school. She was asked to perform a sexual act. She said, 'No.'"

In the Scherzers' house, Paul said, he saw Leslie Faber's mouth on Bryant Grober's penis.

"Did you observe Bryant Grober forcing Leslie Faber?" Zegas asked.

"No—no force at all," Archer said quickly.

He said Bryant was leaning back on the couch with a "straight face—no expression at all." Paul told Zegas that Kevin and Chris were saying, "Bry, why are you doing this? You're crazy!" Archer didn't raise his voice. As the oral sex continued, Paul went on, "Bry put his hand on her shoulder. There was no pressure at all."

After a while, Paul testified, "Bry was resting his hand on her head." Again, he said, no force was applied. When Grober heard the two boys ridiculing him, Archer said, he "became real embarrassed, a look of shame, and pulled up his pants." Grober left the couch and sat down next to Paul, the witness said.

Zegas went on to the rest of the activities in the basement.

Paul said that Leslie sprawled on the couch and "started bragging, 'Look, guys, how many fingers I can put in myself.' She then asked for a beer bottle. Kyle said, 'No.' Kevin turned around and said, 'How about a broomstick?'"

Archer said Kevin handed her the broomstick, and she inserted it into her vagina for "about twenty seconds." Archer testified that Leslie said, "It feels so good, it feels just like a cock." Toneless. It could have been algebra.

Paul said Kevin then handed the broom bristles to Chris, and Leslie continued to "move the broom in and out." It was the first time Paul had mentioned what Chris was doing in the basement.

Next, Leslie asked "for something bigger and Kevin got her a baseball bat," Paul said. "Kyle said to make sure she didn't get hurt." This was Kyle's most important defense, but Zegas didn't dwell on it.

Paul glanced over at his brother as he described Chris's activities. Chris looked back at him. Paul said that as Chris held the handle, Leslie tried to insert the barrel end of the "fungo" bat into her vagina for a "few seconds." "She tried to put it in," he continued. "It didn't work. She was trying to maneuver it."

At the same time, Archer said, Leslie was "looking down at the bat" and "moaning, 'It feels so good. It feels just like a cock.' " Archer had attributed exactly those same words to Leslie in her separate reactions to both the bat and the broomstick.

After Leslie pulled on her pants, Archer testified, she asked him, " 'Don't you like my breasts?' I said, 'No.' She asked me to touch her breasts. I said, 'No.' "

Zegas asked Archer about Leslie's "throwing" stick that she found in the park. Archer said he was "positive" there was no stick in the basement.

Archer told Bryant's lawyer that Leslie was "voluntarily doing everything." Now came the signature line, the headline maker, of Paul's first day of testimony. "*She was totally in control,*" the college senior said. "*She made all the advances. She was the one who did the propositioning. She was the one doing everything. It was all her idea.*"

Three weeks after the encounter in the basement, Archer said, he and Chris were "called" to the Glen Ridge police station. They were accompanied by their mother. "I was scared to death," Archer said; now his words were alive with feeling for one of the few times during his testimony. "I'd never been in a police station." He said he was questioned by Lieutenant Corcoran, "the father of a good friend of mine."

The judge recessed the trial for fifteen minutes before Tom Ford, Chris's lawyer, began. As Paul walked out of the courtroom, his dad's warm smile followed him into the hallway.

Under Ford's questioning, Paul denied that the Jocks had set up chairs before Leslie arrived, as she had testified when she compared the scene in the basement to a movie theater. "Absolutely not," Paul insisted. "There were no chairs."

Ford eased up to the radioactive subject of Chris Archer. Paul said he didn't see anybody walking with Leslie to the Scherzers' house—and he certainly didn't see his brother Chris doing that.

"Did you see any of the four defendants . . . use any threats or force against Leslie Faber?" Ford asked.

"No, none at all," Paul said, his voice rising. "She was fine. She asked us to come back a second day and do it again. She enjoyed it, she said she enjoyed it."

Now the defense lawyer wanted a demonstration from Paul. He went over to the cardboard box containing the broom. Handing it to Paul, Ford asked him to show how Leslie was holding the broom. He stood up and held the broom handle about two inches from the handle end. Paul said that Kevin was holding the broom by its bristles and "she was moving it back and forth."

"Nothing moved from the bristle end?" Ford asked.

"No," Archer said, but added that the end of the broom handle "looked like it was penetrating."

"[Then] Kevin handed it to Chris," Paul said. Chris stared at his brother from the defense table. Bryant Grober put his head in his hands.

Paul Archer said Chris and Kevin each held the broom for a minute. "Then Kevin got the baseball bat," he said.

Ford asked Archer about what he had told Lieutenant Corcoran in the Glen Ridge police station about the bat. "I told him it was a lot smaller than it actually was," Paul admitted. "I told him it was the actual size of a miniature bat they hand out at baseball games—about twelve inches long."

Finally, Judge Cohen asked Archer if he had given an accurate description to Lieutenant Corcoran. "No, I was not being accurate," Archer conceded.

The defense attorney asked about Thursday, June 25, 1992, the day Paul Archer appeared in court to seal his deal with the prosecutors to plea to a misdemeanor and enter the pretrial program. Archer said he knew he was pleading guilty to a much less serious charge than he had faced after he was indicted. In court that day, he said, "my ultimate goal was to enter [the] program."

Ford did not actually ask him what he had said in court on June 25. But at the prosecutors' table, Laurino remembered every word—that Paul had said Chris and Kevin had put the objects into Leslie. It was likely that Paul Archer would be reminded of those words during the prosecutor's cross-examination.

After Archer stepped down at the end of the day, Goldberg was asked whether he was already planning his cross-examination of Archer even though two more defense lawyers had yet to question him. The prosecutor laughed. "This is what I went to law school for," he said.

Michael Querques paused. He let the silence stretch. Archer crossed his legs on the witness stand. Slowly, Querques walked behind where the defendants were sitting. He put his hand on Grober's head. "You like them, don't you?" he asked Paul.

He put his hand on Chris's head. "You know him," he said. "He's your flesh and blood."

He came to Kyle. "A friend of yours, isn't he?"

Paul nodded. His blank expression started to crumble. He looked as though he could cry—if that weren't such an unmanly thing to do. The lawyer came to Kevin. He grabbed a handful of Kevin's hair and yanked his head back.

Querques shook his own head sadly. "Tell us what Leslie was uttering when she was moving the broomstick."

Paul repeated what he had told the two other defense lawyers. "'I feel so good.' She was moaning with pleasure."

Querques wagged his finger at Paul. "I want you to imitate her," he said. "Don't be bashful."

Paul squirmed in his chair, but he gave it a try. "Oh, oh," he moaned. There was no passion in his voice.

At Querques's request, Paul held the bristles of the broomstick to show how Kevin and Chris had held it. "Your friend Kevin over there"— Querques pointed across the room. "What did he do?"

"He held on to the opposite end of the broom," Paul answered.

Would Archer say that Kevin was assisting her? the lawyer asked. Some of the defense lawyers in the case, usually unabashed admirers of Querques, asked themselves: Had he gone one question too far?

Paul Archer answered the lawyer's question. "Yes, he did."

Would he say Kevin had pushed it in her vagina to assist her? Querques asked. That may have been two questions too many. "Yes," Archer said.

Quickly, the lawyer tried to recover: After she inserted it or before?

"Yes, after she inserted it," Paul replied.

Archer's testimony, under Querques's questioning, contradicted his testimony of two days before, when he said that Kevin had only held the broom and not pushed it in.

Querques asked Paul whether he had told the judge, when he was entering the community service program back in June, that he had seen his brother, Chris, and Kevin "put" the broomstick into Leslie's vagina.

"Yes, I did," Paul said. "I mistakenly told the judge they inserted the broomstick. . . . I was nervous."

Querques asked Archer to demonstrate how Leslie looked when the bat and broom were inside her.

Archer's face turned white. He waited a minute, and then he sprawled back in the chair, raised his legs, and leaned his head forward. Up to then,

Leslie had said that her head was flat on the couch when the objects were inserted. The NOW representatives and other women attending the trial often pointed out that it was anatomically impossible for Leslie to have inserted the objects by herself—she couldn't reach the broomstick and bat while lying flat. But Paul's imitation put Leslie into a new head-raised position—setting off a skeptical buzz among many of the women in the courtroom.

Querques asked him what he knew about Leslie's mental development. Archer said she was "slow," but he said he hadn't ever seriously discussed her impairment.

"She was just another kid that you accepted?" Querques asked.

"Correct," he said.

In the basement, the lawyer asked, "did you ever see her on any occasion more pleased . . . happier?"

"It was normal for her," Paul said, not quite answering the question.

When it was Esposito's turn, he couldn't discuss Kyle's concern for Leslie's safety without highlighting what the other defendants did. All he asked was "So what you said today, as it affects Kyle, is it the truth?"

Paul said, "Yes."

In the break before Glenn Goldberg began his cross-examination, some of the defense lawyers assessed Paul Archer's testimony. Esposito said that Querques was "stunned" when Paul acknowledged that Kevin helped Leslie to insert the broomstick. Zegas said he was "appalled" by some of the questions posed to Archer and his responses. He feared that Paul's testimony about Leslie's eagerness to return to the basement for a second go-round would leave an opening for the prosecution. The prosecution could ask Paul why the group of Jocks—a group that included his own client, the ostensibly abashed and embarrassed Bryant Grober—had gathered at Cartaret Park the next day. But the prosecution had already decided not to discuss the activities on the second day for fear that the jury might interpret Leslie's rejection of the Jocks' second invitation as a sign that she was capable of saying "no" to sexual advances.

Goldberg began his cross-examination at a deliberate pace. It had lasted less than an hour when the judge recessed the trial for the weekend, ending the fourteenth week of testimony. The newspaper stories the next day were not about Goldberg's cross-examination. They were about Paul Archer's testimony that Kevin Scherzer had pushed a broomstick into Leslie's vagina.

When Goldberg resumed his cross-examination, his goal was to destroy Archer's credibility. First, the prosecutor noted the times Paul Archer had lied to Lieutenant Corcoran in the Glen Ridge police station. Archer said he was nervous when Corcoran had questioned him because he hadn't been in a police station before. But then Goldberg showed him an arrest report from June 5, 1987, when he had been picked up for buying beer from Richie Corcoran at the Grand Union store. Yes, Archer said, he was in the police station then—but it was a different kind of situation.

Archer had testified that he had never received a *Miranda* warning in his life before Corcoran questioned him on April 11, 1989. Then Goldberg showed him the arrest report from when he and other Jocks were charged with keeping alcoholic beverages in their car. The box on the form headed "*Miranda* Warning" was checked.

Another lie: Archer told the police lieutenant that Leslie had touched several of the Jocks in the park. No, that wasn't true, Paul conceded. She had touched only Bryant Grober, he said.

One more lie: Archer had said to Corcoran that he didn't know how the activities in the basement started. But he admitted to Goldberg that he had seen the oral sex between Bryant and Leslie.

Goldberg turned his back to Archer. He reached into a paper bag and pulled out two miniature bats, one twelve inches long and the other eighteen inches. "This is what you had in mind when you were lying?" he asked.

"Yes," Archer murmured.

Then Goldberg raised the thirty-three-inch fungo bat above his head. "This bat is the truth, isn't it?"

Paul answered, "Yes."

And why did he lie repeatedly to Corcoran? Goldberg asked.

"I just didn't want to tell him anything," Archer answered. "I was trying to evade any involvement. I wanted to evade any involvement of my friends."

Was he telling the truth when he said to Corcoran—and testified to Zegas—that Leslie was doing everything by herself in the basement?

"No, she had help," Archer conceded.

Goldberg scratched his head. He looked puzzled, Seven months before, when Paul was copping a plea, he had said in court that Kevin and Chris in-

serted the broomstick. Now, at the trial, he said Leslie inserted the broomstick herself. Why the change? "Would it be fair to say you have a new
goal—to get your brother out of a jam . . . and to help your friends?"
Goldberg asked him.

"My goal's to tell the truth," he replied. "My only goal is to say what
happened."

Archer began his fourth and last day of testimony on Tuesday morning,
January 26. Archer said he remembered a couple of times when Leslie refused to have sex. He repeated that in 1988 half a dozen guys were hanging out outside the high school and one asked Leslie for a blow job. Leslie said "no," according to Archer, and the boys "went on about their
business."

"Tell us the names of the young men," Goldberg asked.

"I can't remember," Paul said.

"Are you the person who asked her for sex?"

"No," Paul said.

During the time in the basement, Paul recalled, Kevin went to get the
broomstick. "Leslie didn't get up and get the broom?" Goldberg asked.

"No," he said.

"Leslie didn't get up and get the bat?"

"No."

Goldberg reminded Paul that, in his statement to prosecutors that past
June, he said that Kevin and Chris had held the broom for two minutes
each. He reached into his paper bag and took out a clock, placing it where
Paul couldn't see it. Tell me when we get to two minutes, the prosecutor
said. Tick. Tick. Paul sat silently. As Chris watched his brother, Chris's
eyes widened. Paul darted a look at him. Tick. Tick. Chris jerked his head,
nodding. But Paul didn't speed up the count. He waited until it was almost
two minutes before he guessed that time was up. It seemed like forever in
the silent courtroom.

Goldberg picked up the bat and asked which end was bigger. Paul
pointed to the barrel end. "Kyle Scherzer put the plastic bag over the big,
thick, business end of the bat?" the prosecutor asked.

"Correct," said Paul.

Archer had said that he declined to touch Leslie's breasts. Goldberg
asked, referring to phrases Querques had repeated throughout the trial,
"You weren't magnetized to Leslie, to her breasts?"

"No."

Goldberg wondered why the demagnetized Archer hadn't left the basement before the broom was inserted.

"Just curious, I guess," Paul said.

After lunch, Goldberg asked why Archer had told the prosecutors that he didn't want his parents and teachers to find out what went on in the basement. "I did think it was morally wrong," he said, "because there was a girl performing sexual acts on herself and we stood around and watched." Paul had been much more contrite and self-blaming in his earlier statement to prosecutors.

"That's it?" asked Goldberg, in a disbelieving voice.

"Yes," Archer said.

By 2:30 Goldberg was finished with his cross-examination.

Tom Ford was surprisingly succinct. He wanted to give Paul another time test. The defense lawyer set the clock, and waited for Paul to tell him when two minutes had elapsed. Paul was faster when he got a second chance. He guessed two minutes when the clock showed that one minute and twenty-two seconds had passed.

Paul Archer's long-awaited appearance on the witness stand didn't end in a climactic scene, as a courtroom melodrama would in the movies. The defense couldn't transform him into the shining savior of his brother and his buddies. The prosecutor didn't wrench out of him a sobbing admission that the defendants had raped Leslie Faber. But his real-life testimony did leave the jury with a number of hard questions to answer.

Could a witness who admitted that he had lied repeatedly be believed when he said that everything that went on in the basement was Leslie's idea? Was he believable when he disavowed as "nervousness" his own statements that Chris and Kevin had inserted objects into Leslie's body? Was his head-raised, leg-splayed depiction of Leslie with the bat and broomstick credible? Was his fainthearted groaning and moaning a faithful depiction of Leslie's experience with the bat and broomstick? Would the jurors believe Paul's account of his friends as pawns in the hands of a scheming sex bomb after they had seen Leslie testify with their own eyes? Questions. That's what Paul Archer left behind when he stepped down—lots of questions. With their verdict, the jury would answer them.

The defense called three minor witnesses. Then at 1:45 P.M. on Tuesday, February 2, in the sixteenth week of the trial, Alan Zegas stood up and said, "We are calling no further witnesses. The defense rests its case."

Cohen asked the four defendants whether they had agreed to rest the case without testifying. They all said they had.

In their opening arguments, both Ford and Zegas had promised to call Peter Quigley as a witness. Zegas still wanted to call Quigley; he believed that Peter would reaffirm what Paul Archer had said about Grober. But because of what Peter had told the prosecutors back in April 1992, when he was negotiating a plea bargain, some of the other defense lawyers doubted whether Peter would be an effective witness for their clients. In his earlier statement Quigley had said that the guys arranged Leslie's torso before the bat and broom were inserted, and that Chris had held up her legs so Kevin would not be obstructed. So Peter Quigley was not called.

But is wasn't only Quigley who was among the missing. Before the trial began, the defense had listed 199 potential witnesses. These included neighbors from Glen Ridge; teachers and school officials from Maplewood, West Orange, and Glen Ridge; an assortment of Jocks and Jockettes from the Class of '89 and other classes; and even Leslie's father.

Most noticeably absent were witnesses who could testify with firsthand knowledge about Leslie's sexual behavior. For four months the defense had not missed an opportunity to portray Leslie as a slut. In court and outside, they talked of teachers who had witnessed "outrageous" behavior by Leslie; they spoke of neighborhood boys and high school athletes who had been propositioned by her. One defense lawyer privately described Leslie's sexual conduct as "pre-psychotic." They had tried to destroy her reputation with hearsay and innuendo. But where were their eyewitnesses? Where were all the guys who were supposed to have indulged her sexual appetite? Where were all those adults who supposedly observed her profligacy? Where were the educators who supposedly kicked her out of school because of sexual misconduct? The defense produced not one.

Neither did they produce witnesses who could testify to the "good character" of the four defendants. They had a reason for this. If they called character witnesses, the prosecutors could call witnesses who would testify about "bad acts" committed by the Jocks before the incident with Leslie. Investigators for the prosecution had interviewed more than 125 people who knew the defendants, knew how they had treated women, knew all about their lives as Glen Ridge's favorite Jocks. But these witnesses would never be called because the defense did all it could to avoid putting the defendants' character on trial.

On Wednesday, February 3, Judge Cohen excused the jurors early after announcing that closing arguments by the defense would begin the following Monday, February 8. All the witnesses had become memory. Soon it would be time for the jury to speak.

71

Louis Esposito, Kyle's lawyer, was the first of the defense team to deliver closing arguments. In the hard-edged accents of his native Newark, he recalled the testimony of the defense's only major witness, Paul Archer. He said Archer had testified that Leslie was the "instigator and provocateur" on March 1, 1989. Esposito recalled that Archer had said Kyle placed a plastic bag over the baseball bat "so if she was going to do it, she would not hurt herself." It was the closest that Esposito would come to repeating what Kyle told his brother in the basement: "Stop, you're hurting her."

Esposito asked the jury to remember that these were "thirteen boys, not men, not psychiatrists or psychologists—boys in the basement." He straightened a stack of twenty-three psychological and educational evaluations of Leslie and said they often conflicted with each other. "My client, Kyle Scherzer, not being a learning consultant or a psychologist, is in no better position than any of these people." His entire summation took two hours. It was in keeping with the low-profile defense he had favored throughout the trial.

Querques was next. February 9 was Michael Querques's birthday. He was sixty-four years old. He began by repeating the "Lolita," and "girls-will-be-girls" sections of his opening statement. "Did I call her a Lolita?" he asked. "Is she a nymphet, seducing old men? I was talking about a host of other women. I'm not blind and I'm not stupid." Querques wanted to correct any misconceptions about his views. On the other hand, if one holdout juror thought Leslie was Lolita—well, he'd take that, too. Nevertheless, it was an atypically defensive start for a lawyer who was always on the attack.

There was an unaccustomed air of concession when he acknowledged that what Kevin and the others did in the basement was not "a wonderful thing . . . a pretty thing." But Querques was accustomed to representing not the most attractive clients. And he was accustomed to winning by substituting "The Theory" in the place of moral conviction. He was prepared now to unveil his theory of the case. At its center was Rosalind Faber.

He argued that Ros Faber had blinded herself to her daughter's behavior. "She put her head in the sand so she wouldn't know anything." Reminding the jurors that Leslie's mother had used the phrase "ostrich syndrome" to describe how the family ignored newspaper and television accounts of the case, he said, as if he were talking directly to her, "You didn't know anything and you didn't want to know anything."

Querques scowled and said, "The one word I got sick of hearing—she's vulnerable," a reference to how Ros described Leslie. Then using the second-person pronoun as though he were talking directly to Rosalind, he said, "What did you do about her vulnerability? You didn't warn anybody. You share part of the blame."

Switching from the figurative Rosalind Faber to the real jurors, he said, "If you're going to look after Leslie Faber and protect her, ask yourself: What about the boys who came in contact with her before March 1, 1989, on March 1, 1989, and all young men *in futuro?*"

Pointing at the defendants, he said: "The bottom line is if it wasn't these boys, it would have been others."

That was Michael Querques's theory.

When the trial recessed for lunch at 1 P.M., the buzz outside the court-room was about the theory of blaming Ros Faber. It made Laurino furious. "That was low, really low," he said. "This woman taught her child at home, she got tutors and counselors and therapists for Leslie. She took her to dances with other retarded kids and she put her in a million programs, and they never missed a game she played in; and all along she tried to create as normal a life for Les as she knew how. For him to blame her—ahhh."

As the trial moved toward a climax, Doug Archer's composure started to fray. He heard Christine McGoey of NOW saying that the defendants' use of a bat and a broomstick constituted "violent acts." Until then, Archer had never confronted any of the women's rights advocates attending the trial. But now he demanded, "Why do you think that's violent? Tell me why that's violent."

McGoey tried to walk away. But Archer followed her down the corridor, saying, "One thing I just don't get about this case is that what you call violence was consensual. Everybody agreed to do it." McGoey didn't answer him.

In the courtroom Querques went on for two more hours and continued the next morning, Wednesday, February 10. "Oh, I'm excited," he yelped. And pounding his chest, he promised the jury, "I'm not letting anything happen to them [the defendants] as long as I'm alive." He expressed his excitement by clamping Grober in a headlock and pulling his hair and by pinching Chris Archer's nose. "Poor kid, he's a baby," Querques said of

Grober. "He wasn't old enough to go to war. He grew up in a sexual revolution and you want him to resist? . . . Come off it! Come alive!" One of
the jurors, a young woman, wiped tears from her eyes.

Pulling the fungo bat out of a cardboard box, he waved it at the jurors.
"I'm not afraid of it," he said. "It's supposed to meet a baseball. It's not
supposed to meet flesh. It's certainly never, never supposed to meet a
vagina. There are no two ways about it."

But he urged the jury to remember how Leslie had reacted when he had
brought Kevin up to the witness box. "She said she loved him a lot," he
said. "Isn't that good enough for you?" His voice choked as he concluded:
"I never said to you what they did was right. I have said to you what they
did was not criminal in nature. To let the exaggeration of indecent conduct
rise to the level of any degree of crime is an injustice."

In the front row, the blond young women who had come to court to offer their support to Kevin and Kyle started to cry. Querques, who called
himself "the old man," who told the jury he was going to spend tomorrow
with his granddaughter—that gentler Querques also started to cry! He
said, wiping his tears with his pocket handkerchief, that Kevin was entitled
to "common decency and fairness." His voice breaking, Querques ex-
horted: "Have the courage . . . to come out here and utter two beautiful
words: not guilty, not guilty."

Alan Zegas began his summation an hour after Querques finished his
emotional plea. In his analytical style, he described Bryant Grober's role in
the basement as a "very brief moral indiscretion." Bryant, he said, had
done something "absolutely stupid" when he had oral sex with Leslie. "It
was something he should never, never, ever [have] done. . . . [But] Bryant
Grober does not belong in this courtroom. He violated no law." As he
spoke, Dawn Scott, a twenty-six-year-old juror who lived in Glen Ridge's
neighboring community of Bloomfield, nodded her head. She was the
same woman who had wept during Querques's summation.

The next morning, Thursday, February 11, Michaele Archer returned
to the courtroom after an absence of almost two weeks. She listened as Zegas presented a theory of his own about Leslie's almost "insatiable need to
satisfy herself through sex." Zegas said one theory for the jury to consider
was that Leslie came from a "dysfunctional family."

Zegas suggested that "maybe something was going on at home that made her unhappy. . . . Maybe Leslie picked up on some resentment of her mother." No one at the trial had testified that the Fabers were "dysfunctional" and the judge had barred Zegas from discussing his theory further. But he had thrown the line out far enough for the jury to nibble on it.

Ford spoke in a monotone for more than an hour before the judge recessed the trial for four days during Lincoln's and Washington's birthdays. When Ford resumed his closing argument on Tuesday, February 16, he likened the prosecution of Chris Archer to a "legal lynching," and he said the trial resembled a Stalinist "show trial." He used the "replica" broom to sweep the floor of the courtroom, to show how the prosecution had tried to sweep the truth under the rug. None of the jurors laughed.

72

From the back row of the courtroom, Ros and Charlie Faber listened as Glenn Goldberg began to sum up for the state on February 17. This was the first time Charlie had attended the trial. They had a direct view of a quotation that the prosecutor had tacked to the bulletin board above the witness box. The quotation was attributed to Leslie by her friend Dawn Lipinski. It read: "It was a terrible thing. It hurt."

Querques, in fact, provided the spine for Goldberg's closing argument. That was the advantage in being the last lawyer to sum up his case. Responding to Querques's criticism of Ros, and Zegas's references to a "dysfunctional family," Goldberg said, "The young woman isn't on trial and her family is not on trial, either."

Querques had said that teenage boys tend to be pranksters and that their treatment of Leslie was a prank. "This was no prank," the prosecutor said. "You can't commit a prank on a young woman with a bat or a broomstick. Boys can experiment with bugs and frogs and laboratory rats, but they can't experiment with human female body parts."

Querques also had said that some girls like to see "the joy on a boy's face when he ejaculates." Goldberg swung the replica bat. He held up the broom. "A bat doesn't ejaculate and a broom doesn't ejaculate. It's not going to bring joy and pleasure to a girl's face."

Goldberg spent much of his second day of closing arguments describing Leslie's developmental limitations and the taunts she had received from the Glen Ridge boys. Why, he asked, didn't Leslie cry out or try to leave the basement? He compared her reaction to the response of the defendants when Querques slapped and pinched them. The defendants' lawyer was doing this to them in a public courtroom, Goldberg said—How could they complain? For Leslie to protest her treatment by the guys would have been a public "put-down" of her "friends." "How could she complain?" he asked. "How could she cry out or verbalize any discomfort and not lose the friendship of her friends?"

The prosecutor ridiculed Ford for saying that the prosecution had engaged in a "legal lynching" and shown "prejudice" against the defendants. "The only prejudice in this case is from those who call upon the worst of the worst that has ever been said about women to condemn the victim," Goldberg said.

The prosecutor expected that he would take a day more and then the case would go to the jury. But a juror got sick and the trial was delayed a full week. In the week that he waited for the trial to resume, an idea came to him. The idea surfaced in the courtroom as he continued to pull together the strands of the case. He began talking about the "mental imagery" used by the defense lawyers during the trial. He emphasized that Querques, in his opening remarks, said "nothing, absolutely nothing" about what Kevin did to Leslie with the bat and broom. That evoked another mental image for the prosecutor. "I see dark, empty space in the argument," he told the jurors.

Goldberg sometimes liked to spring surprises on juries. Now, without warning, there was staid, calculating, meticulous Glenn Goldberg singing.

"Hello darkness, my old friend, I've come to talk with you again because a vision softly creeping left its seeds while I was sleeping—"

Ford jumped up, fuming. "Jesus—Objection to this, I don't know what this—"

Goldberg kept singing. "And the vision that was planted in my brain, still remains—"

Cohen said: "Overruled."

And Goldberg sang on: "Still remains, within the sounds of silence."

The song he was singing was Simon and Garfunkel's 1966 hit "The Sounds of Silence." Goldberg said it was a "perfect description of the opening statements, . . . silence about what happened with the bat and the broom."

The defense lawyers called for a mistrial because they said Goldberg wasn't really talking about the opening statements, but about the silence of the defendants who had not testified. The prosecutor is not permitted to make note to the jury of defendants who choose not to testify. Judge Cohen said Goldberg was "treading close to the line." He denied the motions because the prosecutor referred specifically to the defense lawyers' opening statements, but he said he would instruct the jury that the defendants are not required to testify. Zegas said, "This is one of the most awful things I've heard any prosecutor do."

At the end of the day, Goldberg held up Leslie's drawings that depicted what she remembered of March 1, four years ago. "Some day these sheets of paper will turn yellow and the drawings will fade, but I submit to you these images will stay in her mind and memory forever," he said.

On his fifth day before the jury, the prosecutor said that Leslie was "spread-eagled in a cramped little basement and raped with sticks wrapped in garbage bags and smeared with Vaseline."

That image brought tears to the eyes of Ros Faber, and she had to leave the courtroom.

On Wednesday, March 3, Goldberg completed his closing arguments. He said that the jurors could convict the defendants of rape even if they concluded that Leslie did not actively resist their advances. "The victim does not have to say 'no,'" he said. "If she just lies there and says nothing, if she doesn't give affirmative consent, you can find them guilty."

Pounding his fist against the railing of the jury box, he told the jurors, "She paid an extraordinary price because of her extraordinary vulnerability. She can be taunted, teased, abused, poked and prodded with sticks, but she matters and her life matters, too."

Goldberg recalled that the defense lawyers had said the case was a "tragedy."

"That's true," he said. "The tragedy is that the defendants attacked Leslie Faber because they thought they could get away with it. The tragedy is that Leslie and the defendants led parallel and separate lives. They [the defendants] had plenty of friends and they were admired by their community. Leslie was retarded and had practically no friends. On March 1, 1989, their lives converged, came together on a little couch when the defendants extended themselves with pieces of wood into the alleged victim's body and their lives became inseparably joined in this American tragedy."

Goldberg's summation took fourteen hours over six days, not as long as the eighteen hours consumed by the defense lawyers. But he had spoken last, and he hoped that what he had to say would remain fresh in the jurors' minds. But there was so much on their minds: a trial that had lasted twenty-one weeks, the testimony of twenty-nine witnesses, dozens of exhibits, and the ambiguity of deciding whether a witness who never said "no" was raped.

73

The next morning Judge Cohen said that the jury was not to consider references to Leslie's sexual history "as an attack on her character or to show in any way that she was a bad or immoral person. She is not on trial here. I've tried to balance her privacy with the defendants' right to a fair trial."

However, it would be difficult for the jurors to keep all of the innuendos about Leslie's background out of their deliberations. For almost five months the defense had argued that it was Leslie's sexual experience that showed she was capable of consenting or refusing to engage in sexual acts.

Similarly, Cohen told the jurors, they were not to consider the defendants' behavior before March 1, 1989. "They are not on trial for allegedly teasing [Leslie] when she was younger. They are not on trial for doing things that were not nice or foolish or may have been immoral."

Cohen looked hard at the jury. "This is a criminal trial," he said. "This is not a morality play. You're not being asked to decide whether what any defendant did is right or wrong in a moral sense."

In legal terms, Cohen was correct: The case was about evidence and laws. But ordinary people, like the people on the jury, might not look at it in legal terms. They might think that the heart of the matter was the morality of the defendants and their friends in Glen Ridge. The jury would make a legal judgment. But no one doubted that it would be, first of all, a moral judgment.

The case went to the jury at 2:10 on the afternoon of Thursday, March 4. The jury of seven women and five men had to reach a decision on nine charges: one charge of conspiracy; four counts of aggravated sexual assault, involving the use of the bat and broom and the act of oral sex; and four counts of sexual contact, in which the defendants were charged with fondling Leslie's breasts and forcing her to masturbate them. The jurors were also given a list of fifteen lesser charges. It was possible for the jury to come up with any number of combinations for each of the four defendants.

In considering these charges, Cohen asked the jury to ponder two central questions:

Was force or coercion used against her?
Was she mentally defective, and did Kyle, Kevin, Bryant, and Chris know that or should they have known it?

Force or coercion is not a matter of subduing someone by brute strength, Judge Cohen instructed the jurors. It could be a more subtle process, he said. The jurors would have to decide whether Leslie was conned into going into the basement; whether she was vulnerable because of her psychological condition; whether the size and layout of the basement intimidated her; whether the number of boys, her previous relations with them, and what they told her before she left pressured her into submitting.

Cohen emphasized that the legal term "mental defective" does not mean that somebody is "slow" or "retarded." It means that a person cannot understand that she has a right to refuse sex or is incapable of refusing. And, again, to convict on this charge, the jury had to agree that the defendants knew or should have known she was defective.

Despite Cohen's lengthy instructions, it was clear that the concept of mental defectiveness was difficult to grasp. Less than two hours after they had retired to the jury room, the jurors asked Cohen to repeat his explanation of the term. The next day, Friday, the jury asked the judge to read back Leslie's testimony about Bryant Grober. Then the jurors scattered for the weekend.

On Monday reporters could hear raised voices in the jury room. Dawn Scott, the juror from Bloomfield who had seemed sympathetic to the defense's arguments during the trial, sent a typewritten note to the judge that she had apparently written over the weekend. In it she complained that another juror, who was a volunteer driver for retarded people, was injecting his experiences into the deliberations. The volunteer driver was supposed to have said, "Retarded children always need love and affection."

Cohen told the jurors that they should not allow what they had "learned and heard outside of this case" to influence their deliberations. At the end of the day, as the jurors filed from the courtroom, Patrick Parker, a truck driver and the juror who had volunteered to help the mentally retarded, attracted the most stares. He was wearing a T-shirt on which was printed: I HAVE VALUES.

On Friday morning, March 12, the jury asked for testimony to be read about what happened after the bat and broom were used, particularly descriptions of the defendants touching Leslie and of Leslie touching their penises. They wanted the term "aiding and abetting" defined. As the judge explained the legal definition of the term, juror Dawn Scott closed her eyes and moved her head from side to side, as if she were saying "no."

Later the sounds of people arguing could be heard through the thin wall of the courtroom. There was the sound of an object banging against something. The red light outside the jury room flashed. As a guard opened the door, a woman's voice could be heard shouting, "I want that bat out of here now."

The judge received two notes from the jurors requesting that the "replica" bat be removed from the jury room. Cohen said he would remove the bat and the broomstick and urged the jury members to be calm. "I ask you to resolve these issues in a rational manner."

At 4:30 the red light went on again. A message was sent to the judge. At that time there were about a dozen people in the courtroom. In the next five minutes every seat and every inch of standing space were filled. Ringing the courtroom were fifteen sheriff's deputies. What you saw first were the guns in their holsters. For so long, the theatricality of the attorneys had created an atmosphere of make-believe, as if this was only a Sunday-night TV "problem movie," not a real crime and a real trial. The men with the guns signaled that the make-believe was over.

Judge Cohen read a note from the jury: "We have reached a decision on five counts. We are still negotiating on four counts."

The defense lawyers looked as though they had been hit by a Joe Louis uppercut. Their first thought was that the jurors had convicted the defendants on the most serious charges—the sexual assault counts. They were convinced that the jury was still undecided on the lesser counts involving sexual contact.

By law, the judge had the discretion to order the jurors to disclose their decision and to continue deliberating on the undecided counts. If he did that, what the jury had already decided could not be changed—the verdict on the five counts would stand.

But Cohen had another option. He could ask the jury to continue deliberating until agreement had been reached on all of the charges. Fiercely, the defense lawyers argued that was what the judge should do.

Cohen left it up to the jurors. They went back to their conference room and five minutes later sent another note to the judge: "No, all at one time."

What the jurors had decided would remain secret until they agreed on all the charges.

Cohen could have kept them there into the evening; he could have sequestered them, and ordered them to continue their deliberations over the weekend. If the weather forecasts were correct, the region could be hit by a blizzard. That might force further delays. But Cohen decided to send them home until Monday.

Zegas was depressed when he drove home with Esposito. He couldn't shake the mood that had prevailed in the courthouse, that the defendants had been convicted of the most serious charges. Esposito tried to raise his spirits. "Suppose we misread this. Suppose they were acquitted on the conspiracy and on the minor charges and they're still arguing about the major ones," he said.

"Maybe you're right," Zegas said, "and maybe they'll change their minds over the weekend. But I'm thinking the worst."

The next morning the subhead on the *New York Times* story read: "Things look bleak for 4 young men in a sex-assault trial."

That captured Zegas's mood when he phoned Bryant Sunday night. "Look, I know that I'm being gloomy, but . . . I just want to prepare you for the worst, because I don't think I'd be doing my job if I didn't."

But it was Grober who tried to cheer up his lawyer. "Well, maybe they're not really thinking the way you're saying," he said. But Zegas could detect the fear in his voice, and he thought: He knows that I could be right.

On Monday morning the jurors trudged into the courtroom wearing thick sweaters, work pants, and waterproof boots. The jury deliberated quietly through the day, asking only for Leslie's testimony about what the other defendants had said while she was having oral sex with Grober.

Among those who waited was a tall, thin woman sitting alone in the front row of the courtroom, head bowed as she clasped her rosary beads. Her name was Kelly Stannick, she was nineteen years old, and she said she was Kyle's girlfriend. Her dad, she said, had given Kyle a job in his floor-finishing business. She herself worked in a tanning salon and attended college, but had taken two semesters off to attend the trial. "I know if I pray hard enough, the jury will hear my prayers," she said. When she graduated from college, Kelly said, she hoped to become a special education teacher.

74

On Tuesday the jury dressed up. All the lawyers thought a verdict was close after twelve days of deliberation. At 10:45 a muffled cheer came from the jury room, followed by a shout of "Yes!" The red light flashed. Tom Ford stuck his head into a room adjoining the courtroom where the defendants and their families had gathered. Ford mouthed the words: "A verdict."

Quietly, the families took their customary seats in the first three rows. Kelly Stannick, Kyle's girlfriend, sobbed as she sat in the front row. The defendants filed in, Kevin resting a hand on Chris's shoulder. Then he and Chris shook hands. The only person missing from the familiar faces of the trial was Michael Querques. He hadn't appeared in court for days.

Ten minutes passed before Judge Cohen entered the courtroom. In that interval the courtroom had quickly filled up: lawyers, cops, county workers, cafeteria cooks—and a dozen sheriff's deputies. The corridor outside was packed with reporters and photographers and TV camera crews from news organizations all over the country.

The judge summoned the jurors into the courtroom. As they made their way to the same seats they had occupied since October, most did not look at the defendants. Michaele Archer closed her eyes. Doug Archer glared at the jurors, then at the reporters seated across the aisle from him. Geraldine Scherzer whispered, "I can't believe this is happening." The color had been drained from the faces of Nathan and Rosemary Grober.

Cohen said to the defendants, "Please rise." Kyle, Kevin, Bryant, and Chris stood up stiffly and faced the jury. Their feet were together, their hands by their sides, backs straight, shoulders squared. They allowed no expression on their faces. They could have been Marines snapping to attention for their drill sergeant.

Cohen asked the forewoman, Judith Deskin, if the verdict was unanimous. "Yes," she said softly.

Judge Cohen read the verdicts:

Christopher Archer: *Guilty* of two counts of first-degree aggravated sexual assault with the bat and broom. One count was for assaulting a "mentally defective" woman. The other count was for using "force or coercion" in assaulting her. He was also found guilty of second-degree conspiracy.

Kevin Scherzer: The same verdict. *Guilty* of two first-degree counts of aggravated sexual assault. The jury convicted him of both the "mental defective" and "force" charges. He was also found guilty of second-degree conspiracy.

Kyle Scherzer: *Guilty* of one count of first-degree aggravated sexual assault—using "force or coercion." *Guilty* of second-degree attempted aggravated sexual assault—the "mental defective" charge. (Kyle had put the plastic bag over the bat, but he had not inserted the bat or the broomstick into Leslie's body.) *Guilty* of second-degree conspiracy.

Bryant Grober: *Acquitted* of the most serious charges of aggravated sexual assault. *Guilty* of the one charge of third-degree conspiracy to commit aggravated sexual assault and aggravated sexual contact.

As the judge repeated the word *guilty,* the defendants did not express any emotion. But their parents, seated a few feet behind them, were incapable of such discipline. Michaele Archer looked sick, her face bleached, drawn. Jack Scherzer slumped over, his head bowed almost to his knees. Even Nathan Grober, who got better news than the rest, looked distraught. His wife squeezed her eyes shut. Some of the defendants' relatives cried each time Cohen read the word *guilty.*

The jurors did not look at the four young men as the judge read the verdicts. Juror Dawn Scott cried openly.

After Cohen finished reading, Chris Archer whispered something to Kevin and laughed.

The jury had decided that Chris, Kyle, and Kevin knew or should have known that Leslie was "mentally defective" *and* that they had used force and coercion against her when the bat and broom were inserted into her body. With their verdict, the jurors had supported the two main themes of the prosecution's case. Grober was convicted of only the lesser charge of conspiracy to commit aggravated sexual assault and aggravated sexual contact. All the defendants had been acquitted of the lesser charges, which involved touching Leslie's breasts and having her touch their penises.

The jurors filed out of the courtroom for the last time. Tears streamed down Scott's face, and she had to lean on the arm of a sheriff's officer as she walked past the defendants and their families.

Laurino wanted the defendants to be jailed immediately. He told the judge that the bail of the three defendants convicted of the most serious charges should be revoked immediately. They had been allowed to go free for four years, he said, and that was enough. "What we have now are convicted rapists," he said. He said that Kyle, Kevin, and Chris faced a maximum of forty years in prison, but they had not shown that they took the charges against them seriously during the trial. "Their attitudes had ranged from boredom to arrogance," Laurino observed.

Referring to the statement given by the college student in Boston, Laurino said, "Chris Archer had been involved in a criminal assault after this case began. We don't want a predatory sex offender on the street."

The prosecutor added, "In the minority community people assumed there would be no convictions. In urban centers it's called wilding. Here it's called rape. Rape is rape—and these defendants have been found guilty. If this was an urban kid, he'd be in jail already."

Cohen did not look pleased when Laurino raised the issue of unequal treatment for white and minority defendants. The judge said that the defendants had roots in their community and that they didn't present a risk of flight. He let them out on bail until their sentencing, which was scheduled for Friday, April 23, more than a month away.

The defendants and their parents were ushered through a back entrance so they wouldn't have to face photographers and reporters waiting outside, a courtesy not usually extended to poor, minority defendants. Inside the courtroom Nathan Grober, asked what he thought, said, "Enough is enough." When some other family members and friends walked out into the corridor, there was an explosion of light. Photographers had formed a tiered wall of cameras. The Ridgers acted as though they had been caught in an ambush in enemy territory. They pounded at the elevator button, and one relative shouted at the reporters, "Drop dead." Downstairs, making their way to their cars in the courthouse parking lot, the four young men did not try to hide their faces as convicted felons sometimes do. They only looked down at the ground to avoid stepping into the puddles of slush. In a few minutes they were gone.

The three prosecutors gave interviews and then separately made their way to the third floor. In a back hallway leading to the prosecutor's office, they met accidentally. Miller-Hall, Goldberg, and Laurino embraced each other and for a moment they appeared to be doing a little circle dance. They hugged and kissed. Goldberg, the normally unflappable chief trial attorney in the prosecutor's office, was flushed and his glasses were askew. "Justice," he laughed. "Justice—it's wonderful."

At noon Sheila Byron was eating lunch at a meeting at the police academy in Verona, New Jersey. A sheriff's officer tapped her on the shoulder. "You got a verdict in your case," he said. Byron dropped her sandwich and followed him into a room where the TV was playing. She got the drift: There had been some convictions, but she had tuned in too late to know whether they had been convicted of first-degree charges. Then her beeper went off. It was Glen Ridge police chief Tom Dugan. He wanted her to go to Leslie's house; Ros had gone out to take her aunt to the doctor, and Leslie was alone. A million reporters were probably on their way over right now.

When Sheila arrived at the house, Ros had already returned. Mother and daughter were sitting on a sofa, watching the television news. Ros was trying to explain to Les what a guilty verdict was all about. But Sheila thought that Leslie clearly didn't want to hear it. "Oh, it's over, the boys are going to get in trouble," Leslie kept repeating.

Sheila tried to say that they wouldn't know what would happen to the boys until the judge decided. But Leslie kept shaking her head. "No, no, I know they're going to jail." Ros put a hand on Leslie's knee to comfort her, but her daughter pushed it away.

To distract her, Sheila said, "Les, let's go upstairs. I've never seen your room."

As they walking up the stairs, the detective said, "Leslie, you can tell your mom things about how you feel about the case. She'll understand."

Leslie shook her head. "She doesn't understand, I can't tell her."

Leslie clearly didn't want to talk about it. In Leslie's bedroom Sheila saw a snapshot the Fabers had taken of Sheila's wedding. "Isn't that nice," Byron said, changing the subject.

When they came back downstairs, Ros said, "We've got to get out of here." Looking out the front window, she saw a TV van with a satellite dish. Other reporters were standing on the sidewalk, staking out the house. The Fabers had packed their car a week ago for just such a moment.

Sheila walked Leslie out the back door, but Les didn't seem in any rush to get into the car. She lingered in the driveway, peering around the house to see what the commotion was. "Leslie, *get* in the car," Sheila said impatiently. Leslie was nodding her head "yes" but walking backward to the front of the house where the reporters were. Oh, no, Sheila thought, if they spot her and Leslie starts talking, and you know she will because Leslie talks to anyone—.

"So, when am I going to see you again, Sheila?" Leslie asked, playing for time. Sheila grabbed her arm and shoved her into the Fabers' car. The detective walked to the front of the house where her own car was parked.

She saw a pile of telegrams on the enclosed front porch. Many were from TV talk shows requesting interviews; a huge bouquet of roses from the Sally Jessy Raphael show had been placed in the entranceway. The messages would go unanswered.

Driving to the Glen Ridge police station, Sheila couldn't really accept that it was all over—the investigation, the trial, the jury deliberations. At times in the past four years, she had felt divided in her loyalties and less than totally confident: when she had to question the hometown kids; when she had to pursue the investigation and still try to get along with the guys on the police force who were buddies of Detective Corcoran; when she nearly lost it on the witness stand during Querques's cross-examination.

But she didn't feel at all ambivalent about the guilty verdicts. Hey, if they ask me, she thought, I'll be the first one to drive them to jail.

75

The jurors had struggled to reach a verdict. Although a majority thought all the defendants were guilty of the most serious charges, there was one firm holdout. A couple of others had wavered. Ultimately, they had to settle for a compromise to come to an agreement. Their compromise was to let Grober mostly off the hook for the oral sex; at the same time, they wanted harsher sentences for the other three defendants, who were involved in the use of the bat and the broomstick. Their discussion over the course of almost two weeks had been clouded by the misimpression that they had to agree on both the "mental defective" charge and the "force or coercion" charge to find the defendants guilty of first-degree rape. Agreement on only one of the two charges would have been sufficient.

How, then, did the jurors bring in their verdict?

When they began to deliberate on Thursday, March 4, most of them believed they would reach a verdict in a couple of days. That afternoon the jurors voted on whether they thought each of the defendants was guilty of at least one of the charges against them. Eleven out of the twelve jurors said "yes." The lone holdout was Dawn Scott, the Bloomfield resident who worked as an administrative aide at a pharmaceutical research organization.

The jurors decided to give over the first few days of deliberations to venting their emotions. That was when Patrick Parker, a truck driver, explained how his volunteer work with retarded children persuaded him that they craved love and affection. That was when Scott expressed her opinion that Leslie seemed "pressured" by the prosecution when she testified and was "relaxed" when the defense lawyers questioned her. Scott angered several jurors when she speculated that Leslie's parents had "abused" her because they ignored her sexual activities, she said later. "The jury screamed at me," Scott said. "I just thought that she had two lives and her parents didn't want to see one of them."

By Tuesday, the fourth day of deliberations, the jurors had agreed that force and coercion had been used against Leslie by the defendants who had wielded the bat and broomstick and that all four defendants had participated in a conspiracy to sexually abuse her. But Scott, joined at different times by one and then two other jurors, insisted that the defendants could not have known that Leslie was mentally defective. "Leslie didn't look retarded," Scott said. "She was a relatively normal person."

A majority of the jurors agreed that the prosecution's expert witnesses—Esquilin, Meyerhoff, and Burgess—were fairly persuasive when they said that Leslie was retarded and mentally defective. "But almost all of us were convinced by Leslie herself," one juror said. With only a few exceptions, the jurors agreed that she was the best witness for the prosecution even when she was giving the defense lawyers the answers they wanted. "You listened to her for an hour and you knew what happened in the basement," Parker said.

Leslie's drawings also influenced the jurors. They weren't evidence that she had been raped. But they constituted a heartrending account of the emotional toll the experience had taken on her, jurors said; the pictures showed what Leslie wasn't able to say on the stand.

The charges against Bryant Grober were the most difficult to resolve. Donald Murray, a salesman for an insurance company, thought that Grober knew as much about Leslie as did the others in the park. "He was their friend," Murray said. "He knew why they were going to the basement. It wasn't just to socialize." But Lawrence Handel, a soft-spoken thirty-nine-year-old plant manager, argued that Grober had oral sex with Leslie as an "initiation rite." He speculated that Grober's friends said, "Let's initiate him into this group by getting him a blow job with Leslie."

Handel said that most of the jurors concluded that there was not sufficient evidence to show that Grober used force against Leslie, but they believed that Grober knew enough about what was happening to warrant a conviction on a lesser charge of conspiracy. Some jurors thought that Scott would settle for a conspiracy conviction against Grober and rape convictions against the others. But Scott, who reportedly referred to Grober as that "baby-faced kid," still held out against convicting the other three on the "mental defective" charges.

Most of the jurors thought that Alan Zegas, as Grober's attorney, had been the most effective defense advocate. They believed that he had created a reasonable doubt about whether force was used against Leslie during the oral sex and about whether Grober knew about Leslie's disability. "He did his homework, he was all business," Handel said. But some jurors thought Querques, by comparison, had treated Leslie like a child when he cross-examined her, eliciting childlike responses from her. His tactics persuaded the jurors that she could be easily manipulated. Ford seemed more interested in pursuing a personal feud with Goldberg, jurors said, and Esposito had not argued vigorously that Kyle had expressed alarm that Leslie might be hurt by the bat and broom.

During their five months together, friendships had developed among different groups of jurors, but some were strained by the disputes in the jury room. Dawn Scott, for example, had written to the judge to complain that she was being pressured; and on the Friday when the jury reached a partial verdict, she had demanded that the bat be taken out of the jury room. But that Friday, other jurors had wanted to meet with the judge because they thought Scott was being "unreasonable" in her unwillingness to compromise.

One friendship that remained strong was between Handel and Scott. During the weekend before the jury agreed on a verdict, Handel talked with his seventeen-year-old daughter. He didn't discuss the case but he talked generally about school and dating and her relationships with boys. His daughter, Handel said, was "immature," as you might expect with a teenager. "But she was still reasonable," Handel said. "She told me she had said 'no' to boys. I compared her to the boys in the basement, and I decided that they just weren't reasonable. The boys who left, they were reasonable enough to walk out. If I were their father, I would have bought them a car."

When the jury came together after the weekend, Handel took Scott aside and told her about his conversation with his daughter. "The bat and the broomstick were not reasonable acts," he said to her. Patrick Parker, the truck driver who was the most adamant in his belief that the defendants were guilty, reasoned that if the Jocks thought Leslie was capable of saying "no" when they entered the basement, surely they must have realized that she was incapable after they put a broomstick into her body and followed that with a bat. "If there was no resistance from her and she didn't fight, they must have known," Parker argued.

As time passed, Handel thought that Scott's opposition to a guilty verdict was softening. The jury had already agreed not to convict on the sexual contact (masturbation and touching) charges. The jury had voted to convict Grober on a third-degree conspiracy charge, although some believed he was guilty of a more serious charge. "Sleep on it," Handel told Scott as the jury dispersed on Monday afternoon, March 15. Scott still believed that the defendants could not have known that Leslie was "mentally defective."

That night, Scott said, she had nightmares that the families of the defendants were "begging me to take back my decision."

On Tuesday morning Handel talked to Scott as the other jurors listened. Handel predicted that if the jury couldn't reach a verdict, the case would be tried again, and the defendants might be convicted of *more serious charges*. "If you don't do it, Dawn, another jury'll hang them," Handel said.

Handel talked and Dawn Scott listened for a half hour while the other jurors bit their nails. Finally, she said: Okay, I'll go along with the verdict: Guilty on the "mental defective" charge as well as the "force or coercion" charge. The others cheered. "That was really disgusting," Scott said later. "What was there to cheer about?"

The one thing that everybody could cheer about was that the trial was over.

76

The jurors were long gone and their seats were taken by the press. Otherwise, all the people who had attended the long trial took their familiar places for the last piece of business, the only exception being the Fabers, who were once again absent. Today, on Friday, April 23, Judge Cohen was going to hand down his sentences.

Cohen said he had received 369 letters about the sentences he was about to pronounce. The judge said the letters were equally split between those who thought he should send the four convicted felons away for a long time and those who urged leniency. In Glen Ridge Doug Archer had led a letter-writing campaign after the guilty verdicts. In a letter he circulated among friends on March 19, he said, "If you believe as we do in the character of the boys and the basic values that they have grown up with, please let the judge know." Archer offered some guidance for letter writers:

"You may also say that the boys are not arrogant about the situation, that they have been truly remorseful . . . have lived a life of hell on Earth . . . and care much more about the girl than the prosecutors who dragged her through the mire over the last four years."

Other letter writers urged Cohen to send the defendants away for as long as the law permitted. The mother of a retarded teenage girl wrote, "I would hope that we don't have to lock her [her daughter] up to protect her from sexual abuse. I would think that society had completely fallen apart if the defendants . . . weren't given the maximum sentence [or] were allowed free on bail."

The letters were compelling to read, and the judge said that he had read them all but that his decisions were governed by statutory mandates and by his inner compass—by what he thought was right.

After Cohen took his place on the bench, the defense lawyers spoke first, appealing for leniency. Ford said that this was Chris Archer's first offense and that "there was little traumatic effect on Leslie . . . upon her life" as a result of the rape. He said Chris was sixteen when he raped her.

Cohen asked Archer if he had anything to say.

This was the first time Chris had publicly talked about the rape. He stood up and said, deliberately, "Your honor, Mr. Ford has advised me not to say anything but I think I've remained silent too long. I'd just like to say that I'm sorry, I'm sorry for Leslie, her parents and the Faber family." He continued, speaking in a near-whisper: "I never intended for any of this to happen. I realize I used poor judgment, but it was a mistake and I ask you to let me learn from my mistake." If you expected Chris Archer to fall to his knees and plead for mercy, you weren't going to see it today.

Zegas was next. He said that Grober came from a family that had raised him with "very strong, good, and moral values" and that what he did to Leslie was "highly aberrational." Zegas read from a letter written by two court-appointed psychologists, who found that Grober had "a capacity for both empathy and introspection." Noting that Bryant had been acquitted of eight of the nine charges against him, Zegas asked the judge to put Bryant on probation—no jail time.

Then Grober got up. His voice was soft and fading as he finished his sentences; he said that what happened on March 1 was "wrong, stupid." He had apologized to *his* parents "many times," he recalled. "You can't go back and change things that happened." Bryant said he hadn't yet apologized to the Faber family. Rosemary Grober bowed her head and cried as Bryant said, "Leslie and her parents, I can't express the sorrow I feel." He looked at Cohen and went on, "I made a mistake and I think it best that I apologize to them through you. They've been through enough already. I hope you accept my apologies and believe my sincerity."

Grober sat down and Querques stood up. He said he empathized with the judge because he, too, was beleaguered by a "media that is attracted by anything which can make sensations and tingling" and by "pressure groups that seem to want to speak out for the entire population when in fact they don't." He urged the judge to pay attention to the victim when she said, "I don't want him [Kevin] or anybody else to go to jail."

Kyle's girlfriend and his other friends had been crying while Querques talked, but now they were bawling when Kevin stood up to talk.

Kevin recited in a soft monotone: "I'd just like to say that I'm very sorry for what happened on March 1, and I think I used bad moral judgment. I was very young at the time. I'd like to apologize to the Fabers for what I put them through, what I put my parents through, I'd like to apologize for that. And I'm just sorry about everything that happened."

Jack Scherzer stared straight ahead. Geraldine Scherzer was bent over almost double, as if she had a terrible pain in her gut.

The three defendants had each taken less than half a minute to speak. Esposito spoke for the last of the four defendants, Kyle Scherzer. He said that the psychiatric tests Kyle had received before sentencing showed that he was "genuinely remorseful." Esposito said that because of Kyle's age when the rape was committed—he had just turned eighteen—and because he had no arrest record, the judge should downgrade the charges to second-degree sexual assault and sentence Kyle to a youthful offenders' institution rather than state prison.

Cohen asked Kyle Scherzer if he had anything to say. "No, sir," said Kyle.

It was Laurino's turn to respond. Only a few days before, he expected that the college student from Boston, who said she had been sexually assaulted by Chris Archer in October 1990, would testify during the sentencing. Without her testimony her sealed affidavit to the prosecutor, describing what she said Archer had done to her, could not be considered by the judge.

The young woman had at first been reluctant to appear publicly because there was no assurance that her identity would be kept secret by the media. But while she was trying to make up her mind, assistant prosecutor Elizabeth Miller-Hall argued to the chief prosecutor that the rape of Leslie Faber was sufficient grounds for the judge to send the rapists away for a long time. Miller-Hall maintained that it would be a bad precedent to influence the judge's thinking by citing a second allegation of assault that was unrelated to the Leslie Faber case.

Goldberg and Laurino didn't agree with Miller-Hall. They had argued vehemently that the young woman's story would demonstrate that Archer was a continuing threat to women. Their position was, if the woman wanted to tell her story, let her. But Miller-Hall's view prevailed, and the chief prosecutor decided not to ask the woman from Boston to testify at the sentencing. The night before the sentencing, Laurino heard from the young woman: She said she had resolved her doubts and she was ready to go into court and describe how Chris Archer had abused her. Laurino had no choice but to tell her that the prosecutor's office had decided, after all, not to call her. Chris was never charged with a crime related to her allegations.

The judge was surprised that the young woman had not appeared. He had been told by the prosecutors that she would speak. So that left Laurino all alone, without the witness who he was sure would seal the argument that the defendants deserved significant jail time. During meetings between the judge and the lawyers from both sides, Laurino sensed that Cohen's judgment was tilting toward the defendants. In the courtroom now, he was arguing with the desperation of a man trying to hold back a tidal wave.

Laurino's voice rose as he said, "They've been getting free rides all their life, and today that free ride must end." Friends of the Scherzers shook their heads in disgust.

Laurino said the Fabers were not vindictive people, but after "enduring personal hell" for years, they recognized "the need for punishment." From the beginning of the case, the prosecutor said, the Fabers had maintained that "to allow these defendants to essentially walk out this door and essentially laugh at this act . . . would be the highest insult of all."

Laurino said that Kevin, Kyle, and Chris should receive prison sentences consistent with "the depravity" of their crimes. Then he came to Bryant. Bryant had been convicted of the least serious charge. Bryant, he said, was "the one who started the fire. He was the one who engaged in the first sexual act, and then everybody else began to jump in." Bryant should get up to a year in prison, he argued, and should do community service in the inner city, where he could "see people suffer."

The prosecutor had anticipated that Cohen might sentence the three defendants convicted of rape to a youthful offenders' facility instead of a state prison because of their age when the rape was committed. He knew that it was customary not to set a minimum term of imprisonment for "youthful offenders." This meant that prison officials would decide when the offenders were eligible for parole. But Laurino argued that the law permitted the judge to set a minimum.

When Laurino finished, Cohen glanced at his notes and started to pronounce sentence. The four convicted felons looked up at the judge; their expressions were placid and composed. As they had when the verdict came in, the parents and relatives seemed solemn and tense. Rosemary Grober bit her lower lip, Michaele Archer dug her nails into her palms.

Theoretically, Chris and Kevin, convicted of two counts of first-degree sexual assault, could have been sentenced to as much as forty years. But Cohen had the latitude to merge the counts into one—which he did. He sentenced them to a maximum of fifteen years in prison, halfway between the ceiling of twenty years and the floor of ten years. Kyle Scherzer, who had been convicted of one first-degree and one second-degree charge, was also sentenced to a maximum of fifteen years.

The kicker was that all three were sentenced to a "young adult offenders'" institution, with an "indeterminate" minimum term of imprisonment. As first offenders, with time off for good behavior they could be released from prison in twenty-two to twenty-seven months. They could actually serve less than two years in prison. If Cohen had set a minimum sentence, they probably would have had to serve eight months longer.

Grober, who was convicted only of the third-degree conspiracy charge, was sentenced to three years of probation and two hundred hours of community service.

When the judge announced the "indeterminate" sentences, Doug Archer wheeled around and gave a thumbs-up sign to his friends in the back of the courtroom.

In the weeks before the sentencing, Cohen had balanced the "heinous" crime committed by Kyle, Kevin, and Chris against their ages when they raped Leslie. In his mind, it added up to an "indeterminate" minimum. When he recalled how they had appeared in court and the distress on the faces of their families and friends, he also thought about how he had acted when he was a teenager. He asked himself, How much sense and discretion did I have? He told himself that there was no excuse for what they did, but then, he thought, if it hadn't been for that one horrible day, they would have been someone's all-American boys. You didn't want to lock up all-American boys and throw the key away. That's the way Judge Cohen thought.

The sentence was only the first act of the day's drama. The other central issue was bail. Cohen decided to allow the Scherzers and Archer to remain free on bail until their appeals were decided—perhaps five or six years from then. Cohen told himself, They're not likely to go off on a rape spree. As far as what the woman in Boston had said in her accusation against Archer, Cohen decided that it had "never been substantiated or corroborated."

The other argument for continuing the defendants free on bail, which the judge found persuasive, was that the trial had raised "substantial" issues to be argued on appeal. These included the testimony on rape trauma syndrome (it was the first time it had been offered in a New Jersey court), Goldberg's singing during his summation, and Cohen's decision to remove three jurors during the trial. "If it should turn out that I am wrong on any one of these issues, then the defendants will have spent . . . a substantial amount of time incarcerated, possibly unjustly," Cohen said.

Laurino said later that in all the years he had been a prosecutor, he had never seen a defendant who was convicted of a first-degree sex crime let out on bail while an appeal wended its way through the serpentine justice system of the state. "What Mrs. Faber feared may come true," he argued in court. "They will walk out of the door, they'll laugh in the face of this court, laugh in the face of the victim, in the face of the victim's family, in the face of the millions of victims, overwhelmingly female, who are subjected to sexual violence."

In fact, Kevin Scherzer was chuckling. He was standing outside the courtroom with the group of young women who had come to court to support him. They hugged each other and laughed as if they were celebrating a victory. Friends of Doug Archer embraced him. Chris's father was beaming. The Scherzer twins' older brother, Paul, said the judge's sentence was "very harsh," but added, "I'm glad that he let them out on bail."

Not everyone agreed. Carole Vasile of NOW said, "The judge didn't have the courage to uphold the verdict of the jury." Patrick Parker, one of the jurors, said that when he heard about the judge's ruling, he couldn't believe it. "To me, it felt like what we did was for nothing," he said.

Ren Scott, a reporter for the New York CBS television station, was thinking along those lines when he left the courtroom after the sentencing. "I thought the judge was going to send a message," Scott said as he entered an elevator. Then he paused briefly and added, "I guess he did: If you're white, it's all right."

Five days later, the *New York Times* said in an editorial that Cohen's sentencing and bail ruling spoke to the letter of the law but not to "the moral and ethical outrage generated by these young men's treatment of that vulnerable young woman." When it comes to crime, the *Times* said, "it seems, there's still nothing like being white, middle-class, and suburban to get the benefit of the doubt."

Cohen might disagree with the *Times*'s judgment on him, but it would be difficult for him to deny that the criminal justice *system* treats defendants unequally. A poor black youngster accused in a highly publicized case—the rape of the Central Park jogger in New York, for example—would have had a much higher bail than the $15,000 to $25,000 that was set for the Glen Ridge guys. Most likely, he wouldn't have been able to come up with the bail money when he was arrested. He would have had to spend months, maybe years, locked up waiting to go to trial or to cop a plea. He wouldn't have been represented by the best legal talent that money could buy. He would have been represented by an underpaid public defender with a huge caseload. After he was convicted of first-degree sexual assault, he probably would have been jailed immediately. Even if a "liberal" judge like Cohen offered to let him out on bail, an impoverished defendant wouldn't have had the money to buy his freedom.

The Glen Ridge guys were fortunate to be born into loyal, white middle-class families. But it wasn't only their race and class that got them a sweet deal. The nature of their crime also had a lot to do with it. The judge's sentence—if it will ever be served—was not unusual: A 1989 study by the U.S. Department of Justice found that prisoners convicted of rape actually served an average of twenty-nine months.

Cohen's sentence was consistent with the consensus reached by judges and parole boards that rape isn't a terribly serious crime, even if it is committed with a bat and a broom against a retarded young woman. Cohen reasoned that March 1, 1989, was one unfortunate anomaly in the otherwise placid adolescence of a group of typical suburban teenage males. Why keep them in jail, he seemed to be saying, when they can be out enjoying a happy, fulfilling life?

At home in Glen Ridge, Ros Faber said to her husband, "He let them go free."

Charlie Faber turned off the television news program. "Makes you wonder," he said. "After all Leslie went through, was it worth it?"

77

In the Glen Ridge case, at the moment of decision, the judge decided that the damage done to this woman weighed less heavily than concern for the futures of the rapists and sympathy for their families. That judgment was not exceptional. As far as the legal system was concerned, Laurino recalled that in his experience sexual offenders usually received lighter sentences when their victims were retarded. In a much broader sense, this judgment, which favored the offenders over the victim, was remarkably similar to the judgments that had been made by people in Glen Ridge and elsewhere all through Leslie's hard life.

Her interests were always being sacrificed to a higher cause, to what collective wisdom held was a greater good. When popular boys from good families made her life miserable as a child, it was easier for adults to look the other way than to confront the boys and their parents.

When Leslie required more comprehensive educational services, the Glen Ridge school system transferred her out of town because caring for her was too great a burden. But the schools never lacked for athletic equipment, never stinted in their celebrations of their young sports heroes.

When, as a twelve-year-old, Leslie was sexually abused by a young man who came from a prominent local family, the boy got off with virtually no penalty and Leslie was painted as a seductress. It was the first time—but not the last—that Leslie was required to expose her private life to strangers in the pursuit of an elusive abstraction called justice.

When Leslie found a high school that she liked and friends who accepted her, she was transferred out because the school couldn't provide the care, attention, and security that she required.

When, as a teenager, she was degraded by a favored clique of hometown jocks, her feelings were ignored in the interest of a higher cause—preserving the tranquility and reputation of Glen Ridge.

When she told an educator that her body had been violated with a baseball bat and a broomstick, teachers, social workers, and school administrators decided that this "incident" was not sufficiently serious to report to the police or the child welfare system for three weeks. To do so would mean taking the word of one retarded youngster above that of the most celebrated and popular guys in the school—not just one or two, but dozens who were centrally or peripherally involved. Once again, Leslie was sacrificed to a greater good—suppressing a potentially devastating scandal that could send the perpetrators to jail, scar their families, and reveal the real values of the community. Therefore, what happened to Leslie was kept quiet, although those who knew the truth must have understood that Leslie could be abused again unless the police intervened.

When it became known that police were investigating what happened on Lorraine Street and arrests were made, many in the community offered their support to the suspects and vilified Leslie. Few residents demanded the kind of inquiry that would have scrutinized the bedrock values of Glen Ridge and its institutions for youth. Leslie's reputation was sacrificed to achieve the greater good of preserving the town's culture as it was.

When the Glen Ridge board of education commissioned a review of its conduct in the case, a retired judge exonerated the school and the town and blamed Leslie's parents for the delay in calling in the police. Again, the good name of the town was judged more important than the reputation of one family and one retarded teenager.

When Leslie was examined and interviewed by the prosecution's psychologists and psychiatrists, she was encouraged to discuss her sexual history, unaware that whatever she said could—and would—be made public at trial and used to shred her privacy. These procedures, it was said, were necessary to establish her infirmity and her incapacity to consent—all done in the interests of serving the higher cause of justice.

When a reporter stumbled across Leslie, she engaged her in conversation and recorded Leslie's utterances in her notebook, which later found their way onto the front page of her newspaper. Whatever reservations the paper might have had about printing the fragmented phrases of a retarded young woman were subordinated, it said, to its higher calling of getting out the news—ahead of the competition.

After the arrests, when Leslie was isolated and ridiculed by neighborhood teenagers, a young woman presented herself as Leslie's one true friend. Mari Carmen Ferraez easily won Leslie's confidence and used it to tape-record Leslie's observations about love, sex, and ice cream. Mari Carmen later explained that she was only a volunteer in the service of a higher cause—protecting the welfare of a group of innocent young men.

Before the trial even started, a judge ruled that to secure a fair trial for the defendants it was permissible to intrude into every private corner of the victim's life; almost nothing was off-limits—not what she told her gynecologist, not what she told her therapist, not what she told the calculating Mari Carmen.

During the trial the defense lawyers tested the limits of their license. Every rumor, innuendo, and unsupported suspicion about Leslie and her family were hung out in public. The lawyers said it was too bad, but they were only doing their job, fulfilling their highest mission of providing the best possible defense of their clients.

Where the jury found guilt, the judge was moved to mercy. He let the defendants go free until some uncertain date in the indefinite future. He was guided by his sympathies and his interpretation of justice. Judge Cohen's compassion may have been misplaced. But his gentle treatment of the defendants was not really surprising.

Throughout the trial Leslie was constantly described as a person who had not progressed beyond the mental age of an eight-year-old. But through her life it appeared that the values of the community around her, the community she grew up in, had not progressed beyond those of a high school pep rally.

Although what happened to Leslie was an act of singular cruelty, she was not the only young woman to be misused in Glen Ridge's gung-ho culture. The indifference in the community to how girls were being treated by young males, especially the favored athletes, stole the childhood innocence away from the most vulnerable young women much as poverty stole the childhood innocence away from the children of Newark.

As children they expected to be accepted as equal human beings by the boys they knew. This was a reasonable expectation for children living in a seemingly placid small town whose appearance invited trust. But they quickly learned it was better not to trust anybody. Treated as inferiors and outcasts when they stood up to the Jocks, these girls learned while they were very young—a lesson that was repeated throughout their childhood and adolescence—that the price of acceptance was submission. They had to submit to whatever the boys asked of them, and, as time passed, the boys kept asking for more.

Suppose the girls refused to submit. Who could they go to for support? Who would defend them against the Jocks' outrageous demands? Who could the girls in the middle school go to when the boys in their class exposed themselves? Who would console and defend Mary Ryan when the Jocks wrecked her house and ruined her youth? When boys masturbated in their high school classes, threatened and harassed their female class-mates, pressured some girls who had barely entered ménarche to provide sexual entertainment, who would stand up for these young women? Who would say to these boys, "This is wrong. Stop it."?

The ultimate effect of the damage these young men inflicted on some young women of Glen Ridge will be difficult to measure until they are adults. But it's not unreasonable to speculate that the experiences with the Jocks established in childhood a pattern of power and submission that would extend into these girls' adult lives. The message was clear: Guys had unchallenged power. Defy them at your peril. But even submitting didn't mean a girl would be treated decently. Just ask Leslie.

One girl, who was frequently humiliated by the Jocks as early as middle school, remembered that their abusive behavior made her mistrust most boys. "All guys were perverts—that was my thought," she said. Such treatment, even when it is ameliorated later by more positive experiences with men, can erode the self-worth of the strongest girls. Because adults did not intervene to stop the abuse, many girls questioned their own worth, not only to boys but also to adults whose judgment really counted. This theme of submissiveness to the abusive demands of the boys, coupled with a sense of adult abandonment, was sounded early and often as the girls emerged from the chrysalis of youth. For those girls who lacked self-esteem to start with, it was potentially devastating: It could undermine their future relations with men and impair their chances of succeeding in school and in the workplace.

Where were the grownups of Glen Ridge while this was going on? The truth was, most of them were on the sidelines. The most common expla-nation they gave for their passivity was that they didn't know. The Jocks, they said, were sustained by an impenetrable, subterranean youth culture whose members were bound by a code of secrecy.

When Leslie's experience in the basement of the Scherzer house was ex-posed, adults responded by asking: Who would have believed that evil could have metastasized among so many youngsters in such a benign set-ting? But this response seems disingenuous. Long before March 1, 1989, the behavior of many boys in the town was evident to adults who bothered to look. It was implicit in what teachers and police officers, clergy and even other parents, told them. The warnings were voiced explicitly in meetings of church groups and town commissions and the board of education. If you didn't go to these meetings, you still could get a good idea of what was going on when you sifted through the human and physical wreckage created by the Jocks and their friends throughout the town.

Adults heard the warnings and saw the evidence, but they chose to ignore them. Partly, this was because they didn't want to taint the town they treasured—the place they considered "Valhalla," as one school official put it—with scandal. But there was another reason: self-protection. The Jocks didn't invent the idea of mistreating young women. The ruling clique of teenagers adhered to a code of behavior that mimicked, distorted, and exaggerated the values of the adult world around them.

These values extolled "winners"—the rich businessmen, the esteemed professionals, the attractive, fashion-conscious wives, the high-achieving children. They denigrated the "losers"—the less affluent breadwinners, the decidedly dowdy wives, the inconspicuous, bashful, ungainly kids.

Glen Ridge placed the elite kids—the kids with masculine good looks, the kids who stood out on the playing field—on a pedestal. But there wasn't much room there for those who didn't fit the Glen Ridge model of achievement. It was doubtful whether there was any space at all on that pedestal for young women or whether it was strictly reserved for boys.

Adults might have forestalled the unfolding tragedy in their town if they had questioned their own values, if they had challenged the assumptions of the culture that defined how people treated one another in Glen Ridge. They could have provided an alternative model of behavior to youngsters, one that emphasized fairness, compassion, humanity, and decency. But that required too much self-examination, too many embarrassing admissions of failure. They weren't up to it. They decided to hope for the best. And they got the worst.

A gung-ho pep rally: That symbolizes much of the culture of Glen Ridge. But these misguided and ultimately dehumanizing values were not exclusive to this one small town. As the continuing revelations of sexual harassment and abuse in the military, in colleges, in the workplace, and in many other spheres suggest, these values have deep roots in American life.

What happened to Leslie Faber is important because it reveals the extreme outcome of the behavior of young men who are made to feel omnipotent. If a culture is measured by how it treats its weakest members, the Glen Ridge case, first to last, revealed American culture at its basest. Many of the people who judged Leslie spoke for a system of values that got it wrong. They never learned how to measure the true goodness of a human being.

The law follows culture, and until we reexamine how we mold children and what we expect of our creations, we don't have a right to hold judges and lawyers to a higher standard than our own. Why should they be different from all those, in and out of Glen Ridge, who were prepared, even eager, to sacrifice Leslie to a higher cause?

EPILOGUE

During the two years after the trial ended, all charges against Richard Corcoran, Jr., were dropped. The chief prosecutor said that he didn't want to put the Fabers through the pain of another trial, but some suspected that, with Leslie's conflicting testimony, the prosecutor didn't have much of a case against Corcoran. His dad, Lieutenant Richard Corcoran, retired from the Glen Ridge police force. Detective Sheila Byron was promoted to the rank of sergeant and became a mother.

The charges were also dropped against John Maher, who had been indicted for allegedly trying to induce Leslie to return to the Scherzers' house. The Archers and Scherzers left Glen Ridge. Kyle and Kevin got jobs; Chris went to college in North Carolina. Charles Figueroa, the black student who first reported the rape to his teacher, went to college in New York. His family moved out of town. The Scherzers' house on Lorraine Street was vacant for a long time; when prospective buyers heard about what happened in the basement, they lost interest in the property.

Tom Ford, Chris Archer's lawyer, died at the age of sixty-four. The other defense attorneys moved on to other important cases. Chris, Kyle, and Kevin were now being represented in their appeals by public defenders. As of this writing, no date has been set for when the appeals will be finally argued and a decision rendered by the higher courts. Chris Archer reportedly sent periodic letters to Judge Cohen describing his academic achievements and proper behavior. Robert Laurino continued as a prosecutor and as head of the Sexual Assault Unit. He was commended for his commitment to justice by advocates for women and retarded people. Glenn D. Goldberg and Elizabeth Miller-Hall were also recognized for their efforts in the Glen Ridge case and remained as prosecutors in Newark. Judge Benjamin Cohen heard other cases.

The Fabers stayed in Glen Ridge. When people asked them why they didn't move, Charlie would answer, "This is where we live. Why shouldn't we stay here?" Leslie worked for a while at a senior citizens center, then got a menial job with a department store in a mall.

In the months after the trial, before the Archers moved, Leslie would occasionally see Michaele Archer drive by. When she recognized the car, Leslie would stop playing basketball and run to the front of her house. Sometimes Leslie would think she saw Mrs. Archer wave to her, but she couldn't be sure because the car didn't slow down. But Leslie waved anyway. "I like Mrs. Archer," Leslie said. "She's a great lady."

Mrs. Archer would turn the corner and go on. Leslie didn't move on. She stayed where she was. Leslie watched with fondness the car disappear.

"I have a good heart," Leslie said. "I was raised that way."

RESEARCH METHODS

During the seven years I spent researching and writing this book, I interviewed 250 people. The majority of them lived or worked in Glen Ridge. These included past and present students at the middle school and high school; members of the high school Class of '89; parents; teachers, school administrators, and other educators; members of the school board; Glen Ridge municipal officials and police officers; clergy; leaders of civic organizations; current and former residents who had been active in school and community affairs; and friends and adversaries of those involved in the case.

My primary purpose in this research was not to gather information about the alleged crime. It was to try to understand and evoke the culture in which these young people grew up. My questions were intended to shed light on why this assault had occurred. My focus was not so much on what had happened. In any event, it soon became clear what had generally transpired in the basement.

In this kind of social and cultural inquiry, an investigator needs to understand why his sources answered his questions as they did, and how their judgments and opinions were formed. Therefore, I spent considerable time with people in Glen Ridge who—although they were not professionals—seemed to have a broad grasp of the social, psychological, and educational dynamics in the community, and, in particular, of child development. I had dozens of conversations with each of these people. With each discussion, each walk around town, each dinner at their homes, each visit to their friends and offspring, each football game I attended, I thought my understanding of Glen Ridge and suburban life generally deepened.

Someone who is examining a bitter conflict of values, as existed in Glen Ridge, must try to avoid becoming a prisoner of the sources who are most responsive to his questions and whose social perspectives most closely resemble his own. I have tried to check this tendency by seeking out many friends and admirers of the defendants and advocates for the high school athletes. Some slammed the phone down when I called them. But others agreed to talk to me. Because a number of the graduates of the Class of '89 had already left for college when I began my research, I visited many of them at their campuses across the country. At a distance from their families and hometown friends, they seemed remarkably open and candid about their experiences in Glen Ridge and their relationships with the young men they called "our guys."

My preference would be to identify and use the real names of people I have interviewed. However, I have changed a lot of the names to protect the privacy of those I interviewed. Some of the individuals I spoke to were concerned that they and their families could become targets of retribution in their community if they were identified as sources. Because of their concerns, I honored their requests to grant them anonymity, or otherwise disguise their identity.

One of the most difficult tasks for a writer is to reconstruct in his narrative a past event whose facts are in dispute. Ultimately, I had to rely on my judgment to render the encounter between Leslie Faber and the group of athletes in the Scherzers' basement. My judgment was certainly influenced by the outcome of the Glen Ridge rape trial. But my description of that encounter was also shaped by interviews with some of those who were present in the basement on March 1, 1989, and those who showed up the next day in Cartaret Park when an effort was made to induce Leslie to return to the basement.

The four defendants declined to be interviewed. But I did speak to their friends who witnessed what occurred, or heard about it soon after, and interviewed as well one of the young men who was later indicted in the case. I also drew from the trial testimony of four eyewitnesses and from Leslie Faber's lengthy testimony. My account of the experience in the basement also reflects the full pretrial statements to prosecutors by Peter Quigley and Paul Archer, statements to law enforcement officials and others by Leslie Faber, Leslie's comments that were tape-recorded by Mari Carmen Ferraez, and other relevant material.

This book explores at length the childhood and adolescence of the young men charged in this case and their friends; it also tries to describe Leslie Faber's childhood. I have sought to confirm controversial or disputed experiences during their growing-up years by speaking to multiple sources, including classmates, teammates, friends, relatives, and educators.

To document each of the most significant experiences, I interviewed as many as a dozen or more sources, often more than once. These interviews have been supplemented by material contained in actual school records, unedited original police reports, legal documents, trial exhibits, and other documentation compiled by investigators, attorneys, and law enforcement officials.

The writing of social history involves interpretation and analysis, for which, in this book, I bear sole responsibility. There are no invented scenes or dialogue. I have drawn on the recollections of those involved, whenever possible, and tried to verify them through additional interviews and documentation. As far as it is possible and practical I made every effort to confirm disputed facts, but I recognize that some facts will always remain in dispute.

In the second half of the book, the terrain shifts from Glen Ridge to the criminal justice system. There, as in Glen Ridge, I tried to investigate the values of those who worked in the system: defense lawyers, lawyers not directly involved in the case, judges, prosecutors, staff members in the prosecutor's office, witnesses, experts, police, investigators, and others. I did this by interviewing many of those who were involved with the case. But in this part of the narrative I had one advantage that I did not have when I tried to reconstruct the past. I could observe firsthand all the court proceedings that were open to the public—hearings, arguments, pretrial motions and rulings, and appeals. I was present, as well, for other events closed to the general public. I also attended every day of the Glen Ridge trial, which lasted more than five months. In short, I was able for more than three years to observe as an eyewitness virtually every step in the criminal justice process.

My understanding of the issues in Glen Ridge and in the outside world was enhanced by books and studies and by conversations with experts. I benefited particularly from discussions with Richard Lapchick, the sports sociologist; Chris O'Sullivan, the social psychologist; and Myriam Miedzian, the social philosopher.

My discussion of character in the Introduction was informed by Peter D. Kramer's book *Listening to Prozac* (New York: Penguin, 1993). The references to poor children are drawn from my book *Tough Change* (New York: Free Press, 1987).

I am indebted to Margaret Kennedy for her research into the history of Glen Ridge and to Susan Schantz for her exploration of comparable upper-middle-class communities in Ohio. *Glen Ridge Heritage*, published by the Glen Ridge Bicentennial Committee in 1976, provided a useful history of the town, as did reports by the U.S. Works Progress Administration in 1936 and 1937. Other works that provided a historical context include a report on the town by the League of Women Voters in 1960 and articles that appeared in the *Glen Ridge Paper,* a weekly newspaper. An excellent historical analysis of the Glen Ridge schools is contained in *The Schools of Glen Ridge: A Survey,* by Clyde Milton Hill, Samuel Miller Brownell, John Seiler Brubacher, Bessie Lee Gambrill, and John Warren Tilton, faculty members of the Department of Education at Yale University (unpublished manuscript, New Haven, 1941). *The Burrow Underground,* a newspaper published by Glen Ridge High School students in the 1970s, sheds light on how some young people felt about the treatment of athletes by the schools and the police.

A number of books and studies enhanced my understanding of male adolescent development, young athletes, and sexual aggression by adolescents. Foremost among these is Peggy Reeves Sanday's *Fraternity Gang Rape* (New York: New York University Press, 1990). Other influential works include Myriam Miedzian's *Boys Will Be Boys: Breaking the Link between Masculinity and Violence* (New York: Doubleday, 1991); *The Men from the Boys: Rites of Passage in Male America,* by Ray Raphael (Lincoln: University of Nebraska Press, 1988); *With the Boys: Little League Baseball and Preadolescent Culture,* by Gary Alan Fine (Chicago: University of Chicago Press, 1987); *Jocks and Burnouts: Social Categories and Identity in the High School,* by Penelope Eckert (New York: Teachers College Press, 1989); *Today's Delinquent,* vols. 4, 5, and 6 (Pittsburgh: National Center for Juvenile Justice, 1985, 1986, and 1987); *WAC Stats: The Facts about Women* (New York: Women's Action Coalition, 1992); and Susan Brownmiller's landmark work, *Against Our Will: Men, Women, and Rape* (New York: Bantam Books, 1976). Other published sources are cited in the text.

Finally, my brief discussion of the Scottsboro case was influenced by James Goodman's enlightening study *Stories of Scottsboro* (New York: Vintage Books, 1995).

INDEX

Page numbers in italics indicate a photograph of the subject.

pairment of, 49, 50, 66, 67, 70, 83–84, 138, 162, 164; obscene phone calls to, 168–69, 170, 322, 349; oral sex performed by, 21, 199, 204, 223, 308–9, 315, 317, 323, 344, 354, 363–64, 377, 380–81, 387; as outsider, 3, 84, 338; personality of, 2, 14, 16, 67, 68, 93, 94, 139, 142, 163, 202, 231, 233, 330; and Lisa Marie Petersen, 249–50; physical appearance of, 12, 205, 340; physical pain experienced by, 26, 348, 359, 376, 377; promiscuity of, 2, 287, 318, 320, 327; and Andrew Provost, 86–87, 329–30; and Michael Querques, 310–12, 313, 364–70, 383; and Peter Quigley, 224, 281–83; and rape shield law, 287, 328; rape trauma syndrome of, 382; religious beliefs of, 84–85; retardation of, 11, 15–16, 25, 31, 32–33, 66, 83, 87, 140, 164–65, 190, 191, 230, 231, 232, 250, 287–88, 291, 304, 308, 315, 317, 319, 323, 327, 341, 351, 367, 422; and Mary Romeo, 84; rumors about, 1, 24–25, 231; and Nick Salerno, 233–34; and Margaret Savage, 26, 187–88, 191–92, 195, 200, 379; and Kevin Scherzer, 15, 89, 185–86, 199, 204, 211, 223, 259–60, 282, 284, 286, 303, 329, 345, 368, 387, 389, 390, 391–92; and Kyle Scherzer, 15, 31, 89, 185–86, 199, 329, 345, 346, 393; as sex-obsessed, 310, 311, 312, 329; sexuality of, 87, 88–89, 210–11; in Special Olympics, 187, 188–89; as student, 15–16, 50, 65–66, 83–84, 138, 162–63, 165, 166; talking and moaning in sleep of, 23, 190; and Benedict Tantillo, 239; and Herbert H. Tate, Jr., 224; as tease, 2, 308; and television, 88; videotaping of, plan for, 185, 186, 196, 199, 235; vulnerability of, 11–12, 68–69, 94, 231, 232, 323, 397, 401; as witness, 341–70, 372, 373–77; in yearbook, 174; and Alan Zegas, 357–59, 360–64

Faber, Rosalind: adoption of children by, 49–50; and Doug and Michaele Archer, 215–16; and Sheila Byron, 90; civic duties of, 47; and Carol Faber, 49; and Charles Faber, 201; and Leslie Faber, 11, 22, 23, 30, 49–50, 90, 190–91, 193, 201–2, 205, 206, 273–74; and Glen Ridge, initial impressions of, 37; gossip about, 48–49; and Robert Griffin, 200–201; and Jocks, 206–7; Samuel Larner on, 280; and Robert Laurino, 217–19, 221;

marriage of, 38; personality of, 47–49, 170, 190–91; and Cherry Provost, 87; and Michael Querques, 396–97; religious beliefs of, 47, 48; in Williamsburg, 37–38; as witness, 331–35

Ferraez, Mari Carmen, 96; as athlete, 263; and Richard Childs, 266; and Leslie Faber, 263–65, 266–68, 269–71, 273, 274, 304, 309, 324, 325–26, 330, 349, 421; indictment of, 273; in Pre-Trial Intervention program, 281

Figueroa, Charles, 97; as athlete, 25; breakdown of, 215; and Sheila Byron, 25, 207, 208; college plans of, 427; and Richard Edward Corcoran, 198–99, 208; defamation-of-character suit brought by, 236; dyslexia of, 196; and Leslie Faber, 185–86, 195–96, 198–99; at graduation, 253, 256; and Robert Griffin, 198–99; and Jocks, 118, 119–20, 137, 185–86, 214–15; and Rose McCaffery, 235–36; phone calls to, 215; report of rape by, 25–26; and Ariel Riviera, 196–97; and Mary Ryan, 131, 132, 135, 136; and Kevin Scherzer, 185, 195, 214, 319; as student, 215; values of, 120, 136; as witness, 318–19

Figueroa, Julio, 118

Figueroa, Mary, 118–19

football in Glen Ridge, New Jersey: and Paul Archer, 16; Susan Atkins on, 62; and John Barone, 92–93; and Richard Corcoran, Jr., 29; and Richard Edward Corcoran, 62; and Gary Cuozzo, 62; and Charles Figueroa, 25; and Bryant Grober, 19, 28; and William Horey, 61–62; importance of, 61–62, 105–9; and Kevin Scherzer, 14, 145, 150; and Kyle Scherzer, 14, 150; and sex, 107; wins and losses of team, 148, 149, 150. *See also* athletes and athletics in Glen Ridge, New Jersey; Glen Ridge High School; Homecoming

force, defined, 403. *See also* rape

Ford, Thomas: and Christopher Archer, 275, 305; and Paul Archer, 388–89, 394; closing argument of, 399; death of, 427; and Leslie Faber, 306–7, 336, 352–57, 358, 359; and gender roles, 275; and Elizabeth Miller-Hall, 330; misogynism of, 330, 384; on National Organization for Women, 384; physical appearance of, 305

Franco, Caroline, 58, 89

Compositor:	G&S Typesetters, Inc.
Text:	10/13 Aldus
Display:	Univers
Printer:	Edwards Brothers, Inc
Binder:	Edwards Brothers, Inc.